BRITISH HISTORY
1714 to the Present Day

BY

HERBERT L. PEACOCK

D1368336

Second Edition

Maps by Boris Weltman

HEB

HEINEMANN EDUCATIONAL BOOKS
LONDON

Heinemann Educational Books Ltd
22 Bedford Square, London,WC1B 3HH

LONDON EDINBURGH MELBOURNE AUCKLAND HONG KONG
SINGAPORE KUALA LUMPUR NEW DELHI IBADAN
NAIROBI JOHANNESBURG EXETER (NH)
KINGSTON PORT OF SPAIN

ISBN 0 435 31716 4

Printed and bound in Great Britain
by Biddles Ltd., Guildford, Surrey

CONTENTS

PREFACE TO THE SECOND EDITION

In this edition I have brought a number of key references up to the beginning of 1979 and have inserted some new material in a number of chapters. This has involved appropriate changes in the date-lists and to chapter headings.

While adopting the chronological approach for basic political information, I have given attention also to topics of economic, technical, scientific and general social importance.

Names and dates when first mentioned are shown in bold type. Summaries, dates and questions are given at the end of each chapter, while numerous diagrams are included as a special aid to learning.

H. L. Peacock

NOTE TO THE 1983 REPRINT

This reprint extends the second edition to the end of 1981. Topics added include the problems faced by the Conservative Government elected in 1979 and its attempts to solve them; the formation of the Social Democratic Party; the independence of Rhodesia as Zimbabwe; and a new constitution for Canada.

H.L.P.

CHAPTER ONE

BRITAIN IN 1714

The Hanoverian Succession

O
N 1st August, **1714, Queen Anne** died and **George, Elector of Hanover**, became King of Great Britain and Ireland. His succession to the English throne had been provided for in the **Act of Settlement (1701)** which named his mother, Electress **Sophia of Hanover** and her heirs the successors of Anne, if the Queen died without children to succeed her. The Electress Sophia was the youngest daughter of **Elizabeth**, the daughter of **James I** of England. She had, therefore, a remote connection with the English crown.

At the time of the death of Queen Anne all her children were dead, as also was the Electress Sophia, and thus George was the legal heir to the throne. He was an unattractive successor. He was a German, spoke little English and was known to be uninterested in English affairs. His appearance was decidedly unkingly. His personal life had been difficult and his marriage to his cousin, **Sophia Dorothea**, had ended in divorce. His only son, George Augustus (later **George II**) was on very bad terms with his father. All this was not an edifying situation for a British monarch.

However his accession occurred without bloodshed. He was accepted by most people as the rightful heir and as Parliament's choice. Moreover, prompt action by the Whigs, the supporters of the Hanoverian succession, prevented any attempt to enthrone the only other possible candidate, the **Old Pretender**, son of **James II**. James II himself had died in exile in France in 1701.

The Jacobites

Those supporting the Old Pretender were known as **Jacobites**. Their strength lay mainly in the Highlands of Scotland and in Ireland, where Roman Catholicism and loyalty to the Stuarts were strong, and where there was intense dislike of the English king. The Hanoverians could expect trouble from these two areas.

In England, however, the position of the Jacobites was less clear. Since the **Glorious Revolution** of **1688**, when James II fled to France and was succeeded by **William III** and **Mary**, there were men and women, many of them in influential positions, who were suspected of

Jacobitism. Some of them, like the **Duke of Marlborough**, may have kept in touch with James as a kind of insurance in case William failed to retain the English throne. Others, either because they were Roman Catholics or because they believed James II to be the lawful King of England, toasted the 'King over the water' and kept up a secret correspondence with him.

At the time of Anne's death in 1714, **Robert Harley, Earl of Oxford** and **Henry St. John, Viscount Bolingbroke**, leader of the Tory party, were in close touch with the Old Pretender. They were, however, uneasy about his refusal to become a Protestant. Bolingbroke was shrewd enough to realize that a Stuart restoration needed support from England as well as Scotland and Ireland. Yet such support was very unlikely while the Old Pretender remained a Catholic.

The Dismissal of Oxford

Oxford and Bolingbroke did not agree on the succession question. The former hesitated to make plans for James's succession while the Pretender refused to grant more than 'reasonable security' for Protestantism. Bolingbroke, on the other hand, cared little for religion and was prepared to go ahead. Just before Anne's death, the two men quarrelled openly in the Queen's presence. Shortly afterwards, on 27th July, 1714, the Queen dismissed Oxford, and Bolingbroke was temporarily in supreme power.

The Fall of Bolingbroke

He seemed to be in a very strong position. He had the support of the Queen who hated the Hanoverians and was known to sympathize with the cause of her exiled brother. He also had a working majority in Parliament. But he lacked the one thing needed for success, and that was time; time in which to complete his plans for a Stuart restoration.

Less than a week after his victory over Oxford, Queen Anne died. At once, power slipped from Bolingbroke's hands. The Whigs sent a special envoy to summon the Elector of Hanover, and on 18th September, 1714, George landed at Greenwich.

One of his first actions was to give all the chief offices to leading Whigs. Then he ordered the election of a new Parliament. *The result was a triumph for the Whigs* who were returned to power with a large majority in the House of Commons.

The election showed unmistakably the popularity of Whig policy. While the Tories were discredited because of the Jacobitism of some of their leaders, the Whigs were associated with the Revolution Settlement of 1689, which secured Protestantism and the supremacy of

Parliament. With such an election appeal they could hardly have failed; and the support given to the Whig party by the grateful George I made their success even more certain.

In March 1715 the new Parliament moved for the impeachment of Oxford and Bolingbroke. The case against Oxford was not very strong, but Bolingbroke's position was dangerous. To avoid impeachment he fled to France where he became for a time Secretary of State to the Pretender. After some years he realized the hopelessness of the Jacobite cause and in 1723 he accepted a pardon under the Great Seal and returned to England.

The Importance of the Whig Victory

The Whig triumph in 1714 began a long period of Whig supremacy lasting nearly half a century. This supremacy was based on the support of the King and the House of Commons. It was the final victory of Parliament in a struggle which had occupied most of the seventeenth century and which had involved England in civil war, the execution of **Charles I** and the banishment of James II. If the Act of Settlement (1701) had been repealed and the Pretender made king instead of George I, the whole struggle would have been in vain and the work of the Revolution Settlement undone. It would have meant the triumph of the *divine right theory of kingship.*

As it was, the monarchy remained a 'constitutional' one. George I was king *not* because he had the strongest claim to the throne by right of birth, *but* simply and solely because he was the heir of the Electress Sophia whom Parliament had named as Anne's successor. Because he did not understand English and because he was not interested in English politics, George I was only too glad to let the Whigs administer the country with the minimum of royal interference. This led to a further and continuing increase in Parliament's power, exercised through the development of cabinet government and the office of Prime Minister.

Whig Policy

The maintenance of the Hanoverian succession was essential both for the Whig party and for the general good of the country as a whole. Whig policy, therefore, was aimed at providing the kind of government likely to satisfy the majority of people so that they would give no support to Jacobite movements.

In 1714 Britain had emerged from the **Spanish Succession War (1702–1713)** war-weary and in need of a prolonged period of peace in which to build up her trade and industries. Because of the abandonment of her allies in **1713** when she made a separate peace with France,

HANOVER AND EUROPE IN 1714

Britain was without a friend in Europe. A cautious foreign policy to preserve the **Utrecht Settlement**, which had ended the war, was therefore also necessary and this the Whig ministers were patiently to pursue. Peace and prosperity were their aims; a cautious foreign policy, protection and expansion of trade were their methods of achieving them.

Parliament

In framing their policies, the Whig ministers had to consider not so much public opinion (the views of ordinary men and women) as the opinion of Members of Parliament. This was because they depended for their position on the support of the House of Commons, and in those days the Commons did not represent the ordinary men and women of Britain but only certain sections of the population—landowners, clergy, merchants and professional men.

The large majority of the people of Britain had no vote. In the counties, only those who owned land bringing in a rent of 40/- per annum and upwards could vote. Usually, the county members were the nominees of the local landlords. In the boroughs, there was no uniform system of election. In some cases individual Whig magnates were easily able to control elections. They could buy up land in places where a borough had once existed and where the right to vote still belonged to the tenants or the owners of the land, though the town had long since disappeared. They could influence the choice of *freemen* in towns where the right to vote belonged only to those chosen by the corporation. For example, the Duke of Bedford was usually asked to approve lists of new freemen prepared by the corporation of the borough of Bedford. In other boroughs the corporations elected and determined the members, and here again an influential magnate could often secure the election of a member of his choice. Sometimes he would influence individual members of the corporation to vote the way he wished. At other times he might attempt to get his way by providing some public amenity for the borough such as a park or a new school. In the few boroughs where every ratepayer or every resident had a vote, *open bribery was often employed.*

There was no secret ballot. Voting was often by a show of hands, and electors could therefore be intimidated. Yet on the whole, except in times of crisis, elections took place with the minimum of disturbance, and there was no demand for Parliamentary reform. The political system, like the social structure of the country, was accepted as unchangeable by a generally contented people.

News and Opinion

This does not mean that no interest was shown by the public in how the country was governed. The steady increase in the number of newspapers published, and the large quantity of political pamphlets issued each year, testified to the growing demand for news and comment on the affairs of the day. The first daily newspaper, the *Daily Courant*, appeared in **1702**. Seven years later **Steele** founded *The Tatler,* to which Addison contributed. Practically every writer of importance, notably **Daniel Defoe**, the author of *Robinson Crusoe*, and **Jonathan Swift**, the author of *Gulliver's Travels*, was concerned with politics.

In the coffee houses of London men met and talked about the latest speeches in Parliament (the right to publish debates was not conceded by the two Houses of Parliament until 1771), the policy of ministers, new plays and books, and a wide variety of business topics. London was then one of the greatest centres of commerce in the world. It was in a London coffee house that *Lloyd's,* the famous marine insurance corporation, had its origins. Its founder, **Edward Lloyd**, kept a coffee house in Lombard Street (1691), which was the resort of business men. They went there to obtain information about shipping and business transactions of all kinds. Some of them were willing to subscribe ('underwrite') policies insuring against sea risks, and Lloyd's coffee house soon became a place where those wanting to insure knew they would find insurers. It was at that time the only means of placing marine risks.

Other coffee houses became popular for different reasons. The *Windsor* at Charing Cross supplied translations of the latest Dutch newspapers. Another was famous for the witty conversation of the literary men who gathered there.

Those who frequented coffee houses belonged on the whole to the wealthier classes. They were the well-informed, the educated, and very often the 'landed' section of the community, the men of property. Many of them travelled abroad regularly. Some owned large private libraries. Nearly all could afford to spend time and money on keeping abreast of the latest trends and fashions. These were the merchants, landowners, lawyers, members of Parliament and the 'men about town', who exercised the greatest influence, quite out of proportion to their numbers.

As for the ordinary people in town and country, they were generally less well-informed and had little direct influence on policy. In the towns, the 'mob' could demonstrate, and if the demonstration was sufficiently impressive the opinion of the demonstrators could not be ignored. But such occasions were rare. Quite a large proportion of people could read and write, though most of them, particularly in country districts, seldom saw a newspaper or read a book. They were dependent for their news mainly on letters, the gossip of friends, and the weekly sermon. Clergymen preached almost as much on political subjects as on religious doctrine.

Agriculture

Britain was still predominantly a rural and agricultural country. There were few large towns apart from London and the main ports. The population of England and Wales in 1714 was about five and a half million, the majority of whom lived in villages or country towns. More than half were engaged in agriculture. At first sight the face of the country seemed to have changed little since Tudor times. There was more land under cultivation and more wheat, barley, rye and oats were being grown. But the majority of the fields were unenclosed, and *agricultural methods were those of the Middle Ages*. Sheep and cattle were small and thin. Little was known about selective breeding; and most animals had to be killed at the end of the summer, since there was so little feed for them beyond meadow-hay.

A closer look at the countryside, however, reveals a somewhat different picture. In certain areas, mostly in the west and south, the rate of enclosure was speeding up. The large open fields, divided into strips and cultivated separately by each village farmer, were being made into compact, hedged or walled fields.

A few progressive farmers were beginning to experiment with crops on their newly-enclosed farms. **Jethro Tull (1674–1741)** invented a seed drill which sowed the seed in rows at a uniform depth. Before then, seed was scattered by hand. The seed drill saved seed, made weeding easy and improved yield. Soon afterwards, when he returned from travelling in France and Italy, Tull experimented on his Berkshire farm with various theories of plant nutrition, and made a horse-hoe. His experiments were so successful that he published a book about his work, *The New Horse-Hoeing Husbandry: or, an Essay on the Principles of Tillage and Vegetation*. At the time he gained little support for his ideas and methods.

Another early pioneer was **Charles ('Turnip') Townshend (1674–1738)** brother-in-law of **Sir Robert Walpole**, who introduced on his Norfolk farm a new four-course rotation of crops: wheat, root crop, barley and clover. In this way winter feed could be provided and land did not have to be left fallow.

But it was not until later in the century when the enclosure movement was at its height, and more farmers were able to try out new methods, that widespread improvements began. New crops, better live-stock, and a scientific approach to farming introducing modern techniques, brought about a revolution in agriculture.

Industry

Equally great progress was to be made in industry and trade, and by the mid-eighteenth century an industrial revolution had begun. This was to continue as Britain acquired more colonies in North America and in the East, resulting in a big expansion of overseas trade.

It was Whig policy to encourage industry and promote trade. When they came to power in 1714, therefore, the Whig leaders worked to maintain peace abroad and stability in domestic affairs, so that the popularity of their rule would ensure the permanence of the Hanoverian succession, and give the necessary confidence for business men to develop new enterprises. The **Bank of England** had been founded in **1694** and this had already gone a long way towards providing financial security for trade and investment.

The woollen cloth industry was still, after agriculture, Britain's greatest source of wealth. It was run mainly on domestic lines. Spinning was done in the cottages by women and children. Weaving was usually the work of men, in cottages or in small workshops in villages and towns. Middlemen travelled round the country collecting and delivering wool and cloth which was eventually sold to merchants, many of whom exported large quantities.

As the century wore on, inventions to speed up spinning and weaving processes led to a great expansion of the industry. The trend was towards factories and towns, and away from cottage industry.

There was great development also in other industries. Coal-mining, ship-building, the luxury industries, such as the silk industry in London, all benefited eventually from the long period of Whig rule which began in 1714.

In most industries the apprenticeship system still operated with all its advantages and disadvantages. It was a time when everything seemed to be on the side of the employer. There were no trade unions, no inspectors to see that working conditions were satisfactory, and no limits fixed for hours of work and pay. Parliament's policy could be summed up in the phrase *'laissez-faire'*, which implied non-interference in private enterprise.

Trade

In the sphere of trade, Parliament was less tolerant. It was considered essential to maintain a favourable *balance of trade*, and to do this Britain had to export more than she imported so that she might build up a stock of gold which could be used in an emergency. This was the policy of *mercantilism* held by most European governments at the time, and it stemmed generally from a fear of war.

Various regulations were passed to protect and stimulate the cloth industry, which provided the country with its main exports. Restrictions were placed on goods like calico and muslin brought in by the **East India Company**; and the Lancashire cotton industry was encouraged. So also was the linen industry in Ireland. In the American colonies measures were taken to prevent the growth of textile industries which might compete with those in Britain.

Yet in spite of restrictions, and erroneous economic theories, Britain's trade was in a thriving condition in the early part of the eighteenth century. The **South Sea Company** was founded in **1711**. This, and other trading companies brought great wealth to the country. The ports of London, Bristol and Liverpool had never been busier. British sea power, and the acquisition of more colonies during the eighteenth century, were to lead to an even greater expansion of overseas trade.

Transport

Economic progress is dependent to a great extent on a good system of communications. In the early part of the eighteenth century, goods had to be transported either by road or by sea or river, and in each case there were dangers and delays. The roads were in a very bad state. They became muddy and full of holes in the winter, and dry and rutted in the summer. Many of them were extremely narrow and little more than tracks. Others, in lonely parts, were dangerous because of the robbers and highwaymen who were known to frequent them. It took six days to travel by stage-coach from London to Newcastle.

A system of *turnpikes* had been devised whereby the users of a road had to pass through a gate where they were charged a sum of money or 'toll' to pay for the upkeep of the road. The local Justice of the Peace was usually responsible for the turnpikes, but sometimes special turnpike trustees were set up. They did not provide the answer to the problem, however, and the state of the roads continued to remain generally bad until later in the century when a vast new programme of road improvement began.

Largely because of the poor state of the roads, heavy goods were usually sent by sea or river. London's coal came mostly by sea from the Tyneside mines. Agricultural products often went by river from one part of the country to another, and many rivers were being specially widened and deepened for the purpose. Towards the end of the reign of George I the country had over a thousand miles of navigable rivers. Soon, the age of canals was to begin.

London

In many respects, the London life of this period was typical of the economic and social conditions of the country at the time of the Hanoverian succession. *London was the business centre of Europe.* To the port of London came ships carrying cargoes from the Mediterranean, the Far East, America and Africa. London merchants and London markets were among the wealthiest and most important in the world and London was also the centre of banking and of the law.

In London there were some of the best shops and theatres in Europe, filled with men and women anxious to keep abreast of the latest fashions and of literary developments. There was much drinking and gambling, and sometimes immense sums of money were won and lost over cards and dice. Occasionally an evening's gambling would end in a duel fought at dawn in some secluded field or garden. The wearing of swords was still quite common among gentlemen.

Many gentlemen, from dukes to squires, spent only a few months of the year in the capital. The rest of the time they lived on their country estates, attending to their land and bringing up their families in the best traditions of the English gentry. They entertained neighbouring gentry, went hunting or fishing, and sometimes, as local landlords, showed an interest in a game of football or cricket played on the village green.

The ownership of land gave social and political standing, and it had long been the practice of successful merchants to buy a country estate with their profits from trade. They built fine houses with panelled rooms, high ceilings and sash windows. They filled them with delicately-carved furniture made of mahogany imported from the American Indies. They sent their sons to the nearest grammar school or to the public schools such as Eton, Winchester, Harrow or Westminster, while their daughters were taught domestic subjects at home. It was unusual for a girl to be educated up to the standard of her brother, or to take an interest in politics, although there were exceptions.

Finally, no mention of London would be complete without reference to the thousands of skilled and unskilled workmen, shopkeepers, doctors and others who gave the city its real character. Like all cities, London was a place where there were extremes of wealth and poverty. There were slums and mansions, beggars and rich merchants. The London 'mob' could not be roused easily, but when it was provoked it was a force which could not be ignored. London's magistrates and her constables and militia were always prepared to defend the city's privileges, and it was a very unwise person who under-estimated its strength.

Scotland and Ireland

While Londoners welcomed George I, there were Jacobites in Scotland and Ireland who supported the Stuart cause. The **Act of Union (1707)** which united England and Scotland satisfied most of the Lowland Scots and others who realized the solid benefits brought to Scottish trade and industry. The Act provided for the union of the two **Parliaments**. The crowns of England and Scotland had been united in 1603 when **James VI** of Scotland became also **James I** of England. But there were many people, particularly in the less law-abiding Highlands, who did not appreciate the advantages of the Union. They were prepared to support the son of James II in his attempt to regain the English throne, though their chance of success was small, the union being too beneficial to Scots and English to be in serious danger.

In Ireland the position was different. There was no union between the countries, and a tradition of bitter hostility towards England had recently been made worse by the breaking of the **Treaty of Limerick (1691)**. In this treaty, the Irish, who had been supporting the banished James II against William III, had been promised better treatment after their surrender to the Dutch **General Ginkel**. The promise was not kept.

The majority of Irish were Roman Catholic, and for centuries they had been deprived of political power and subjected to a harsh penal code. *The Irish Parliament was exclusively Protestant.* No Catholic could vote; nor could he educate his children in his own religion. Over the years, much of their land had been confiscated and given to English Protestants. When, therefore, the Irish were promised some alleviation of their condition in 1691 and there was, in fact, no improvement, hatred of the English grew more intense.

Unlike Scotland, Ireland did not enjoy free trade with England. The English Parliament passed measures to restrict the development of any Irish industry which might compete with English manufactures.

The result of oppression in Ireland was large-scale emigration. The population almost halved during the eighteenth century. Some went to European countries, others to America. Everywhere they went they carried with them a burning hatred of England because of the injustice done to their country, and they were willing recruits for any army formed to fight against the English.

Britain and Europe

Britain had no friends in Europe in 1714. The War of the Spanish Succession had only just ended and Britain's principal allies, Holland and the Empire, felt they had been extremely badly treated when Britain concluded secret peace terms with the French. In the **Treaty of Utrecht (1713)**, which ended the war, Britain gained the Hudson's Bay territory, Nova Scotia and Newfoundland from France, and Gibraltar and Minorca from Spain. She also received by the **Asiento Treaty (1713)**, permission to export 4,800 negroes a year to Spanish America for the following thirty years, and the right to send one trading ship a year to Porto Bello on the Isthmus of Panama. By comparison, Britain's allies gained very little, and it was no wonder they felt betrayed.

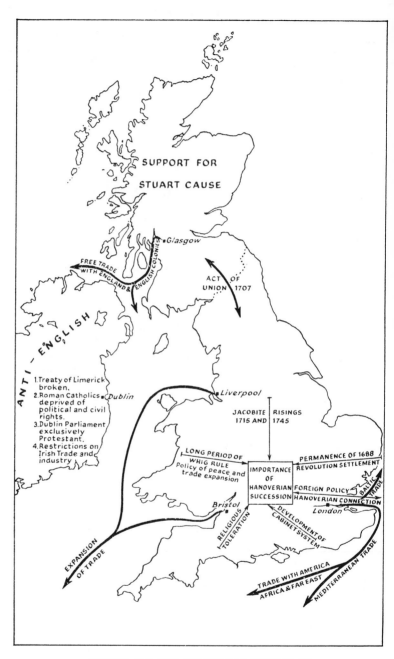

Text within the map:

SUPPORT FOR STUART CAUSE

Glasgow

FREE TRADE WITH ENGLAND & ENGLISH COLONIES

ACT OF UNION 1707

ANTI-ENGLISH

1. Treaty of Limerick broken.
2. Roman Catholics deprived of political and civil rights.
3. Dublin Parliament exclusively Protestant.
4. Restrictions on Irish Trade and industry

Dublin

Liverpool

JACOBITE | RISINGS
1715 AND | 1745

LONG PERIOD OF WHIG RULE
Policy of peace and trade expansion

PERMANENCE OF 1688 REVOLUTION SETTLEMENT

IMPORTANCE OF HANOVERIAN SUCCESSION

FOREIGN POLICY
HANOVERIAN CONNECTION

BALTIC TRADE

Bristol

RELIGIOUS TOLERATION

DEVELOPMENT OF CABINET SYSTEM

London

EXPANSION OF TRADE

TRADE WITH AMERICA AFRICA & FAR EAST

MEDITERRANEAN TRADE

BRITAIN AND THE HANOVERIAN SUCCESSION

In view of Britain's unpopularity in Europe, the Whig government would need to proceed with great caution in foreign affairs, and even try to become friendly with France, England's former enemy and her maritime and colonial rival. The Whigs would also have to guard against any attempt by the disgruntled powers, notably Spain, to overturn the Utrecht settlement. This was not to prove too difficult, since Britain had emerged from the war with a heightened military prestige as a result of Marlborough's great victories.

Apart from Britain's isolation, the Whig ministers had also the Hanoverian connection to consider. However desirable it might seem to steer clear of European entanglements, the Hanoverian kings were sure to be ever watchful of their German electorate, and many people thought this might involve England in wars to defend purely Hanoverian interests. But Britain was not, in fact, involved in any very large-scale fighting on land in Europe during the eighteenth century. Wars were fought in the colonies and on the sea, and subsidies were paid to support allied armies on the Continent.

Britain and the World

Already Britain's interests were world-wide. The British flag flew in North America, the West Indies, the west coast of Africa, in India, and in the important naval bases of Minorca and Gibraltar in the Mediterranean. Spain and Holland, both of which had once been leading maritime powers, were in decline; and Britain, at the time of the Hanoverian succession, had a clear lead as a colonial and commercial power over her only possible rival, France. French power had been considerably weakened by the wars of Louis XIV in which he attempted to gain the mastery of Europe; and, although it was not apparent in 1714, France had already chosen in favour of Europe rather than an empire.

The attitude towards colonies during the early part of the eighteenth century was that they existed solely for the benefit of the mother country. Their main purpose was to supply the mother country with raw materials for her industries and become markets for her manufactured goods. *Trade and not the possession of land was the important thing.* There was little appreciation of the political and strategic value of colonies, and no idea that they might develop to become independent.

Summary

On the death of Queen Anne in 1714, George the Elector of Hanover became King of England in accordance with the terms of the Act of Settlement (1701). The Hanoverian succession assured the permanence of the Glorious Revolution (1688) which finally established the supremacy of Parliament over the King. It also began a long period of Whig rule during which important constitutional and economic progress was made.

Whig supremacy was based on the support of Parliament and of the king. The Tory party had been discredited because of its association with Jacobitism. But the Whig ministers could not afford to be complacent. Support for the Old Pretender, the son of James II, was strong in Ireland and in parts of Scotland; and a Jacobite attempt to regain the throne for the Stuarts might also receive help from sympathizers in England, unless Whig policy could popularize the Hanoverian succession by providing a long period of peace and prosperity. Agriculture and industry were modernized as the century progressed, and overseas trade expanded.

In Europe, Britain's strength was respected but her reputation was low. The secret negotiations with France towards the end of the Spanish Succession War, which led to Britain obtaining extremely favourable peace terms for herself at Utrecht, had left her without allies. The Whig ministers found it necessary to adopt a cautious foreign policy in order to preserve peace and the Utrecht settlement, and at the same time to safeguard the interests of Hanover. Britain's future was to lie not in Europe but in maritime and colonial strength, France being her only serious rival.

Important Dates

1711 **South Sea Company founded.**
1713 **Treaty of Utrecht.**
         The Asiento Treaty.
1714 **Accession of George I.**
1715 **Whig Parliament.**
         Oxford and Bolingbroke impeached.

QUESTIONS

(*1*) *How do you account for the successful establishment of the Hanoverian Succession?*

(*2*) *Explain the importance of the Whig victory on the death of Anne in 1714.*

(*3*) *Describe the social and economic condition of Britain at the start of the Hanoverian period.*

(*4*) *Write notes on three of the following:* (a) *Jethro Tull;* (b) *the fall of Bolingbroke;* (c) *turnpikes;* (d) *Jacobitism;* (e) *Whig policy in 1714;* (f) *The coffee houses.*

CHAPTER TWO

THE AGE OF WALPOLE

The Whig Leaders

THE period of Whig rule which began with the Hanoverian succession and ended in 1760, extended over the reign of two kings, George I (1714–1727) and **George II (1727–1760)**. Both these kings felt themselves to be foreigners in Britain and they were glad, therefore, to leave most of the work of government to the Whig ministers. Neither of the kings took much part in the administration of domestic or colonial affairs, though they did, occasionally, as Electors of Hanover, try to influence foreign policy particularly when Hanoverian interests were at stake. Each king expected his ministers to 'do his business', by which he meant his Hanoverian business.

The Unpopularity of George I

George I was accepted by the majority of his subjects but he inspired no affection. He was probably the most disliked king ever to occupy the English throne. The fact that there was no uprising against him when he arrived in England is a measure not of his popularity but of the strength of anti-Stuart feeling in the country. People feared a return of the Stuarts more than they disliked the notion of a foreigner on the throne. The Stuarts were associated with Roman Catholicism and arbitrary rule, while the Hanoverians represented the triumph of Protestantism and of Parliamentary government.

Yet in spite of this, there were some who were prepared to support the Stuart cause. Throughout 1715 there was unrest and rioting in places. This was kept in check by the magistrates who had been given more power under the **Riot Act**. The Act was passed in **1714** following disorders in Scotland and elsewhere. It authorized magistrates to order troops to fire on rioting crowds if they refused to disperse within an hour of being ordered to do so.

But if unrest was curbed to some extent, it was by no means cured, and Jacobitism was a force which neither the King nor his Whig ministers could afford to ignore. *In Scotland lay the greatest danger.* Highland clans were known to support the Stuarts, and there was still dissatisfaction with the Union.

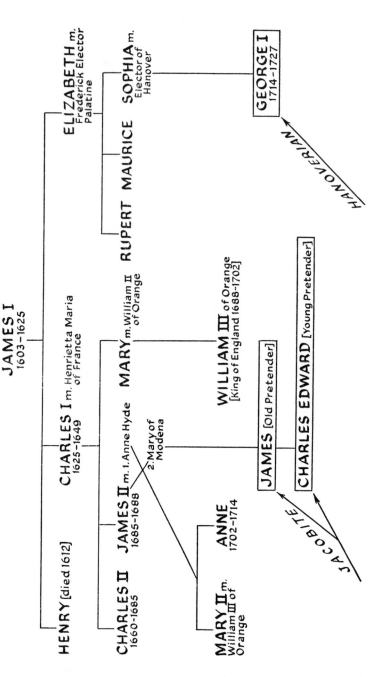

The descendants of James I, showing Hanoverian and Jacobite claims

The Jacobite Rising of 1715 (The Fifteen)

George I had been on the throne less than a year when news reached England of a plot to overthrow him and to enthrone **Prince James Edward, the Old Pretender.** The plot was formed in France at the court of the Pretender at St. Germain. There were to be three simultaneous risings. One in the Highlands under a Scottish nobleman, the **Earl of Mar**; a second in Northumberland to be led by **Mr. Forster** and the **Earl of Derwentwater**; and a third in the west of England under the leadership of the **Duke of Ormonde**. James himself was to land in Scotland to lead the revolt, and he was to be helped by French troops.

On 6th September, **1715**, the Earl of Mar raised his standard at **Braemar** and the rebellion began. At first it looked quite promising. About 8,000 Highlanders joined Mar. By October, he had occupied **Perth** and was in control of all the central Highlands. Meanwhile, a Jacobite rising had occurred in Northumberland under Forster and Derwentwater.

But success was short-lived. On 13th November, Mar's army fought an indecisive battle against the forces of the Whig **Duke of Argyll** at **Sheriffmuir**; and on the same day the Jacobites in the north of England were compelled to surrender at **Preston**. Mar's army fell back on Perth, while Forster's supporters returned to their homes. All hope of a successful rising had vanished. James arrived in Scotland in December only to find the Jacobite cause dead, and within six weeks he had returned to France taking Mar with him.

The Causes of Failure

The main reason for the failure of the Fifteen rebellion was the lack of English support. The rising planned in the west under Ormonde never took place at all, and very few joined Forster and Derwentwater in the north. Even in Scotland support for the Stuarts was not as strong as expected.

The appearance of James himself in Scotland, after the battle of Sheriffmuir, did nothing to revive Stuart hopes. He was an uninspiring leader who clearly had no confidence in himself or his cause. Further, he brought no French help with him. The French King Louis XIV had died in 1715 and the Regent, Orleans, who was governing France during the minority of Louis XV, was anxious to maintain friendship with Britain. He refused help to the Jacobites and ordered the seizure of supplies which they had obtained.

From a purely military point of view the rebellion was doomed from the start. The British Ambassador in Paris, **Lord Stair**, reported fully on every move made by the Pretender and his friends. The Whigs therefore had early warning of the revolt and took the precaution of garrisoning key points, while the navy patrolled the coasts.

If Mar had acted quickly after taking Perth, and moved southwards to join up with Forster, the rising might not have collapsed so quickly, though its ultimate failure was certain. As it was, he hesitated, giving his enemies time to consolidate their position.

Finally, the Catholicism of James led even the most enthusiastic of Protestant Jacobites to have misgivings, and without complete unity and fixity of purpose the rising could not hope to succeed. As for the bulk of people in England and Scotland, they were opposed to a return of Stuart rule. Some feared financial ruin and a repudiation of the National Debt. Others feared a return to despotic royal government and an end to constitutional monarchy. Nearly all were opposed to civil war and in favour of the established Hanoverian government under Whig direction.

Results of the Fifteen

The rebels were treated fairly leniently by eighteenth-century standards. Many of them were transported to the colonies. Probably about fifty were executed. Seven peers were impeached and found guilty, though four were reprieved. Of the remaining three, Lords Derwentwater and **Kenmure** were beheaded, but **Lord Nithsdale** managed to escape disguised as a woman.

The defeat of the Fifteen rebellion strengthened the Whigs and secured the Hanoverian succession. But Jacobitism still survived, and it was thought advisable not to risk an early election. The **Septennial Act** was therefore passed in **1716** to extend the life of Parliament from three to seven years. The Septennial Act remained in force until 1911 when five years became the maximum period without a general election.

Continuing Jacobite Activity

Disappointed in their hope of help from France because of the pro-English policy of the Regent, Orleans, the Jacobites looked for help elsewhere. **Charles XII** of Sweden seemed a likely friend, but he died in **1718** and domestic problems prevented Sweden giving any aid.

Spain was another possible supporter of the Jacobite cause. **Alberoni**, Spain's chief minister, was anxious to destroy the Utrecht settlement by recapturing Gibraltar and seizing Sicily. James visited Madrid and persuaded the Spanish to send a small force to Scotland in 1719. The expedition reached Loch Duich in the West Highlands and a few hundred Highlanders rose to support it. But they were quickly defeated and **Marshal Wade** was sent to the Highlands to build roads and forts so that order could be maintained. No further Spanish help was given to the Jacobites. The Spaniards had suffered a naval

THE 1715 JACOBITE RISING

defeat off **Cape Passaro** in Sicily in **1718** and the power of Alberoni was waning. He disappeared entirely from the political scene two years later.

However, the birth of a son to the Old Pretender in 1720 helped to keep Jacobitism alive in Britain. In **1722** there was a Jacobite plot to seize the King and the Prince of Wales. News of it leaked out and the organizer of the plot, **Atterbury, Bishop of Rochester** was banished. There was a further plot in 1727 when George I died, but nothing came of it.

Meanwhile, Jacobite hopes centred on **Prince Charles Edward**, son of the Old Pretender. As he grew up, the number of Jacobite societies increased, particularly in Scotland. But as each year passed, and Whig rule brought stability and increasing prosperity to the country, contentment with the Hanoverian succession grew and the chances of a successful Jacobite rising declined.

The Whigs and the Crown

The Whigs were quick to strengthen their position after the defeat of the Fifteen. They were helped considerably by their use of Crown 'patronage', which allowed them to reward their supporters with promotions and titles. Normally only the sovereign could confer these favours, but George I knew little about English domestic affairs and was glad to let the Whig ministers have their way. Naturally, they used their power to obtain supporters, and soon it became extremely difficult for a man to rise in his profession, or to obtain social advancement unless he was a loyal Whig.

Though George I never allowed himself to be dominated by his ministers, he lost a considerable amount of influence in politics through his inability to speak or to understand English. At Cabinet meetings during the early part of his reign, his only son, the Prince of Wales, later to become George II, interpreted proceedings to the King. But by 1718 father and son, never on good terms, had quarrelled openly, and George I avoided attending cabinet meetings not so much because he was bored with English politics, but because he did not wish to see his son who attended the meetings as heir to the throne. By then it had become customary for most of the work of the cabinet to be done without the Sovereign being present, though under Queen Anne, George I's predecessor, it was still usual for the Sovereign to attend cabinet meetings once a week.

The practice, therefore, grew up of a leading minister taking the place of the Crown and presiding at cabinet meetings. The minister would then report proceedings to the King. George I understood and spoke French fluently, and this was the language commonly used by Whig Ministers when they discussed affairs with him.

The Prince of Wales and the Opposition

The feud between the heir to the throne and his parents was a continuing feature of Hanoverian family life. In 1718, the Prince of Wales and his wife, **Caroline of Anspach**, set up their own court at Leicester House, and all who visited them were forbidden to appear at the King's court of St. James. Leicester House became a centre of the political opposition.

When George I died and his son succeeded him as George II in 1727, the traditional hostility of the heir to the throne was continued through George II's son, **Frederick Louis, Prince of Wales**. Frederick's court attracted leading writers and wits of the day, for example, Swift, Pope and Gay, as well as discontented politicians and place-seekers.

The Prince of Wales, by patronizing the opposition, was looked on as its nominal head. Encouraged by members of the opposition, he quarrelled with his parents, demanding a higher allowance on his marriage in 1736. His father, George II, called him a 'puppy, fool and rascal', while his mother said: 'My dear first-born is the greatest ass and the greatest liar and the greatest *canaille* and the greatest beast in the whole world, and I heartily wish he were out of it.'

Frederick Louis died in 1751. Perhaps, in view of his reputation, it was just as well he never succeeded to the throne. On the death of George II in 1760, Frederick's son became **George III**. Like the two previous kings, George III was on extremely bad terms with his eldest son.

While the continuing connection of the Prince of Wales with the opposition was of political significance, it was not as important as it would have been had it occurred earlier in British history. *By the Hanoverian period the power of the Crown had been considerably reduced.* We are concerned in the eighteenth century more with the rise and fall of ministries than with the reigns of Kings and Queens.

The Whigs and Parliament

The support of the Crown would not have been sufficient on its own to maintain the Whigs in power. They needed also the support of Parliament, and particularly the House of Commons. The Whigs had a majority in the Lords, and were careful always to keep a clear majority in the Commons. This was not difficult. About a quarter of the Commons were '*placemen*', that is, members who held minor posts on condition that they continued to vote for the government. Many other seats were held by men whose election was arranged. They were either the nominees of Whig noblemen, who controlled the elections in their areas, or were elected as a result of the *bribing of electors*. There were a few members from free boroughs, but they were in such a minority that they had little influence on the House as a whole.

Both Whigs and Tories used bribery at election times. But in the first half of the eighteenth century, the Whigs, wielding the patronage of the Crown, were able to use it more effectively.

Stanhope's Foreign Policy

At the time of George I's succession, the Whigs were led by **Lord Sunderland, the Earl of Stanhope, Viscount Townshend** and **Sir Robert Walpole**. In 1717 Walpole and Townshend resigned because they did not agree with the foreign policy of their colleagues, and Stanhope was chief minister until his death in 1721.

Stanhope, who had fought in Spain under the **Earl of Peterborough** during the War of the Spanish Succession, was in favour of strong measures to preserve the Utrecht settlement and with it, the balance of power in Europe. This was being challenged by **Philip V of Spain** and his ambitious minister Alberoni. They were dissatisfied with the terms of the Treaty of Utrecht, and wanted to recapture Gibraltar and Sicily. The Spanish King was also known to support the Jacobite cause. Stanhope was determined to check Spanish ambitions and in this he was supported by France and Holland.

The Regent of France, the **Duke of Orleans**, who governed during the minority of **Louis XV**, feared that the delicate Louis XV might not live long and the next heir in the strict line of succession was Philip of Spain, whose succession was forbidden by the Treaty of Utrecht, but who still coveted the French crown. As a descendant of a brother of Louis XIV, Orleans could have a claim to the French throne on the death of Louis XV, if Philip were excluded. The Dutch, on the other hand, were alarmed at the prospect of a union of the French and Spanish Crowns, which would threaten their independence.

Britain, France and Holland, therefore, formed the **Triple Alliance** in **1717** to maintain the Utrecht settlement. It was a great diplomatic triumph for Stanhope, though it was at this point that Walpole, Townshend and **Pulteney** resigned. They were against Britain becoming involved in European alliances since they considered Britain's true interests lay in developing the colonial and commercial gains made at the Treaty of Utrecht.

The argument that Britain was primarily a colonial and maritime power and, as such, ought to devote her attention to overseas expansion rather than to European affairs, was supported by many members from both political parties. Even today, the same kind of controversy exists about Britain's role in Europe and the world, though the issue has been sharpened by the looser ties of the Commonwealth, and the urgent need for Britain to re-examine her position.

In the eighteenth century, the great age of empire building was only just beginning, and there was strong pressure from the rapidly-developing business section of the population to acquire more markets for manufactured goods and sources of raw materials for Britain's expanding industries. Stanhope was aware of this need, but he also knew that European peace was essential for the development of British trade. Britain has never been able to afford to ignore Europe for long, and in the early eighteenth century there were two additional strong reasons why it was impossible for a policy of isolation to be pursued. The first was the Hanoverian connection. The second was the growing rivalry between Britain and France at sea and in the colonies. Any major changes in the European political scene were bound to have important repercussions, for example, in America and India, where the interests of English and French colonists clashed and where fighting was certain to break out in the event of a European war.

Stanhope's policy of alliance with France proved to be a wise one. As was foreseen, Spain, encouraged by the friendship of the warrior King of Sweden, Charles XII, made a determined attempt to destroy the Utrecht settlement. Spanish forces occupied Sardinia and attacked Sicily. In 1718 a British naval victory off **Cape Passaro** prevented a Spanish conquest of Sicily. This was followed by two further blows to Spanish hopes. Charles XII was killed in fighting against the Norwegians and the Austrian Emperor joined Britain, thereby turning the Triple into the **Quadruple Alliance.**

In the following year (1719), Alberoni resigned and Philip agreed to abandon the Stuart cause and to accept the terms of the Treaty of Utrecht. The only important change in the settlement was that the **Duke of Savoy** received Sardinia instead of Sicily, and Sicily went back to Austria. The strong policy of Stanhope had been justified. British sea power and the Franco-British alliance had succeeded in giving Europe a much-needed period of peace, during which both France and Britain were able to develop their trade.

It was unlikely that the two countries would remain on friendly terms indefinitely, since maritime and colonial rivalry was becoming acute. Furthermore, France and Spain were almost certain to draw closer together, finding they had a common interest in opposing Britain. Yet this does not detract from Stanhope's achievement. It is generally agreed that he suggested the right policy for the time, and deserves much credit for the part he played in maintaining the general peace of Europe for some twenty years.

The Protestant Interests Act

Stanhope's ministry is notable not only for its successful foreign policy, but for the passing of the **Protestant Interests Act** in **1719**, which gave more freedom to nonconformists. The Act repealed the

Occasional Conformity Act (1711) and the **Schism Act (1714)**. The former punished with a heavy fine anyone who had taken the Anglican sacrament in order to qualify for office, and afterwards attended nonconformist services. The latter forbade nonconformists to have their own schools and teachers.

Both the Occasional Conformity Act and the Schism Act had been passed by the Tories. Their repeal helped to make the Whig party popular among the increasing number of nonconformists in the country on whom the Whigs partly depended for political support. At the same time it expressed the growing demand for more toleration in matters of religion among the educated sections of the population.

The Peerage Bill

The Whigs had a safe majority in the Lords and they wanted to make sure that this favourable position continued indefinitely. In **1719**, therefore, the **Peerage Bill** was introduced to prevent the creation of new peers.

Walpole spoke against the Bill and it was rejected. He pointed out that if it were passed no Commoner could ever become a peer, and the House of Lords would become a lifeless, purely hereditary body. It would also mean that in future no sovereign could create new peers to ensure the passing of a Bill in the Lords which had been passed by the Commons, and which the ministry in power considered to be of vital importance. The House of Lords would thus become a closed community of peers with the power to block indefinitely measures passed by the Commons. It was just as well for English constitutional development that the Bill was dropped.

The ability shown by Walpole in the debates on the Peerage Bill led to the offer of a post in the Stanhope ministry. He became, in 1720, Paymaster-General of the Forces. He had held this position for a short time once before, just after the accession of George I.

The Early Career of Sir Robert Walpole

Walpole was born in 1676 at Houghton in Norfolk. He was the third son of a country gentleman, Robert Walpole, the member of Parliament for Houghton. Like many other sons of the gentry, he received a public school education, spending five years at Eton College. From there he went as a scholar to King's College, Cambridge, but resigned his scholarship when he became heir to the family estates on the death of his two elder brothers.

In **1701** he entered Parliament for the family borough of **Castle Rising** in Norfolk, and soon afterwards became member for **King's Lynn**, a constituency he was to represent until **1742** when he was raised to the peerage as the **Earl of Orford**.

Soon after becoming a member of the Commons, Walpole was appointed Lord High Admiral of England. In **1708** he succeeded Henry St. John (Bolingbroke) as Secretary at War, and for a time also held the treasurership of the Navy. In **1712** he was accused of corruption, expelled from the Commons, and sent to the Tower. This was the work of his political opponents. But his fortunes changed with the Hanoverian succession when he became Paymaster-General of the Forces.

He was appointed First Lord of the Treasury and Chancellor of the Exchequer in 1715, but withdrew from the ministry in 1717 after differences with the Whig leaders, Sunderland and Stanhope. It was then that Walpole became a leading member of the opposition Whigs and spoke against the Peerage Bill. Not long afterwards the Stanhope ministry fell, and Walpole emerged as the leading Whig minister, a position he was to hold for the next twenty years.

The South Sea Bubble

His rise to power was the direct result of a serious financial crisis which affected England, France and the European countries in 1720. Its cause was the mania for speculation which began as a result of the rapid growth in all kinds of commercial enterprise about the beginning of the eighteenth century.

In England the trouble began in **1719** when the **South Sea Company**, which had been founded in 1711 by Harley to trade with South America, offered to take over the National Debt. The South Sea Company was by then extremely prosperous, having benefited greatly by the terms of the Asiento Treaty. It seemed, therefore, an admirable idea for the government and the Company to come to an agreement in 1720 by which those who had subscribed to the Debt would receive shares in the Company in place of government stock. The Company paid the government £7 million for the arrangement, and interest payable on the Debt was reduced to five per cent.

The interest shown by the Government in the South Sea Company, and the protection of its merchandise was a powerful advertisement. Shares in the Company soared in price, and the Company expanded with great speed. The King became a governor of the Company in 1718. Walpole, who had foreseen a rise in the value of the shares, bought some himself and also obtained £30,000 worth for the Prince and Princess of Wales.

There followed a boom in speculation. Scores of new companies, many of them fraudulent, were founded. At one time there were 140 companies being advertised in London alone, and the shares found a ready market. There was a company for 'a wheel of perpetual motion'; another 'for extracting silver from lead'; and strangest of all, a company 'for importing a large number of large jackasses from Spain to improve the breed of British mules'. There seemed no end to the ingenuity of promoters and speculators. However, not all the companies launched were dishonest. Many dealt with foreign trade and with insurance. On the whole, it was the poor people who became most heavily involved in the fraudulent projects. Stocks were sold to them for deposits of sixpence or a shilling. Walpole sensed a financial storm. He had earlier advised the government against speculative investment in the South Sea Company, but his advice had been ignored.

In August 1720 the storm broke, and all his warnings were proved justified. The panic began when the South Sea Company, annoyed at the founding of so many rival companies, prosecuted some of them. Immediately there was a rush to sell stock. Thousands of small investors were ruined. The South Sea 'Bubble' had burst, though the shares of the Company did not fall below the original purchase price, and the Company continued to make a profit until 1732. The *London Gazette* was filled with bankruptcy notices; and suicides occurred practically every day.

The End of the South Sea Affair

Although the South Sea Company weathered the storm, there was such an outcry against the directors and ministers responsible for making the arrangements about the National Debt that a committee of the House of Commons was set up to enquire into the scandal. Its report showed that at least three ministers had accepted bribes and speculated in stock, and that many directors had made enormous profits.

In February 1721 Stanhope collapsed and died, after bursting a blood vessel when in a rage during a South Sea debate in the House of Lords. The Chancellor of the Exchequer, **John Aislabie**, who appeared to have made a profit of £1,000,000 on the South Sea scheme, was expelled from Parliament and sent to the Tower. In April, Sunderland resigned, his political career ruined in spite of his acquittal on the charge of having received a bribe of £50,000. Another minister, **James Craggs**, committed suicide. Most of the estates of the South Sea directors were confiscated, though the majority of them managed to repair their broken fortunes later.

Walpole, the man who had foreseen the crash, and who had kept aloof from the disaster, having sold his South Sea stock in good time, was swept into power. He became First Lord of the Treasury and Chancellor of the Exchequer and, not long after, Chief Minister of the Crown.

Most of the measures he had planned for the country's recovery were never put into effect. England's economy was basically sound. All that was needed was a restoration of confidence and once this had been achieved no further action was necessary.

Walpole's Character and Policy

Few men could have been better qualified to inspire confidence than Sir Robert Walpole, the shrewd 46-year-old Norfolk squire, who had disapproved of the South Sea scheme and had remained calm throughout the crisis. He was a brilliant financier and an experienced administrator. He knew the House of Commons well, having served as a member for King's Lynn since he was a young man; and he showed great skill in debate. Members had learned to respect his judgment. Essentially a practical man, he seemed to know exactly when to press a point and when to abandon it or to compromise. Even his physical appearance was impressive. He weighed over twenty stone.

Yet in 1721 he was only just beginning the most important part of his career. As a practical business man, who was also a landowner and a Whig, *Walpole was determined to pursue a policy of peace and trade expansion.* This was essential to restore business confidence, to ensure the safety of the Hanoverian succession, and to make the rule of the Whigs popular. He had the ability to carry out his policy, but his position as Chief Minister depended on the continued support of the Crown and of the Commons. The ways in which he obtained their support for the next twenty years of his administration must now be examined.

Walpole and the Crown

George I quickly recognized the value of Walpole as a competent Chief Minister. He was deeply grateful to him for the way in which he had restored calm at the time of the South Sea crisis. He therefore left the conduct of domestic affairs entirely to him and his colleagues, and only showed an interest in foreign affairs when questions arose which concerned the safety of his beloved Duchy of Hanover.

It is a measure of the strength of Walpole's position that, on the death of George I in 1727, he remained securely in office in spite of George II's opposition to him. It seems that George II bore Walpole a grudge for not continuing to support him when he was Prince of Wales after Walpole resumed office in 1720. But on the advice of his wife, Queen Caroline, George II allowed Walpole to remain. The Queen became one of Walpole's closest supporters, and for the next ten years he relied upon her to obtain the King's agreement on all important issues. It was said that Walpole and the Queen discussed the various matters of state first and arrived at a decision. Then the Queen discussed them with the King and cleverly made him think he had reached the decision himself, when in fact he was following her ideas or those of Walpole.

On the death of Queen Caroline in 1737, Walpole seriously thought of retiring. It was 'the greatest blow that ever he received'. But it was the Queen's wish that he should continue, and he also felt it his duty to the country to remain in office.

Walpole and the Commons

While no chief minister could remain in office against the wishes of the Crown, even more important to him was the support of the Commons. Walpole knew the strength of the House and always took the trouble to explain his policies to the members. He listened to their advice and on more than one occasion changed his mind on a proposal when convinced by arguments raised against it.

Throughout his ministry he was fortunate to have the services of the **Duke of Newcastle**, the greatest of all Whig borough-mongers. Newcastle took an active part in every election from 1715 to 1761, particularly in the constituencies he controlled in Sussex, Nottinghamshire, Yorkshire and Lincolnshire. By the skilful use of patronage and persuasion he was always able to secure a comfortable majority. In both Houses of Parliament he exercised powerful influence. Members knew that their loyal support would be rewarded by favours and pensions, but that their opposition would result in loss of prospects, and even possibly the ruin of their careers.

The House of Commons was by no means representative of the whole population. (See page 5.) Yet on important issues it often reflected public opinion with surprising accuracy. Powerful as he was, the Duke of Newcastle could not turn the Commons into a completely subservient assembly. On several occasions, various small groups of members showed an independent spirit which no amount of persuasion or bribery could subdue. At the time of the Peerage Bill, and later when Walpole tried to get an Excise Bill passed, opinion in the country prevailed, and the measures had to be dropped.

Walpole was the first Chief Minister to choose to sit in the Commons rather than in the Lords. By recognizing the predominance of the House of Commons in the British system of government, he did much to raise its prestige. His views are summed up in the following remarks made during a debate in the Commons: 'I have lived long enough in the world, Sir, to know that the safety of a minister lies in his having the approbation of this House. Former ministers, Sir, neglected this, and therefore they fell; I have always made it my first study to obtain it, and therefore I hope to stand.'

The Cabinet

In the time of Walpole, the official position of 'Prime Minister' was unknown in the British constitution. Yet Walpole is considered to have been in fact the first British Prime Minister. In the absence of the King from cabinet meetings, Walpole acted as chairman and co-ordinated the work of all government departments. Any minister who disagreed with him was compelled to resign. **Carteret**, Pulteney and Lord Townshend all had to resign after disagreements with Walpole. In this way the idea was born, though it was not regularly practised until much later, that there should be *unanimity in the cabinet*.

Many people believed that no *one* minister should exercise control over his colleagues, and one of the accusations levelled against Walpole in 1741, when he came under attack in Parliament, was that he had tried to make himself a 'Prime Minister'. Walpole always denied the accusation.

Finance and Trade

When he came into office after the South Sea crisis, Walpole's first task was to set the national finances in order. This he did by a series of measures which established his reputation as a great finance minister.

The National Debt stood at £50 million. He was able to reduce it by cutting down the rate of interest, and at the same time establishing a *Sinking Fund* which was to accumulate until the sum obtained was equal to the Debt. When that happened, the fundholders were to be paid off. The scheme was not very successful, though by the time Walpole resigned, the National Debt had been reduced by about £10 million.

Walpole's greatest contribution lay in his *reform of the tariff system*. He kept taxation as low as possible, and removed or reduced customs duties on many articles of export and import. To clarify the position he issued a new **Book of Rates**. All duties on the export of agricultural produce were abolished, and over a hundred manufactured articles which sold well were freed from export duty. Bounties were given for the export of grain, spirits, silk and refined sugar. To help home industries, he lifted import duties on certain raw materials such as flax, dyes, and raw silk. The result of all these measures was a substantial increase in overseas trade.

Walpole further stimulated trade by developing the *bonded warehouse system*. Under this system, imported goods were taken to a government warehouse and kept there until required either for re-export or for sale to retailers in England. No duty was levied on goods re-exported, but on those sold to retailers for home consumption excise duty had to be paid. The system benefited both the importer and the government. The importer did not have to pay duty on cargo coming into the country for re-export, and the Exchequer gained from the effective check on smuggling. In 1723, Walpole applied the system to tea and coffee, and the results were most encouraging. Ten years later he decided to extend the warehouse plan to wine and tobacco.

This time he was unsuccessful. His **Excise Bill (1733)** had to be withdrawn after the second reading. For six years his political opponents had conducted a campaign against excise. With the new plan to extend the system they succeeded in arousing nation-wide hostility to the Bill. It was alleged that armies of excise men would invade the privacy of shops and homes, since the Bill contained a proposal to collect the duties on wine and tobacco in the shops where the articles were sold, instead of at the ports. Angry crowds marched through the streets, crying 'No slavery, no excise'. It was a triumph for uninformed opinion over sound finance, but it was never Walpole's policy to press a point in the face of opposition of such magnitude. Some forty years later, a similar excise scheme to Walpole's was introduced by Pitt and it proved very beneficial.

Wood's Halfpence

Walpole's withdrawal of the Excise Bill was not the first occasion on which he yielded to public pressure. In **1722** a patent was granted to Wood of Wolverhampton to produce a new copper coinage for Ireland. **Dean Swift (1667–1745)**, the Irish author of great influence, attacked the new coinage in the satirical 'Drapier's Letters'.

The Irish resented the administration in Ireland for many reasons, and it was not difficult to stir up a bitter outcry against the new coins which were referred to contemptuously as 'Wood's Halfpence'. Rather than face serious trouble in Ireland, Walpole withdrew the coinage. A better reaction would have been an attempt to remedy some of the very considerable grievances of the Irish.

The Porteous Riots

Scotland remained quiet during most of Walpole's rule. Scottish industry was benefiting from the Act of Union (1707), which gave Scotland free trade with England and the colonies; and the defeat of the Jacobite Rebellion in 1715 had for a time at least discouraged any further attempt by the Highlanders to dislodge the Hanoverians from the British throne.

But the quiet was shattered for a brief period in **1736** when a smuggler was hanged in Edinburgh, and a large crowd gathered to protest. **Captain Porteous** unwisely ordered his troops to fire on the crowd. He was condemned to death, but the government granted him a reprieve. This infuriated the people of Edinburgh. They seized Porteous and hanged him. Unable to tolerate such defiance, Walpole fined the city of Edinburgh. He thereby lost the support of Scottish members in the Commons, and at the same time stimulated anti-English feeling in Scotland where Jacobitism was by no means dead.

Walpole's Religious Policy

Walpole was never able to ignore the possibility of a revival of Jacobite activity. This explains to some extent his determination to make Hanoverian rule popular. One way in which this could be done was to avoid any measures which might arouse religious animosity. Walpole had no strong religious convictions himself, and he therefore pursued a policy of toleration, hoping to satisfy both the Nonconformists and Anglicans. He would have liked to repeal the **Test Act (1673)** and the **Corporation Act (1661)** which made it illegal for any man to hold office under the Crown, or to be a member of a town Corporation, unless he took Holy Communion according to the rites of the Church of England. But he feared such a step might alarm the High Church party. He therefore placated Nonconformist opinion by introducing an annual **Indemnity Bill** to relieve those who had accepted public office of any penalties they had incurred under the Test and Corporation Acts.

This solution was a wise one in the circumstances. Although religion was no longer a major issue in English political life, it was still sufficiently important to be respected. It was not until a century later, in **1828**, that the Test and Corporation Acts were eventually repealed.

Walpole and the Colonies

In dealing with the colonies Walpole was guided mainly by economic considerations. Colonial trade was becoming increasingly important as the capacity of the colonies to supply Britain with raw materials grew along with their ability to absorb British manufactured goods. British merchants were becoming less dependent on European trading connections, and were anxious to extend their trade with the colonies.

Walpole relied for much of his support on the merchants. These men, though still relatively few in number, were extremely powerful both inside Parliament and in the country. They exercised as strong an influence on government policy as members of the old landed aristocracy did, and Walpole had their interests constantly in mind.

In order to protect British industries, the colonists were forbidden to manufacture goods which might compete with those produced in Britain. For example, they were not allowed to manufacture copper.

All copper ore had to be sent to Britain to be smelted. The colonists were also forbidden to make hats. However, Walpole took steps to encourage colonial trade. Under the **Molasses Act (1733)** duties on foreign sugar were to be levied in colonial ports. This was done to destroy colonial trade with the French West Indies, and help the sugar producers in the British West Indies. Colonial goods sent to Britain for re-export were not subject to duties. Walpole further encouraged colonial trade in **1729** when the **Rice Act** allowed producers to ship rice direct to any port south of Cape Finisterre instead of sending it first to Britain. A similar concession was made for sugar in 1733.

Walpole's colonial policy had been criticized on the grounds that he made no really constructive attempt to draw the colonies closer to Britain or to improve their administration. He did not enforce the laws and regulations governing colonial trade. Smuggling was allowed to continue unchecked. No steps were taken to see that suitable governors were sent out. The colonists managed their own domestic affairs through the colonial assemblies, and they frequently criticized the conduct of governors appointed by the Crown, many of whom were incompetent.

Bearing all these points in mind it must nevertheless be said that Walpole's attitude towards the colonies was typical of the time. It was considered that colonies existed primarily for the benefit of the mother country. The economic and political development of the colonies themselves was thought to be of secondary importance.

The Patriots

An opposition to Walpole had existed for some time. Its members included discontented Whigs as well as Tories. They were led for ten years by Bolingbroke, who returned from exile in 1723 and conducted a campaign against Walpole in his weekly paper, 'The Craftsman'. Other important members of the opposition were William Pulteney and **Lord Carteret**, both of them Whigs.

Bolingbroke retired from politics in 1735 but in the same year a much more formidable man, from Walpole's point of view, entered Parliament and joined the opposition. His name was **William Pitt.** He was twenty-seven years old, the grandson of Governor Pitt of Madras. He had been educated at Eton and Oxford, and had obtained a commission in a cavalry regiment.

Pitt's maiden speech made a profound impression on members of the House of Commons. In those days the standard of oratory was high and his achievement was therefore all the more remarkable. Walpole, sensing danger, and hoping to silence the talented young newcomer, struck his name from the Army List. But this only increased the determination of Pitt and the powerful minority of opposition

Whigs to bring about Walpole's fall. Pitt's followers called themselves the 'Patriots' but Walpole referred to them as the 'Boys'. It was on questions of foreign policy that Walpole was perhaps most open to criticism, and it was here that the opposition concentrated its attack. Pitt and the Patriots accused him of neglecting Britain's interests abroad by pursuing a policy of peace at any price.

Foreign Affairs under Walpole

On Stanhope's death in 1721, Britain and France were in close alliance, and Spanish attempts to destroy the Utrecht settlement had been curbed. But a new, and potentially dangerous situation was arising in Europe. In the first place, Russia, under **Peter the Great,** had defeated Sweden and by the **Treaty of Nystad (1721)** had become the predominant power in the Baltic. In future, no statesman could ignore the entry of Russia into European affairs. Secondly, the Duke of Orleans, Regent of France, died in 1723. For three years power was in the hands of the Duke of Bourbon until the peace-loving, seventy-three-year-old tutor of Louis XV, **Cardinal Fleury,** was made Chief Minister. Thirdly, Philip V of Spain abdicated in 1724. From then until his death in 1746 supreme power was exercised by his scheming wife, **Elizabeth Farnese,** who revived Spanish ambitions in Italy. She was determined to obtain Italian duchies for her sons, and also had an eye on Gibraltar and Minorca which Britain had acquired at the end of the Spanish Succession War. Fourthly, there was always the danger of a breakdown of the Anglo-French alliance as rivalry grew between English and French colonists in America and India, and as France and Spain found they had a common interest in opposing Britain's naval and commercial supremacy.

The first crisis came in **1725,** when Spain and Austria surprised Europe by coming to an agreement in the **Treaty of Vienna.** Spain undertook to give special facilities for trade in the Indies to the Ostend Company, a company founded by the Emperor, **Charles VI,** to develop the foreign trade of the Austrian Netherlands. In return, Austria agreed to help in the reconquest of Gibraltar and Minorca. Once again, Spain became the centre of anti-British activity. Plans were drawn up for a Jacobite invasion, and Spanish sympathizers in France renewed their attacks on the British alliance.

But the alliance held. Both Fleury and Walpole were determined to maintain peace. In **1725** the **Treaty of Hanover** was signed between Britain, France, Hanover, Sweden and Prussia. Following this show of solidarity, Walpole sent British fleets to the Mediterranean and the West Indies in order to impress Spain further. Four years later, in **1729,** after the failure of a Spanish attempt to re-take Gibraltar, Britain and Spain reached an understanding in the **Treaty of Seville** by which

Tuscany and Parma were to go to the sons of Elizabeth Farnese when the existing rulers died. The Emperor **Charles VI** agreed to this arrangement and in **1731** Britain signed the 'Pragmatic Sanction', a solemn pledge to support the right of the Emperor's daughter, Maria Theresa, to succeed to the throne of Austria on his death. In return, Austria abandoned the Ostend Company, which was thought to be a serious threat to British trade in the East Indies.

So far so good. Walpole by painstaking diplomacy and a determination to avoid war for as long as possible, had succeeded in overcoming each crisis as it arose. But he had not evolved any clear lines of policy or long-term solutions. Sooner or later Britain would have to face a breakdown of the Franco-British alliance and the closer understanding between France and Spain. This was a new and dangerous situation for which Britain was largely unprepared.

The War of the Polish Succession

The first major crisis occurred in **1733** on the death of **Augustus II**, King of Poland. The Polish throne was elective, and the great powers of Europe were concerned with the election of a new King. There were two candidates. The first was **Stanislaw Leszczynski**, father-in-law of Louis XV, and supported by France. The second was the **Elector of Saxony**, son of Augustus II, and championed by Austria and Russia.

A European war broke out over the disputed election. French troops overran the Austrian Netherlands, while Spain, coming to the assistance of France, attacked Austrian lands in Italy. The war dragged on until **1735** when, by the **Treaty of Vienna**, the Elector of Saxony became **Augustus III**, King of Poland, and Stanislaw Leszczynski was compensated with the Duchy of Lorraine.

Although pressed by many to intervene, Walpole doggedly refused to involve Britain in the war. 'Madam, there are fifty thousand men slain this year in Europe,' he told the Queen, 'and not one Englishman.' There was some justification for his attitude to the war, since British interests were not directly involved. But the war marked the real end of the Franco-British alliance.

The First Family Compact

In **1733** came the first of three secret agreements made between the Bourbon powers, France and Spain, which came to be known as **'Family Compacts'**. The two Kings pledged themselves to eternal friendship and guaranteed each others' possessions in Europe and overseas. They promised mutual trade concessions and annulled all previous treaties which affected their relations, including the Treaty of Utrecht. France undertook to support Spanish claims in Italy and to help in the recapture of Gibraltar.

Although France and Spain had come together over the Polish question, they were not really concerned with the fate of Poland. *Their agreement was aimed against Britain.* They had decided to join forces in the great struggle which lay ahead for maritime and colonial supremacy.

War and the Resignation of Walpole

For many years, tension had been rising between Britain and Spain. The Spanish challenged Britain's right to Gibraltar and Minorca, and fiercely resented British colonial and trade expansion. They accused British merchants of abusing the privileges granted to them by the Asiento Treaty, in sending more than the stipulated number of slaves to Spanish colonies in South America, and in re-loading the single trading ship allowed annually into Porto Bello harbour.

On the British side, it was claimed that Spanish coastguards and sailors were unnecessarily harsh, and often cruel. There were tales of British seamen captured and tortured by the Spaniards. As for Gibraltar, it had become a question of British pride, as well as a naval necessity, to keep it.

In **1739** matters came to a head after a certain **Captain Jenkins** showed members of the House of Commons his mutilated ear for which he blamed the Spaniards. War fever seized the country, and on 19th October, 1739, Walpole was reluctantly forced to declare war against Spain. 'It is your war,' he told Newcastle, 'and I wish you joy of it.' He foresaw French intervention in the war and an extension of the conflict. Yet he did not resign at this point, as might have been expected.

Instead, he directed the **War of Jenkins' Ear** which was almost entirely naval. **Admiral Vernon** took **Porto Bello**, while **Admiral Anson** sailed round the world attacking Spanish ports and ships. But the attacks yielded little profit, and in 1740 the war became merged into a general European war, as Walpole had feared.

The occasion was the death of the Emperor, Charles VI, in **1740**. Although the Emperor had obtained the signature of almost every ruler in Europe to the Pragmatic Sanction which guaranteed the succession of Maria Theresa, trouble at once arose. **Frederick the Great of Prussia**, in spite of signing the Pragmatic Sanction, seized the opportunity of invading the rich territory of Silesia, which belonged to Austria. In the war which followed, France, Spain and Prussia fought against Austria, Britain and Holland. But by the time Britain entered the **War of the Austrian Succession**, Walpole was no longer Chief Minister.

He resigned in 1742 after a defeat in the Commons on a minor issue. He had become very unpopular because of his failure to achieve victories in the war against Spain, and lacked the qualities required of a war leader. It was typical of Walpole to resign not over some major policy question, but over a relatively unimportant Commons' issue. He was, above all else, a 'House of Commons man'. Walpole retired to the House of Lords as Earl of Orford. His political career was over. Meeting another newly-created peer, Pulteney, in the House of Lords he said, 'You and I, my lord, are now two as insignificant men as any in England.' He died three years later.

Walpole's Place in History

A man's contemporaries are not necessarily the best judges of his worth. They stand too close to events to be able to see them in perspective. On his death in **1745**, Walpole must have seemed to many to have failed. The war he had dreaded had broken out; he had not succeeded in destroying the Jacobite threat; and the Whig supremacy was being challenged by a revived Tory party.

Walpole's enemies accused him of neglecting Britain's home interests, and of aspiring to become 'Prime Minister', an office which was declared to be unknown in the British constitution. There was some truth in these charges, and in the accusation of corruption, which Pitt levelled against him.

In his foreign policy, Walpole failed to realize the dangers of maritime and colonial rivalry with France and Spain. He did nothing to prevent the signing of the Family Compact, nor did he build up the strength of the army and navy. Colonial policy, though less open to criticism, was unconstructive. The same might be said of various aspects of his domestic policy. He tended to let things drift. On occasions, he gave way to public pressure, as in the case of Wood's Halfpence, when he ought perhaps to have remained firm. On the charge of corruption he stands guilty. But in those days, bribery was common practice, and until the Parliamentary reforms of the nineteenth century, large sums of money continued to change hands at election times.

In defence of Walpole it can be said that he gave the country twenty years of much-needed peace. His rule established the Hanoverian succession securely, and his measures for tariff reform led to a great expansion of British trade. His tolerance in religious matters was admirable. Finally, by remaining a member of the House of Commons, and by insisting on unanimity in the Cabinet, he did much to promote the development of Parliamentary government.

These achievements entitle Walpole to rank as a great peace minister and a wise financier. However, the view is widely held that he was more a politician than a statesman. To reach a conclusion on this point it is necessary to be clear about the meaning of the two terms. The 'politician' tends to supply temporary solutions for the various problems which face him. He is more concerned with day-to-day politics and immediate results. The 'statesman', on the other hand, shows vision, and has the ability to devise sound long-term policies which are in the best interests of the country. He does not fear unpopularity, and never allows Party or personal interests to cloud his judgment. On these grounds Walpole surely ranks as a statesman.

Summary

The Hanoverian Succession led to a long period of Whig rule. It lasted throughout the reigns of George I (1714–1727) and George II (1727–1760). The Whigs were able to maintain their supremacy because (*a*) they had the support of King and Parliament, and (*b*) the Tory Party was discredited through its association with Jacobitism, and because it lacked good leadership.

Although the majority of people were contented under Whig rule, Jacobitism continued. In 1715 the Earl of Mar led a rebellion in Scotland in favour of Prince James Edward, the Old Pretender. Jacobites also rose in the north of England. Mar was defeated at Sheriffmuir, and the English Jacobites at Preston. The failure of the Fifteen was due mainly to the lack of English support, to poor Jacobite leadership, and to the unpopularity of the Old Pretender who refused to give up his Roman Catholicism. His defeat strengthened the Whigs and secured the Hanoverian Succession, though Jacobite activity continued, leading to another and more dangerous revolt in 1745.

Both George I and George II left the control of government largely in the hands of the Whig ministers. From 1717–1721 Stanhope was Chief Minister. His ministry is notable mainly for the signing of the Triple and Quadruple Alliances (based on Franco-British understanding), which succeeded in preserving the Utrecht settlement and the general peace of Europe for twenty years. On the fall of Stanhope at the time of the South Sea Bubble crisis, Walpole became Chief Minister, a position he held until his resignation in 1742.

Walpole's policy was to make Hanoverian rule popular in order to safeguard the succession, destroy Jacobitism, and prolong the rule of the Whigs. This he hoped to achieve by giving the country a long period of peace and prosperity.

Walpole's ministry saw the end of the French alliance and the concluding of the Family Compact between France and Spain, which was to lead to a period of bitter struggle, between Britain on the one side and France and Spain on the other, for maritime and colonial supremacy.

1676 Born at Houghton in Norfolk

1690-95 Eton College

1696 King's College, Cambridge

1701 Entered Parliament

1708 Secretary at War

1712 Sent to Tower on charge of corruption

1714 Paymaster-General of The Forces

1715 First Lord of The Treasury and Chancellor of The Exchequer

1717 Resigned

1720 Paymaster-General of The Forces

1721-1742 CHIEF MINISTER

ACHIEVEMENTS	AT HOME	FAILURES
Secured Hanoverian succession and continuance of Whig rule		Wood's Halfpence
Developed Parliamentary Government.[Cabinet Office of Prime Minister]		Excise Bill
Put Britain's finances in order [Sinking Fund, Tariff Reform]		Porteous Riots
Suppressed Jacobite activity		

ABROAD

Colonial Trade encouraged		No constructive Colonial Development Policy
England at peace from 1713 –1739		No long-term Foreign Policy [Failed to prevent Family Compact or to strengthen Armed Forces]

THE CAREER OF SIR ROBERT WALPOLE

Important Dates

1715	Jacobite Rebellion (The Fifteen).
	Battles of Sheriffmuir and Preston.
1716	Septennial Act.
1717	Triple Alliance.
1718	Battle of Cape Passaro.
1719	Protestant Interests Act.
	Peerage Bill.
1720	South Sea Bubble.
1721–1742	Walpole's Ministry.
1722	Wood's Halfpence.
1725	Treaty of Vienna.
1727	Death of George I.
	Accession of George II.
1733	Excise Bill.
	Molasses Act.
1733–1735	War of the Polish Succession.
1736	Porteous Riots.
1737	Death of Queen Caroline.
1739	War of Jenkins' Ear began.
1740	War of the Austrian Succession began.
1742	Resignation of Walpole.

QUESTIONS

(1) Describe the Jacobite rising of 1715. Why did it fail?

(2) How do you account for the long period of Whig rule which followed the accession of George I?

(3) What were Walpole's principal achievements at home and abroad?

(4) Explain the importance of the following: (a) *the Quadruple Alliance;* (b) *the Peerage Bill;* (c) *the South Sea Bubble;* (d) *Frederick Louis, Prince of Wales, and the opposition;* (e) *the War of Jenkins' Ear.*

CHAPTER THREE

THE WAR OF THE AUSTRIAN SUCCESSION

THE resignation of Walpole in February 1742 did not mark the end of Whig rule. Nor did it open the way for Walpole's critics to assume power. Pitt, **Lyttleton** and the **Grenvilles** were all excluded from office, while members of the old ministry, Newcastle and his brother **(Henry Pelham), Hardwicke, Harrington** and the **Duke of Devonshire** still remained in the government. The only important change was the return of Carteret as Secretary of State.

Carteret

It was a time when foreign affairs overshadowed domestic questions. Britain was at war with Spain, and fighting had broken out in Europe between Prussia and Austria. Between the years 1742 and 1744 Carteret conducted Britain's foreign policy almost single-handed.

He appeared to have all the qualities necessary to become a great Foreign Minister. He spoke French, German and Spanish, and had a good grasp of the Scandinavian languages. He had shown himself an able diplomat in missions to Copenhagen and Stockholm in 1719 and was an efficient Foreign Secretary from 1721–1723. His knowledge of German affairs assured him of the support of George II but, as a man, Carteret was never popular. His aristocratic manner, his refusal to take even his colleagues into his confidence, and his scornful disregard of public opinion, made him seem overbearing and proud. He over-estimated the value of royal support, believing that with the Crown on his side he need never stoop to seek understanding or popular approval for his actions. But if he respected the British King, he showed little regard for foreign rulers. Frederick II of Prussia observed that Carteret treated princes as '*petits garçons*' (little boys). This haughty attitude to foreign royalty was unlikely to win him friends in Europe. Yet during his relatively short term of office, under extremely difficult circumstances, he achieved notable success.

The Foreign Situation

In order to understand the foreign situation and to assess Carteret's achievements, it is necessary to return to the year 1740, when two important European rulers died. The first was **Frederick William I,** King of Prussia, who left to his successor **Frederick II (the Great)** a strengthened kingdom and the most efficient army in Europe. The second was the Emperor Charles VI, who bequeathed to his daughter, **Maria Theresa,** all the hereditary dominions of the Hapsburgs and the Pragmatic Sanction guaranteeing her inheritance, which had been accepted by all the states of Europe except Bavaria.

Frederick II was a man of immense energy and ambition; Maria Theresa a woman of great pride and courage. Both were determined to make the most of the new situation; Frederick to extend Prussian power, Maria Theresa to defend the scattered Hapsburg dominions against her ambitious neighbours. It was well known that France had her eye on the Austrian Netherlands; Spain wanted to acquire Naples and Milan; and the rich territories of Silesia and Bohemia tempted Prussia.

The Invasion of Silesia

At first it seemed as though the European powers intended to respect the Pragmatic Sanction. Maria Theresa succeeded to the Hapsburg inheritance quietly, and Frederick II even revived his father's promise to support the Queen if help was needed. But within months he had shown his true intentions by sending an army into the duchy of Silesia. His action encouraged all the other greedy claimants to Hapsburg lands to abandon the Pragmatic Sanction and to take advantage of Maria Theresa's weakness. Bavaria, France and Spain all joined in the war against the Austrian queen. Holland eventually joined the side of Austria, while Russia, too involved in domestic trouble, stood aloof. Britain alone, of the more important signatories of the Pragmatic Sanction, remained loyal to the bond, although not entirely for unselfish reasons. Merchants in Britain welcomed a policy which might weaken the French and Spanish, their commercial rivals. They were supported in Parliament by officers of the armed forces who were eager to uphold Britain's prestige.

George II, however, was against entering the war immediately since he feared a Prussian attack on Hanover. From the outbreak of the Austrian Succession War in 1740 until the resignation of Walpole in 1742, Britain did no more than continue the war against Spain, subsidize Maria Theresa, and build up the army and navy for the inevitable struggle against France.

Carteret's Policy

With the entry of Carteret into the government, Britain's policy

changed from one of half-hearted support for Austria to active partici-
pation in the war. By then, Austria had been decisively defeated by
Prussia at the **Battle of Mollwitz (1741)**, and an alliance had been signed
between France, Spain and Prussia to divide up the Hapsburg lands
between them, leaving Maria Theresa with only Hungary and a part
of Austria. Carteret, recognizing France as 'the enemy always aiming
at our destruction', decided to exploit the European situation to promote Britain's interests. His aim was to reconcile Austria and Prussia,
and unify the German Electorates and Kingdoms into a compact state
so that Germany would then be strong enough to prevent French
expansion.

Dettingen

In July 1742 he succeeded in persuading Maria Theresa to come to
terms with Frederick in the **Treaty of Berlin**. Frederick agreed to
remain neutral in return for the cession of Silesia. The following year,
Austrian troops occupied Bavaria and turned out the Elector, who
had been chosen Emperor, Charles VII. Shortly afterwards, an army
of British, Dutch and Hanoverian troops defeated the French at
Dettingen, George II himself fighting with great bravery. It was the last
time an English King took part in a battle.

The Fall of Carteret

The victory, far from enhancing the reputation of Carteret, seemed
to make him very unpopular. Members of Parliament denounced his
German policy, accusing him of subordinating British interests to those
of Hanover. There was no truth in the accusation, though Carteret's
aim of a united Germany was clearly impossible to achieve at that
time. His unpopularity increased with the failure of the British navy
to destroy the French and Spanish fleets when they emerged from the
port of Toulon in February 1744. Less than two weeks later, a French
fleet appeared off Dungeness to provide cover, it was thought, for a
Jacobite invasion. France and Britain were still nominally at peace,
and it was not until March 1744 that the two countries formally
declared war. France and Austria also declared war on one another,
and in the same year, Prussia re-entered the war against Austria by
invading Bohemia and occupying Prague.

The policy of Carteret, now **Earl Granville**, appeared to have failed.
Henry Pelham and his brother, the Duke of Newcastle, together with
other members of the cabinet, demanded Granville's dismissal.
George II would have liked to retain him; but, on the advice of Orford
(formerly Sir Robert Walpole) who held that no ministry could stand
without the support of the Pelhams, he gave way and accepted Gran-

ville's resignation. A new ministry, known as the 'Broad Bottom Administration' because it included Tories and others, was then formed under the Pelham brothers. This ministry which William Pitt joined, lasted from 1744-1754 except for a brief interval in 1746.

Fontenoy

Under the new ministry, Britain's policy remained much the same as before, to subsidize Maria Theresa and to prevent France from occupying the Austrian Netherlands. In **1745** the most important battle of the war was fought in the Low Countries at **Fontenoy**, where the French under **Marshal Saxe** won a great victory over a mixed army of British, Dutch, Austrians and Hanoverians. The British troops were led by the **Duke of Cumberland**, 24-year-old second son of George II.

As a result of the Battle, Tournai fell, then Ghent, Oudenarde, Ostend and Nieuport. Marshal Saxe was master of the Austrian Netherlands, and Holland was in great danger of a French invasion. It was at this point that Britain had to recall her troops to fight against the Young Pretender, who had been encouraged, by the French victory at Fontenoy, to launch a carefully-planned Jacobite rising from the Highlands of Scotland.

The Young Pretender

Charles Edward, the Young Pretender, who was twenty-five years old, seemed to possess all the qualities which his father, the Old Pretender, lacked at the time of the ill-fated Jacobite rebellion in 1715. He was handsome, adventurous and confident of success. Ever since the failure of the Fifteen, Jacobite hopes had centred on the young Stuart prince. His magnetic personality secured him many devoted followers: it was hoped he would attract thousands more when he appeared in Britain to claim the throne.

His Chances of Success

In some ways, the political and economic condition of Britain made a Jacobite success in 1745 more unlikely than in 1715. Firstly, when the Old Pretender landed in Scotland, the union between England and Scotland was only eight years old, and ill-feeling was still strong. Secondly, the War of the Spanish Succession had just ended and Britain was experiencing some of the usual economic difficulties which invariably follow a long period of war. Thirdly, George I had only succeeded to the throne in 1714. No one knew whether the Hanoverian succession would be a success and bring the promised improvements. *By 1745, however, it was obvious that the Union had brought im-*

mense economic and political benefits for both England and Scotland.
The Hanoverian Succession and Whig rule were not only generally
accepted, but were also popular. They had brought stability and prosperity, and few were likely to be prepared to sacrifice everything to
support Charles Edward, a Roman Catholic prince, who as a Stuart
might be expected to reintroduce the old system of arbitrary government and a policy of alliance with France.

Yet there were circumstances which encouraged the Young Pretender to launch his attack. Britain was engaged in the war of the
Austrian Succession, and most of her best troops were out of the
country. The French victory at Fontenoy had made the Hanoverians
less popular, and had shown up George II's military weakness. Finally,
it was such a long time since a Stuart had sat upon the English throne
that many people had forgotten their unattractive qualities. These
people, it was thought, might possibly be won over to the Jacobite
cause by the strongly romantic appeal of the Young Pretender.

In 1744 the French planned to help the Jacobites by an invasion of
England, but they were prevented by the strength and readiness of
the navy. Despairing of any effective aid from France, Charles Edward
decided to wait no longer.

The Forty-Five

In August 1745 he landed with a few supporters at Moidart in the
West Highlands and raised his standard at Glenfinnan. Camerons,
Macdonalds and others flocked to join him. They were charmed by the
Pretender's kingly manner, his courage, confidence, and readiness to
share the hardships of the men he led. Marching swiftly southwards
he soon took Perth, and in less than a month from his landing at
Moidart, was on the outskirts of Edinburgh.

The Scottish capital surrendered immediately, and on 17th September, Charles Edward rode triumphantly down the High Street loudly
cheered by the citizens. That night, a ball was held in the palace of
Holyrood, the ancient home of the Scottish kings.

Meanwhile, **Sir John Cope**, Commander of the government forces in
Scotland, who had shipped his troops from the Highlands to Dunbar,
was hurriedly advancing towards Edinburgh. Charles Edward left the
capital to meet him, and inflicted a crushing defeat on Cope at **Prestonpans**. The English troops, terrified by the wild rush of the Highlanders,
were scattered within minutes. Cope retired towards Berwick. The
Highlanders, instead of following up the victory, returned to Edinburgh
where a further round of celebrations began.

Derby

It was not until six weeks later that the Pretender's army set out from

Edinburgh to continue the march south. Carlisle was captured in November. Shortly afterwards, Manchester fell. By then, only about 200 recruits had joined the rebel army, and it was obvious that no general rising of English Jacobites would take place. Nevertheless, Charles Edward proceeded southwards reaching Derby on the 4th December 1745.

The news that he was only 130 miles from London caused a panic in the city. There was a run on the Bank of England, people actually demanding coins in exchange for banknotes, because they feared the Pretender, on seizing the throne, might repudiate the National Debt and destroy the credit of the Bank. To save the situation the Bank paid out in sixpences. It was the first Friday in December, and the day became known as 'Black Friday'.

Like most Londoners, George II thought the Jacobites were very near to victory. He made hasty preparations to leave the capital. But they were never put into effect. At a meeting of chiefs Charles Edward failed to convince his followers of the necessity for an immediate march on London. The chiefs, led by **Lord George Murray**, were disheartened by the lack of English support, and by the return to their homes in Scotland of many of their men. They advised withdrawal, and Charles Edward had no alternative but to agree. The retreat from Derby began.

Culloden

Government forces made little attempt to stop the retreating army, though some of Cumberland's troops routed the rebels at Penrith. The march northwards continued. On 20th December Charles Edward was across the border again, and six days later was in Glasgow. More recruits joined him the further north he went. After a spectacular battle at **Falkirk** when government troops under **General Hawley** were defeated, the Jacobites besieged Stirling Castle. But they were unable to take it and, in February 1746, decided to retreat to the Highlands.

They were pursued by Cumberland's army. On 16th April **1746** the decisive battle of the rebellion was fought, in a snowstorm, on **Culloden Moor** near Nairn. The Highlanders were tired, hungry and dispirited, yet they fought bravely, only yielding when all hope of victory had gone and the Prince himself had left the field of battle. The moor was covered with dead and dying. Edward Lynn of the Royal Scots Fusiliers remarked: 'I never saw a field thicker of dead.' The government claimed they lost 50 dead and 259 wounded. Rebel losses are harder to assess. Some reports put the dead at 2,000, which would be nearly half the number engaged. The figure was certainly not less than 1,200.

The heavy loss of life was due partly to the ferocious way in which Cumberland's soldiers behaved once they had achieved victory. An

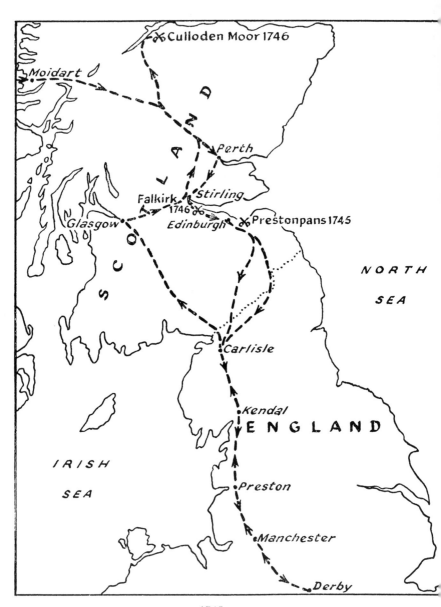

THE 1745 JACOBITE RISING

officer described how they bayoneted or shot clansmen trying to struggle from the heaps of dead; the men, he said 'looked like so many butchers rather than Christian soldiers'. For three months the killings continued as fleeing rebels were caught and executed. It was this slaughter that earned for Cumberland his nickname 'The Butcher'.

Causes and Results of the Jacobite Failure

Some eighty prisoners were sent for trial and executed, among them the **Lords Kilmarnock, Balmerino** and **Lovat**. Charles Edward, however, went into hiding in the Highlands where, for nearly six months he was hunted relentlessly by government troops. Helped by the loyal Highlanders, notable among them **Flora Macdonald**, he managed eventually to escape to France. It says much for the integrity of the Highlanders that not one of them betrayed him, although there was a price of £30,000 on his head.

So ended the last rising of the Jacobites. It had been well enough planned from the military point of view, and there was no lack of good leadership, but it was doomed from the start for political reasons. The rule of the Whigs had been so efficient and popular that Charles Edward gained practically no English support. Other reasons for the failure were the lack of French help and the strength of the government forces. At Culloden, more Scotsmen fought in Cumberland's army than in the army of the Young Pretender; and in the killing after the battle, the Lowland Scots were just as merciless as the most zealous of Cumberland's men.

The triumph of the Hanoverians marked the end of much that was traditional in the life of the Scottish Highlanders. Measures were taken to destroy the clan system; chiefs were deprived of their powers of jurisdiction; and common law was enforced throughout the country for a time. The wearing of Highland dress was forbidden. Within a few years, hundreds of former rebels had been recruited into the new Highland regiments specially formed to absorb the warlike clansmen. These regiments soon became famous for their bravery in almost every part of the world.

Over the years, new roads and bridges were built to open up the Highlands, and Scotland achieved a degree of unity between Highlands and Lowlands which had been unknown before.

The Long Administration

In 1746, while the Young Pretender was still at large in Scotland, the entire Cabinet resigned. The reason for this unprecedented step was the determination of the Pelhams to force George II to agree to have Pitt in the ministry. Pitt had been widely consulted by all concerning the rising, and was regarded as the wisest and most forceful of contemporary politicians. The King, however, disliked Pitt who had called his beloved Hanover a 'despicable Electorate', but he was unable to keep him out. After two days in which **Bath** and Granville tried, at the King's request, to form a government and failed, the Pelhams returned with Pitt as Paymaster of the Forces.

The Pelham government is of constitutional importance since it marked the first time that a ministry had resigned as a body on a question of policy.

The War in Europe and Overseas

Meanwhile, the War of the Austrian Succession dragged on. In 1745, on the death of the Emperor Charles VII, Maria Theresa secured the election of her husband, Francis of Lorraine, as Emperor, and made an alliance with Saxony. Frederick was driven out of Bohemia, and in December **1745** signed the **Treaty of Dresden**, by which he retained Silesia and withdrew from the war. By then most of the combatants would have welcomed peace, but the war continued for nearly three years more.

In **1747** the French, who already controlled the Austrian Netherlands, invaded Holland. They seized the great border fortress of Bergen-op-Zoom and defeated the allied army under Cumberland at **Lauffeldt**.

The British, however, had secured a notable victory in America in 1745 when the French fort of **Louisburg** on Cape Breton Island was taken. Louisburg not only controlled the entrance to the St. Lawrence River but threatened the safety of British fishermen off Newfoundland. Its capture encouraged British colonists to prepare for an attack on Quebec.

In India, where Britain and France each had a number of trading stations, the war at first went well for the British, but in **1746** the important British fort of **Madras** fell into French hands.

The War at Sea

Throughout the war the Royal Navy performed its dual function of protecting the shores of Britain and of carrying men and supplies to and from Britain and her overseas territories. In 1747 Admiral Anson captured many French warships as the French fleet emerged from port with convoys for Canada and the East Indies. Only a small detachment of the fleet destined for the relief of the French garrison of Pondicherry reached India.

Some months after Anson's successful engagement, **Admiral Hawke** attacked a convoy on its way to the West Indies. All but two of the

French warships surrendered, and later, forty of the ships in the convoy, which had escaped, 17 were taken as they approached the islands.

*The British naval victories of 1747 had driven the enemy fleets off
the seas*; had deprived their colonies of badly-needed supplies and
reinforcements; and had seriously damaged their commerce. France,
already in grave difficulties owing to a bad harvest, faced economic
ruin.

The Peace of Aix-la-Chapelle

Britain, in spite of her victories at sea, and the capture of Louisburg,
was equally ready for peace. She had achieved practically no success
on land, and was feeling the strain of keeping up the payment of subsidies to her continental allies. Even the capture of Louisburg had
been counterbalanced by the loss of Madras.

In October **1748** the war came to an end with the signing of the
Peace of Aix-la-Chapelle, by which:

(1) Frederick II kept Silesia,
(2) Maria Theresa's husband was recognized as Emperor of the
Holy Roman Empire,
(3) Louisburg was restored to the French,
(4) Madras was restored to Britain,
(5) The sea defences of Dunkirk were to be destroyed,
(6) France recognized the Hanoverian succession and repudiated
the Pretender,
(7) Holland recovered the territory lost to France, and
(8) The French withdrew from the Low Countries.

The only country satisfied with the Peace of Aix-la-Chapelle was
Holland. Britain and her American colonists resented the handing back
of Louisburg. In India, differences between the French and English
East India Companies had not been settled. The original dispute with
Spain over the right of search of British ships was not even mentioned
in the peace settlement; although, by the **Treaty of Madrid** in **1750,**
Britain abandoned her trading rights in South America for a lump sum.

Maria Theresa and Frederick II were also dissatisfied with the peace
terms. Maria Theresa was determined to get back Silesia one day,
while Frederick wanted to add Bohemia and Saxony to the Prussian
Kingdom. As for the French, they still hoped to extend their frontiers
to the Rhine; and intended to renew the maritime and colonial struggle
with Britain.

Pelham's Financial Measures

The Peace of Aix-la-Chapelle was nothing more than a truce, but it provided a much-needed breathing space before the decisive struggle for world leadership began. During the first six years of the truce, Henry Pelham, who was First Lord of The Treasury and Chancellor of the Exchequer, did much to restore the country's finances. Expenditure on the armed forces and on subsidies paid to foreign princes was reduced. By 1752 the budget was balanced at £1,112,048 instead of £9,819,345; and Pelham was able to reduce the land tax, and to tackle the problem of the growing National Debt. In 1739, when the war against Spain broke out, the debt stood at £46 millions. By the end of the war it had risen to nearly £79 millions. Pelham succeeded in reducing the rate of interest paid to holders of stock; so that, by his death in 1754, a saving of over £250,000 per annum had been secured. Other measures taken by him to improve the economy included the encouragement of the fishing industry and a scheme to abolish restrictions on the export of wool and other raw materials from Ireland.

Newcastle and Kaunitz

While Pelham struggled to improve Britain's financial position, Newcastle, as Secretary of State, exercised control of foreign policy. He showed little talent for the job, failing to realize that times were changing, and that when war broke out again, as everyone expected it would before long, both Austria and France were likely to be Britain's enemies.

The Austrian minister, **Kaunitz**, was known to be gradually persuading Maria Theresa to turn to France instead of to Britain for help to regain Silesia. Yet Newcastle, who had refused Frederick's offer of an alliance in 1748, took no steps to prevent Austria and France from coming to terms.

In 1755 Kaunitz made proposals to the French for an alliance. He suggested that the Austrian Netherlands should go to Louis XV's son-in-law **Don Philip**, and that, in exchange, Austria should receive the Italian territories of Parma and Piacenza. The proposed change was sure to please the French since it would go far towards giving them a frontier on the Rhine. The second part of Kaunitz's scheme, however, was even bolder. It was for a concerted attack by France, Austria, Russia, Saxony and Sweden on Prussia, and the partitioning of the Kingdom between them.

The Convention of Westminster

Rumours of Kaunitz's proposals reached the Prussian Court towards the end of 1755, and although France had not then agreed to them, Frederick became convinced that an attack was to be made on his territory. Already Russia and Britain had come to an agreement, by

PEACE OF AIX-LA-CHAPELLE, 1748

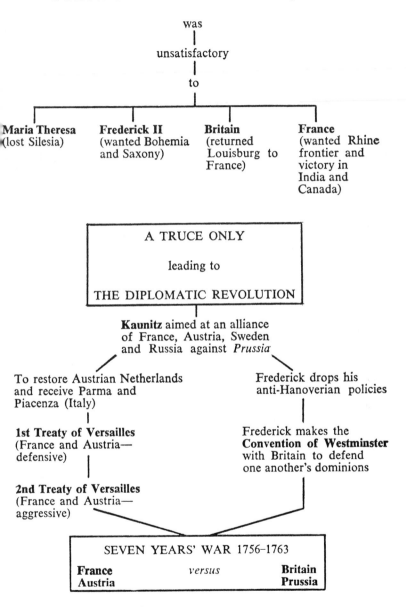

was

unsatisfactory

to

Maria Theresa
(lost Silesia)

Frederick II
(wanted Bohemia
and Saxony)

Britain
(returned
Louisburg to
France)

France
(wanted Rhine
frontier and
victory in
India and
Canada)

A TRUCE ONLY

leading to

THE DIPLOMATIC REVOLUTION

Kaunitz aimed at an alliance
of France, Austria, Sweden
and Russia against *Prussia*

To restore Austrian Netherlands
and receive Parma and
Piacenza (Italy)

Frederick drops his
anti-Hanoverian policies

1st Treaty of Versailles
(France and Austria—
defensive)

Frederick makes the
Convention of Westminster
with Britain to defend
one another's dominions

2nd Treaty of Versailles
(France and Austria—
aggressive)

SEVEN YEARS' WAR 1756–1763

France   *versus*   **Britain**
Austria   **Prussia**

which Britain was to subsidize Russia in return for military and naval support if Britain or any of her allies, notably Hanover, were attacked. According to this treaty, some 55,000 Russian troops were to be kept in readiness on the Livonian frontier, and about fifty warships anchored off the coast. The treaty was never put into operation, but the prospect of a Russian army so close to Prussian soil, coupled with the danger from France, made Frederick drop his anti-Hanoverian policy and turn towards Britain.

Britain, for her part, was seeking an ally. It had become clear that her old ally, Austria, was coming to terms with France, and that an alliance with a strong continental power was essential in order to defend Hanover and to fight a successful war against France both in Europe and overseas. Prussia, with its huge army and great military tradition, was the obvious choice. In January **1756**, therefore, Britain and Prussia secretly signed the **Convention of Westminster** to guarantee each other's dominions.

The Treaties of Versailles

News of the Anglo-Prussian agreement leaked out, and within six months, Austria and France had signed a defensive alliance known as the **First Treaty of Versailles**. A year later, the alliance became an offensive one with the signing of the **Second Treaty of Versailles**.

Europe was once again divided into hostile power blocs poised for war, Britain and Prussia on the one side and Austria and France on the other. This changed grouping of the bigger powers from the positions they held during the Austrian Succession War, had become known as the *Reversal of Alliances* or the *Diplomatic Revolution*. It was the prelude to one of the most widespread and decisive wars of modern times.

Summary

On Walpole's resignation in 1742, the Pelhams continued in office and Carteret joined the government as Secretary of State. Britain had been at war with Spain since 1739 (War of Jenkins' Ear); and this war merged into the War of the Austrian Succession, which broke out in 1740 as a result of Frederick II's invasion of Silesia. Britain, Austria and (later) Holland fought against Prussia, France, Bavaria and Spain.

Carteret directed foreign policy from 1742–1744. An expert in German affairs, he helped to reconcile Austria and Prussia, and unite the German kingdoms to provide a strong bulwark against France. In 1742 he persuaded Maria Theresa to sign the Treaty of Berlin with Frederick, by which Prussia retained Silesia but withdrew (temporarily) from the war. Shortly afterwards, the allies defeated the French at Dettingen. By 1744 Carteret, always suspected of subordinating Britain's interests to those of Hanover, had become very unpopular, and was forced to resign in spite of having the support of George II.

The Broad Bottom Administration (1744–1754) was then formed under the Pelham brothers. Overseas the war went badly for the allies, France winning the Battle of Fontenoy (1745) and occupying the Austrian Netherlands. At home, a Jacobite rebellion broke out in the Highlands of Scotland under the leadership of Prince Charles Edward, the Young Pretender. After a victory at Prestonpans, near Edinburgh, the Prince led his army into England. But he gained practically no English support, and was compelled to turn back on reaching Derby. The Jacobites were finally defeated at Culloden (1746). The rising failed mainly for political reasons. People were too contented under Whig rule to support the Jacobites, and the promised help from France did not materialize.

The War of the Austrian Succession eventually ended in 1748 with the signing of the Treaty of Aix-la-Chapelle. Frederick II retained Silesia, and France and Britain restored their colonial gains. The powers, who regarded the Treaty of Aix-la-Chapelle as no more than a truce, began at once to prepare for a renewal of war. In the Diplomatic Revolution, Britain allied with Prussia, and Austria with France.

Important Dates

1740	**Death of Frederick William I, King of Prussia.**
	Accession of Frederick II (the Great).
	Death of Emperor Charles VI.
	Accession of Maria Theresa.
	Prussian invasion of Silesia.
1740–1748	**War of the Austrian Succession.**
1741	**Battle of Moliwitz.**
1742	**Resignation of Walpole.**
	Treaty of Berlin.
1743	**Battle of Dettingen.**
1743–1748	**England and France at war.**
1745	**Battle of Fontenoy.**
	Capture of Louisburg.
	The Forty-Five Rising.
	Battle of Prestonpans.
	Treaty of Dresden.
1746	**Battles of Falkirk and Culloden.**
	The Long Administration.
1747	**Battle of Lauffeldt.**
	British naval successes.

1748	Treaty of Aix-la-Chapelle.
1754	Death of Pelham.
1754–1756	Newcastle's ministry.
1756	Convention of Westminster.
1756–1757	Treaties of Versailles.

QUESTIONS

(1) Explain Carteret's foreign policy. How successful was it?

(2) What part did Britain play in the War of the Austrian Succession?

(3) Which Jacobite rebellion had the greatest chance of success, the Fifteen or the Forty-Five?

(4) Write briefly on three of the following: (a) *the Broad Bottom Administration* (b) *the battle of Fontenoy;* (c) *the Long Administration;* (d) *Kaunitz;* (e) *the Convention of Westminster.*

CHAPTER FOUR

TRADE AND EMPIRE

THE Treaty of Aix-la-Chapelle, which ended the War of the Austrian Succession in 1748, provided no permanent solutions to European or colonial problems. In Europe it did little more than mark the end of the first phase of the struggle between Austria and Prussia for leadership in Germany. Overseas, it only provided a short pause in the conflict between Britain and France in America and India.

Mercantilism

The colonial struggle was not so much for territorial gain as for trade. It was believed that foreign trade could bring unlimited wealth, and that the state should regulate trade in order to stimulate the nation's industry, strengthen its defences and increase its supply of bullion. In those days a country's greatness was often measured by the amount of gold and silver it possessed. For a healthy economy, there had to be a favourable balance of trade, that is, exports had to exceed imports. Furthermore, it was thought that a country could only expand its trade at the expense of another.

The **mercantilist theory** when applied to the colonies meant the passing of regulations to control colonial trade and industry in the interests of the mother country. Under the seventeenth century **Navigation Acts**, goods coming from Asia, America or Africa to any part of England or her Empire had to be carried in English or colonial ships. All colonial products had to be sent to England, and the manufacture in the colonies of goods which might compete with those produced in Britain was forbidden.

It was thought that colonies existed primarily for the strengthening and enrichment of the mother country. They were expected to supply her with raw materials which she could not produce herself, and to buy her manufactured goods.

British Colonies in North America

At the beginning of the eighteenth century, the whole coast of North America from Maine to the borders of Florida was in British hands.

BRITAIN'S OVERSEAS POSSESSIONS IN 1714

Map labels:
Equator
British Isles
Newfoundland
Nova Scotia
American Colonies
Hudson Bay
Bermudas
Bahamas
St. Kitts
Jamaica
Barbados
Slave Trade
Asiento Treaty
Gibraltar
Minorca
Guinea Coast
Fort James
Cape Coast Castle
St. Helena
India
Bombay
Calcutta
Madras

Under the terms of the Treaty of Utrecht (1713), Britain acquired further territory in America when France gave up all claims to Hudson's Bay, Nova Scotia and Newfoundland.

Some of the American colonies were founded in the seventeenth century by religious exiles (Puritans, Catholics and Quakers), who went to America to escape religious persecution at home. Others were founded for trade reasons, or were obtained as the result of war. In most cases the cost of the enterprise was borne by **'joint stock companies'** who obtained royal charters giving them authority to develop and govern the area. Initially, the home government showed very little interest in the establishment of colonies and played no direct part in founding them. This attitude changed later with the full appreciation of their commercial, strategic and political importance. Overseas possessions came to be regarded as an index of a country's greatness.

The first successful attempt to establish a colony in America was made in 1607 when the **Virginia Company** landed settlers at **Jamestown**. This was followed by the foundation of many other settlements, which may be divided broadly into three main groups.

First, there was the New England group of colonies. The earliest was **New Plymouth** founded by the Pilgrim Fathers who sailed from England in the *Mayflower* in 1620. They were financed by a London group of merchants called the **Plymouth Company**. The foundation of **Massachusetts** followed in 1628. This was one of the most successful of the New England colonies, though the intolerance of the Puritan administrators caused many people to leave the colony and found new settlements at **Connecticut** (1633), **New Haven** (1638), and **Rhode Island** (1636).

Most of the New Englanders were engaged in farming, ship-building or in the fishing and timber industries. They were a hard-working people, noted for their piety and independent spirit. Most colonies had their own separate assemblies elected by the colonists, and a governor and a council nominated by the crown; but in Connecticut and Rhode Island they also chose their own governors and officials.

Secondly, there were the Plantation colonies of **Virginia (1607)**, **Maryland** (a Catholic settlement founded by Lord Baltimore in 1632) and **North** and **South Carolina**, founded during the reign of **Charles II**, when Lord Clarendon and others obtained a royal charter in **1663** to develop land south of Virginia. In the eighteenth century a fifth Plantation colony, **Georgia (1732)**, was founded by the philanthropist, **General Oglethorpe**.

The economy of this group of colonies was based largely on the production of tobacco and rice, for which African slave labour was introduced. The planters became extremely rich. Compared with the New Englanders they lived a life of luxury, in a sunny climate, with slaves to do all the hard manual work.

The New England colonies were for a time separated from the Plantation colonies of the South by Dutch settlements round the mouths of the Hudson and Delaware Rivers. These were seized by the English at the beginning of the Second Dutch War, and these territories became the states of **New York, New Jersey,** and **Delaware**. This third group of colonies, which may be called the **Middle Colonies,** came to include **Pennsylvania,** founded in **1681** by the Quaker leader, **William Penn**.

The West Indies

At the time of George I's accession in 1714, Britain, Spain and France all had strong interests in the Caribbean. Britain owned the Bermudas, the Bahamas and Jamaica. **Jamaica** had been seized in **1655** during **Oliver Cromwell's** rule. It was the first time that the government had set out deliberately to acquire territory beyond the Atlantic. In the Leeward and Windward Islands, Britain possessed the Virgin Islands, Barbuda, St. Kitts, Antigua, Montserrat and Barbados. Most of the islands had developed on the lines of the Plantation colonies with large sugar plantations run by slave labour. Towards the end of the seventeenth century an English settlement grew up on the mainland near the Belize River, the area which now forms part of Honduras.

Spain held Cuba, Trinidad, Porto Rico and shared San Domingo with France. The French occupied the rich islands of Guadeloupe and Martinique, and also owned Dominica, St. Lucia, St. Vincent, Granada and Tobago.

Most of the British islands had originally been granted to companies or individuals under charter from the Crown. But by the end of the seventeenth century, the Crown had rescinded nearly all of the charters and was exercising complete royal control. In 1714, the Bahamas was the only privately owned British colony still left in the West Indies; but by 1735, the proprietors had surrendered most of their rights to the Crown.

English Trading Posts in Africa and India

Trade was the main motive for the establishment of English settlements in Africa and India. Both the climate and local conditions made colonization in these areas unattractive and impracticable. Unlike America, with its temperate climate and relatively small indigenous population, Africa and India were tropical areas with large populations. It was too hot for Europeans to wish to make permanent homes there, and even if they had wanted to do so, they would have been faced with the necessity of seizing already-inhabited territory which they could only have acquired by force. They contented themselves with establishing trading posts at suitable places along the coasts, and making trade agreements with local rulers. Both Africa and India were known to contain immense wealth in the form of natural resources, and trade possibilities were also thought to be immense.

English traders visited West Africa in the sixteenth century, and early in the Stuart period a settlement was formed around the estuary of the Gambia River. In **1663 Fort James** was built by the **Royal African Company** as a depot for the slave trade. This Company also built fortified trading posts at **Accra** and **Cape Coast** in the Gold Coast (now Ghana), which was at that time the centre of the slave trade. Slaves were brought from the interior by Arab or native traders and lodged in the Company's forts before being shipped, tightly-packed below decks, to work on the plantations in America and the West Indies. The terrible sufferings of the slaves during the 'Middle Passage', as the voyage across the Atlantic was called, resulted in many deaths, but it was not until 1807 that the lucrative slave trade between Africa and America was abolished.

During the reign of George II, Parliament granted the Royal African Company £10,000 a year for the upkeep of the Gold Coast forts. They were needed not so much for protection from the local peoples as for defence against attacks from French and Dutch competitors in the trade. Both France and Holland had established trading posts at various points along the coast of West Africa, and keen competition existed. In **1750** the Royal African Company was superseded by the **Company of Merchants Trading to Africa** which any British merchant could join for a fee of forty shillings; and the Parliamentary grant for forts was continued to the new company.

In the Far East, there was bitter Anglo-Dutch rivalry during most of the seventeenth century. After the **massacre of Amboyna** in **1623**, when English merchants were murdered by the Dutch in the Spice Islands, the **English East India Company** directed its commercial activity towards the mainland of India. **Surat**, founded in **1612**, was already a flourishing trading centre. Other important trading posts were established during the course of the seventeenth century, among them **Masulipatam (1622)** and **Madras (1639)**. In **1668** Charles II handed over **Bombay** to the East India Company. He had received it from the King of Portugal as part of the dowry of his wife, Catherine of Braganza. Bombay soon superseded Surat as the most important trading centre on the west coast of India. Finally, **Fort St. David** to the south of Madras was founded in **1690**, and Fort William (Calcutta) in **1696**. So profitable did the Indian trade become that a rival East India Company was formed in **1698**. The two companies amalgamated in **1708** as the **United Company of Merchants Trading to the East Indies**.

The Board of Trade and Plantations

Colonial affairs were the responsibility of the Secretary of State for the South, assisted by the Board of Trade and Plantations set up in 1696 by William III. Under Walpole's administration the Board did little work, since colonial business was largely ignored, but when the **Earl of Halifax** was made President of the Board in **1748** its activities increased and it was treated with more respect. An important milestone in its history was reached in 1757, when Halifax succeeded in securing a place for himself in the cabinet.

The French in North America and India

By then, Anglo-French colonial rivalry had brought a renewal of fighting in America and India, and the official attitude towards the colonies had changed from apathy to keen interest.

While English settlements were being formed along the American coast, the French were colonizing the banks of the St. Lawrence. **Quebec** was founded in **1608**. During the second half of the seventeenth century, the **Great Lakes** were explored by **La Salle**, and the greater part of **Louisiana** was occupied by the French. Gradually, the French built forts at various points from the St. Lawrence to the Gulf of Mexico, and established claims to all the territory which lay between them. The chain of forts included Louisburg, established in 1716, Quebec, Montreal, Crown Point, Fort Frontenac, Fort Niagara, Fort Chartres, and in 1754 (most important of all) Fort Duquesne, built at the junction of the Ohio and Allegheny Rivers.

These French forts prevented any expansion westwards by the British colonists. Their security was also threatened, since the French might at any time attempt to expand eastwards driving a wedge between the British settlements, splitting them into two groups, and conquering each in turn. The position was made worse by the absence of definite frontiers between the two lines of settlement, and by the uncertain loyalty of the Indians. On the whole, the Indians were on the side of the French but the French colonists lacked two vital things, the strong support of their government, and the command of the sea, both essential if supplies and reinforcements were to reach them.

In India Anglo-French competition was just as acute, both for the expanding trade and for the friendship of the native rulers. Competing with the British-owned trading stations of Bombay, Calcutta and Madras were the three great French settlements of **Pondicherry, Chandernagore and Mahé**. When English and French trading posts were first established in India there seemed to be plenty of scope for the merchants of both countries to expand their business without interfering with each other, but by the middle of the eighteenth century this phase was over. The rapid growth of British and French trading

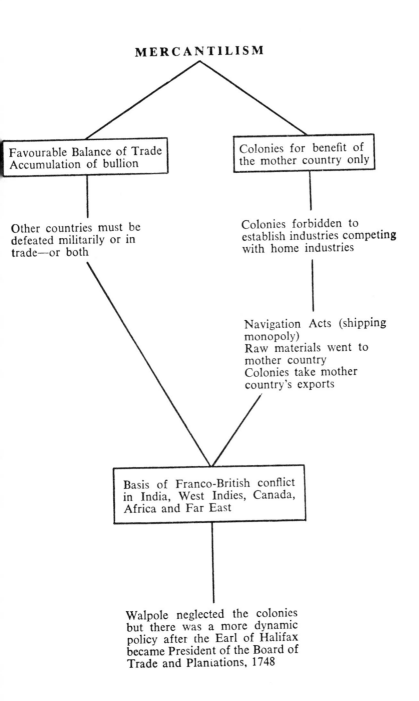

MERCANTILISM

Favourable Balance of Trade
Accumulation of bullion

Colonies for benefit of
the mother country only

Other countries must be
defeated militarily or in
trade—or both

Colonies forbidden to
establish industries competing
with home industries

Navigation Acts (shipping
monopoly)
Raw materials went to
mother country
Colonies take mother
country's exports

Basis of Franco-British conflict
in India, West Indies, Canada,
Africa and Far East

Walpole neglected the colonies
but there was a more dynamic
policy after the Earl of Halifax
became President of the Board of
Trade and Plantations, 1748

companies had led to intense rivalry which could ultimately only be resolved by war.

Between the Wars

It will be remembered that during the War of the Austrian Succession (1740–1748), British and French colonists fought in America and India. In America, the British seized Louisburg on Cape Breton Island, while in India the French took the important British trading post of Madras. Both Louisburg and Madras were handed back to their previous owners in the Treaty of Aix-la-Chapelle which ended the war.

But this was not the end of the trouble. Between the end of the Austrian Succession War and the start of the **Seven Years' War** in **1756**, the French and British continued the struggle for supremacy overseas. In America French colonists were already, in 1748, crossing the Allegheny mountains and entering the valley of Ohio in an attempt to drive the British from the region. It was then that work began on the building of Fort Duquesne at the strategically important point where the Ohio and Allegheny Rivers meet.

In **1753** and **1754 Governor Dinwiddie** of Virginia sent forces into the disputed area, but they were repulsed by the French and the Indians. In general, the Indians supported the French rather than the British because it seemed the French only wished to trade while the British wanted their land.

General Braddock was sent to Virginia in **1755** with two British regiments. He hoped to raise a strong colonial force to augment his small army, but so great were the differences and jealousies between the separate colonies that no united effort against the French was possible, and when Braddock did eventually set out for Fort Duquesne his army was ambushed a few miles from the fort. Braddock's regular soldiers, accustomed to fighting in close, well-disciplined ranks, were no match for the scattered French and Indians who attacked from behind trees and ridges and fired from all sides. They were decisively defeated. Braddock himself, three-quarters of his officers and half of his men were killed in the battle.

The Ohio region was not the only trouble area. The French were making determined efforts to undermine British rule in Nova Scotia. This territory had been colonized by a group of Scotsmen during the reign of James I. But the French claimed it as their province of Acadia, and in 1632 their claim was recognized. It remained French until 1713 when it was handed over to Britain under the terms of the Treaty of Utrecht. Most of the inhabitants were French and belonged to the Roman Catholic Church, owing allegiance to the Bishop of Quebec. It was, therefore, a comparatively easy matter for French agents and priests to stir up anti-British feeling.

By 1755 the country was in a state of revolt, and the British, in desperation, decided to deport a large part of the disaffected population. About 8,000 Nova Scotians were sent to live in the older colonies, and their places were taken by British settlers.

Dupleix and Clive

In India, there was scarcely a pause in the fighting between French and British between the wars. **Dupleix**, the French governor of Pondicherry, who had been mainly responsible for the capture of Madras during the Austrian Succession War, seemed for a time to be in control of most of southern India. His success had been due in large measure to his policy of training Indians to fight for him. These **sepoys**, as they were called, were used by Dupleix against both the British and any local ruler who challenged his power.

But Dupleix's success was short-lived. He met his match in the person of **Robert Clive**, a clerk in the service of the East India Company, who had fought during the Austrian Succession War, and who was determined to resume his military career as soon as possible. The opportunity came in a war which broke out between two rival Indian claimants for the throne of the Carnatic. The French supported **Chunda Sahib**, and the British the other claimant, **Mohammed Ali**. Clive joined the army and was given charge of a company. At that moment, Mohammed Ali was being besieged in **Trichinopoly** by the French. Clive, in order to draw off the French forces, marched on **Arcot**, the capital of the Carnatic. He captured it in **1751** and managed to hold it during a fifty-three day siege until relief arrived.

It was the turning point in the fortunes of both Clive and Dupleix. The British candidate, Mohammed Ali, was placed on the throne of the Carnatic, and Clive returned in glory to England for a short spell. Dupleix was recalled to France, where he ended his days, poverty-stricken, in a garret.

Clive's triumph at Arcot and Dupleix's recall, showed the way in which the fighting between the French and British in India was likely to end, but when Clive returned to India in 1755, years of struggle lay ahead.

Summary

The struggle between Britain and France for commercial and colonial supremacy continued throughout most of the eighteenth century. It was the age of 'mercantilism', when the government regulated and encouraged colonial expansion in order to increase the nation's wealth and strength.

The main areas of Anglo-French rivalry were in:

(1) *North America*

By the reign of George II, Britain held Hudson's Bay, Nova Scotia and all the Atlantic coastline to the borders of Florida. The French possessed Quebec, Montreal and Louisiana, and claimed the greater part of the country around the Ohio and Mississippi Rivers. They built a chain of forts linking their territories in the St. Lawrence area to the Gulf of Mexico, thus preventing British expansion westwards, and threatening the security of the British eastern seaboard colonies. With the building of Fort Duquesne and Braddock's defeat in 1755, it was clear that full-scale war between British and French in America would begin.

(2) *The West Indies*

Britain, France and Spain all owned islands in the Caribbean. Most of them had developed on the lines of the Plantation colonies with large sugar plantations run by slave labour.

(3) *Africa and India*

Trade rather than land was the main motive behind European expansion in Africa and India. Britain and France each established trading posts along the coasts of West Africa and the Indian mainland. In Africa, Britain had fortified trading posts at Cape Coast, Accra, and the estuary of the Gambia River. From there the Royal African Company exported slaves to America and the West Indies. In India, the three main British trading posts were Madras, Calcutta and Bombay, while the French held Pondicherry, Chandernagore and Mahé. Intense rivalry developed between British and French trading companies. At first Dupleix, using sepoys, achieved some success; but with the capture, by Robert Clive, of Arcot (1751) the tide turned in favour of the British.

Important Dates

1607	Virginia founded.
1612	Surat founded.
1620	Sailing of the 'Mayflower'.
1622	Masulipatam founded.
1623	Massacre of Amboyna.
1628	Foundation of Massachusetts.
1632	Foundation of Maryland.
1633	Foundation of Connecticut.
1636	Foundation of Rhode Island.
1638	Foundation of New Haven.
1639	Madras founded.
1655	Seizure of Jamaica.

1663	Foundation of North and South Carolina.
	Fort James built.
1665	Acquisition of New York, New Jersey, Delaware.
1668	Bombay acquired by East India Company.
1681	Foundation of Pennsylvania.
1690	Fort St. David founded.
1708	United Company of Merchants Trading to the East Indies.
1750	Company of Merchants trading to Africa formed.
1751	Capture of Arcot.
1753–1754	Dinwiddie expeditions.
1754	Fort Duquesne built.
1755	Braddock's defeat near Fort Duquesne.

QUESTIONS

(*1*) *Explain the meaning of 'mercantilism', and show how it influenced British colonial policy during the first half of the eighteenth century.*

(*2*) *Describe the situation in North America and India which led to the outbreak of war between Britain and France in 1756.*

(*3*) *Write briefly on three of the following:* (a) *the Royal African Company;* (b) *Fort Duquesne;* (c) *the Board of Trade and Plantations;* (d) *General Braddock;* (e) *Dupleix.*

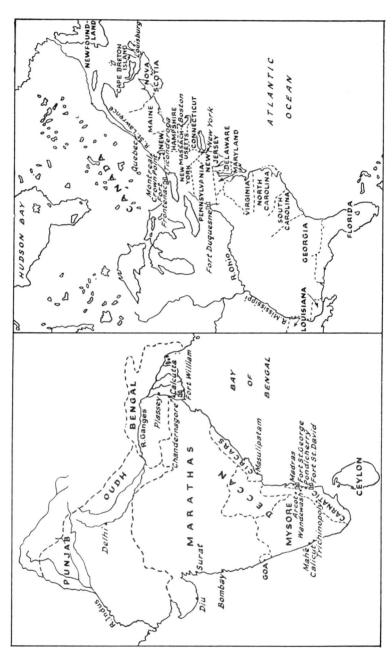

INDIA AND NORTH AMERICA AT THE TIME OF THE SEVEN YEARS' WAR

CHAPTER FIVE

THE SEVEN YEARS' WAR
1756-1763

The War in Europe

ENGLAND'S ally, Frederick the Great, was under attack from France, Austria and Russia. But the efficiency of his army and the strategy of speedy manoeuvre enabled him to weather the storm. In an aggressive campaign he conquered Saxony in 1756, but the following year was one of immense danger to Prussia. George II's son, the Duke of Cumberland, in command of British and Hanoverian troops, was defeated at **Hastenbeck** by the French, who then occupied Hanover. Cumberland was forced to surrender and sign the **Convention of Kloster-Seven.** Frederick now showed his military skill at its highest and completely retrieved the situation. By speed of manoeuvre and forced marches he first defeated the French at **Rossbach** and then the Austrians at **Leuthen.** In 1758 he followed up these victories by driving the French from Hanover and defeating both the Austrians and Russians. In **1759** he was once again on the verge of disaster when he was defeated by the Russians and Austrians at **Künersdorf,** but **Ferdinand of Brunswick** defeated the French at the **Battle of Minden** and thus prevented them moving against Frederick. In **1762** the **Czarina Elizabeth** of Russia died and Russia withdrew from the war. This greatly eased the pressure on Frederick the Great. In **1762** he made a separate peace with Austria at **Hubertusburg,** by which Frederick retained Silesia. Frederick's survival is explained by (1) the power of the Prussian army as developed by his father, **Frederick William I,** (2) his own military genius, (3) the financial support given to him by Pitt—an annual subsidy of £650,000, (4) the change of Russian policy in 1762, (5) the falling apart of the opposition to him, (6) the cessation of all French attacks after the defeats by Britain in Canada and India and the signing of peace with Britain in **1763**.

The War at Sea between Britain and France

On becoming Secretary of State in 1757 in Newcastle's government, Pitt became the real directing force in the war. Previously Britain had suffered disasters through Newcastle's neglect of the navy and its wrong deployment. In **1756 Admiral Byng** had evacuated the important island of Minorca, which fell to the French. He claimed that he would have risked defeat by the superior French force and that his withdrawal safeguarded Gibraltar. However, Byng was tried and shot on the quarter-deck of his flagship.

William Pitt determined to pursue the naval war more vigorously. *His policy was to keep Frederick in the field by financial help, thus occupying the French in Europe while Britain conquered the French in Canada and India.* By the policy of blockading the French naval ports, he seriously interrupted their communications with Canada and India. In 1759 the French collected transports at Le Havre with the aim of invading Britain. For this purpose they needed the junction of their Toulon and Brest fleets in order to command the Channel. The Toulon fleet managed to pass through the Straits of Gibraltar, but was overtaken by **Admiral Boscawen** and almost completely destroyed off **Lagos**. The Brest fleet was also defeated by **Admiral Hawke** at **Quiberon Bay** in 1759. It should be noted that both Boscawen and Hawke were chosen by Pitt, who had an uncanny capacity for appointing the right men for the right tasks. These two naval victories gave Britain command of the Atlantic and severely reduced French trade. At a critical point the French commander in Canada, **Montcalm**, had his communications with France cut. In **1760 Admiral Rodney** destroyed another French fleet at **Le Havre**, and the French lost most of their West Indian islands in 1761.

In 1761 Pitt, knowing that Spain was about to declare war on Britain, demanded action against her. **George III** refused, and Pitt resigned. Even so his Tory successor, the **Earl of Bute**, declared war on Spain in **1762**. Such was the naval power built up by Pitt that Britain captured both Havana (Cuba) and Manila (Philippines), thus rendering useless the Spanish support of France.

The War in India

In 1751 Clive's successful defence of Arcot (see p. 63) had been a blow to French prestige in India, and Dupleix returned in disgrace to France in 1754, whereas in the previous year Clive had been fêted in London as a hero. However, French influence in Bengal was still very great. Bengal was ruled by **Surajah Dowlah**. In 1756, when the British in Calcutta refused to surrender a refugee under sentence of death by Surajah Dowlah, the latter seized control of the British settlement. Then occurred the notorious affair of the **Black Hole of Calcutta**, when only twenty-three out of one hundred and forty-six British prisoners survived after being confined for one night in a room only twenty feet square. Pitt now sent back Clive to Bengal and he succeeded in wringing compensation from Surajah Dowlah.

In 1757 a plot against Surajah Dowlah aimed at placing **Mir Jaffir** on the throne in his place. This plot was supported by Clive. Then **Omichund**, a native, threatened to reveal the plot to Surajah Dowlah unless he had a written and signed promise of a large sum of money— the signatures to be those of Clive and Admiral Watson who commanded the British fleet in the Hooghli river. Watson refused, but Clive forged his signature. However, after Clive's victory over Surajah Dowlah at **Plassey (1757)** and the placing of the pro-British Mir Jaffir on the throne, the agreement with Omichund was repudiated. Chandernagore was also captured by the British at this time.

In 1758 **Count Lally** was appointed French Governor of Pondicherry and attempted to retrieve the position for France. He failed in his attempt to capture Madras and the French abandoned Hyderabad when its ruler made a treaty with Britain. In 1760 Lally was defeated by **Colonel Eyre Coote** at the battle of **Wandewash** and Pondicherry was also taken. By 1760 Clive had made British power supreme in the Carnatic, at Hyderabad and in Bengal.

The War in North America

The position was extremely dangerous for the British American colonists in 1756. The French controlled important posts on the great rivers which were the main lines of communication. These posts were on the St. Lawrence, the Great Lakes, the Ohio and the Mississippi, and ran from Louisburg on Cape Breton Island to New Orleans. Also, Quebec, Montreal and Toronto were in French hands. The French aimed at preventing further British expansion westward and themselves advanced eastward in such a way as to cut the British colonies in two. The British had very little support from the Indians. However, the British naval victories at Lagos and Quiberon Bay seriously hampered the French plans, for they received insufficient arms and other supplies. Pitt's policy was to use Britain's command of the Atlantic to send increased forces and supplies to the colonies from 1757 onwards. This led to the British capture of **Louisburg (1758)** and **Forts Oswego, William Henry, Frontenac** and **Duquesne**. The French commander **Montcalm** decided to defend Quebec, but a British fleet under Admiral Saunders took **General Wolfe's** forces up the St. Lawrence and the British troops scaled at night the supposedly impossible **Heights of Abraham**. In the ensuing battle, which gained Quebec for Britain **(1759)**, both Wolfe and Montcalm were killed. After the capture of Montreal by **General Amherst** in **1760** Canada was completely under British control.

The Peace of Paris, 1763

On the death of George II in 1760 his successor George III, wishing

THE SEVEN YEARS' WAR
1756-1763

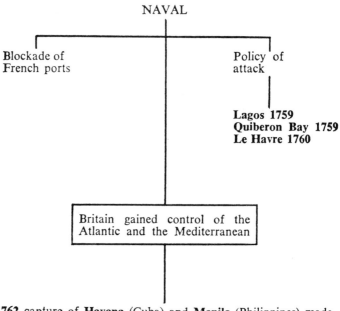

POLICY OF PITT THE ELDER

He aimed to conquer Canada and India while subsidizing Frederick against France

NAVAL

Blockade of French ports

Policy of attack

Lagos 1759
Quiberon Bay 1759
Le Havre 1760

Britain gained control of the Atlantic and the Mediterranean

1762 capture of **Havana** (Cuba) and **Manila** (Philippines) made Spanish alliance useless to France

It was extremely difficult for the French to get adequate military supplies and men to India and Canada. British *naval control* of the St. Lawrence River made Wolfe's capture of **Quebec, 1759,** possible

o reassert the royal power which the Whigs had reduced during the
two previous reigns, aimed at the removal of Pitt as soon as possible.
As already stated, Pitt resigned in 1761 over the King's refusal to
declare war on Spain. In 1762 the Tory Earl of Bute was in office. He
was anxious to bring the war to an end on the grounds that Britain
had gained all she wanted and also because of the great expense and
consequent increase of the National Debt.

In 1763 peace terms were signed. Concessions were made to France,
who regained Pondicherry, Chandernagore and Mahé in India, but
with the proviso that they were to be unfortified and used only for
trade. In America France lost all her possessions except New Orleans.
It was also agreed that French fishermen could still fish in the Gulf of
St. Lawrence and use part of the coast of Newfoundland for drying
their nets. In the West Indies, Britain gained Tobago, Dominica,
St. Vincent and Grenada, but Guadeloupe, Martinique and St. Lucia
were returned to France. In West Africa the French regained Goree,
while Britain retained Senegal. In the Mediterranean Britain regained
Minorca, but Belle Isle was returned to France. The French also
agreed to dismantle the fortifications of Dunkirk.

Comments on the Treaty

In the House of Commons the vote for opening peace negotiations
had been 311 to 65. Some critics declared that this was the result of
bribery by the King's government, but in fact these were merely
malicious stories put out by Bute's opponents. The cost of the war,
including the huge annual subsidy to Frederick the Great, was proving
a great burden and was increasingly unpopular with the trading
interests. Financial considerations were, in fact, a sound reason for
bringing the war to an end.

On the other hand, some details were open to adverse criticism.
Manila was returned to Spain and Martinique to France without
equivalents, while Havana, which was also returned to Spain in
exchange for Florida, was far more valuable than the latter. The French
were favoured by the return of several West Indian Islands, which prevented Britain from obtaining a monopoly of the sugar trade. France
also retained Goree and her former trading towns or *factories* in
India. If the restitution of the French factories had not been made, the
East India Company could have controlled all trade with Europe.
The French concessions in the Newfoundland fisheries, which were
training grounds for their sailors, were criticized at the time. The
desertion of Frederick the Great, who was left to make his own terms,
was also open to criticism, for the annual subsidy was withdrawn just
at the time when a complete victory of Prussia over Austria and France
was imminent. Nevertheless, the question remained: Could Britain

have continued the war and have imposed a completely one-sided settlement? This is doubtful. In any case, the gains of Britain laid the foundation for the British Empire and were all of great value. Again, it must be remembered that many British politicians and traders were opposed to the idea of complete monopoly of the eastern trade by the East India Company and some French competition was considered healthy.

Summary

The Seven Years' War saw the decisive victory of Britain and her allies over France and Austria. The British Empire gained strength and territory through the skilful deployment of naval and military resources by the Elder Pitt. Britain's naval power reached a new peak and her command of the seas ensured her success in North America and India. Pitt's promotion of talent in both the army and the navy was brilliantly justified. Britain's subsidies to Frederick the Great were made possible by the great advance in wealth which Walpole's earlier commercial policies had brought about. The Treaty of Paris, which ended the war, was the subject of much criticism, but probably the most regrettable action was Britain's over-hasty desertion of Frederick the Great, which prevented him making gains which in any way matched up to those of Britain.

Important Dates

1757   **Convention of Kloster-Seven.**
        Frederick's victory over French at Rossbach.
        Frederick's victory over Austrians at Leuthen.
1758   **Frederick drove French from Hanover and defeated both Austrians and Russians.**
1759   **Combined Russian and Austrian forces defeated Prussians at Künersdorf.**
        Ferdinand of Brunswick defeated French at Minden.
1762   **Peace of Hubertusburg between Frederick and Austria.**

At sea

1757   **Execution of Admiral Byng.**
1757   **British naval blockade of French ports.**
        onwards.
1759   **Boscawen destroyed French fleet off Lagos.**
        Hawke's victory at Quiberon Bay.
1760   **Rodney destroyed French fleet at Le Havre.**
1761   **Pitt resigned.**
1762   **Britain captured Havana and Manila.**

India

1756 Black Hole of Calcutta.
Pitt sent Clive back to India.
1757 Battle of Plassey.
Capture of Chandernagore.
1758 Count Lally failed to capture Madras and French also lost Hyderabad.
1760 Lally defeated by Eyre Coote at Wandewash.
British captured Pondicherry.

North America

1758 British captured Louisburg and Forts Oswego, William Henry, Frontenac and Duquesne.
1759 Capture of Quebec. Deaths of both Wolfe and Montcalm.
1760 General Amherst captured Montreal.
1763 Peace of Paris.

QUESTIONS

(*1*) *How would you explain the military survival of Frederick the Great?*

(*2*) *Describe Pitt's general strategy, with special reference to naval power.*

(*3*) *How would you account for British success in India and North America?*

(*4*) *On what grounds could the Peace of Paris, 1763, be criticized? Give the case for and against.*

CHAPTER SIX

INDIA IN THE TIME OF ROBERT CLIVE AND WARREN HASTINGS

Robert Clive (Third Period in India)

IN 1765 Clive returned to India because of serious developments there. Trouble had arisen with **Mir Cossim**, the successor of his father-in-law, **Mir Jaffir**, in Bengal. Mir Cossim had formed an alliance with the Nabob of Oudh against the British, but had been defeated at Buxar by Major Munro. However, there was great discontent owing to the corruption of English traders and officials, and a firm hand was needed.

Clive determined to consolidate further British power in India. His achievements are generally considered as the real foundation of the British Empire in India. By an agreement with the Mogul Emperor he secured control for the **East India Company** of Bengal, Behar and Orissa, containing thirty million people and giving the Company an annual revenue of about four million pounds. This agreement, signed at Benares in 1765, was a vast extension of British power in India. Clive had taken full advantage of the real weakness of the Emperor, surrounded as he was by ambitious and independent princes. At the same time Clive obtained an imperial charter for the Company's assets in the Carnatic and the Deccan.

Clive then proceeded to reform the general administration by improving the salaries of British officials and forbidding them to receive gifts from the local people. He also stopped the practice by which officials took part in the inland trade. These reforms led to outright mutiny by á number of British officers, which Clive suppressed, and then reformed the army itself by dividing it into three brigades, each of which could meet on its own terms any native army brought against it.

Clive returned to Britain after having expended a good deal of his own fortune in the service of the British in India, but his reforms had aroused intense opposition from the corrupt officials of the old school. Clive was elected M.P. for Shrewsbury, but his enemies, led by **General Burgoyne**, who was later to surrender to Washington at Saratoga, induced the House of Commons to impeach him on charges of corruption, and especially of having received large sums from Mir Jaffir.

74

His trial before a committee of the House of Commons led to his being censured for receiving gifts of £234,000 during his first administration in Bengal, but the committee unanimously passed a resolution 'that Robert, Lord Clive, did at the same time render great and meritorious service to his country'.

The very fact of his trial and its methods brought about a fatal depression. 'I have been examined by the Select Committee more like a sheep stealer than a member of this House.' He committed suicide in 1774.

Clive had established British ascendancy in India by the defeat of the French in the Seven Years' War, by the extension of the East India Company's control and by his insistence on honesty in administration. Although not of military background he proved himself a military genius, but he always generously recognized the great services he received from his commanders in India. After the siege of Arcot he was offered by the Company a sword worth £700, but he refused it unless **Major Lawrence**, his great supporter, received the same. He transferred the sum of £75,000 left him by Mir Jaffir in 1765 to a fund for the support of invalided officers and soldiers and their widows. He used much of his own fortune during his work in India. He admitted that he used oriental methods of craft and deception, as in the case of Omichund, but regarded this as permissible in view of the great issues at stake. Altogether, he was one of the greatest men of the period of British expansion.

Lord North's Regulating Act, 1773

The East India Company was in poor financial condition and nearly bankrupt. This led to demands for more control by the home government. Under this act (1) a loan was made to the Company by the government, and it could export tea to America free of duty at the English ports, (2) the Governor of Bengal now became Governor-General of India, with a Council of Four, presided over by the Governor-General who, in a case of equal division, had a casting vote, (3) a court of supreme jurisdiction was set up in Calcutta to try legal cases arising in India. This was presided over by English judges, (4) the British Crown was to give final approval to all military, political and financial arrangements.

Warren Hastings, First Governor-General

Warren Hastings had gone to Calcutta in 1750 as a clerk in the East India Company, but had rapidly risen to important posts under the Company through the recognition by Clive of his great ability. He became successively a member of the council of Madras and then of

Bengal, and was named Governor-General in **Lord North's Regulating Act of 1773**.

He aimed at extending still further British power in India and especially to prevent the threatened rise of the Mahrattas to take the place of the weakened Mogul Emperor. He was also expected by the directors at home to clean up the financial position of the Company and secure a high rate of profit.

He made a number of fundamental changes in administration. He abolished the 'dual system' established by Clive and secured control for British officials of both the internal and external affairs of Bengal. Thus he no longer relied on native administration as much as Clive had done. On the financial side he reduced the Company's allowances to the Nabob of Bengal and to the Mogul Emperor at Delhi. He deprived the latter of the two provinces of Corah and Allahabad and sold them to the Nabob of Oudh for £300,000 and also loaned him the services of British troops against the Rohillas for a payment of £400,000. By this means he hoped to strengthen Oudh as an ally against the Mahrattas. In two years he had increased the Company's income by £410,000 and its capital by £1,000,000.

He achieved these improvements despite the fact that he had much opposition in the new **Council of Four**, and it was not until 1777 that Hastings had a clear majority support.

Hastings found that widespread corruption and gift-taking had occurred again after the departure of Clive, but he now ruthlessly enforced Clive's rulings against private trading by officials and the taking of presents. Native tax-collectors were replaced by British and this led to less extortion and malpractice.

In 1777 the French made an alliance with the Mahrattas, and a British force was defeated at **Poonah**, and in 1780 **Hyder Ali of Mysore**, expecting assistance from the French who were now supporting the American colonists, captured Arcot. But Hastings retrieved the situation by sending a British force under **Eyre Coote**, who defeated Hyder Ali at **Porto Novo**. Hastings now had to raise money to meet the costs of this campaign, and in 1781 he deposed the Nabob of Benares, **Cheyte Singh**, who had refused his annual payments to the Company, and seized the royal treasure. At the same time £1,000,000 was extorted from the **Begums of Oudh**, whose attendants were subjected to torture. Hastings was not directly concerned with the cruelties inflicted, but his name was naturally associated with them and he could have ensured that they did not occur. This was followed by the affair of **Nuncomar**, who, in the first years of Hastings as Governor-General, had brought charges of corruption and injustice against him in support of his enemies, especially **Philip Francis**, a member of the Council of Four. Nuncomar was of doubtful character, and in 1781 was brought before the supreme court at Calcutta on charges of forgery, which was a capital crime. He was sentenced to death and executed. The enemies of Hastings accused the Chief Justice of having conveniently removed an enemy of Hastings. This was an unjust charge, for Hastings had nothing to do either with the accusations or the sentence.

The Trial of Warren Hastings

The opponents of Hastings in Britain were now preparing accusations against him and demanding his recall. He returned in 1785 and was impeached in 1788, his trial continuing until 1795, the prime movers against him in the Commons being the playwright and M.P. **Richard Brinsley Sheridan** and his more famous contemporary **Edmund Burke**, author of *Reflections on the Revolution in France* and the opponent of the radical ideas of **Thomas Paine**. The charges against him centred upon the extermination of the Rohillas by the Nabob of Oudh with the assistance of troops lent by Hastings (see p. 76), the cases of Cheyte Singh and of the Begums of Oudh. The trial served the useful purpose of emphasizing that Europeans could not ride rough-shod over native peoples, but Hastings was acquitted on all charges although ruined by the expenses of the trial. He was granted a pension by the Company and died in 1818.

Hastings had given sound and uncorrupt government to Bengal and, by transferring all departments of government to Calcutta, had greatly improved efficiency. His alliance with Oudh had successfully checked the Mahrattas. He had strengthened the work of Clive and had a profound understanding of the Indian people. He was a fine linguist and spoke both Persian and Arabic. He had also saved the East India Company from complete bankruptcy.

Pitt's India Act, 1784

It had become clear that the East India Company had too much independent power in India and was inclined to put profit before good government. The Whig leader **Charles James Fox** had attempted to bring in a bill limiting the Company's powers, but had been defeated. The next effort was by the Prime Minister, William Pitt the Younger, in 1784. This was accepted by Parliament and the Act made the following changes: (1) A Board of Control of six members was to control the *political* affairs of India; (2) the company kept control of *trading* matters, but the Crown could veto the appointment of a Governor-General of whom it did not approve; (3) the Governor-General was given wide discretion to deal with crises which might arise; and (4) a Court was set up in Britain to try offences committed in India.

Summary

After 1765 Clive successfully extended British power in India by securing control of Bengal, Behar and Orissa for the East India Company; he improved the Company's administration and reduced corruption with ruthless determination. His impeachment led to his own conviction for having received immense gifts, but his services to Britain were acknowledged. His methods were unscrupulous in an unscrupulous age, but he had qualities of military brilliance clearly recognized by all. Lord North's Regulating Act, 1773, greatly increased the powers of the home government over Indian affairs, and Warren Hastings became the first Governor-General under its terms. In the new Council of Four he had much jealous opposition; but Hastings defeated French attempts to re-assert their influence at the expense of Britain, greatly improved the revenues of the Company (sometimes by ruthless means), reduced corruption, and improved the whole administration. He was acquitted on all charges brought at his impeachment. With Clive he was the founder of British power in India.

Important Dates

1765   **Clive returned to India.**
        Bengal, Behar and Orissa came under Company rule.
        Imperial Charter for Company's trade in the Carnatic and the Deccan.
1772   **Warren Hastings abolished dual system set up by Clive.**
1773   **North's Regulating Act.**
        Warren Hastings Governor-General.
1774   **Hastings lent British troops to Nabob of Oudh to crush Rohillas.**
1781   **Eyre Coote defeated Hyder Ali at Porto Novo.**
        Execution of Nuncomar.
1784   **Pitt's India Act.**
1788   **Impeachment of Warren Hastings.**
1795   **Hastings acquitted.**

QUESTIONS

(1) *What were the main achievements of Clive in India?*

(2) *Explain the terms of North's Regulating Act, 1773, and of Pitt's India Act, 1784.*

(3) *Describe the main achievements of Warren Hastings.*

(4) *Why were both Clive and Warren Hastings impeached? Did these impeachments serve any useful purpose?*

CHAPTER SEVEN

GEORGE III, 1760–1820

George's Theory of Kingship

THE Whigs had been the ruling influence in Britain for nearly fifty years. They regarded themselves as the protectors of the country against the Jacobites, who wished to restore the descendants of James II to the throne. The Tories had become associated in the public mind with Jacobitism and, especially under Walpole's premiership (1721–1742), had been completely eclipsed by the success of his policies, which had given the trading classes peace abroad and security at home. The art of parliamentary management through bribery was carried to effective lengths by the Duke of Newcastle, and even the Elder Pitt had accepted this function of Newcastle during the Seven Years' War. Both George I and George II had been prepared to accept the Whig monopoly of power and, through the practice of the Prime Minister presiding at cabinet meetings in place of the monarch, royal influence had declined. *George III had different ideas on the rights and duties of the king.* The Tories had hoped that George's father, Frederick Prince of Wales, would have come to the throne and restored the Tory fortunes, but he died in 1751. However, the Dowager Princess of Wales undertook George's education through the Tory **Earl of Bute**, who was his tutor. George III was determined to be above party, and *especially to assert his right to control the composition of governments.* He had the advantage with parliament and the public that his life was highly moral. He was not interested in Hanover, and was proud to be king—'I glory,' he declared, 'in the name of Britain.'

George's first action was to take back patronage (i.e. the distribution of money and offices for services rendered) for the Crown. In doing this he dismissed Newcastle, who for many years had used patronage to keep parliamentary support for the Whigs. Pitt also resigned over the Spanish question (see p. 68), and Bute became head of the government in 1761 and proceeded to make the peace settlement in 1762–1763. George now began to use royal patronage to form a core of royal supporters in parliament—a group who came to be known as '**The King's Friends**'. By this means George III hoped to be able to control parliament by throwing the weight of the 'King's Friends' on one side

GEORGE III

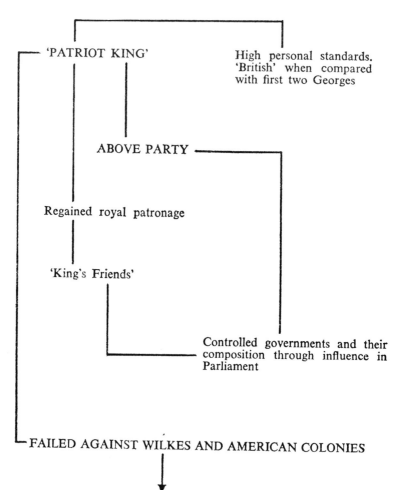

'PATRIOT KING'

High personal standards. 'British' when compared with first two Georges

ABOVE PARTY

Regained royal patronage

'King's Friends'

Controlled governments and their composition through influence in Parliament

FAILED AGAINST WILKES AND AMERICAN COLONIES

(a) Preserved the rights of voters against the Crown
(b) Defeated dangers to liberty of general warrants of arrest
(c) Increased the liberty of the press

or the other as he thought best. However, George had no intention of being dependent on the Tories, and in 1763 he accepted the resignation of Bute through his unpopularity over the Peace of Paris. He then accepted **Grenville**, a Whig (but not of the old school) as Prime Minister. When he was compelled by parliament's decision to accept the Old Whig **Rockingham** as Prime Minister in 1765 the 'King's Friends' promptly voted Rockingham out of office. In 1766 George III actually accepted Pitt (then Earl of Chatham) as Prime Minister in a mixed government of Whigs and Tories, and then the Whig **Grafton** until **Lord North** became Prime Minister in 1770. From then until North's resignation in 1782, George was able to wield real control of the government, for North was prepared to accept the King's will on most matters. North had the continued support of the 'King's Friends' in parliament. The effects of this on British history we shall see in connection with the American War of Independence.

Wilkes and Liberty

John Wilkes was editor of the *North Briton*, a journal designed to counteract the policies of *The Briton*, whose owner was the Earl of Bute. Although Wilkes himself was somewhat disreputable, he became the centre of important issues which directly involved George III himself.

General Warrants. In No. 45 of the *North Briton* Wilkes attacked the King's Speech as containing a false statement about the Peace of Paris, 1763. The King took this as a personal insult to himself and ordered the prosecution of Wilkes. A General Warrant was issued by the Secretary of State by which forty-nine persons were arrested, but no individual charge was made against them. Wilkes was among those arrested, but he was released on claiming privilege as an M.P. As a result of this affair, the *Lord Chief Justice declared general warrants illegal*, and Wilkes received £2,000 in damages.

But neither George III nor the government let the matter rest there. The House of Commons voted No. 45 of the *North Briton* a 'seditious libel' and for this offence parliamentary privilege did not apply. Wilkes then fled to France and did not appear before the House of Commons when summoned. In 1764 he was expelled from the Commons and declared an outlaw.

In 1768 Wilkes returned and was elected M.P. for Middlesex, where his support was very strong. He was now fined £1,000 and sentenced to twenty-two months' imprisonment on the charge of seditious libel. But the House of Commons now committed two serious errors. The first was in 1769, when the Commons expelled him for a libel against a minister of the Crown, **Lord Weymouth** (this case should have been tried in the ordinary courts); and the second was that a libel against a member of the House of Lords was not a breach of privilege of the House of Commons. After this, the Commons declared him incapable of sitting as an M.P.—thus going much further than expelling him. The Commons were not justified in this sweeping declaration.

The Middlesex electors now replied by electing Wilkes as their member against the King's candidate, **Colonel Luttrell**, who was then declared M.P. for Middlesex by the Commons. *In this again they were acting illegally themselves, for they were denying the rights of the voters.* Riots now broke out in London in support of 'Wilkes and Liberty', and Wilkes was made an alderman of London. In 1774 Wilkes was again elected for Middlesex, took his seat in the Commons, and eight years later the Commons erased from their Journal the motion which in 1769 had declared him incapable of being an M.P.

Some Comments on the Wilkes' Case

This was a very important case. It resisted the attempts of George III and his government to oppose the legal decisions of the voters of Middlesex. Moreover, the liberty of the people was considerably safeguarded by the defeat of the dangerous practice of issuing general warrants of search and arrest without specifying charges or naming individuals.

During his remaining time as an M.P. and a member of the corporation of London, Wilkes fought hard to secure the right of reporters to report and of printers to print, the proceedings of the House of Commons. Wilkes successfully defended in 1771 two printers whom the Commons were attempting to arrest, and *this resulted in the Commons accepting the reporting of debates.* In this way, Wilkes increased the liberty of the press and brought Parliament under closer public scrutiny. Wilkes had also successfully opposed the extension of arbitrary power by the King who had declared that 'the expulsion of Wilkes is highly expedient and must be effected'. The London and Middlesex riots had shown the government that popular opinion was alive to injustice, and Wilkes contributed to the development of a new 'public opinion' which, under radical influence, was later to alter the whole system of election to Parliament.

Summary

George III had a clear notion of the royal prerogative and was anxious to reassert those powers which George I and II had been incapable of sustaining. He aimed to be above party, but to exercise a clear role in the choice of governments and in the decisions of Parliament. His views brought him into conflict with Wilkes, whose activities served to protect a number of important liberties against royal encroachment. He also rigidly interpreted his rights in relation to the American colonists and proved unyielding at times when compromise might have succeeded.

Important Dates

1761   Bute becomes Prime Minister.
1763   Peace of Paris.
      No. 45 of 'North Briton'.
      Wilkes arrested, but general warrants declared illegal.
      Wilkes fled to France.
1764   Wilkes expelled from House of Commons and declared an outlaw.
1768   Return of Wilkes and his election for Middlesex as M.P.
1769   Again expelled from Commons.
1774   Wilkes again elected for Middlesex, and took seat in Commons.
1782   Motion debarring him from Commons (1769) expunged from the Journal of the House.

QUESTIONS

(1) What was George III's view of the monarch's rights?
(2) Describe some of the activities of the 'King's Friends'.
(3) What were the main stages in the Wilkes' case?
(4) What was the real importance of the Wilkes' case?

CHAPTER EIGHT

THE AMERICAN WAR OF INDEPENDENCE 1775-1783

General Background

THE mercantile theory of trade demanded a favourable balance of trade to the mother country, and this balance was to be paid for in actual money, the possession of which was regarded as wealth. But parliament had only regulated trade with the colonies and had not imposed direct taxation upon them. In general, the colonists had been free to conduct their internal trade as they wished. In a number of commodities the colonies were allowed a monopoly of trade with England, and Walpole had allowed them to carry on a smuggling trade with the French and Spanish colonies, much to their advantage. Britain had lost revenue in customs duties by allowing this contraband trade, especially the trade in timber and cattle.

Grenville, who succeeded Lord Bute as Prime Minister in April 1763, decided to stop the contraband trade and to impose *internal taxes* on the colonists in order to meet the costs of the successful defence of the colonies against the French. The British National Debt had risen to £140,000,000 because of the Seven Years' War, and it was thought only right by the home government that the colonies should contribute to the cost of maintaining troops in the colonies. The British parliament now passed the **Stamp Act (1765)** which imposed a stamp duty on paper and legal documents. Immediately the colonists denounced the principle of taxation without representation in the British parliament—'No taxation without representation' became the slogan. Riots occurred in Boston; and the Assembly of Virginia, led by the strongly anti-British **Patrick Henry**, took the lead in demanding the repeal of the Stamp Act. The Congress of New York, representing thirteen colonies, recognized England's right to regulate trade, but otherwise accepted the views of the Virginian Assembly. In fact, *the Stamp Act was quite legal, for England had sovereign rights over the colonies*; but, in view of the colonies' great development of their own independent life, it was unwise. In the following year, 1766, the Stamp Act was repealed by the Rockingham ministry which succeeded Grenville's; but at the same time parliament passed the **Declaratory Act**, which affirmed that parliament had full rights of taxation of the colonies as well as law-making. George III supported the Declaratory Act and was opposed to the repeal of the Stamp Act. He was determined to maintain every legal right of the Crown against all odds. In 1767, **Townshend**, the Chancellor of the Exchequer in Chatham's ministry, imposed import duties at the colonial ports upon tea, glass, paper, white and red lead and painters' colours, with the purpose of raising about £40,000 annually to pay the salaries of various colonial officials. But the colonists objected to this on the grounds that the duties were taxes for the raising of government income and not merely trade regulations, and were therefore to be opposed as strongly as the Stamp Act.

The strains between the home government and the colonies became daily greater. In 1767 the Assembly of New York was dissolved for refusing to accept the Townshend duties. The government also revived an Act of the reign of Henry VIII which enabled offenders to be brought to England for trial. This was not enforced, but it was alarming to the colonists. In March, 1770 occurred the **Boston Massacre**, when three colonists were killed by soldiers during a riot. In 1772 some colonists captured and burnt a revenue cutter.

In 1770 Lord North removed all the Townshend duties except that on tea, mainly because they had failed to raise the required revenue. To the colonists the maintenance of the tax on tea really meant that the home government had not abandoned their idea of taxing the colonies—they still retained the 'right to tax'. In 1773 Lord North permitted the East India Company to export tea directly to the colonies without first paying a duty in Britain. They would still pay the small colonial tax, but tea would be cheaper to the colonists. However, agitation against the tea tax continued and on 16th December, **1773**, there occurred the famous **Boston Tea Party**, when a crowd of Bostonians, disguised as Red Indians, boarded a ship of the East India Company in Boston harbour and threw its cargo of tea overboard.

The government of Lord North replied by closing the port of Boston in 1774, cancelling the Charter of Massachusetts and converting it to a Crown Colony ruled from Britain. These moves were directly inspired by George III. The colonists were further alarmed by the passing of the **Quebec Act** in **1774** which made their neighbour Canada a Crown Colony, and they feared the extension to themselves of royal power. When the famous **Congress of Philadelphia**, representing all colonies except Georgia, met in the same year, it denied Parliament's right to tax for revenue purposes and condemned the action taken against Massachusetts. In Massachusetts itself, a Provincial Congress of the Assembly delegates met and arranged the enrolment of '*minutemen*'—that is, a militia composed of men ready to serve against Britain at a minute's notice.

In **1775** tension grew worse. A force sent by the British authorities from Boston to Concord, to take over military stores which they feared

WAR OF AMERICAN INDEPENDENCE: CAUSES (

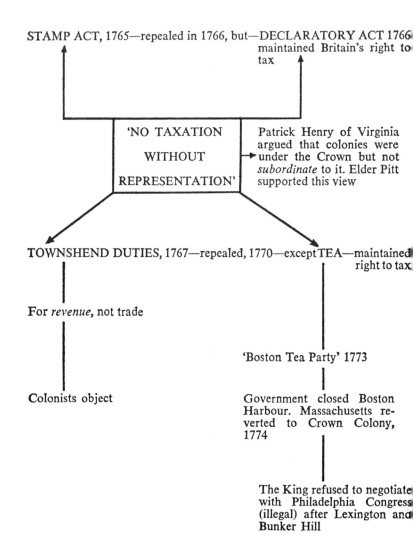

POLITICAL

STAMP ACT, 1765—repealed in 1766, but—DECLARATORY ACT 1766
maintained Britain's right to
tax

'NO TAXATION WITHOUT REPRESENTATION'

Patrick Henry of Virginia argued that colonies were under the Crown but not *subordinate* to it. Elder Pitt supported this view

TOWNSHEND DUTIES, 1767—repealed, 1770—except TEA—maintained
right to tax

For *revenue*, not trade

Colonists object

'Boston Tea Party' 1773

Government closed Boston Harbour. Massachusetts reverted to Crown Colony, 1774

The King refused to negotiate with Philadelphia Congress (illegal) after Lexington and Bunker Hill

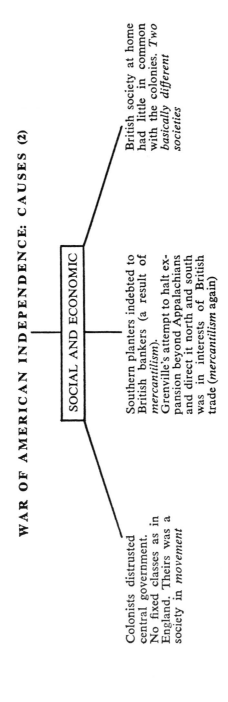

WAR OF AMERICAN INDEPENDENCE: CAUSES (2)

SOCIAL AND ECONOMIC

Colonists distrusted central government. No fixed classes as in England. Theirs was a society in *movement*

Southern planters indebted to British bankers (a result of *mercantilism*). Grenville's attempt to halt expansion beyond Appalachians and direct it north and south was in interests of British trade (*mercantilism* again)

British society at home had little in common with the colonies. *Two basically different societies* might fall into colonial hands, was attacked on its way back at **Lexington**. The force got back to Boston, but the colonists occupied **Bunker Hill** outside Boston with the purpose of blockading it. They were counter-attacked and forced to abandon the position. The battles of Lexington and Bunker Hill need not have led to outright war, but George III refused to negotiate with the illegal Philadelphia Congress, and in April 1776 the Congress opened American ports to the traders of all nations, thus destroying the British mercantile system at one blow. On **4th July, 1776**, the Congress issued the **Declaration of Independence**.

Some very important considerations about the war are the following:

Although economic reasons connected with trade and taxation have often been declared the causes of the American Revolution, it is possible that *social* causes were stronger. There was a basically different outlook—the colonists were impatient of government interference of any kind—they had a revolutionary distrust of government. For this reason they disliked central authority and were not prepared to work together for one cause. This was especially the case during the Seven Years' War, when Britain was fighting on their behalf against the French. Indeed, many colonists had continued to trade with the French, to the great annoyance of the British government. The colonies had many trading squabbles among themselves. The traders of New England wanted to continue their smuggling activity—it was their way of life, and the men on the frontier least of all wanted interference from Britain or anyone else. As the pioneers began to move westward (there were a few even beyond the Appalachian Mountains by 1776) they became even more independent and separated from European ideas and ways of life. In Britain itself, however, there was a settled government, with clearly defined classes, but in the colonies fortunes came and went rapidly—there was little of a set class structure—it was a society in *movement*. In the deep South there was more of a class structure based on cotton plantations and negro slaves, but a system based on slavery was far different from that of the Englishman's country estate.

Yet the trading connection with Britain was important, and special bounties were given to colonial exporters of commodities to England in return for the latter's much-needed manufactures. However, the New England states had insufficient farming products to send to England, and this was one reason why cheap French sugar was smuggled in from the West Indies and re-sold to Britain. Yet the anti-smuggling laws of Grenville were designed to stop this. Again, the southern planters were heavily financed by British banking agents, and as early as 1760 the Virginian planters owed over £2 million to Britain—a situation very galling to them. The indebtedness was a result of the British mercantile system which controlled colonial trade in the interests of Britain.

The Grenville government attempted to fix the western frontiers and prevent movement beyond the Appalachians, with the purpose of encouraging expansion to the north towards Nova Scotia and south towards Florida, where trading prospects were better and, under the mercantile system, would benefit Britain. This policy, which involved leaving the Indian tribes well alone, would cost Britain about £370,000 a year to administer, and it was to raise this money that the Stamp Act was imposed. The westerners disliked the Indian policy, and, besides the objections we have noted (p. 84), the Stamp Act hit hard the editors of newspapers who were in a position to make the maximum fuss. The Act was not illegal, but it was unwise.

Patrick Henry of Virginia claimed that the elected assemblies of the colonies were separate and sovereign under the Crown, but not subordinate to the Crown and the British Parliament. He claimed that it was not sufficient for the British Parliament to enact taxation for the colonies without their consent, for colonial assemblies existed and had the right to resist. This attitude was accepted by the other American colonies. In Britain they had the strong support in this view of William Pitt, Earl of Chatham. However, when Chatham became Prime Minister, he proposed a system of *requisitions* on the colonies—that is, a request to each of the separate colonies for money, to be made by the King and not by parliament. But the colonists also took objection to this because it still gave financial power to the King and took it out of the hands of the colonial assemblies. In general, the colonists had an intense fear of English interference, and this was the underlying cause of their opposition to Britain. They had developed their own forms of local trade and social life and were determined to maintain them. In many ways they were independent before the War of Independence began. This, of course, was in absolute conflict with George III's claim of complete sovereignty for Britain over the colonies.

Stages of the War of Independence, 1775-1783

After Concord and Lexington the Congress of Philadelphia adopted the name of 'United Colonies' and **George Washington** was appointed Commander-in-Chief. Washington's task of creating an effective army was immensely difficult. The colonists were quite unused to acting together and there was much jealousy among them. They lacked supplies of arms and lacked trained officers. At his training ground at Valley Forge, Washington had to create an army from a rabble and instil into them a true revolutionary fervour. One of his most important assistants in this work was the Englishman, **Thomas Paine**, a radical and a fervent supporter of the American cause against George III. His propaganda pamphlets were of great importance in building up the colonial anti-British morale. He later wrote an important work *The Rights of Man*; and in the French Revolution of 1789 he was presented with the key of the royal fortress of the Bastille after its capture by the revolutionaries—some of whom in these earlier years fought under the **Marquis de Lafayette** on the side of the colonists.

After the battle of Bunker Hill, where the British under **General Gage** lost eight hundred men, **General Howe** succeeded Gage and decided to evacuate Boston altogether. This decision greatly encouraged the colonists. They hoped to gain the support of the Canadians and invaded Canada and captured Montreal, but their commander was killed at Quebec, and the expedition proved a failure (December 1775). In the south an English force under **Lord Dunmore** burnt the town of Norfolk. **General Clinton's** attempt to capture Richmond failed. The general effect of these moves was to unite the Southerners against Britain. They had previously been better disposed to Britain than the North.

On 4th July, 1776, the Declaration of Independence was issued. The Founding Fathers were greatly influenced by the democratic ideas of Thomas Paine. The Declaration broke all political connection with Britain. This is one of the most important documents ever written. The detailed wording of the Declaration was in great part the work of **Thomas Jefferson** who was later to be President of the United States. It contained the following famous announcement: 'We hold these truths to be self-evident, that all men are created equal, that they are endowed by their Creator with certain inalienable Rights, that among these are Life, Liberty and the pursuit of Happiness. That to secure these Rights, Governments are instituted among Men, deriving their just powers from the consent of the governed. That whenever any Form of Government becomes destructive of these ends, it is the Right of the People to alter or abolish it. . . .'

The Declaration then went on to list all the charges against George III and, under Jefferson's influence, was careful to avoid any charges against the people of Britain.

The war now developed rapidly. At first the colonists suffered setbacks, especially when General Howe defeated Washington at **Brooklyn** in **August 1776** and captured Long Island. But Washington's army managed to extricate itself. New York now became the British centre of operations. In New York itself there was much support for Britain from those merchants who had benefited from their monopoly of the British market. New York was easy of access to the British navy. Despite these initial advantages, Howe failed to pursue Washington after the Brooklyn defeat; this gave Washington time to strengthen his forces, with the result that he defeated the British at **Trenton** in

AREAS OF FIGHTING DURING THE AMERICAN WAR OF INDEPENDENCE

December, 1776 and again at **Princeton**, in **January 1777**. Thus Washington was able to raise the colonial morale considerably at a critical point. George III's employment of German mercenaries to assist the British forces also tended to harden even further the colonial resistance.

A British plan of campaign was now devised to secure a quick victory. **Burgoyne** was to advance from Canada along Lake Champlain and to join General Clinton's force from New York on the Hudson River. By this means it was hoped to separate the New England states from the remainder, and General Howe was to attack Philadelphia. This important plan was a failure. Howe defeated Washington at **Brandywine**, but then went into winter quarters at a time when Washington's army was in very bad condition at Valley Forge. General Burgoyne, in his advance from Canada, captured Saratoga, but Clinton had insufficient forces to leave New York and join him on the Hudson River. The Indians now deserted Burgoyne and he was forced to surrender to General Gates at **Saratoga** on **17th October, 1777**.

Importance of the Surrender at Saratoga

The British plan was a good one, but the home government had failed to give the commanders sufficient forces to carry it out. There had been waste of valuable time by Howe, and it was clear that the British had underestimated the difficulty of their task. They apparently were not prepared for a winter campaign. Saratoga was the decisive event which brought the French into the war to help the colonists, who now had the support of the French Atlantic Fleet **(February 1778)**. Saratoga made agreement with the colonists almost impossible, for their determination was strengthened. *North, the British Prime Minister, proposed to abandon all direct taxation of the colonists, but he was too late.* William Pitt the Elder (Lord Chatham), who had shown much support for the colonists' case, opposed the granting of independence and wished to continue the war against the old enemy France. These points he made clear in a speech in the House of Commons on 7th April, when he had an apoplectic fit, and he died on 11th April. Thus Saratoga and its results made agreement with the colonists impossible in conditions which had suddenly worsened for Britain.

Besides assisting the Americans with their fleet, the French allowed American privateer captains, such as **Paul Jones**, to use French ports from which to sally forth in their attacks on British shipping. In America itself the French under General Lafayette gave great help to the colonists. The French government of Louis XVI gave direct help both in arms and money, for now was the opportunity to avenge the Seven Years' War and regain much that they had lost. In **1779** Spain, who had the Family Compact with France, entered the war and began the **Siege of Gibraltar**. Holland, another of the old commercial rivals of Britain, was also helping American privateers in the Dutch West Indies, and Britain declared war against the Dutch in 1780. In that year was formed the **Armed Neutrality** consisting of Sweden, Holland, Prussia, France, Spain and Russia to resist the British claim to search neutral vessels for contraband of war.

With this accession of naval powers to the colonists' side, Britain lost command of the sea. The old strategy of Chatham was not used, and there was a failure to blockade the French ports, which enabled supplies to reach the colonists. However, the years 1780–1781 saw successes for British forces in the Southern States, especially in Carolina under Clinton, who also captured Charleston, South Carolina. **General Cornwallis** captured Camden and Guilford in 1781. But here Britain's loss of naval supremacy brought immediate difficulty, for it was impossible for **Cornwallis** to strengthen his rather small force from the sea and he decided to join Clinton's force. At **Yorktown** he was attacked by Washington from the land while the French fleet under **de Grasse** held the approaches from the sea. Clinton was unable to join Cornwallis by sea, nor was Cornwallis able to escape by sea. *He was forced to surrender in October 1781.* This was the virtual end of the war in America.

The General War to the Treaty of Versailles, 1783

The only compensation for Britain had been the defeat of the Spanish fleet off **Cape St. Vincent** by **Rodney** in 1780. But in **1782** the French captured all the British West Indies with the exception of Jamaica, Barbados and Antigua, and in the Mediterranean the French and Spanish captured Minorca.

However, despite her desperate position, Britain rallied sufficiently to retrieve the situation. Already in 1781 the ally of the French in India, Hyder Ali of Mysore, had been defeated by General Eyre Coote at Porto Novo, and this put an end to the French threat in India. On 12th April, 1782, Admiral Rodney defeated de Grasse off the **Isles des Saints** in the West Indies, and the French fleet was destroyed. The war was proving a great strain on France's finances, and this defeat made her willing to negotiate. Another favourable factor for Britain was the successful defence of **Gibraltar** by **General Eliot** since **1779** and its relief by **Admiral Howe** in **October, 1782.**

The Treaty of Versailles

All parties were now ready to negotiate, and the treaty was signed in 1783. (1) The U.S.A. was recognized as an independent state; (2) Minorca and Florida went to Spain; (3) France gained St. Lucia, Tobago (West Indies), Senegal (West Africa), St. Pierre and Miquelon

(St. Lawrence River) and three trading stations in India which she could now garrison; and (4) Holland and Britain exchanged conquests.

Summary of Reasons for Britain's Loss of the American Colonies

(1) The colonies were distant and unfamiliar to the British commanders; (2) British officers clung to European military ideas; (3) there was no real attempt by Britain to rally the loyal elements in the colonies, and they were not protected by the Treaty of Versailles—many were driven into Canada by persecution; (4) the employment of German Hessian troops by George III stiffened colonial resistance; (5) the intervention of other powers after Saratoga and the loss of British command of the seas aggravated the situation. *Results.* The short-term results were bad for Britain, whose National Debt had increased by £100 million. Many people considered that Britain's greatness was finished. *In the long-run, however, some of the results were good.* The old mercantile system based on the Navigation Acts had received a blow from which it never recovered, and this led on to the eventual free development of other British colonies. *In Ireland the patriots seized the opportunity to gain the grant of an independent parliament in 1782.* Before 1783 Britain had used North and South Carolina and Virginia for the transportation of convicts, but now had to look elsewhere. *In 1788, the first convicts arrived at Botany Bay, Australia,* under **Captain Phillip**, and from further settlements the future Australian colonies were to develop.

The Gordon Riots, 1780

It was during Lord North's ministry, and at the height of the American War of Independence, that serious disorder broke out in London. This took the form of a violent anti-Catholic movement led by **Lord George Gordon**, a swashbuckling political adventurer who was M.P. for a Wiltshire borough. He combined a hatred of Lord North with fanatical Protestantism. He believed, quite wrongly, that Catholic influence was increasing in every department of political and social life. This feeling had grown to a point of delusion since the passing by parliament of **Sir George Savile's Catholic Relief Bill** in **1778**. This enabled Catholics to purchase and inherit land, prohibited the imprisonment of Catholic priests for exercising their religion and allowed Catholic recruits to the forces to take a modified oath of fidelity to the Crown. But even this tolerant and enlightened law provoked riots in the Presbyterian Lowlands of Scotland, which prevented a similar law being passed for Scotland.

Lord George Gordon and his supporters now formed the **Protestant Association** with the aim of getting the Act of 1778 repealed, and on

2nd June, 1780, a huge mob attempted to invade the House of Commons where Gordon demanded that an anti-Catholic petition should be heard. As the day went on this mob became larger and more riotous. The chapel of the Sardinian Embassy in Lincoln's Inn Fields was destroyed as also was that of the Bavarian Embassy. The magistrates were under the mistaken impression that a mob could not legally be fired upon by the soldiery without the previous reading of the **Riot Act**. This delayed action, and the rioters rampaged through the City doing immense damage to the property of Roman Catholics, attacking the Bank of England and creating numerous fires. The terrified citizens were saved from further horror by the action of George III himself who issued Orders in Council to use military force. The number of people killed was 458 (mostly rioters) and twenty-one were hanged. Gordon was acquitted of treason and somewhat later joined the Jewish faith, but died in prison of gaol fever, having uttered a libel against the Queen of France and not being able to find sureties for his future good behaviour. This episode made the opponents of the government very reluctant to employ mob pressure against it in the future; and in the election of 1780, Lord North's supporters increased their representation. The riots also were a salutary warning against the evils of religious bigotry, but at the same time they made the ruling classes extremely nervous of mass movements and demonstrations of any kind—an alarm which greatly increased after the French Revolution of 1789.

Important Dates

1765 **The Stamp Act.**
1766 **Stamp Act repealed.**
       Declaratory Act passed.
1767 **Townshend Duties imposed on colonies.**
       Assembly of New York dissolved.
1770 **Boston 'Massacre'.**
       Townshend duties removed, except that on tea.
1773 **The Boston Tea Party.**
1774 **Port of Boston closed.**
       Massachusetts Charter cancelled.
       Congress of Philadelphia met.
1775 **Battle of Lexington.**
       Battle of Bunker Hill.
1776 **Congress opened ports to traders of all nations.**
       4th July: Declaration of Independence.
       August: Howe defeated Washington and captured Long Island.
       December: Washington defeated British at Trenton.

1777   January: Washington's victory at Princeton.
       Burgoyne-Clinton-Howe campaign.
       Howe defeated Washington at Brandywine.
       Burgoyne captured Saratoga.
       Clinton failed to join Burgoyne.
       17th October: Burgoyne surrendered to General Gates at Saratoga.
1778   France joined colonists.
1779   Spain also declared war on Britain.
       Siege of Gibraltar began.
1780   Gordon Riots.
       Britain declared war against Holland.
       The League of Armed Neutrality formed against Britain.
       Britain lost naval supremacy, but Rodney gained a victory off Cape St. Vincent.
1781   Cornwallis defeated Americans at Camden and Guilford.
       October: forced to surrender to Washington at Yorktown.
1782   French captured most of British West Indies, and (with the Spanish) Minorca in the Mediterranean.
       Rodney defeated French off the Isles des Saints, West Indies (Battle of the Saints).
       Gibraltar relieved by Admiral Howe.
       French willing to negotiate.
1783   Treaty of Versailles.

QUESTIONS

(1) *What specific actions of the British governments led to the War of American Independence?*

(2) *What economic and social conditions favoured the break from Britain?*

(3) *What were the main reasons for the American victory?*

(4) *Describe the Versailles Treaty of 1783.*

(5) *What were the short and long-term results for Britain of the loss of the American colonies?*

(6) *What were the causes and results of the Gordon Riots?*

CHAPTER NINE

THE AGRICULTURAL AND INDUSTRIAL REVOLUTIONS

The Agricultural Revolution

DURING the eighteenth century great changes occurred in the English countryside, with increasing rapidity after 1760. These changes altered the whole system of agricultural production. The term 'revolution', if we accept the fact that the changes took many years to bring about, is no exaggeration.

The old system derived from the Middle Ages was the *Open Field* system. Each village cultivated two or three large fields which were sub-divided into strips separated by low ridges of earth known as 'baulks'. Each farmer had a number of these strips scattered in the big fields. The original idea of scattering was to give each villager a share of both good and poorer land. In general, fixed customs decided the type of crop, times of sowing and harvesting. As only two of the three fields were cultivated each year and one was left fallow to recuperate, a simple rotation of crops (very commonly wheat and barley) moved round each year, with a different field fallow each time.

In 1760 this system prevailed mainly in the South and East Midlands —the middle belt of counties running across England. In other parts of England the system had generally been abandoned in favour of compact or enclosed farms.

Faults of the System

The grain crops were poor. Broadcast sowing was wasteful and produced crops impossible to weed in the early stages of growth. Even if some farmers had wanted to adopt improved methods, they needed the agreement of the whole community—almost impossible to obtain. The separation of strips led to waste of time and labour and, in any case, no man was interested in improving land which might be allocated to someone else the next year. The low ridges between the fields harboured weeds and, in the absence of drainage, held water on the land and produced swampy conditions. The cattle in the old-style village were of poor quality, mixed up as they were on the common grazing grounds and having no root crops provided for them. The common practice was to kill most of the animals in the autumn and salt down the meat for the winter. Those left for breeding produced another generation of poor quality.

Causes of Change

Such a system sufficed for the static population of the Middle Ages and of the modern period up to the eighteenth century. Each isolated village could feed itself and, as the great majority of the people lived on the land or in trades connected with it, food supplies were sufficient. *But between 1750 and 1810 the population doubled from about five to ten million.* This increase was mainly in the towns which now needed far more agricultural produce. But the old system could not produce it. Another important change affected agriculture. Under the old system a farmer improved his earnings by employing his wife and children to card and spin wool for the middlemen who supplied the cloth manufacturers. But with the decline of the old domestic system and the growth of the factory system, this source of income was slowly dying out. If the land was to earn its occupants a livelihood without this addition, it would need great change and improvement. Up to the late eighteenth century England had been an exporter of corn, but now there was insufficient to feed herself. This became even more apparent during the **Revolutionary** and **Napoleonic Wars (1793–1815)**, when it became almost impossible to import grain to make up for deficiencies. It was now necessary for Britain to feed herself—and the Open Field system couldn't do it. Another important factor was *farming for profit*, which began to dominate farming in the eighteenth century. The capitalist who wanted land either for profit or as a means of entering parliament, or both, was sure to be a supporter of new methods in agriculture.

The Agricultural Pioneers

A great stimulus to enclosure was the work of a number of important improvers of agricultural methods. In the early eighteenth century **Jethro Tull (1674–1741)**, on his farm at Howberry near Wallingford invented in 1701 the machine drill which replaced the old broadcast sowing, by rows sufficiently separated to allow for hoeing during the whole period of growth. In 1711–1714 he travelled in France and Italy studying agricultural methods. In his work *Horse-hoeing Husbandry (1731)* he emphasized the importance of proper manuring and breaking up of the soil. Another important pioneer was **Charles ('Turnip') Townshend (1674–1738)** who was the brother-in-law of Robert Walpole and served in the latter's government until 1730, when he retired and devoted himself to the improvement of his Norfolk estates at Raynham. He ended the waste of fallow land by introducing the famous

Norfolk rotation of crops. This was a four-year course which cut out the fallow land altogether; and he alternated corn with clover and root crops, *e.g.* wheat, clover, barley and roots, in that order. The root crops gave winter feed for cattle which increased in number and gave valuable manure for the land. To fertilize the land he used *marl*, a mixture of clay and carbonate of lime. He greatly improved drainage and used better implements. He derived many of his practices from Jethro Tull. The Norfolk rotation was not his invention—it had been used before, but he encouraged its wider use. Another great innovator in Norfolk was **Thomas Coke (1752–1842)**, later Earl of Leicester. When he succeeded to his father's estates at Holkham he found them almost barren, with a light sandy soil of no value. By applying the new methods of marling and manuring he transformed it into rich corn-growing land. Altogether he spent over one million pounds on his estates, but his returns (from his tenants as well as from his own estates) were so great that he made a fortune. His influence was enhanced by the fact that he was M.P. for Norfolk for many years, a popular sportsman and a great advocate of enclosure. **Robert Bakewell (1725–1795)** was no less important. On his Leicestershire farm at Dishley he produced a new breed of sheep, the *New Leicesters*. These were characterized by weight as well as by the excellent quality of their wool, and he brought his sheep to peak condition in two years instead of the old four. He was also a very important breeder of horses, which were characterized by thick, strong bodies and short legs. These horses replaced the old, cumbersome ox-team in the South and Midlands. In all these experiments Bakewell was greatly aided by the use of the new root crops for winter feeding which the Norfolk pioneers had introduced. George III himself ('Farmer George'), by establishing a model farm at Windsor, greatly encouraged the new agriculture and the movement towards enclosure.

The great writer on English agriculture, **Arthur Young (1741–1820)** did more than any other individual to promote the new agriculture and the enclosure movement. By making tours of England and publishing his *Farmer's Letters to the People of England* in 1768 he became the national advocate of enclosure. His *Annals of Agriculture*, begun in 1784, ran into forty-five volumes, and George III himself contributed under the pseudonym of 'Ralph Robinson'. He was appointed the first secretary of the new **Board of Agriculture** in **1793**—a private society for the promotion of agriculture and not a government concern.

Such was the prosperity of Norfolk that in 1760 there was a thriving wheat export through such ports as Yarmouth, Blakeney and King's Lynn. Yet in many other parts of Britain agriculture had not changed. Even in Middlesex, with London as its market, there had been no progress whatever. Yet, between 1760 and 1820 the enclosure movement swept away the old system.

The Enclosure Acts

Between 1760 and 1800 over fifteen hundred Enclosure Acts were passed by Parliament, and about three million acres enclosed. Before an Enclosure Act could be introduced four-fifths of the village land-holders had to agree to enclosure. After the Act was passed, Commissioners were appointed to supervise enclosure. In general this appears to have been done fairly, but there were difficulties. When the land was re-allocated the expenses of hedging, ditching, etc., forced the small farmer to sell to the better-off. Some yeoman farmers who had owned their own land remained as tenants of the new landlord who had acquired most of the land. Others became labourers or drifted to the towns. The villagers also lost their right to graze cattle on the common, which was now enclosed. This right had been by custom and not by law, and they had no legal redress. The same applied to the right of wood-cutting, which in the past had helped both yeoman and labourer. Another important result of enclosure was the rise in the value of land by six times in thirty years. The capitalist, the man with money to invest, now found the countryside to his liking, especially during the war years, 1793–1815, when prices and profits were high. On the other hand, the number of small, independent farmers, the 'yeomen', declined rapidly. At the same time farming for profit and for the markets provided by the growing industrial towns also brought about a great improvement in farming methods. On balance, the change was progressive, but many suffered. The high price of bread did not mean higher wages; and such was the poverty of the labourers that, in 1795, the magistrates of Speenhamland in Berkshire decided to add to the workers' wages from the Poor Rates on a scale decided by the price of bread and the number in a family. This was the famous **Speenhamland System** of poor relief which spread to many other parts of Britain in the war years. It was designed to prevent starvation and rebellion.

The Industrial Revolution

The Industrial Revolution was the change in methods of industrial production which occurred in the eighteenth and nineteenth centuries. This was a change from the old domestic system of production to the factory system, from small-scale to larger scale industry, aided by new sources of power and by new inventions. Together with these changes there occurred great improvements in communications both by land and water, of which the canal and railway systems were the most important. The revolution produced a new class of capitalist owners making great incomes from the work of masses of wage-earners in factories and mines.

THE AGRICULTURAL REVOLUTION

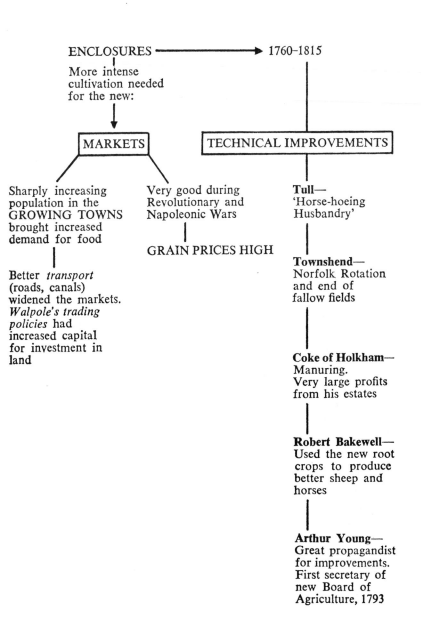

ENCLOSURES ──────────────▶ 1760–1815

More intense
cultivation needed
for the new:

MARKETS   TECHNICAL IMPROVEMENTS

Sharply increasing
population in the
GROWING TOWNS
brought increased
demand for food

Very good during
Revolutionary and
Napoleonic Wars

GRAIN PRICES HIGH

Tull—
'Horse-hoeing
Husbandry'

Better *transport*
(roads, canals)
widened the markets.
*Walpole's trading
policies* had
increased capital
for investment in
land

Townshend—
Norfolk Rotation
and end of
fallow fields

Coke of Holkham—
Manuring.
Very large profits
from his estates

Robert Bakewell—
Used the new root
crops to produce
better sheep and
horses

Arthur Young—
Great propagandist
for improvements.
First secretary of
new Board of
Agriculture, 1793

During the early eighteenth century British trade, under Walpole's guidance, had expanded enormously. Both merchants and bankers had great wealth ready to invest in new directions. Britain's defeat of France and Spain, leading to the Treaty of Utrecht, had given her new colonies and thus new markets for trade. But the old domestic system at home was not efficient enough to provide the demands of these new markets. Another important development after 1750 was the *growth of population* at home which in itself created more demand and at the same time provided more labour for industry. This increase was from five million in 1700 to six million in 1750 and nine million by 1800. All these factors led men to attempt to improve on the old system, and in these attempts both capitalists and inventors were involved. After the Peace of Paris in 1763, Britain added still more colonies to her possessions and the market was thus widened even further. After 1760 the Industrial Revolution gradually speeded up.

Difficulties of the Old System

In the woollen and cotton industries the manufacture of cloth was carried on in houses and very commonly in farmhouses. The travelling 'packman' provided the weavers with the yarn, collected the finished product and sold it at fairs or directly to a merchant. This was a simple and inexpensive system not requiring much capital, and it could be carried out on a family or small workshop basis. But the system was slow and production was irregular. There was no supervision of the weaver and quality varied considerably.

Inventions in the Woollen and Cotton Industries

An important early invention was the *flying-shuttle* by **John Kay** in **1733**, which enabled one man to throw the shuttle mechanically from one side of the loom to the other instead of two operators being needed, one at each side. This enabled broadcloth to be woven by a single weaver. But this invention had little use until after 1760, because for many years yarn was scarce and spinning could not keep pace with the demands of weavers. At last, in **1764, James Hargreaves** of Blackburn invented a *spinning-jenny* which turned eleven spindles at the same time and was worked by hand. In general use by 1767, it produced a yarn which was suitable only for the 'woof' or cross thread in the cloth. It was used at first for cotton only. In **1769 Richard Arkwright** produced a spinning machine worked by water power, and it was called *the water-frame*. The yarn produced was suitable for the 'warp'. Arkwright established a factory at Cromford in Derbyshire for producing yarn for stockings. Arkwright's water-frame was too large and expensive for the domestic worker, and a factory was needed for it. Then in **1779 Samuel Crompton's** 'mule' was an improvement on the water-frame and produced a yarn that was both fine and strong. This enabled muslins to be woven in England instead of being imported from India. The next great development was the manufacture by **James Watt** of an improved steam engine in 1782, and from that time *steam began to replace water-power in both cotton and woollen mills*—though much faster in cotton. In fact, all these early inventions were applied first to the cotton industry and not to wool. The supply of the latter was limited for many years to English pasture, whereas cotton came in abundance from the West Indies and later from the United States as well. The cotton industry entered the factory system much faster than wool. The steam engine enabled factories to be moved from streams and rivers into towns, and the unreliability of a water-supply was overcome.

Other industries underwent great change. In the iron industry up to 1750 smelting was done by the charcoal process in the Weald of Sussex. This was slow and production was slight. Owing to the great wastage of wood needed for ship-building the industry had been restricted and was declining. **Abraham Darby** of **Coalbrookdale** invented about 1709 a method of smelting by first turning coal into coke (a process improved by his son about 1730); and, as these methods became known, the iron industry moved to the coal-fields and iron-fields. As the demand for iron increased with the Industrial Revolution the industry revived in the new areas and the Sussex centres died out.

Developments in Communications

Great developments in communications helped to expand the market for manufactures and also led to an increasing demand for coal and iron especially. The **Bridgewater Canal** was built by **James Brindley** between **1759 and 1761**. This connected the Duke of Bridgewater's coal-mine at Worsley with Manchester and enabled coal to be carried cheaply to the city. This stimulated the construction of other canals such as the **Grand Trunk Canal** in **1766** and the **Grand Junction Canal** in **1790**. The canals enabled farm produce to be carried to the towns and raw materials to the factories. **Josiah Wedgwood** had established his famous pottery of Etruria in 1762, and the clay was transported to it from Cornwall by canal. Wedgwood himself put much of his capital into canal construction. The canals enabled export goods to reach the ports more rapidly than by road and were much superior for the transport of bulky loads such as coal, or fragile manufactures which rough roads would have damaged. In the 1790s there was a 'canal mania', and more canals were constructed than either before or since. As numerous private companies were concerned, the width of the canals varied considerably and this set limits to the size of the craft that could be used, and made transport slower than it need have been. Only a national or 'nationalized' system from the start could have overcome this difficulty, but *laissez-faire* or free enterprise and competition was the developing theory as against the old idea of monopoly.

The roads had fallen into neglect, for the parishes no longer carried out their duties of repair derived from the Middle Ages. But improvements to the main roads were brought about in the eighteenth century by the development of the **Turnpike Trusts** financed by private individuals. These companies took over stretches of main road, improved them and charged a toll. Many of these Turnpikes employed the great road inventors of the later years of the century. Probably the most important of these was **Thomas Telford**. Between 1800 and 1820 he built nearly a thousand miles of good roads and twelve hundred bridges, many of which still carry road and rail traffic today. Another great pioneer was **John Metcalf—'Blind Jack of Knaresborough'**. In Yorkshire he built his first three miles of road in 1765 using small compressed stones. This was so successful that he gained other contracts and built over 200 miles of roads. Another pioneer was **John Macadam**, who used granite chippings for the surface of roads and employed the camber for drainage. All these improvements meant that good main roads linked most large towns by the beginning of the nineteenth century, but the by-roads were still as bad as ever. On the main roads regular coaching services developed, one of the most famous being **John Palmer**'s mail-coach service between London and Bath and Bristol, introduced in 1784. Another greatly improved route was the London to Holyhead road rebuilt by Telford. (A considerable part of it is the present-day A 5.) Not only was this valuable for trade between England and Ireland, but it was also pleasing to the Irish M.P.s who could reach London so much more quickly.

The railways were the next great development. The pioneer was **Richard Trevithick** of Cornwall. He invented a number of locomotives which were used to haul coal at the pitheads. But the main credit belongs to **George Stephenson**, whose father was an engineman at a Newcastle colliery. By experimenting at the Killingworth colliery he at last built a locomotive which hauled coal on iron rails. Stephenson was appointed the engineer for the **Stockton to Darlington Railway,** opened in **1825**, on which his locomotive was used. This was the first railway to use a steam locomotive. In **1829**, the **Liverpool to Manchester Railway** was opened and **Stephenson's 'Rocket'** came off best in competition with others.

General Results of the Industrial Revolution

It led to a vast increase of Britain's wealth and a *great increase in population.* England gradually became a manufacturing instead of an agricultural country, and this especially enabled her to weather the storm of the wars against France and Napoleon from 1793 to 1815. The manufacturing towns grew rapidly and in an unplanned way that produced slum conditions for masses of the people. Men, women and children were employed for excessively long hours in the factories, and this was to lead to discontent and the growth of trade union organization against the employers. Indeed, *a great proportion of our modern social and political problems resulted from the Industrial Revolution.* The great economist, **Adam Smith,** in his work *The Wealth of Nations* (1776) had argued for free trade, free enterprise and the sweeping away of old, hampering regulations both in industry and in trade. This policy of *laissez-faire* suited the factory and mine owners, but it meant that the workers and reformers had to fight to get new regulations to protect their interests.

The Industrial Revolution also gave Britain a fifty-year start over other countries, which was not seriously challenged until the late nineteenth century. At the same time new towns arose which were unrepresented in Parliament and the new class of capitalist factory owner would naturally demand a place in political life. *Parliament became out-of-date*, and a great struggle to reform it was sure to break out between the landowners and the new middle class.

Summary

The Agricultural and Industrial Revolutions transformed Britain into the first modern industrial state and gave her great early advantages over her trade and industrial rivals in the nineteenth century. In agriculture, farming for the market became the key motive for change leading to extensive enclosure, with great increase of output but much attendant suffering. In industry, market considerations forced on new methods and inventions which had their most important applications in the developing factory system which gradually replaced the domestic system. As in agriculture, output greatly increased, but the displaced domestic workers suffered greatly. The demands of industry led to equivalent transformations in travel and communications—the improvement of roads and rivers, the development of canals and railways being the most important. Population increased rapidly after 1760 and difficult social problems arose from the pressure of this population on housing space in the growing industrial towns. The social problems of Britain since 1760 have been closely related to the Industrial Revolution.

Important Dates

Agriculture

1701   **Tull's invention of the machine drill.**

1731	Tull's 'Horse-hoeing Husbandry' published.
	Townshend began development of Norfolk rotation.
1725–1795	Robert Bakewell.
1752–1842	Coke of Holkham.
1768	Arthur Young published his 'Farmer's Letters to the People of England'.
1784	Young began his 'Annals of Agriculture'.
1793	Young became first Secretary of the new Board of Agriculture.
1795	Speenhamland System of poor relief.

Industry

1730	Abraham Darby Junior improved iron-smelting process, begun by his father in 1709.
1733	Kay's flying-shuttle.
1761	Brindley completed Bridgewater Canal.
1764	Hargreaves' spinning-jenny.
1766	Grand Trunk Canal.
1769	Arkwright's water-frame.
1776	Adam Smith's 'Wealth of Nations'.
1779	Crompton's 'mule'.
1782	James Watt's improved steam engine.
1784	John Palmer's mail-coach service, London-Bath-Bristol.
1790	Grand Junction Canal.
	Canal 'mania' begins.
1760–1820	Main work of Macadam, Metcalf and Telford within this period.
1825	Opening of Stockton to Darlington Railway.
1829	Stephenson's 'Rocket' gives best performance at opening of Liverpool to Manchester Railway.

QUESTIONS

(*1*) *For what reasons did agricultural change speed up after 1760?*

(*2*) *What were the good and bad results of the Agricultural Revolution?*

(*3*) *What was the importance of Jethro Tull, Coke of Holkham (Earl of Leicester), Lord Townshend, Robert Bakewell and Arthur Young?*

(*4*) *What were the main causes of the Industrial Revolution?*

(*5*) *What was the importance of Richard Arkwright, James Watt, Adam Smith, Richard Trevithick, George Stephenson?*

CHAPTER TEN

WILLIAM PITT THE YOUNGER AND THE NAPOLEONIC WARS

Pitt becomes Prime Minister, 1783

AFTER the loss of the American colonies there were three changes of government in two years, the last being a coalition led by the Whig, Charles James Fox, and the Tory, Lord North. This government came to an end with the rejection of Fox's India Bill in 1783, and George III now brought forward a Prime Minister of his own choice, the son of the Earl of Chatham, **William Pitt the Younger (1759–1806)**, who was only twenty-four when appointed. His position was difficult. His age alone brought the jibe, 'A kingdom trusted to a schoolboy's care.' He had no clear majority in the House of Commons and all his ministers except himself were members of the House of Lords. In the parliamentary sessions of 1783–1784 he was defeated again and again, but refused to resign or dissolve parliament. He determined to hold on until the tide turned against the Whigs. His main supporters in parliament were the Tories and the King's Friends. But he was not a Tory of the old school, and he was not merely subservient to the King. At last, a general election was held in 1784 and 160 of Fox's supporters lost their seats—'Fox's Martyrs' as they were called. In general, Pitt had managed to gain the support of the trading classes and, as the son of the great Chatham, he was popular.

Pitt's Domestic Policies

Pitt had a genuine hatred of corruption which was so common in the public life of the century. He refused to accept unpaid offices from the King—for example, he was offered and refused the Clerkship of the Pells, a sinecure, which would have brought him an annual income of £3,000. In parliament he relied on the support of a section of the Whigs who supported his father, on the more progressive Tories, and on the King's Friends. This was not therefore a completely Tory grouping, although it became regarded as a Tory party mainly because Fox and the Whigs consistently opposed it in parliament.

The first task facing him was to restore Britain's finances, which were in a bad state. The American war had raised the National Debt to £250,000,000. Taxation was very heavy, there was a vast amount of smuggling, and the budget was unbalanced. The interest on the National Debt was very high because the old practice was to get money from government favourites who could demand a high price. Pitt now introduced a system of public loans by public tender of subscription, which, through the competitive principle, lowered the rate of interest and saved the government money. He also saved a great deal by abolishing many sinecure offices. For the first time the national accounts were properly audited and the government and nation knew the exact state of the national finances. This was reassuring to both financiers and traders. He also established a *Sinking Fund* with the purpose of paying off the National Debt, when the £1,000,000 put aside annually at compound interest equalled the amount of the debt, a device used much earlier by Walpole. Unfortunately the outbreak of war with France in 1793 ended this scheme.

On trading matters Pitt was influenced by Adam Smith's *Wealth of Nations* (1776) which advocated the end of monopolies and of the mercantile system and the introduction of free trade between nations. Pitt realized that the total volume of trade mattered greatly, and the greater the volume the greater the benefits all round. In all these respects he was influenced by Adam Smith. He encouraged trade by simplifying the collection of customs duties and making the system fairer for the merchant by extending the system of bonded warehouses in which the importer could keep his goods free of duty until they were actually distributed in the country. In 1785 he attempted a free trade treaty with Ireland, but British manufacturers, led by Josiah Wedgwood, were so alarmed at the possibility of competition, that the scheme was defeated in parliament and had to be abandoned. He was more successful with his trade treaty with France in **1786**, the **Eden Treaty**, named after the British negotiator. British cotton goods, cutlery, and ironware were admitted to France at reduced duties, and in exchange Britain reduced duties on French wine, brandy and olive-oil. Up to 1793 there was a great increase of Franco-British trade. This treaty was a defeat for those, led by the Whig leader **Charles James Fox**, who maintained that Britain and France were natural and permanent enemies.

To increase government revenue Pitt introduced a number of tax reforms. In the first place, he improved the efficiency of tax collection by a system of government inspection of the collectors. Previously much government money had gone into private pockets. To reduce smuggling he made it less profitable by reducing duties on spirits and tea—the latter from 112% to 25%. To meet the temporary loss of income he introduced what were called *assessed taxes*, falling mainly on the wealthier classes, including a tax on houses with more than six windows and on servants and racehorses.

Other Reforms

Pitt's **India Act, 1784** (see p. 77) and **Canada Act, 1791** (see p. 350) were distinct improvements on the previous situation in those colonies. In 1785 he introduced a Bill in the Commons to disfranchise thirty-six *rotten boroughs* and transfer their parliamentary representation (seventy-two seats) to unrepresented towns. He proposed to pay £1,000,000 compensation to those landowners who had the right to nominate and secure the election of any candidate who paid enough to gain the nomination. But the 'rotten borough' system was so firmly established that his bill was heavily defeated and he made no further attempts to change the system. The French Revolution also had the effect of preventing such reforms. As we shall see, Pitt's fear of the Revolution led him to introduce a number of serious restrictions on the liberty of the people. Pitt brought about the union of the Irish and English parliaments, 1800-01, but he had promised Catholic Emancipation in Ireland, which would have given real political equality between Protestants and Catholics. When George III refused to agree to this Pitt resigned in 1801. He supported the efforts of the anti-slave trade movement, but it was not until a year after his death that Britain made slave-trading illegal **(1807)**.

Ireland before Pitt's Act of Union

By the **Treaty of Limerick, 1691**, which ended the struggle between William III and the Irish Catholic supporters of the Stuarts, the Catholics were promised the same rights as they had in the reign of Charles II. In 1695, however, the entirely Protestant Irish Parliament had gone against the letter and spirit of the Treaty and imposed serious disabilities on the Catholics. They were not permitted to carry arms, to marry Protestants or to purchase land. These disabilities made Ireland a country almost entirely dominated by a Protestant minority of landowners, and they created perpetual ill-will between the majority of Irishmen and England. Strong laws were passed also against the Nonconformist minority. Thus the Protestant landlords and the English Church in Ireland were in effective control, consolidated by the fact that no Catholic could hold any important political post.

Even the Irish Protestant parliament did not possess the right to pass laws of which the English Parliament disapproved. The Catholic peasantry paid tithe to the Anglican Church and their rents were paid to landlords who in many cases were absentees from Ireland. Ireland also suffered trade restrictions in order that English interests could be protected—for example, the export of Irish cattle to England was forbidden.

Changes after 1780

The American War of Independence had important results for Ireland. British troops were withdrawn to fight in America. The **Irish Volunteers** were formed under the inspiration of **Henry Grattan** to defend Ireland against a threatened French invasion. The volunteers were a Protestant force and were used by Grattan to bring pressure upon Pitt the Younger to grant the Irish Parliament the right to pass laws independently of the English Parliament. This, of course, was pleasing to the Protestants, but scarcely affected the Catholic position.

In 1785 Pitt succeeded in passing through the Irish Parliament a Bill which would bring Ireland into the whole colonial trading system. This involved giving Ireland either free trade with England or, where customs duties existed, on the same terms as other colonies. These proposals led to panic opposition from English manufacturers and traders led by Josiah Wedgwood, and Pitt was forced to modify them in such a way that the Irish Parliament rejected the whole scheme. This was a most unfortunate failure of a progressive and enlightened measure and, of course, affected not only Protestant but Catholic manufacturers and traders also.

An important development in Ireland was the formation of the **Society of the United Irishmen** containing both Catholics and Protestants. The founders and leaders were **Lord Edward Fitzgerald** and **Wolfe Tone**. The society's policy was deeply affected by the French Revolution of 1789 and itself became revolutionary in its aim of complete Irish independence. It took to military preparations to achieve this aim. Pitt responded to these pressures by moderate reforms—for example, in 1793 Catholics with the approved property qualifications were allowed to vote in elections, but were still unable to become M.P.s. In 1795, **Earl Fitzwilliam**, an avowed sympathizer with Irish grievances, was appointed Lord Lieutenant of Ireland. He made strenuous efforts to achieve Catholic Emancipation—that is, the removal of all Catholic disabilities which had existed since 1695, but he was completely frustrated in these efforts both by the Irish Parliament itself and by opposition in Britain. The Irish had hoped much from him, but his failure increased Irish discontent very sharply. This led the United Irishmen to seek direct French help in achieving their aims, and in 1796 an invasion of Ireland under **General Hoche** was planned. A French force reached **Bantry Bay**, but bad weather and lack of immediate mass support in Ireland prevented a landing. In **1798 a rising in Ulster** under the United Irishmen was suppressed with great ruthlessness. Another attempted rebellion in **Wexford at Vinegar Hill, 1798**, was defeated by **General Lake** on 21st June. In the same year a French force which landed in Ireland was defeated, and this brought the efforts of the Irish at armed rebellion to an end.

The Union, 1800–1801

Pitt arrived at the conclusion that the union of the Irish and English Parliaments with Roman Catholic Emancipation were necessary for the following main reasons: (a) the separation of the parliaments gave too much freedom of action to Ireland; (b) the dangers of foreign intervention as shown by the French efforts were increased without union; (c) with Catholic Emancipation, a united parliament could better guarantee the rights of the Protestant minorities; and (d) bribery and corruption were notoriously great in the Irish Parliament, and Pitt hoped that the Union would greatly reduce this.

The **Act of Union** of **1801** provided that one hundred members would be elected to the Commons for Ireland, and thirty-two peers (of whom four would be bishops) would sit in the House of Lords. Free trade was to be allowed and the established Churches of Ireland and England were to be united. To achieve the passage of this Act through the Irish Parliament much money changed hands, over £1,000,000 being paid to supporters of the measure, and many titles were bestowed.

The Roman Catholics supported the measure because they expected Emancipation, but this was prevented by George III's personal opposition, which led to Pitt's resignation. Thus Pitt's aims were not entirely achieved, with the result that much unnecessary discontent continued in Ireland.

Pitt and the French Revolution

The **French Revolution** of **1789** was one of the most important events of world history. The revolutionaries overthrew the monarchy and the old system. The French monarchy was a despotism without any effective checks. **Louis XIV** had announced '*L'état, c'est moi*'—'I am the State'. But by the reign of **Louis XVI** France was no longer the powerful state she had been one hundred years before. Discontent was widespread, especially among the peasantry, from whom the nobility exacted feudal taxes of various kinds, and among the wealthy middle class or *bourgeoisie*, who had little political influence. At Versailles the king had collected an aristocracy who had left their estates, the *absentee landlords*; while the ardent supporter of all their privileges, the Queen of Louis XVI, **Marie Antoinette**, was widely disliked both as an Austrian and the supporter of privilege in church and state. She was instrumental in defeating the social and political reforms proposed by the King's more enlightened ministers. In 1788 a bad harvest and food shortages made matters worse, and Louis was compelled to summon the **States General** in May, **1789**. This comprised representatives of the church, the nobility and the commons, or middle class, voting separately by estates. When in 1789 the Third Estate, or commons, declared themselves the National Assembly and invited the First and Second Estates to join them, the Revolution had really begun. The Revolution came to be dominated by the **Jacobins**, and this led to the establishment of the **Republic in 1792** and the execution of the King and Queen in 1793.

We are not concerned in these notes with the details of the causes and events of the Revolution, but rather with its effects on Britain. At first its outbreak was well received in Britain. Not only was the French monarchy the ancient enemy of Britain, but the form of government in France was totally unlike the parliamentary system developing in England. The Whigs above all saw in it an imitation of the English Revolution of 1688 against James II, when parliament was strengthened against the monarchy. The fall of the **Bastille, 14th July, 1789**, was widely acclaimed in Britain. The Revolution was seen by the great poets, especially Wordsworth and Coleridge, as the dawn of liberty for mankind. English societies, especially the **London Corresponding Society** and the **Friends of the People**, both of which advocated the reform of the British parliamentary system, greeted the Revolution enthusiastically and sent their congratulations to the revolutionary leaders.

However, public opinion in Britain gradually changed during the years 1789–1793. This was due to several factors: (1) As the Revolution took a more extreme and violent course, the fears expressed by the English politician and writer, **Edmund Burke**, seemed to be justified. In his work, *Reflections on the Revolution in France*, he argued that the French Revolution was totally different from the English Revolution of 1688, and, far from extending the liberties of the people, would lead to another despotism. (The later rise of Napoleon seemed to prove his point.) His chief literary and political opponent was **Thomas Paine** (see also p. 89) who replied to Burke in a work which became almost the gospel of the radicals in years to come—*The Rights of Man*. It had such a wide circulation that Pitt took measures to suppress it, and Paine was indicted for treason. With the help of **William Blake**, the poet, he escaped to France, where he was elected to the revolutionary Convention, was imprisoned for a time by Robespierre, but was liberated on the latter's fall and remained a member of the Convention until 1795. (2) In 1792 the revolutionaries declared war against Austria, who was supporting the activities of the *émigrés* or nobles who had fled from France. Pitt was anxious to keep out of war, as he was afraid of Russian expansion and had formed the **Triple Alliance of Great Britain, Holland and Prussia** in **1788** to counteract Russia's aims. But now in 1792 the French armies overran the Netherlands, which was a breach of the Treaty of Utrecht of 1713 signed by Britain and France, among others. More alarming to Pitt and his supporters was the French declaration that the River Scheldt was open to the rade of all nations, not only the Dutch. This was a breach of the Treaty of Westphalia of 1648, but what really alarmed Pitt was the fact that the French could now use Antwerp as a base for naval and military activity against Britain. (3) In **November 1792**, the French issued the **Edict of Fraternity**, in which they offered help to all peoples struggling to gain their liberty. In effect, this was an attempt to spread the Revolution. (4) The execution of Louis XVI in January 1793, brought strong protests from Pitt and King George III himself. The French ambassador in London was dismissed. The French reply was a declaration of war against Britain on **1st February, 1793**. From now on Britain was to be almost continuously at war with France until 1815, and one of the most difficult and perilous of her national struggles had begun.

Pitt's Domestic Policy from 1793

Pitt feared the spread of revolutionary ideas to Britain. He now dropped all thought of parliamentary reform and opposed an attempt of the Whigs in 1792 to disfranchise a number of 'rotten boroughs' and redistribute their seats—the very changes which Pitt himself had advocated earlier. In Scotland in 1793 two radicals, Muir and Palmer, were transported to Australia as convicts for advocating parliamentary reform. The judge in this case, the notorious **Lord Braxfield**, was so alarmed at the thought of revolution that he put forward the theory that the English system of government was perfect and that anyone trying to change it was a traitor. These tactics, however, told against Pitt and his government, and a special convention of Scottish and English radicals was called to demand an end to the war against France. Twelve of the convention leaders were tried for treason, but the jury acquitted them. Things became difficult for the government when a bad harvest in 1794 caused widespread radical agitation against Pitt and his supporters.

Pitt now decided that individual prosecutions were failing and, indeed, provoking sympathy for his opponents. He therefore decided to alter the law. In **1794**, the **Habeas Corpus Act** was suspended, thus allowing political suspects to be held without trial. The **Aliens Act** of the previous year restricted the rights of foreign visitors and was aimed especially against agents of the French government. In 1795, the **Seditious Meetings Act** was passed, after political demonstrations in London; and, for the next three years, all meetings of more than fifty persons were to be licensed by a magistrate. The **Treasonable Practices Act** of the same year imposed up to seven years' transportation for attacking the British system of government, plotting to help invaders or 'devising evil against the King'. By the **Seditious Publications Act** of **1793** radical newspapers were put under close watch, and in 1795

PITT THE YOUNGER
DOMESTIC POLICIES
1783–1801

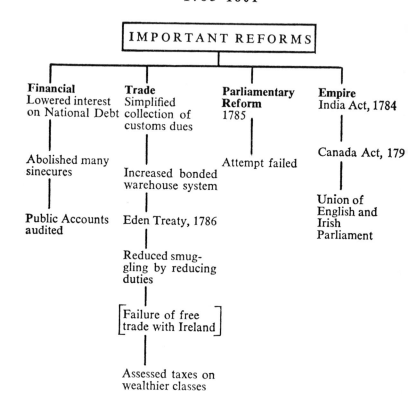

IMPORTANT REFORMS

Financial
Lowered interest
on National Debt

Abolished many
sinecures

Public Accounts
audited

Trade
Simplified
collection of
customs dues

Increased bonded
warehouse system

Eden Treaty, 1786

Reduced smug-
gling by reducing
duties

[Failure of free
trade with Ireland]

Assessed taxes on
wealthier classes

**Parliamentary
Reform**
1785

Attempt failed

Empire
India Act, 1784

Canada Act, 179

Union of
English and
Irish
Parliament

FRENCH REVOLUTION
War with France, 1793

Pitt imposed
restrictive
measures

Habeas Corpus
suspended.
Aliens Act
Seditious Meetings
Act

Pitt dropped all
idea of Parliamentary
Reform

Treasonable Practices Act
Seditious Publications Act
Stamp Duty
Trade Unions illegalised,
1799–1800

a **Stamp Duty** was imposed on publications. In addition to this a **Newspaper Publication Act** was passed which enabled the local magistrates to supervise newspapers, and any offending editor or printer could be tried by two magistrates—a very serious extension of the power of magistrates.

These repressive measures were not widely applied, but they served as a sufficient threat to make the radicals more restrained in their activities. The Whig leader, Charles James Fox, protested in parliament, but parliamentary opposition to the new acts was not strong. Pitt made it clear that they were only temporary. However, the government of Pitt greatly exaggerated the dangers of revolution, and this was particularly seen in 1799–1800 when Pitt introduced the **Combination Laws** which made trade unions illegal.

The War

In **1793** Pitt organized the **First Coalition against France**. It consisted of Britain, Spain, Holland, Austria and Prussia. Pitt used British money to subsidize these continental allies. But by 1797 the French had completely defeated the Coalition. How did this come about? In the first place, the allies underestimated the military power and enthusiasm of the French Republic. Above all, they were unable to change their military tactics to meet the new methods adopted by the French. They also underestimated the power of French patriotism and determination to defeat the foreign invader. (Rather as Hitler in the twentieth century underestimated the power of Russian patriotism in the Second World War.) The French also produced a military organizer of genius in **Carnot**, who rallied the retreating armies of France in 1793, raised new forces by conscription and threw back the Austrians and Prussians. The allies of the Coalition also failed to produce a united leadership, and they were weakened by the selfishness of their aims—for example, Prussia was anxious to take part in the Partition of Poland and was watching Russia, who was not a member of the First Coalition. Prussian troops entered Poland in 1793 during the war against France, and her Austrian ally also resented this. Thus there was much division among the allies of the First Coalition. In any case, Prussian aims were not merely anti-revolutionary, for she also hoped to gain French territory on the Rhine.

Although the French were at first defeated in 1793 and were driven from the Austrian Netherlands (Belgium), Carnot's organizing work brought about recovery. In the following year the French re-occupied the Austrian Netherlands and, in 1795, Holland also—which became the **Batavian Republic**. At this point both Prussia and Spain made peace, and Spain joined France, which now had control of both the Dutch and the Spanish fleets—a great challenge to Britain. In 1796

Carnot planned and achieved the defeat of Austria. This was brought about by the brilliant Italian campaign of **Napoleon Bonaparte**, who forced the Austrians to sign the **Treaty of Campo Formio in 1797**. The French had also formed the **Cisalpine Republic**, comprising most of northern Italy and, of course, under French control. Thus the First Coalition was utterly defeated and Pitt's efforts were in ruins.

Faults of Pitt's War Policy, 1793–1797

He underestimated the strength of the French Republic, and thought that a series of isolated blows would be enough to bring France to her knees. He also joined with Austria in order to keep France at war on the Continent while Britain seized French islands in the West Indies and elsewhere—a very limited view of the war and a poor imitation of his father's strategy in the Seven Years' War. A force sent to the Netherlands in 1793 under the Duke of York was utterly defeated. Pitt had no war minister in his cabinet for six months after the war began, and there was no supreme commander of the allies. Pitt frittered away the power of the small British army of only 20,000 men on futile expeditions—such as the **capture of Toulon** in **1793** (later retrieved for the French by Bonaparte), an attack on Dunkirk and an expedition to the West Indies. A calamitous failure was the landing of 3,000 French royalist *émigrés* at **Quiberon Bay** in **1795** to assist the royalist movement in La Vendée. This force, too weak, badly equipped and organized, was overwhelmed by the Republican forces and massacred.

British Naval Action, 1793–1797

During these years British naval action was more effective. On 1st June, 1794. **Lord Howe** defeated a French fleet convoying grain ships from America (The **'Glorious First of June'**), although the grain supplies reached harbour. However, by 1797 Britain's general position was very bad. *There was a run on the* **Bank of England** *and Pitt suspended cash payments.* Many banks closed their doors throughout the country. To raise funds for the war *Pitt introduced Income Tax* and imposed other taxes as well. England was threatened with invasion, and the French attempted to give help to the Irish independence movement under Wolfe Tone by sending a French force under **General Hoche**. This was hindered by storms and bad management and was scattered and defeated by the British navy. However, another serious development was the outbreak of **mutiny in the British fleets at Spithead and the Nore**. The Spithead mutiny in April 1797 was caused by the appalling conditions of the Service—bad food, poor pay, brutal discipline, embezzlement of funds by the pursers, and inadequate medical care. Complaints were wisely listened to by the Admiralty, promises of reform made, and the mutiny ended. At the Nore the mutiny was under the leadership of a revolutionary, **Richard Parker.** This was suppressed and Parker was executed. Soon afterwards, **Admiral Duncan's** Nore Fleet defeated a Dutch invasion fleet at the **Battle of Camperdown** off the Texel River. This fleet was also now used to blockade the French fleet in Brest and other ports. Just before the mutinies, in February 1797, **Admiral Jervis,** with **Nelson** second in command, utterly defeated a Spanish force of twenty-eight vessels off **Cape St. Vincent.** This prevented their junction with the French fleet, and the remnants which escaped were blockaded in Spanish ports.

Pitt now made overtures for peace to the French Directory, even agreeing to the French possession of the Netherlands. But these offers were rejected. It appeared that the French were determined to control Europe, and that Pitt's idea of a limited war was wrong. Even the Whigs under Fox, who had frequently pressed for an end of the war, were disconcerted by the French attitude. Pitt now prepared for a wider and longer war. His change of attitude was further confirmed by Bonaparte's expedition to Egypt in 1798, with the aim of conquering that country, hampering Britain's trade with India, and with the possibility of the ultimate restoration of French power in India. Here British naval power was again decisive, for Nelson's destruction of the French fleet in **Aboukir Bay (Battle of the Nile)** left Bonaparte stranded in Egypt. When he then marched through Syria to defeat the Turks and open the land route into Europe, the British navy was able to reinforce the coastal town of **Acre** which was defended by Sir Sidney Smith. Bonaparte, who could not take it and dared not leave it in his rear, retreated. He himself left the French forces marooned in Egypt under **General Kléber** and made his way back to France, where he succeeded in having himself created **First Consul, 1799.**

Pitt Forms the Second Coalition, 1799

Instead of mere financial assistance and no clear aims, as with the First Coalition, Pitt now made concrete offers to Britain's allies. Russia was promised control of the Knights of St. John in Malta (an astonishing change in Pitt's attitude to Russia), and Austria was to have Lombardy in Italy in return for giving up Belgium. *Pitt succeeded in forming a* **coalition of Britain, Russia, Austria, Naples and Turkey.**

During Bonaparte's absence in Egypt, the Second Coalition achieved considerable successes. The Russians under **Suvorof** drove the French from northern Italy and from Switzerland. Unfortunately, disputes arose between Russia and Austria, especially when the latter withdrew her forces in order to gain control of Suabia. Russia then withdrew from the Coalition. As a result, the French regained control of Switzerland

(Helvetic Republic). But there were still 70,000 Austrian troops in northern Italy, and Bonaparte (now First Consul) decided to take command of the campaign against them. In May 1800, he took his army over the Great St. Bernard Pass into northern Italy and defeated the Austrians at **Marengo.** In Germany also, **General Moreau** defeated the Austrians at **Hohenlinden, December 1800.** The Austrians now recognized defeat and signed the **Treaty of Lunéville, February 1801,** by which France regained all the territory allotted to her by the Treaty of Campo Formio.

Another serious difficulty for Britain was the formation in 1800 of the **League of Armed Neutrality** by the new **Czar of Russia, Paul I,** who admired Napoleon. This aimed to resist the right claimed by Britain to search neutral vessels for contraband of war, and consisted of Russia, Prussia, Denmark and Sweden. Denmark also seized the port of Hamburg to prevent British trade with northern Germany. Britain's reply was to send a fleet under **Sir Hyde Parker,** with Nelson second in command, to **Copenhagen, April 1801.** The Danish Fleet, which might have made a dangerous addition to French naval forces, was destroyed. This ruthless action helped to bring the League to an end, and when when Paul I was murdered and succeeded by **Alexander I,** the latter chose neutrality.

Besides defeating the League of Armed Neutrality, Britain had two other compensations for the defeat of the Second Coalition. **General Abercromby** defeated Napoleon's forces left in Egypt, and in India **Arthur Wellesley** (later, **Duke of Wellington**) gained control of the Carnatic from its pro-French ruler and also defeated the Nizam of Hyderabad and the French troops which had been sent there. By his defeat of the Mahrattas, in 1803, Wellesley had consolidated British power in India and French designs had been defeated.

Peace of Amiens and Addington, Prime Minister

Pitt, who had expected a quick Coalition victory in 1800, resigned in 1801 and was succeeded by **Henry Addington** (later **Lord Sidmouth**), who opened negotiations with France and concluded the **Peace of Amiens, March 1802.** There were several reasons for peace. English trade with the Continent had seriously declined, there were riots in the country owing to scarce bread and high prices, and a financial crash seemed imminent because of the drain of gold away from Britain to pay the large subsidies to our allies of the Second Coalition. More-over, a situation of real stale-mate had arisen. Bonaparte controlled Europe and Britain controlled the seas. The peace also suited Bona-parte, as it gave him a breathing space to consolidate his power in France and in Europe. By the treaty, Britain agreed to restore all conquests to France, Spain and Holland, with the exception of Trinidad and Ceylon. Malta was to be restored to the Knights of St. John and no French or British Knights were to be admitted to the Order. British troops were to leave Malta within three months and the island's independence was to be guaranteed. In return France agreed to find compensation for the deposed royal family of Holland and to evacuate central and southern Italy and Naples. Pitt gave his support to this peace, on condition that French expansionist ambitions ceased. But difficulties soon arose. In Northern Italy, Piedmont was annexed by France; and Napoleon intervened in Switzerland with armed force. Britain also failed to evacuate **Malta**; mainly because French spying continued in Egypt, and the King of Spain, an ally of Napoleon, seized the property of the Knights of St. John in that country. Addington was planning to reduce the expenditure on the British navy, but at the same time Napoleon began to plan an increase of the French navy by half. He also, despite promises of freer trade, prohibited English exports to Holland and Italy. These developments led to the resumption of war—the strict beginning of the Napoleonic War, as such, by Britain's declaration of war in May **1803**. Addington resigned in the following year (May 1804), and Pitt formed a new government.

Invasion Preparations and Trafalgar

Pitt now succeeded in forming the **Third Coalition** of Britain, Russia, Austria and Sweden. Napoleon became Emperor in May 1804. He now prepared invasion forces in huge camps at Boulogne, Flushing, Nieuport, Ostend, Dunkirk, Gravelines and Calais. He hoped at first to send these forces over the Channel in a surprise attack, but the preparations were badly managed and he lost the initiative. He then decided that the force should be convoyed across under the protection of the combined French and Spanish fleets, and any others he could use. At the same time he seized control of Hanover and declared the whole coastline from the Baltic to the Mediterranean closed to British trade. The French Admiral, **Villeneuve**, succeeded in breaking the British blockade of Toulon and drawing Nelson across the Atlantic, with the purpose of slipping back, joining the Spanish fleet and gaining command of the Channel long enough to enable the invasion to succeed. But Nelson warned the British government in time and Villeneuve put in at Cadiz. Napoleon ordered him to put out, and on **21st October, 1805**, the combined French and Spanish fleets were smashed by Nelson and Collingwood at **Trafalgar**, Nelson himself falling a victim. It should be noted that Trafalgar did not save Britain from immediate invasion, as Napoleon had abandoned his plan almost a month before, but it did prevent any future French revival of such a scheme.

On the Continent Napoleon went from strength to strength. The crushing defeat of the Austrians and Russians at **Austerlitz, 2nd December, 1805,** led to the **Peace of Pressburg** with Austria, by which Austria lost all influence in the German states of Baden, Bavaria and Wurtemburg, and French control was established. Austria also gave up the Tyrol and her provinces in Italy and Dalmatia. The news of Austerlitz was the final blow to William Pitt, who had been ill through overwork and exhaustion for some time. He died in January 1806 at the age of forty-six. He was succeeded by **Grenville,** who formed the **'Ministry of All the Talents',** and through the Foreign Secretary, **Fox,** attempted negotiations with Napoleon, who rejected British efforts. Fox himself died in September 1806. The **Duke of Portland** became Prime Minister in 1807.

Napoleon's victories over Prussia (who had suddenly entered the war) **at Jena, October 1806,** and over the Russians at **Friedland, June 1807,** ended the war of the Third Coalition.

The Treaty of Tilsit, July 1807

In July 1807 Napoleon and **Alexander I** of Russia met on a raft on the River Niemen at **Tilsit.** Alexander agreed to close Russian ports to British trade. There were also secret clauses of this agreement which involved the forcing of Denmark, Sweden and Portugal into this system of trade embargo. The British government got to know of these clauses, and realized the danger that the Danish fleet would be used for enforcing the embargo. Britain requested the Danes to hand over their fleet, promising its restoration at the end of hostilities. This was refused, and British forces were landed on Zeeland and besieged Copenhagen from the landward side, while naval forces bombarded it from the sea. After the destruction of a considerable part of the city, *the Danes handed over their fleet, which was sailed by British sailors to England.*

At Tilsit Napoleon and Alexander agreed on their respective 'spheres of influence'. Napoleon made it clear that he would not oppose Alexander's seizure of Finland from Swedish control, and he promised Alexander a share of the Turkish empire at the end of the war. But more important for Britain, Alexander agreed to enter Napoleon's Continental System if Britain refused to make peace.

The Continental System

This was Napoleon's effort to ruin Britain by stopping her trade with Europe. It was not invented by Napoleon, however. Such efforts had been a part of French policy since 1793. In 1798 the Directory had ordered the seizure of neutral vessels trading with Britain. The *new* situation was France's complete control of Europe in 1807, and the greater opportunity of ruining British trade which this presented.

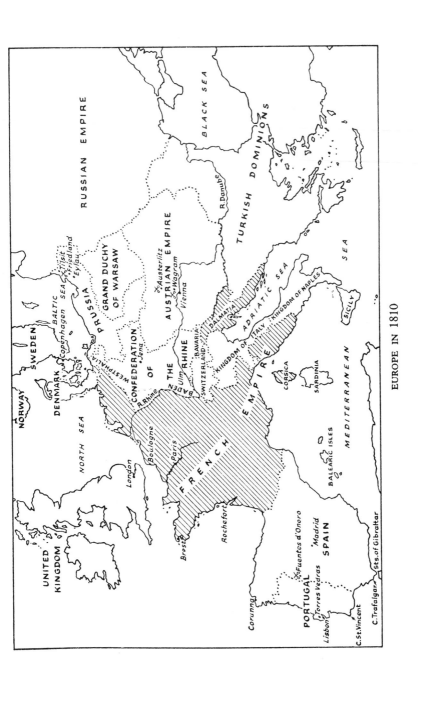

EUROPE IN 1810

Earlier French efforts had been unsuccessful and in fact British exports doubled between 1790 and 1800.

(1) **The Berlin Decree, 21st November, 1806.** By this decree Napoleon declared Britain in a state of blockade, and no vessels coming direct from Britain or her colonies could enter ports under French control. This was dangerous to Britain, especially as Napoleon now controlled the ports of northern Europe.

(2) **Britain replied by Orders in Council, 1807.** Neutral vessels trading with enemy ports were to come to Britain first, pay customs and purchase licences to proceed. From this arrangement Britain could derive considerable profit and neutrals might prefer it to the danger of having their ships seized by the British.

(3) **The Milan Decrees, 17th December, 1807.** These ordered the seizure of any vessels trading with British ports. Thus all vessels obeying the British Orders in Council were in danger of seizure by the French. The U.S.A. suffered greatly, and in 1807, in an effort to make both Britain and France change their minds, put an embargo on all trade with both.

Effects of the Continental System

The effects of Napoleon's system on Britain were severe at first. In 1808 British exports fell by one-eighth compared with 1807, and some trades were very hard hit. The import of raw cotton into Liverpool fell by five-sixths and grain imports to only one-twentieth of those of 1807. This led to high prices of grain and bread, and to unemployment, riots and disturbances in a number of English towns,—the very situation which Napoleon wished to produce. However, British exporters attempted various means of counteracting this by expanding their trade with South America, with Turkey and with the Middle East. But the curious situation arose that France began to suffer from her own system and began to relax it before its full effects were felt in Britain. Napoleon was particularly embarrassed by the fact that the customs duties received by the French from states under their control fell disastrously—in 1809 this income to the French exchequer fell by five-sixths of the income of the previous year. The French also needed various imports from the colonies of other powers (including Britain) and in 1809 the Batavian Republic (Holland) allowed the import of American supplies under French control. Eventually Napoleon was compelled to introduce a system of licences to trade, and this applied to a number of British products. The strains imposed on Europe were very great, and unemployment was widespread—in 1810 the great port of Hamburg was almost at a standstill and grass was growing in the harbour streets. *In 1811 many firms all over Europe were bankrupt.* This led to increased national resistance to Napoleon and was a cause of his downfall. The system began to break down, and British trade with Europe gradually increased and certain trading cities, such as Leipzig in Saxony, became centres from which British goods penetrated Europe. And then in 1811 Russia, whose merchants suffered severely by the severance of trade with Britain, broke away from the system. British trade revival was seen in 1812 when exports were twenty-eight per cent higher than in the previous year. Finally. *Napoleon's defeat in the* **Moscow campaign** *of* **1812** *made it impossible for him to extend his system in Europe.*

It would be wrong to think that Britain easily overcame Napoleon's efforts to strangle her economically, for even as late as 1811 conditions were very bad in a number of centres. In the summer of that year Manchester, for example, was working only a three-day week. But the system produced more problems for Napoleon than he himself was able to cope with.

The War from 1808 to 1815

(1) *The Peninsular War.* In October 1807 Napoleon's forces moved through Spain, invaded Portugal and captured Lisbon. This move was especially directed against the trade between Portugal and Britain which was causing a breach in the Continental System. In January 1808 the King of Spain was replaced by Napoleon's brother Joseph. At this time Portugal appealed to Britain for help, and Wellesley, recently returned from India, was sent out with a British force which defeated the French at **Vimeiro**. But the **Convention of Cintra** was negotiated by a General senior to Wellesley, and the French were allowed to withdraw from Portugal. In 1808 the British commander, **Sir John Moore**, landed in Spain with a force intended to assist the native guerrilla movement against the French, but he was forced to retreat to **Corunna**, where he successfully evacuated his forces but was himself killed. The effect of his diversion had been to weaken the French movement against both the Spanish and Portuguese, and it gave time for Wellesley, who took command of British and Portuguese forces in 1809, to strengthen the defences of Lisbon. The defensive emplacements around Lisbon known as the **Lines of Torres Vedras** were supported by a 'scorched earth' area up to thirty miles from Lisbon, in which the French could not adopt their usual methods of living off the country. The Portland government had greatly increased the training and efficiency of the British army, and the forces under Wellesley were far superior to those previously used. They proved, by all accounts, as good as, if not better than, the forces Napoleon could bring against them. From the Lisbon base Wellesley (easily supplied from the sea by the navy) drove the French back towards Madrid, and the **Battle of Talavera, July 1809**, was an important victory. The

French were now beginning to lose battles, and an ominous change was coming over the war. The very geography of Spain itself was against them, for they had to move their supplies *across* the main valleys and rivers—a slow and difficult operation which gave the Spanish guerrilla forces ample opportunity for harassing action. The most significant change occurred in 1810 when **Masséna**, one of the most brilliant of Napoleon's generals, succeeded in advancing to Lisbon, but completely failed to penetrate the Lines of Torres Vedras. He commenced a siege of Lisbon, but the French suffered terribly from the lack of food supplies and about 30,000 died of fever. Masséna was now forced to retreat, and this was the decisive turning-point of the Peninsular War. Wellesley's success had been achieved by the endurance of his forces and his skilful alternation of attack and retreat in order to draw the French deeper into the country. He now followed up his success at Lisbon by defeating the French at **Almeida, 1811**, and capturing the key fortresses of **Ciudad Rodrigo** and **Badajoz** in **1812**.

The Moscow Campaign, 1812

In **1809** the Austrians again attempted resistance to Napoleon, but were defeated at **Wagram**. From 1809 to 1812 Napoleon dominated Europe. In 1812 the Czar Alexander broke away from the Continental System, which had ruined Russia's important trade with Britain. Rather than see his whole system collapse, Napoleon determined to invade and defeat Russia. The Grand Army of 600,000 men consisted not only of French but also of the troops of other countries under Napoleon's control, including 20,000 Prussians and 30,000 Austrians. Forces were also withdrawn from the war in Spain at a time when Wellington was becoming increasingly effective there. In June 1812, Napoleon launched his invasion of Russia. The Russians employed a scorched earth policy and systematically retreated, with occasional important battles which began to wear down the invading forces. When Napoleon reached Moscow in mid-September, Alexander made no effort to negotiate peace, the Russian winter had set in, and fires broke out in the deserted city. In mid-October the French retreat began, harassed by Russian forces under **General Kutusov** and by guerrilla bands. The retreat was a disaster, despite the heroic rearguard actions fought by **Marshal Ney**. Napoleon himself left his army to struggle over the frontier, and not more than 60,000 men found their way back again into western Europe.

Results of the Moscow Campaign

(1) Napoleon's Continental System was fast breaking up.

(2) The withdrawal of troops from Spain strengthened Wellesley's position there, and in **1812** he won the **Battle of Salamanca** and in

1813 that of **Vittoria** (after which he was made Duke of Wellington). In April 1814 he reached **Toulouse** in southern France, where he again defeated the French.

(3) Napoleon's enemies were now encouraged to form the **Fourth Coalition** of Britain, Prussia, Austria and Russia.

Napoleon now raised new armies and conducted a brilliant campaign, but he was faced by well-trained troops in superior numbers, while many of his own young recruits had to be trained even as they marched towards battle. *The new feeling of nationalism in the states of Europe was strong*, and this phase of the war is known as the **War of Liberation**. At the battle of **Leipzig** in **October 1813** Napoleon was forced to retreat over the Rhine. In **March 1814** by the **Treaty of Chaumont**, the allies pledged themselves to remain united and not, as in the past, to sign any separate peace with Napoleon. On 6th April, 1814, Napoleon abdicated and was sent a prisoner to the island of **Elba**, between Italy and Corsica. A conference of the allies was called at Vienna to make a new European settlement.

The Battle of Waterloo, 18th June, 1815

The conference at Vienna disclosed many differences and quarrels among the allies, and Napoleon was encouraged to think that he might yet be successful, and he succeeded in escaping from Elba and reached France on **1st March, 1815**. At once his supporters flocked to his side and the restored monarchy, in the person of **Louis XVIII**, was forced to flee. However, the allies now re-affirmed the Treaty of Chaumont and Wellington became the supreme commander of a force of 100,000 in the Netherlands. Napoleon's force consisted of about 120,000 men, but the Prussians under **Blücher** amounted to another 100,000 in addition to Wellington's. On 18th June, the decisive battle was fought at **Waterloo**. Wellington's force withstood the repeated attacks of the French until Wellington ordered a general advance, on the arrival of Blücher and the Prussians. Even Napoleon's famous Imperial Guard was unable to stem the tide.

The **'Hundred Days'** between Napoleon's escape and the battle of Waterloo ended with his exile to St. Helena in the southern Atlantic, where he died in 1821. The new terms imposed on the French by the **Second Treaty of Paris (1815)** were harsher than before. France's boundaries were to be the more restricted ones of 1790 and not those of 1792 as in the **First Treaty of Paris of 1814**. She was also forced to pay the allies a war indemnity of £28 million and an army of occupation was stationed on her soil for five years.

Reasons for Napoleon's Defeat

The following points should be considered:

(1) The financial and industrial power of Britain which enabled her to remain in the war and finance her allies at appropriate times.

(2) The failure of Napoleon to make the Continental System effective against Britain.

(3) The strength of the British navy throughout the wars, and especially after Trafalgar.

(4) The campaign in Spain and the special difficulties it produced for the French. Napoleon said he could hold Spain with 30,000 men, but nearly ten times that number were engaged there.

(5) The burdens of taxation on the conquered states, and especially the economic sufferings which the Continental System produced, gave rise to a wide national resistance to Napoleon. The national resistance in Spain was the earliest and it became stronger as the years passed.

(6) His Russian campaign proved a costly mistake and showed a decline in his powers of judgment.

Summary

Pitt's earlier years of office were characterized by important financial and economic changes and by attempts to reform partially the electoral system and improve the position of Ireland. These reforms were retarded by Britain's involvement in the war against France after 1793. In his second phase Pitt was less successful and, despite the naval supremacy of Britain, his policies were unable to prevent the victorious march of the Revolution and later of Napoleon. The latter's success continued without pause until the beginning of the Peninsular War in 1808. Napoleon's Continental System did damage to Britain, but his allies increasingly chafed under its severities. Alexander I's break from the system led on to Napoleon's disastrous Moscow campaign, the increase of national resistance to him as seen in the War of Liberation, and his ultimate defeat. By her industrial, agricultural, financial and naval power, and by her military successes in Spain, Britain played a great part in the defeat of Napoleon.

Important Dates

1783	Pitt the Younger became Prime Minister.
1784	Electoral defeat of the Whigs under Fox.
	Pitt's India Act.
1786	Commercial Treaty with France.
1789	Outbreak of the French Revolution.
	Favourable view of Revolution taken in Britain.
1792	French declaration of war against Austria.
	French overrun Netherlands and open the Scheldt to general commerce.

	November: Edict of Fraternity.
1793	January: Execution of Louis XVI.
	February 1st. French declared war against Britain.
	Pitt forms the First Coalition.
1794–1800	Pitt's various acts restricting personal liberty.
1793–1797	Defeat of the First Coalition and Treaty of Campo Formio.
	Failure of British isolated expeditions against France.
	Compensating naval successes for Britain.
	Mutinies at Spithead and the Nore, 1797.
1798	Battle of the Nile.
1799	Pitt formed Second Coalition.
1800	French victories of Marengo and Hohenlinden.
1801	Treaty of Lunéville.
	Nelson at Copenhagen.
	Pitt resigned. Addington Prime Minister.
1802	March: Peace of Amiens.
1803	May: War resumed.
1804	Pitt again Prime Minister. Forms Third Coalition.
1805	21st October. Battle of Trafalgar and death of Nelson.
	December. Napoleon defeated Austrians and Russians at Austerlitz.
1806	January: Death of Pitt.
1807	Treaty of Tilsit between Alexander I and Napoleon.
	Continental System now in force.
1808	Opening of the Peninsular War.
1809	July: (Wellesley's) victory at Talavera.
	Napoleon defeated Austrians at Wagram.
1810	Masséna's retreat from Lines of Torres Vedras.
1811	French defeated at Almeida.
1812	The Moscow Campaign.
	Fourth Coalition formed.
1813	Napoleon defeated in Europe.
1814	March: Treaty of Chaumont.
	April: Napoleon exiled to Elba.
1815	18th June. Battle of Waterloo.

QUESTIONS

(1) Give an account of the reforms carried out or attempted by William Pitt the Younger from 1784 to 1789.

(2) Describe Pitt's policy towards Ireland from 1784 to 1800.

(3) What circumstances changed the attitude of Pitt towards the French Revolution?

(4) *What restrictions were placed on liberty in Britain in the years 1793 to 1800?*

(5) *Why was the year 1797 an extremely critical one for Great Britain?*

(6) *How can Pitt's war policy in the years 1793 to 1797 be criticized?*

(7) *For what reasons was the Peace of Amiens concluded in 1802 and why was war resumed in 1803?*

(8) *What part did Britain play in the downfall of Napoleon?*

(9) *What reasons could you give for the great length of the war against France from 1793, with only two brief interludes before 1815?*

CHAPTER ELEVEN

BRITAIN AFTER WATERLOO
1815-1821

Britain in 1815

IN 1815 Britain was still mainly an agricultural country. Most towns were small and surrounded by unspoilt countryside. The population numbered about thirteen million, and, although many lived a hard and difficult life, conditions were far better than a century before. Medical developments and better food supplies had lowered the death rate, and this mainly accounts for the doubling of the population in about fifty years.

After 1815, however, change became more rapid, and *by 1830 half the population lived in towns.* New industrial towns grew rapidly. Sheffield and Birmingham doubled their population in these fifteen years. These towns produced slums and crowded and unhealthy living conditions. Many houses put up for the factory workers were little more than hovels, often being built without damp courses and with walls of single-brick thickness. They were mostly back-to-back houses, poorly lit and badly ventilated.

Changes in the Countryside

As we have seen, the great change in the countryside came about through enclosure of the open fields. The small farmers were disappearing fast, although the high prices of grain during the Napoleonic wars gave them a temporary prosperity. But when the war ended and foreign grain was able to come in, prices fell and many small farmers were ruined, especially if they had borrowed money from the banks in times of prosperity and were now unable to pay. In 1813 many hundreds were in the debtors' gaols. The small farmer often moved to the towns or became an agricultural worker. This change was lamented by **William Cobbett** in his famous work *Rural Rides*. He regarded the yeoman farmer as the backbone of England, but now saw him being pushed out by wealthier men, who might be farmers themselves or who might be men who had made their money in trade and commerce, bought up land, and now attempted to live the life of the hunting, shooting and fishing squire. These new men were aiming first and foremost at profit from the land and had not the same interest in their tenants as the older generation of squires. Class division was becoming sharper in the countryside between the wage-labourer and the new class of capitalist farmer and landlord. Of course, the old gentry, descended from men who had held land for many generations, disliked intensely the new 'upstarts'.

Poverty in the Countryside

Although grain prices fell sharply at the end of the war, the labourers did not benefit to any great extent. Their wages remained appallingly low. In Sussex wages only rose from nine shillings to thirteen shillings in the twenty years from 1790 to 1810, and prices had far outstripped wages. Moreover, the spinning and carding of wool by the small farmer's, or labourer's, wife and children, which added to their income, was fast giving way to the factory system. Thus the possibility of supplementing their income was disappearing. In these circumstances, the magistrates of Speenhamland in Berkshire in 1795 introduced what became known as the **Speenhamland system of poor relief**. To prevent the threat of starvation they added to the labourer's wages poor relief money based on a scale which took into account the price of bread and the number of persons in the family. Assistance was also given to the unemployed in their homes. Many other parishes in England followed suit, and by 1815 the whole of southern England had adopted the system. While it kept the poor from outright starvation, the system also had bad effects. The farmers, knowing that their labourers would receive relief, paid low wages, while the system also encouraged large families which became an increasing burden on the middle- and upper-class ratepayers. It also encouraged a loss of self-respect and independence by many labourers who came to rely on charity.

The Factory System and its Effects

By 1815 the factory system had made much progress in the North and Midlands, especially in the cotton industry. During the Napoleonic wars the hand-loom cotton weavers had seen their wages halved as the factory system pushed out the hand-loom weavers. This caused much social discontent in the North, especially when, at the end of the war, there was a very sharp decline in wages to an average of only 8/- a week in 1818, whereas in 1805 their wage had been 23/-. The workers were forced by necessity into the factories, which they resented, for it entailed the loss of a certain independence which they had enjoyed before. Whole families were involved, and young children worked as much as fourteen hours a day.

In 1815, the end of the war threw more than 200,000 soldiers and sailors on to the labour market at the same time that government contracts for armaments and clothing came to an end. Prices also fell sharply and manufacturers were forced to shut down their mills and reduce production. Thus *unemployment was widespread*. Natural forces added to distress, for in 1816 the Baltic Sea was frozen over and our trade with northern Europe was brought to a standstill. In 1817 William Cobbett declared that in the town of Coventry eight thousand of the twenty thousand inhabitants were 'miserable paupers'.

Regency Society

London was the centre of social fashion led by the **Prince Regent** (to become George IV in 1820 on the death of his father George III, who had become insane). The social life was a great contrast to the lives of the poorer people in the countryside and the industrial towns. The Regent was a patron of the arts, but he led a disreputable and immoral life. His language was so bad that even Wellington declared that he was ashamed to enter a room in his company. The Prince Regent was also the patron of horse-racing, of prize-fighting and of gambling. He was, however, the subject of much lampooning by the very outspoken cartoonists of the day.

In architecture, painting and literature the Regency period saw some outstanding achievements—such as the fine houses of Regent's Park, London, designed by **John Nash**, the magnificent portrait-painting of Sir Thomas Lawrence, the poetry of Byron, Keats and Shelley, and the novels of Sir Walter Scott. The 'dandies' and 'dandizettes' of the fashionable London salons prided themselves on their appreciation and patronage of the arts. The Prince Regent's best-known contribution to the architectural scene was the Brighton Pavilion.

The lives of the Prince Regent and his circle tended to emphasise the growing gulf between rich and poor. This was dangerous for the monarchy itself, which had sunk to a low level in public opinion. The Regent's father, George III, was regarded by many as the reason for Britain's loss of the American colonies and as a prime cause of our having entered the gruelling war against the French Revolution and Napoleon. As social discontent increased, the monarchy became more unpopular and it took the reign of **Queen Victoria** to restore it to popular favour.

British Freedom in 1815

Despite the points made above, many foreign visitors looked at Britain with envious eyes as the home of progress and freedom compared with many states on the Continent. They especially praised the *freedom of newspapers*, and the *freedom of cartoonists to attack even the monarchy itself*. They praised the absence of a censor's office to which newspaper articles had to be submitted before publication, although heavy stamp duties were imposed to prevent the growth of radical or revolutionary papers by making their price prohibitive. Magistrates and juries proved very reluctant to impose penalties on editors and printers who broke the laws of libel.

Government Action, 1815–1821

The Prime Minister from 1812 to 1827 was **Lord Liverpool,** and the most important members of his cabinet were **Lord Sidmouth** (Home Secretary) and **Lord Castlereagh** (Foreign Secretary). They were intensely opposed to anything which remotely resembled the Jacobinism of the French Revolution of 1789, and were prepared to suppress popular discontent wherever it arose. At this time there was much machine-breaking both in the towns of the Midlands and the North and in the agricultural counties of the South. The machine-breakers, known as **Luddites** after a certain Ned Ludd, who is supposed to have been one of their leaders, regarded the new machines as the cause of unemployment. Lord Liverpool's answer to this was to make machine-breaking liable to the death penalty, and in 1815 and 1816 a number of Luddites were hanged.

Liverpool and his government adopted a *laissez-faire* attitude—natural laws must take their course, and government could do little. Lord Sidmouth declared in 1817: '*The alleviation of the difficulties is not to be looked for from the intervention of Government and Parliament.*' However, when it came to the interests of the farmer and landlord, so heavily represented in the House of Commons, their attitude was different; and in **1815** the **Corn Laws** were passed. With the resumption of grain imports at the end of the war the price of wheat had fallen to 65/7 in 1815, whereas in 1812 it had been 126/6 a quarter. The aim of the Corn Laws was to prohibit the import of wheat until British wheat rose above 80/-. The price of 96/11 was reached in 1817, but in the years 1821–1825, despite the Corn Laws, the price fell to a little over 44/-. The general effect of the Corn Laws was to give a price which kept the farmer in business, but in fact the level of 80/- was not reached, and 73/- was the highest for many years. But this price meant dear bread to the labourer, and caused much discontent.

Liverpool's Financial Policies

Under pressure from the wealthier classes, *Liverpool removed Income Tax in 1815*, even though it was bringing into the Treasury nearly a quarter of the government's whole revenue. To meet the loss of nearly £15,000,000 taxes were imposed on many articles of ordinary household consumption (even including candles), and thus the expenses arising from the war were in part transferred to the poorer classes—a fact strongly denounced at this time by William Cobbett.

Agitation of the Radicals

There was no strictly radical party, but rather a number of influential individuals who had considerable effect on the political scene. They all detested the evils of poverty which the war had produced for some, and they denounced most of the policies pursued by Lord Liverpool. They particularly demanded changes in the way parliament was elected and the extension of the vote to a much wider public. In parliament, **Joseph Hume** and **Sir Francis Burdett** were important members of the radical wing of the Whig party. Outside, some of the most prominent agitators at this time were **'Orator' Henry Hunt, Francis Place** and **William Cobbett**. A most important figure was **Robert Owen**, factory-owner and early socialist. It is important to consider the lives of the more prominent of these men.

William Cobbett (1763–1835)

He exercised very great influence over the workers of both town and countryside. He had had a varied and colourful life—as a ploughboy, then as a teacher of English (he later wrote a very entertaining grammar), and a pamphleteer against the American colonies, against the French Revolution and against Jacobinism. His political journal, the *Political Register* was at first established to combat revolutionary ideas, but gradually Cobbett's views changed, particularly when he became convinced that the Tories could not improve the condition of the people as he had hoped. During the Napoleonic Wars, he was fined £2,000 and sent to prison for criticizing the Duke of York's sale of army commissions to royal favourites and for denouncing the brutal floggings in the army. He now entered the radical camp, and printed a twopenny version of the *Political Register* within the means of the working class. This 'twopenny trash', as his opponents called it, kept up a running fight for reform of the parliamentary system, for abolition of the Corn Laws, and for the ending of the Poor Law and of the Speenhamland system. In 1821 the *Political Register* began to publish his *Rural Rides*, in which, as a result of an extensive tour of England, he described the sufferings of the labourers and deplored the decline of the yeoman farmer whom he regarded as the backbone of England. Throughout the years 1815-1821 he was leader of the opposition to Lord Liverpool's repressive policies.

The Spa Fields Riots

Increasing demonstrations occurred in the years 1815–1821. One of the earliest of these was in **1816** at **Spa Fields, London**, when there was great distress and unemployment. One of the leaders was **Arthur Thistlewood**, a republican; 'Orator' Hunt also addressed the demonstrators in favour of parliamentary reform. After this meeting a huge mob marched through the London streets (some wearing the red revolutionary 'caps of liberty' of 1789), and seized guns from the gunsmiths' shops. Their avowed aim, in which they did not succeed, was to capture the Tower of London.

Liverpool replied to these demonstrations by *suspending the Habeas Corpus Act* which guaranteed the subject the right of trial without lengthy imprisonment. In 1817, Lord Sidmouth, the Home Secretary, declared that all public meetings were to be licensed by magistrates, as also were coffee houses, reading rooms and public houses. He also increased the number of government spies operating throughout the country. However, these measures were not as effective as Sidmouth hoped. A London jury acquitted the organizers of the Spa Fields riots on charges of treason; but many radical leaders were fined.

The Blanketeers

Many weavers of the northern towns decided to make their own protest to Lord Liverpool, and in 1817 a march was organized from Manchester to London by the northern radicals. The weavers were to march in groups of ten, with blankets on their backs and a petition to the Prince Regent fixed to their arms. The main request was for something to be done to improve the bad state of the cotton industry. Of the six hundred men who set out only one reached London and presented his petition—the others were dispersed by the soldiery sent against them. Lord Sidmouth was convinced that they had intended to raise an army of supporters as they marched south. Soon after this occurred the insurrection of the unemployed frame-knitters of Derbyshire under **Jeremiah Brandreth**, who aimed to overthrow the government. The insurrectionists marched on Nottingham, but were met by a band of soldiers and captured. Brandreth and two others were hanged at Derby.

The Peterloo Massacre, 1819

In 1818 general economic conditions improved and there was less unemployment, but in 1819 a further depression set in. This was the signal for another outbreak of agitation. In August 1819 the

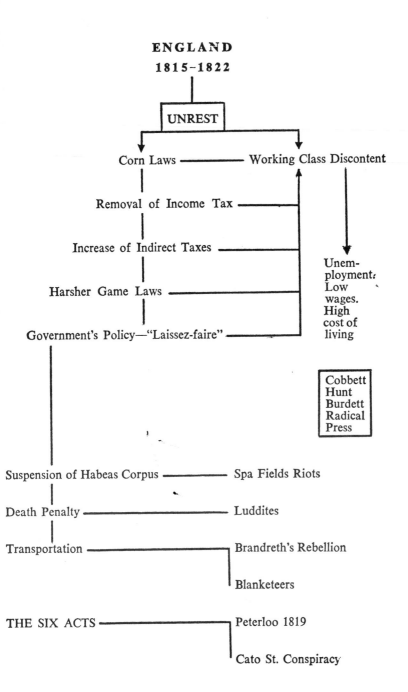

ENGLAND
1815-1822

UNREST

Corn Laws ———————— Working Class Discontent

Removal of Income Tax ————

Increase of Indirect Taxes ————

Harsher Game Laws ————

Government's Policy—"Laissez-faire" ————

Unem-
ployment.
Low
wages.
High
cost of
living

Cobbett
Hunt
Burdett
Radical
Press

Suspension of Habeas Corpus ———————— Spa Fields Riots

Death Penalty ———————— Luddites

Transportation ———————— Brandreth's Rebellion

Blanketeers

THE SIX ACTS ———————— Peterloo 1819

Cato St. Conspiracy

Manchester radicals decided to hold a monster meeting in **St. Peter's Fields**, at which the principal speaker was to be **'Orator' Hunt**. The magistrates, alarmed by local rumours, held the Yeomanry in readiness, although the huge crowd of men, women and children proved entirely peaceable. Half-way through the meeting the magistrates decided to arrest Hunt, but the Yeomanry had difficulty in reaching the platform and were surrounded by an angry crowd. The soldiers drew their sabres and some hussars were sent in to help them. They now struck out in all directions and a panic flight of the crowd ensued. *On the field were left 400 wounded and 11 dead.*

The Six Acts

There were immediate nation-wide protests, but Lord Liverpool congratulated the magistrates. Henry Hunt was greeted in London by a crowd of 25,000. Cobbett described the state of England at this time as 'Gaols ten times as big as formerly; houses of correction; treadmills; the hulks; and the country filled with spies of one kind and another.' The effect of Peterloo, far from deterring the radicals, was to increase their agitation, and against this Lord Sidmouth now imposed the **Six Acts** in **1819**, introduced in Parliament by **Lord Castlereagh**. These regulations were far more severe than those of 1817. Meetings for the purposes of presenting petitions were restricted to the residents of the parish in which the meeting was to be held. Magistrates were able summarily to convict offenders without resort to the Assizes. They were given powers to search houses, to suppress all armed drilling and to prohibit any meeting. The newspaper tax was extended to all publications—aimed especially at Cobbett's *Political Register*; but Cobbett continued to publish it without the official stamp, as did many other radical newspaper editors. This led to fines and imprisonments, but the radical press flourished.

The 'Queen's Affair'

In 1820 Arthur Thistlewood and a group of supporters planned the murder of Liverpool and his cabinet as the prelude to the revolutionary seizure of London. A government spy named Edwards assisted in their preparations, and police raided their headquarters at a barn in the Edgware Road. There was a skirmish in which one police officer was killed. Thistlewood and his principal assistants were hanged. This affair tended to swing a good deal of sympathy towards Liverpool's government and seemed to justify the stringency of the Six Acts. On the other hand, the government again lost sympathy over the **'Queen's Affair'**. The Prince Regent had married Mrs. Fitzherbert secretly, then he committed bigamy by marrying the Princess Caroline of **Brunswick**.

The Prince had tried to divorce her by making charges against her moral conduct, but this led to an official inquiry into the conduct of both himself and Queen Caroline—which did neither of them any good. In 1820, on the death of his father, the new king determined to prevent Caroline becoming Queen, and Lord Liverpool was persuaded to introduce a **Bill of Pains and Penalties** against her in the House of Lords, but the majority was so narrow that he dared not put it before the Commons. At the Coronation, supported by a large and sympathetic crowd, Caroline attempted to gain entry to the Abbey, but failed. She died a month later. This affair did harm to the Royal Family and to Liverpool's reputation, and the radicals exploited it in their own favour. Cobbett had become an adviser of Queen Caroline.

Thus the government relied upon *laissez-faire* economics in this period and did very little of a constructive kind to pull the country out of its difficulties. Of course, parliament was mostly composed of the landed interests, who had insufficient knowledge of industry and commerce and, indeed, despised the new factory-owning and industrial class. At the same time they feared the labouring classes, and any social agitation was likely to be denounced at once as 'Jacobinism'. Thus the government fell back upon the restriction of liberty as shown in the Six Acts, even using spies and *'agents provocateurs'* when it suited their purpose. The years 1815–1821 were some of the most distressful and difficult ever experienced in Britain.

Summary

The period immediately after Waterloo was an extremely difficult one. The Liverpool government assisted agriculture and industry by the Corn Laws and removal of income tax, but adopted a purely repressive policy towards social discontent. The unfortunate 'Peterloo Massacre' showed up the fears and limitations of the repressive policy. The severity of the game laws and the narrowness of the franchise were also causes of agitation and discontent. The monarchy itself sank further into disrepute, from which only the reign of Queen Victoria was to raise it again.

Important Dates

1815 Corn Laws passed.
1816 Repeal of income tax (Property Tax).
   Spa Fields riots.
1817 Suspension of 'Habeas Corpus'.
   Lord Sidmouth's restrictions on meetings, coffee houses, etc.
   Jury acquits Spa Fields leaders of treason charges.
   The Blanketeers.
   Brandreth's rebellion,

1819 **The Peterloo Massacre.**
       The Six Acts.
1820 **The 'Queen's Affair'.**

QUESTIONS

(1) *Give an account of the general condition of Britain in 1815.*

(2) *Why did the financial and economic policies of the government prove unpopular?*

(3) *What was the importance of William Cobbett and Henry Hunt in this period?*

(4) *What case can be made for Liverpool's repressive policy?*

CHAPTER TWELVE

THE ENLIGHTENED TORIES
1820-1830

New Trends

IN 1820 British trade began to improve and there was an increase of forty per cent in exports during the next four years. This reduced radical agitation to a certain degree, and Liverpool began to give more attention to matters of trade and industry. New appointments of younger men were made to the cabinet. **Sir Robert Peel** became Home Secretary in place of Sidmouth in 1822, **George Canning** succeeded Castlereagh as Foreign Secretary, and **William Huskisson** became President of the Board of Trade. These new men were not to the liking of the old Tories such as Wellington, Eldon (Lord Chancellor) and Lord Sidmouth. The new men all recognized the importance of doing everything possible to expand Britain's trade and to sweep away hampering restrictions, as advocated by Adam Smith in his book, *The Wealth of Nations* (see also p. 105). They were also prepared to take note of 'public opinion' and especially of the new industrialists of the growing factory system. In this respect they were very different from their older colleagues. It is to Liverpool's credit that he appointed these so-called 'enlightened Tories' to important posts.

British Trade

Under William Huskisson, M.P. for the great trading centre of Liverpool from 1823, Britain's trading system underwent important changes. Although not a complete free trader himself, he began the process by which Britain ultimately became a free-trade country. His policy actually led to a small decrease in prices to the consumer in these years: (1) Many commodities which had been excluded from Britain altogether were now allowed entry at moderate duties. (2) He reduced taxation on ordinary manufactures by 30 per cent, thus easing the burden of the numerous taxes which had been placed on ordinary commodities during the war. (3) He reduced very high customs duties to a level at which smuggling, which was very extensive, became unprofitable. (This also reduced the cost to the government of having to employ thousands of customs officials.) (4) He imposed small duties on a number of basic imports, such as raw cotton, wool and silk in place of the very high duties previously levied. (This encouraged manufacturers to expand their businesses both for home and for overseas consumption.) (5) He negotiated a number of Reciprocal Treaties with foreign countries by which we agreed to reduce our tariffs in return for reductions of their tariffs on our exports. (6) The old Navigation Acts, first passed in the seventeenth century against the Dutch and aimed at preventing any British trade except in British vessels, were now drastically modified. Some foreign nations were, in fact, retaliating by preventing British ships entering their ports. (By his **Reciprocity Act of 1823** he achieved agreements with these countries by which British ships could freely enter their harbours in return for the same facilities for them in Britain.) (7) He encouraged the idea of the British Empire as a great trading community. (To safeguard the Canadian timber industry he maintained import duties on timber from foreign countries—a preferential system which he applied to many commodities from other British colonies.) (8) He gave facilities for cheap emigration to the colonies. (9) He put an end to the old Mercantile System denounced by Adam Smith and defied by the American colonies, for he now abolished all regulations which prevented British colonies trading directly with Europe. All these changes showed Huskisson's confidence that British industry and trade could compete to advantage with any other country, and British trade expansion in the next few years owed a great deal to his encouragement. He was killed in 1830 by stumbling in front of a locomotive at the opening of the Manchester and Liverpool Railway. (10) Huskisson is also associated with the **Repeal of the Combination Laws of 1799 and 1800** which, under Pitt's government, had made trade unions illegal.

The main agitation for this change came from outside Parliament, and was organized by **Francis Place**, a radical tailor of Charing Cross. He was supported inside Parliament by two M.P.s, **Joseph Hume** and **Sir Francis Burdett.** When Hume secured a special parliamentary committee of inquiry into the trade unions in 1824, Place rehearsed working men to give their evidence, and the impression they made was very favourable. *The Combination Laws were repealed in 1824.* Place had always argued that free trade unions would be beneficial to both employers and workers and co-operation rather than strife was more likely. But when there was trade recession in 1825 and a rise in the cost of living, the unions, hundreds of which had now come into the open, put forward demands for higher wages and there was a rash of strikes in the industrial towns. Immediately a demand arose in parliament for a return to the position of 1800, but Place and his supporters succeeded in preventing this. However, an **Amending Act of 1825** was passed which made the position of the trade unions difficult. Trade unions were not permitted to 'molest' or 'obstruct' either employers or other workers. This wording was vague and could easily be interpreted against the unions in case of strike action. However, the legality of trade unions had been achieved.

Legal and Prison Reforms

Under Sir Robert Peel, the son of a wealthy Lancashire cotton manufacturer who had himself shown great interest in improving factory conditions for the workers, the Home Office sounded a progressive note. For many years there had been much agitation for the reform of the barbarous penal system by such men as **John Howard** (1726-1790), **Sir Samuel Romilly** (1757-1818), **Jeremy Bentham** and **Sir James Mackintosh**. Sir Samuel Romilly had succeeded in getting rid of the death penalty for picking pockets in 1808, and in 1812 for a member of the armed forces to beg without a licence. But these were small, hard-won reforms, and hundreds of petty crimes were still liable to the death penalty. Sir James Mackintosh had succeeded in securing the abolition of man-traps and spring-guns on country estates, but he had achieved little else, despite years of effort. Peel was open to persuasion on all these matters, and he consulted both the great radical reformers Jeremy Bentham and **Henry Brougham**. In 1820 over two hundred offences were still liable to the death penalty, and four hundred (including the formation of a trade union) were punishable by transportation to the criminal settlements of Australia. Actually, juries increasingly refused to convict, even when a man was guilty, and this was bringing the law into further contempt. In 1823 Peel persuaded Parliament to remove 180 capital offences. He also introduced some important prison reforms which involved the proper classification and separation of prisoners. In 1829, he established the **Metropolitan Police Force**, which became the model for other police forces throughout the country. This was a change much needed, for the old night watchmen and the Bow Street Runners (often in collusion with the criminal) were quite inadequate for maintaining law and protecting property. As Secretary for Ireland in 1812 he had already introduced a police force there. The principle of an unarmed police force was adopted from the beginning.

Catholic Emancipation

Since the Union between the English and Irish Parliaments in 1800, discontent had increased in Ireland. In a country four-fifths Catholic, no Catholic could hold a post in the administration at Dublin nor could a Catholic become an M.P. The disabilities of the Catholics derived from the seventeenth century when in 1688 William III replaced James II on the English throne. Although a number of

PROGRESS

1820-1830

IMPROVEMENT OF TRADE
LIVERPOOL'S GOVERNMENT CHANGES – CANNING – Foreign Policy

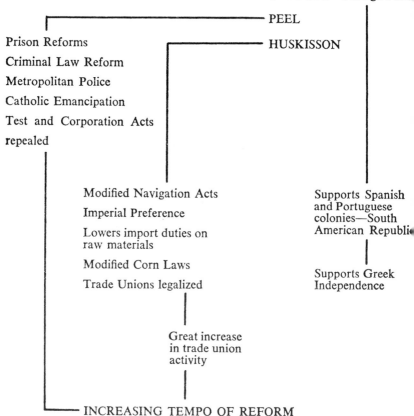

PEEL

Prison Reforms

Criminal Law Reform

Metropolitan Police

Catholic Emancipation

Test and Corporation Acts
repealed

HUSKISSON

Modified Navigation Acts

Imperial Preference

Lowers import duties on
raw materials

Modified Corn Laws

Trade Unions legalized

Great increase
in trade union
activity

Supports Spanish
and Portuguese
colonies—South
American Republic

Supports Greek
Independence

INCREASING TEMPO OF REFORM

grievances had since been relieved, the main grievance of a Catholic country ruled by a small number of Protestant families remained. The leadership of the Irish movement was gained by **Daniel O'Connell**, an Irish lawyer. He aimed at the creation of an Irish Parliament with a Catholic majority which should govern all the internal affairs of Ireland, although he was prepared to see a number of matters, such as foreign policy, remain in British hands. In 1823 he formed the **Catholic Association,** which collected the 'Catholic rent' of a penny a month. The Association had the wide support of the priesthood and soon became powerful. In 1828 O'Connell put himself forward illegally as a candidate in the County Clare election. His opponent was **Vesey Fitzgerald**, a Protestant landlord who in fact supported Catholic Emancipation. O'Connell was elected.

Before O'Connell's election the **Test and Corporation Acts** had been repealed by the British Parliament. These laws from the reign of Charles II were designed to prevent anyone who was not a communicant member of the Church of England from holding high office in the state or being a member of a corporation of a town. In fact, for many years Protestant Dissenters had been able to ignore these acts, and an annual **Act of Indemnity** had been passed to legalize their holding of office. Now this also was swept away. Thus, the growth of religious toleration also strengthened the case for Catholic Emancipation. Sir Robert Peel, Home Secretary in 1829 in Wellington's government, had up to this time been opposed to Emancipation, but O'Connell's movement had gained such support that there was danger of bloodshed. Both Wellington and Peel reluctantly decided to persuade King and Parliament that Emancipation was necessary and, with the help of the Whigs, the **Emancipation Bill** was passed. Even then, when the first Catholic barristers were appointed in Ireland, Peel refused to appoint O'Connell.

Political Position in 1830

Catholic Emancipation divided and weakened the Tory party. The more progressive Tories had also been angered by Wellington's dismissal of Huskisson on becoming Prime Minister in 1828. Thus Wellington had offended both the 'enlightened' Tories and the old Tories. In 1830 he offended those progressive Tories who sympathized with the Belgian revolt against the Dutch which broke out in that year, for he was known to distrust even a liberal revolution which apparently had justice on its side. There was also trouble in England itself when a labourers' revolt broke out in the southern counties and the Whigs demanded a reform of the methods of electing Parliament. When **Lord Grey** raised the question of parliamentary reform Wellington refused to countenance any change. This led to a combination of the reforming Whigs and Tories, together with the disgruntled Tories of the old school, to defeat Wellington. The new King, **William IV,** then asked Lord Grey to form a government and, for the first time in nearly fifty years of Tory rule, the Whigs gained power. This was to have dramatic effects for the political and social future of Britain.

Summary

After 1821 trade and industry improved and unemployment lessened. Liverpool promoted a new group of Tories to important posts and their progressive activities have given them the collective title of the 'Enlightened Tories' in contrast to the policies of 1815–1821. Huskisson removed many remnants of the old out-of-date mercantile restrictions on trade and he also improved the legal position of the trade unions. Peel's legal and prison reforms were also important while the later achievement of Catholic Emancipation caused severe divisions among the Tories which contributed to their defeat in 1830 after a very long period of political power.

Important Dates

1824   **Peel's reform of the penal code.**
       Trade Unions freed from Combination Acts of 1799–1800.
1825   **Trade Union Amending Act.**
1828   **Repeal of Test and Corporations Acts.**
       County Clare Elecion.
1829   **Catholic Emancipation (Catholic Relief Act).**
1830   **Defeat of Wellington.**
       Whigs take office under Grey.

QUESTIONS

(1) What conditions favoured progressive legislation after 1821?
(2) Explain the importance of the work of Huskisson.
(3) Describe Peel's reforms in this period.
(4) What circumstances led to Catholic Emancipation in 1829?

CHAPTER THIRTEEN

BRITISH FOREIGN POLICY
1815-1830

The Congress of Vienna, 1814–1815

THE purpose of this Congress was to decide the new frontiers of Europe and to make arrangements against any revival of French aggression. Those attending the congress included **Lord Castlereagh** for Great Britain, the **Czar Alexander I** for Russia, **Prince Metternich** for Austria, **King Frederick William III** for Prussia and **Talleyrand** for France.

In the north the Austrian Netherlands (Belgium) were united to Holland. This arrangement strengthened the barriers against France in the north-east; but it proved unsatisfactory to the Belgian people and led to the Belgian Revolution of 1830. In northern Italy the **King of Sardinia** (who also ruled Piedmont) was given the formerly free republic of Genoa, and on the Rhine the Prussians gained control of certain territories. Sweden gained Norway from Denmark. Austria gained control of Venetia and Lombardy in northern Italy, an arrangement which was to give rise to great opposition by the Italians. In Germany the number of states was reduced to thirty-nine. Britain herself gained Cape Colony, Ceylon, Mauritius, some islands in the West Indies, Malta, a protectorate over the Ionian Islands, and Heligoland as a naval base in the North Sea.

In eastern Europe, the Czar had hoped to gain control of the whole of the Duchy of Warsaw created by Napoleon, but Castlereagh, Metternich and Talleyrand were all concerned to prevent such a great increase in Alexander's power, and they combined to reduce his demands. Here British policy aimed at *a balance of power in Europe.*

Castlereagh's part in the various settlements was important. Besides reducing Russian gains, he had also succeeded in reducing the demands of Prussia. The principle involved was to make it impossible for any one power to dominate the Continent, and for this purpose he had temporarily brought Britain to the side of Austria and France. This was a revival of the 'balance of power' principle. He was opposed to any policy of revenge against France, and he successfully opposed the idea that she should be put back to the frontiers of 1789. Ultimately, the wider frontiers of 1792 were accepted. He anticipated the need for

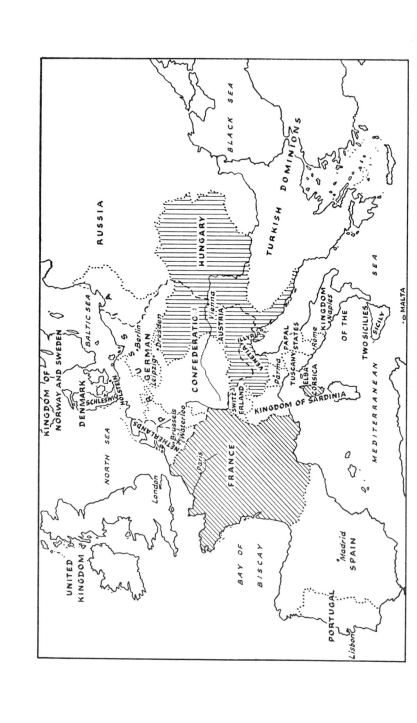

the revival of France as an important element in the balance of power, especially between East and West.

In 1815 the Czar Alexander put forward his idea of the **Holy Alliance** of all the great powers which would keep them united and pledge them to rule their countries on Christian principles. Britain did not sign the declaration, which Castlereagh described as a 'sublime piece of mysticism and nonsense'. Be that as it may, British policy was clearly concerned to prevent Alexander regarding himself as the leader of the great powers and to prevent his ambitions carrying him too far. Castlereagh was here carrying on a foreign policy which had been anticipated by the Younger Pitt.

Castlereagh was one of the principal authors of the more definite **Quadruple Alliance** of **November 1815**, by which Britain, Russia, Prussia and Austria pledged themselves to guarantee the settlements of Vienna and to renew their meetings from time to time to discuss matters of common interest. Their avowed aim was to maintain the peace of Europe, and the 'repose and prosperity of nations'. The latter phrase clearly implied, in the word 'repose', the freedom of nations from revolution. This was a clear reference to France (who was not admitted to the alliance), but the radical critics of Castlereagh at home regarded him as the 'reactionary' opponent of all movements for freedom in Europe.

Castlereagh's Foreign Policy

British policy under Castlereagh was particularly concerned to maintain good relations between the great powers, and the first test of this came at the **Congress of Aix-la-Chapelle** in **1818**. Castlereagh pressed for the admission of France to the Quadruple Alliance, which thus became the **Quintuple Alliance**. France was apparently settling down internally under the cautious government of Louis XVIII and Castlereagh wished her to be once again within the European political system. The occupation troops were also withdrawn. However, important issues faced the Congress and showed division between the powers. Alexander wished to send Russian forces to intervene in Spain where a liberal revolution had broken out. Castlereagh, although an avowed opponent of revolutions, opposed the idea of intervention in Spain, especially by Russia, whom he wished to discourage from any unilateral intervention in western Europe. *In this respect Castlereagh and the Austrian minister, Metternich, were in agreement*, for Austria also was afraid of Russian expansion, especially in the Balkans. Castlereagh succeeded in obtaining a declaration from all the great powers that they would not intervene in the affairs of other states. A further test of this principle came in 1820-1821, when liberal revolutions broke out against despotic rulers in Naples, Portugal and

Spain, and the *South American colonies of Spain and Portugal broke away to form their own independent states.* Castlereagh agreed to Austrian intervention in Naples on the grounds that a treaty with Naples gave Austria this right, but he opposed a French proposal that they should intervene in Spain to suppress the revolution there. His motives were the traditional opposition of Britain to any French control of Spain which would threaten Gibraltar and other British Mediterranean interests. Moreover, the new South American states were free to trade with Britain and any attempt to bring them back to their allegiance would be against British interests. He therefore opposed Alexander's proposal that a joint expedition should be sent against them. In these matters Castlereagh gained the support of Austria and Prussia against France and Russia—a skilful use of the balance of power principle.

However, at the **Congress of Troppau** in **1820** Austria, Russia and Prussia issued the famous **Troppau Protocol** which declared their right to intervene in any state where a revolution threatened other states. Castlereagh opposed the Protocol on the grounds that it would lead to 'extensive interference in the internal transactions of other states'. The next congress was at **Laibach**, which was the adjourned Congress of Troppau.

The Monroe Doctrine

Castlereagh committed suicide in 1822 and was succeeded as Foreign Secretary in Liverpool's government by George Canning. At the **Congress of Verona, 1822**, the Duke of Wellington represented Britain, and British policy under Canning at first followed the same lines as that of Castlereagh. Canning continued to resist French intervention in Spain, as he feared that an attempt would be made to destroy the independence of the South American Republics. He also continued to oppose Alexander's desire for intervention across the Atlantic and made it clear that the British navy would stop such a venture. He was strengthened in this policy by the statement of the **Monroe Doctrine** by President Monroe of the United States in **December 1823**. This made it clear that any interference by European powers in the affairs of the American continent would be regarded by the U.S.A. as an unfriendly act. This effectively ensured the continued independence of the South American states. Canning's policies were only partly effective, however, for in 1823, a French army crossed the Pyrenees and restored royal power in Spain.

The Greek War of Independence

In 1821 the Greeks rose in rebellion against their overlords the

Turks, and Alexander wished to give direct assistance to the Greeks, but was restrained by both Canning and Metternich. In 1825 Alexander died and was succeeded by the **Czar Nicholas I**, who was even more determined to intervene in the Greek struggle. The Russian policy of doing anything possible to increase Russian influence in the Balkans and to weaken Turkey presented Canning with a difficult problem. In Britain itself and in Europe there was great sympathy for the Greek cause and merely to oppose Russian intervention was not enough. He therefore decided to keep control of the situation by assisting the Greeks in collaboration with Russia. This would also prevent a unilateral action by Russia. In **1827** he brought about the **Treaty of London** between Britain, Russia and France, by which the powers proposed that the Greeks should be given self-government though remaining within the Turkish Empire. Neither the Greeks nor the Turks accepted this, and the Turks refused to negotiate. In the same year the Turkish Fleet was destroyed at **Navarino** by a joint British, Russian and French naval force.

Canning, who was Prime Minister for a few months in 1827 on the death of Liverpool, himself died before the Battle of Navarino and, after the brief premiership of **Lord Goderich**, Wellington became Prime Minister in 1828. He now apologized to the Turks for Navarino, for he considered that the battle had dangerously increased Russian naval power. This weakening of the Treaty of London led on to a declaration of war by Russia against Turkey and the expulsion of Turkish forces from Greece with French help. The Turks gave in and signed with Russia the **Treaty of Adrianople, 1829**. In 1832 Greece became independent under her first king, **Otto of Bavaria**. The situation which both Canning and Wellington feared had now arisen, for Russian influence in the Balkans had increased immensely and her threat to the Turkish Empire was greater than ever. As we shall see, this was left as a major problem for Palmerston to deal with.

Summary

After 1815 British foreign policy had a variety of aims—the Balance of Power, opposition to intervention in the internal affairs of other states as shown especially in Castlereagh's opposition to the Troppau Protocol of 1820, the promotion and maintenance of British commercial and naval power. Castlereagh's opposition to Russia stemmed above all from the latter considerations while Canning also resisted Russian aims to intervene against the South American Republics. Canning supported Greek independence in conjunction with Russia, but Wellington's later policies led to Russia herself bringing about the Treaty of Adrianople. Canning gradually withdrew Britain from the Congress system, which faded out after Verona.

Important Dates

1815	**Congress of Vienna.**
1818	**Congress of Aix-la-Chapelle.**
1820	**Congress of Troppau.**
	Troppau Protocol.
1821	**Congress of Laibach.**
	Outbreak of Greek War of Independence.
1822	**Congress of Verona.**
1823	**French intervention in Spain.**
	The Monroe Doctrine.
1825	**Czar Alexander I succeeded by Nicholas I.**
1827	**Treaty of London.**
	Battle of Navarino.
1829	**Treaty of Adrianople.**
1832	**Greece achieved full independence.**

QUESTIONS

(*1*) *What problems were dealt with at the Congress of Aix-la-Chapelle?*

(*2*) *Explain the foreign policy of Castlereagh.*

(*3*) *What difficulties arose in the operation of the Congress System and why did it decline?*

(*4*) *What circumstances gave rise to* (a) *The Treaty of London, 1827;* (b) *the Battle of Navarino;* (c) *the Treaty of Adrianople, 1829?*

(*5*) *What differences and similarities can be detected between the policies of Castlereagh and Canning?*

CHAPTER FOURTEEN

THE FIRST REFORM BILL
1832

The Old Parliamentary System

B Y the early nineteenth century the electoral system no longer met the real needs of the times. In the first place, a new industrial middle class was developing. It had little voice in Parliament compared with that of the great landed families. Secondly, population growth and redistribution were making parliamentary representation very uneven. Some large towns which had expanded rapidly still returned M.P.s on a small borough basis only, while newly developed towns such as Leeds, Manchester and Birmingham, which were not boroughs, had no representation at all. At the other end of the scale there were the *decayed* or *rotten boroughs* which, although almost uninhabited, had representation in Parliament. Such instances were Old Sarum near Salisbury which returned two M.P.s and Dunwich on the east coast which, although it had mostly fallen in the sea, also returned two members.

The *pocket boroughs* were in the possession of wealthy landowners who, through their influence, could ensure the nomination and election of the candidate they wanted. These patrons often sold the right of nomination to the highest bidder, taking full advantage of the fact that entry to the House of Commons in those days meant a desirable rise into the ranks of London society. In those boroughs where there were a considerable number of voters, the latter could be bribed, and they did everything they could to prevent other voters being added to the lists, thus keeping up the bribery value of their votes. In 1811 £200,000 was spent by the candidates in the election for the County of York—the most expensive election ever. In some boroughs only members of the Corporation were allowed to vote, and this also kept the number of voters small. *Altogether fifty-six towns had less than forty voters each, and about 160 landlords nominated half the membership of the House of Commons.*

In the county constituencies in England there were more voters, for the forty-shilling freeholder (a widespread class of farmer) had the vote; but in the Scottish counties the number of voters was very small and open to bribery.

The distribution of seats was very uneven. The very thinly popu-
lated county of Cornwall returned forty-two M.P.s, whereas Dorset
and Somerset returned only eighteen and sixteen respectively. This
meant that *a very small number of voters decided the composition of
the House of Commons.*

The Parliamentary Reform Movement

The French Revolution, the Napoleonic Wars and the unrest of the
years 1815–1821 kept the new middle class from demanding reform,
which became synonymous with revolution. After 1821, however, with
trade expansion and a lessening of extreme agitation, the reform movement took on wider scope. A radical movement developed within the
Whig party, strongly represented by **Henry Brougham** and **Lord
Durham** ('Radical Jack'), who wished to see the new middle class
fully represented in Parliament. Further still to the 'left' of Brougham
and Durham were the **'Philosophic Radicals'**, followers of the doctrines
of **Jeremy Bentham**, who demanded not merely the middle-class vote
but manhood suffrage—the vote for all men over twenty-one. Both
sections of the radicals wished to make a clean sweep of the 'rotten'
and 'pocket' borough system, and the middle-class manufacturers outside Parliament came increasingly to accept them as their leaders
against the entrenched and favoured landlord class. Their chief spokes-
man in the House of Commons was **Joseph Hume**. Within the Whig
leadership division appeared, for the **Grenville** section tended to join
the Tories on important issues, whereas **Lord Grey** and **Lord John
Russell** took a more progressive view, although they did not go as far
as the radicals. At first they hoped that a Whig aristocracy would
replace the Tory aristocracy, and that this would satisfy the middle
class. However, in the 1820s, a considerable reforming stir began to be
felt.

On the more purely working-class sector, William Cobbett, Henry
Hunt and Francis Place were demanding manhood suffrage, and
they established a society, the **National Political Union**, to agitate for
this change. In the northern towns the more revolutionary society, the
National Union of the Working Class, founded in **1830**, had considerable support.

Other reform movements of the 1820s naturally encouraged the
parliamentary reformers. Catholic Emancipation showed that even the
most entrenched interests could be shaken, and that Tories of the old
school, such as Wellington, could be forced to change. Even the
revolution in France in 1830 against the despotic **Charles X** contributed to the general feeling of change, for Wellington's sympathy with
Charles X tended to swing opinion against Wellington even more.
Wellington's influence at this time as Prime Minister began to

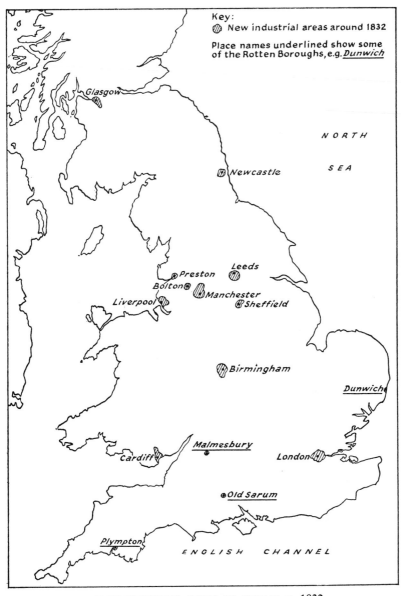

NEW INDUSTRIAL AREAS OF BRITAIN C. 1832

weaken and divide the Tory Party, the main defenders of the 'rotten' and 'pocket' borough system.

The Climax of the Reform Movement, 1830–1832

In 1830, the Birmingham banker, **Thomas Attwood**, set up the **Birmingham Political Union** and other industrial towns followed. Finally a national society, the National Political Union, was formed, with Francis Place as one of its leaders. Their policy was a union of the working and middle class to put forward candidates for Parliament. They had been encouraged by the election of Henry Hunt as M.P. for Preston in 1829. They also demanded, under Attwood's inspiration, a refusal by the middle class to pay taxes until parliamentary reform had been achieved. This was an alarming possibility, which helped to force Lord Grey to move from his previous half-hearted position on reform.

Another social pressure on the Whigs at this time was the *widespread labourers' revolt in the southern counties*, caused by semi-starvation and unemployment. Harshly suppressed by hangings and transportations, the revolt nevertheless raised the spectre of revolution and made the arguments of those Whigs, such as the great historian **Lord Macaulay**, even more cogent—namely, that parliamentary reform was a safeguard against revolution such as was seen on the Continent.

The Passing of the Reform Bill, 1832

Lord Grey, now Prime Minister, appointed Lord Durham chairman of the Special Committee of Four which drew up the Reform Bill, and Lord John Russell introduced it in the House of Commons in March 1831. The Bill proposed the complete abolition of the 'rotten' and 'pocket' borough system. In the Committee Stage the Bill was defeated on two items. Grey resigned, an election was held, and the Whigs increased their majority to 136. The Bill was passed by the Commons but rejected by the House of Lords.

The action of the Lords led to rioting throughout the country, and in the northern counties there was actual drilling and arming by the workers. At Bristol the mob burnt down the Bishop's Palace. There was definite fear of revolution among the upper classes, and a demand arose for the King, William IV, to create sufficient Whig peers to pass the Bill in the Lords. This was partly the effect of the popular campaign being conducted throughout the country by Attwood, Place, Cobbett, Hunt and many others.

After further Tory opposition in the Lords, Grey asked the King to create fifty Whig peers to give a clear majority, but when he agreed to

THE FIRST REFORM BILL, 1832

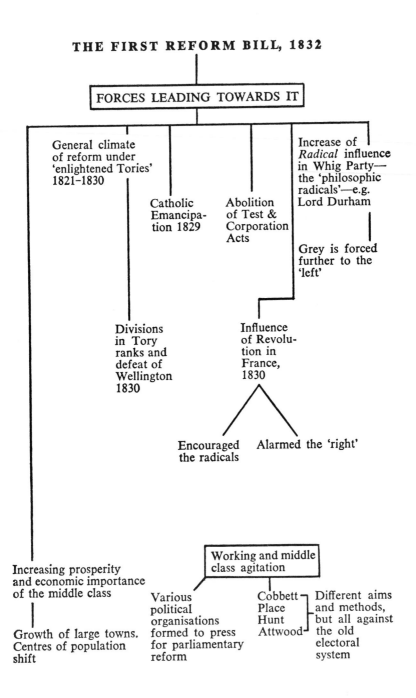

FORCES LEADING TOWARDS IT

General climate of reform under 'enlightened Tories' 1821–1830

Catholic Emancipation 1829

Abolition of Test & Corporation Acts

Increase of *Radical* influence in Whig Party— the 'philosophic radicals'—e.g. Lord Durham

Grey is forced further to the 'left'

Divisions in Tory ranks and defeat of Wellington 1830

Influence of Revolution in France, 1830

Encouraged the radicals

Alarmed the 'right'

Increasing prosperity and economic importance of the middle class

Growth of large towns. Centres of population shift

Working and middle class agitation

Various political organisations formed to press for parliamentary reform

Cobbett
Place
Hunt
Attwood

Different aims and methods, but all against the old electoral system only twenty, Grey resigned and Wellington attempted to form a government. When Wellington agreed to put forward an amended Reform Bill, his 'diehard' supporters deserted him and he was unable to form a government. Grey then returned to office and the **Reform Bill** was passed in **June 1832.** Wellington and a number of Tories had absented themselves from the debate, and they had thus saved the Tory House of Lords but not the 'rotten' and 'pocket' borough system.

Changes made by the Reform Bill

(1) The vote was given to townsmen owning or occupying a house of £10 annual value. This restricted the franchise to the middle class and excluded the working class. In the countryside the franchise was given to freeholders with land of 40/- annual value, to copyholders of £10 annual value, and to leaseholders of land of £50 annual value. In general, these were the better-off sections of the farming community.

(2) Boroughs with less than 2,000 inhabitants lost two M.P.s, and those between 2,000 and 4,000 lost one. The 143 seats in the House of Commons thus released were redistributed to the counties and large towns. More seats were allotted to the counties which had previously been limited to two members each.

Results of the First Reform Bill

Not all who had agitated for parliamentary reform were satisfied. The specific working-class agitation was not successful in gaining the vote for any section of the wage earners. *The new franchise had added a middle-class vote.* The total electoral roll was now 652,000 as against 435,000 before, which meant that only one-sixth of the male population had the vote. Nor is it strictly true to say that the 'pocket borough' entirely disappeared, for some time after the Reform Bill about forty members of the House of Lords were able to nominate members of the Commons. Although the middle class gained in influence, they were not dominant, for the county members increased from 188 to 253—thus the landed interest of the aristocracy increased, as Lord Grey and his supporters had wished. This counteracted the new representation of the great industrial towns. The maintenance of open voting (there had been only one vote in the Commons for the secret ballot) meant that the great landowners could still largely determine the way in which their tenant-farmers voted. *Open voting therefore led to the continuance of both intimidation and bribery of voters,* although the fact that Parliament made official inquiries into a number of glaring cases in the next thirty years tended to reduce malpractices. The system of compiling the lists of voters was left to the parish overseers who were frequently both illiterate and inefficient.

However, the Reform Bill was the real beginning of the process which has led to parliamentary democracy in Britain; but the process was not completed until 1928, when women over twenty-one gained the vote. It had, however, some important effects on the party system. *Both Whigs and Tories now had to take account of a wider public opinion* and the rudimentary beginnings of our present party organizations were seen. After 1832 the Tory **Carlton Club** became the party centre, from which a number of unpaid party officials worked and kept contact with party workers in the country. They were particularly concerned to see that their qualified supporters were on the local electoral rolls. Sir Robert Peel especially encouraged this better organization. In the same way the Whigs, with their centre at the **Reform Club** in London, also began to employ local agents and a number of central officials. Parliament after 1832 became more sensitive to social pressures of all kinds from outside, and *this led on to a spate of social reforms which would not have been possible under the system existing before 1832.*

Summary

During the 1820s conditions became more favourable for a measure of parliamentary reform. Pressure from both the middle and working classes increased greatly. The old system was no longer representative of the country, which had been drastically changed by the Industrial Revolution. Conflicts within both Tory and Whig elements assisted the demand for reform. The Tory divisions which led to the defeat of Wellington and the accession to power of Grey in 1830 were a direct cause of the Reform Bill. The year 1830 was a decisive point of political change after a very long period of Tory rule. Within the Whig party itself the Radical elements were gaining strength and ultimately forced Grey himself to move further forward than he had intended. The Reform Bill of 1832 gave representation to the middle class but did not give it dominance. In some ways, the influence of the landed interests actually increased.

Important Dates

1830   Grey's Whig government formed.
      Attwood formed the Birmingham Political Union.
      Francis Place formed the National Political Union.
1831   March: Bill defeated.
      General election increased Grey's majority.
      Bill passed by Commons, but rejected by Lords.
      Widespread reform riots.

1832 **7th May: Grey resigned owing to opposition of Lords.**
Wellington failed to form a government.
4th June: First Reform Bill passed when Wellington and his
supporters in the Lords abstained.

QUESTIONS

(1) *Why had the political situation become more favourable to parliamentary reform by 1832?*

(2) *What were the main defects of the old system, and to what extent did the Reform Bill remedy them?*

(3) *What part was played by Lord Durham, Henry Hunt, Thomas Attwood, and Francis Place in the reform agitation?*

CHAPTER FIFTEEN

THE WHIG REFORMS
1832-1841

General

THE election after the passing of the Reform Bill returned a decisive majority of Whigs to the Commons. The radicals of both middle and working classes were expecting reforms, and the next six years were marked by a spate of legislation which further modified the old *laissez-faire* attitudes. There was an increasing influence on Parliament of the **Utilitarians** and the **Humanitarians**.

The originator of the philosophy of Utilitarianism was **Jeremy Bentham** (1748-1832). His views affected English social reforms throughout the nineteenth century. He had been a keen critic of English law and government as soon as he left Oxford, to which he had been admitted at the age of thirteen. In his work *A Fragment on Government* (1776—the year also of the publication of Adam Smith's *Wealth of Nations*), he challenged the prevailing idea that English law and government could not be improved upon. *The Philosophy of Utilitarianism* was first expressed in 1789 in his *Introduction to the Principles of Morals and Legislation*. He reduced all human motives to the 'pain and pleasure' principle, by which happiness consists of the avoidance of pain and the achievement of pleasure. All laws should enable man so to live and should also aim at *'the greatest good of the greatest number'*. Every law should be judged on the question of its usefulness and, if it did not achieve this, should be swept aside. Such principles, especially the 'greatest good of the greatest number', would undermine class privilege and take into account the welfare of the whole nation and not just a section of it. Bentham also attacked the evils of the English penal system (see also p. 141) and directly influenced Sir Robert Peel. He also attacked the Poor Law as seen in the Speenhamland system because it encouraged large families which could not be supported, deprived the labourer of independence and was wasteful of the country's money. In 1817 he published his *Catechism of Parliamentary Reform* and demanded annual elections, the vote for all men over twenty-one, the secret ballot and constituencies equal in size. These latter demands were not fully met until the twentieth century though his followers, the **Philosophic Radicals**, had much to do with the passing of the 1832 Reform Bill. His influence is to be seen very clearly in the social reforms of 1832–1841.

Other great men of this period had considerable influence on social reform. They were particularly horrified by the condition of the working people and their children, and their outlook and activity has been given the natural name of *Humanitarianism*. Such men were **Robert Owen**, the socialist and factory reformer (see special note, p. 165), the **Earl of Shaftesbury**, Tory social reformer and campaigner on behalf of children in mine and factory and other employments, **William Wilberforce**, the founder of the anti-slavery movement (see also p. 58), and **Richard Oastler** and **John Fielden**, factory reformers.

The following main reforms were carried out by the Whigs in this period. The governments of the period were:

(1) Earl Grey (November 1830 to July 1834)
(2) Lord Melbourne (July 1834 to November 1834)
(3) Sir Robert Peel (Tory) (November 1834 to April 1835)
(4) Lord Melbourne (April 1835 to September 1841)

The Whigs were in power for eleven years, with the exception of the first short ministry of Sir Robert Peel.

(1) The Abolition of Slavery, 1833

Slave trading by British subjects had been abolished in 1807, but **William Wilberforce** and his supporters of the **Evangelical Movement**, including **Lord Ashley** (later **Earl of Shaftesbury**), were determined to secure the ending of slavery in the British colonies. Wilberforce established the **Anti-slavery Society** in **1823** and had the support in the House of Commons of **Thomas Fowell Buxton**.

There was strong opposition among the sugar planters of the West Indies. A slave was worth at least £50 to his owner, and they also feared the social dangers of freeing the slaves. The 'enlightened Tories' had shown sympathy with the anti-slavery demands, but the only change of any importance before 1833 was the granting in 1828 of legal equality between whites and those coloured people who were not slaves. The Humanitarians kept up their campaign, and on **7th August, 1833**, the Whig government secured the passing of the **Emancipation Act**. The slave-owners were compensated to the amount of £20 million and slaves were gradually to be freed over a period of seven years. The owners were dissatisfied with the compensation and claimed that it met only half the value of their slaves. Many West Indian planters went out of business and in South Africa the Boers, who adopted a biblical justification for slavery, began their trek away from the British Cape Colony in 1836. However, the Act was a great triumph for the Humanitarians and other countries followed Britain's example during the nineteenth century.

(2) The Factory Act, 1833

For many years the working conditions in the new factories had been attacked by such enlightened employers as Robert Owen and John Fielden, by radicals such as Cobbett and by Evangelicals such as Ashley. The factories were not 'new' in the strict sense and were mostly old buildings into which machinery had been placed with inadequate protection for employees. Ventilation and proper hygiene were missing. Owen told the Commission of Inquiry that he had found children as young as four years working in the factories, and Lord Shaftesbury brought very young and crippled children before the Commission. The worst treated were the 'workhouse apprentices' or children hired out to the factories by the workhouses. But worst of all were the long hours worked. Hours of sixteen a day were quite common, giving no possibility of proper breaks for food and rest.

A Factory Bill was introduced into the Commons by **Lord Althorp** and was passed. It became known as the 'Children's Charter'. It laid down that no child under nine was to be employed in textile factories; that those between nine and thirteen were not to work more than nine hours a day or forty-eight a week, and those between thirteen and eighteen, twelve hours or sixty-nine a week, and night work was prohibited for all workers between the ages of nine and eighteen. Four inspectors were appointed to supervise the carrying out of the Act.

Previous factory acts had applied only to cotton factories and no proper means of enforcement had been introduced. *The factory inspectors were an important innovation.* Four were not enough, but the principle was important. There was much evasion of the Act, for it was often impossible to check the age of a young child, and many parents were anxious for their children to work with them in the factories to supplement their own wages.

(3) First Government Grant to Education, 1833

There was little elementary education for working-class children. Dame Schools and Charity Schools gave some instruction for a small charge, but more important work was done by **Andrew Bell** and **Joseph Lancaster**, pioneers of the monitorial system by which the better pupils became monitors and taught the others. Lancaster, being a Nonconformist, had the support of the **British and Foreign Schools Society**, and the Church of England's **National Society** supported Bell. It was these societies that the Whig Government decided to support, and in 1833 a grant of £20,000 was given, to be shared by the two societies. In 1839 this was increased to £30,000 annually, with the important creation of a *Committee of the Privy Council* to supervise its use. *At the same time school inspectors were appointed.*

FORCES BEHIND WHIG REFORMS

UTILITARIANISM HUMANITARIANISM

Bentham

Chadwick, etc.

Shaftesbury

Owen

Wilberforce

Fielden, etc.

Poor Law Amendment Act Abolition of Slavery

Municipal Corporations Act

Post Office Reform

Registration of Births and Deaths Report on the State of towns

Paper Duties lowered

Special Commission on
employment of children
in mines

'Greatest good of the
greatest number'

Efficiency and Reason
applied to government

Factory Act

Grants to Education

1833 1841

These changes were approved by a majority of Whigs and Tories alike. They both feared an illiterate populace, which might be either criminal or revolutionary or both, while the Humanitarians had a genuine desire to see ignorance lessened. To the Utilitarians such advances were in line with their doctrines of 'the greatest good of the greatest number', although Bentham himself had advocated a complete state system of elementary education in no way tied to the religious societies. Indeed, the struggle between Nonconformists and Anglicans in the field of education was to have bad effects during the nineteenth century.

(4) The Poor Law Amendment Act, 1834

The Speenhamland system of poor relief was started in 1795 and spread throughout the country. In the northern industrial districts it was mainly used as unemployment relief and not as additions to wages. The reasons for its introduction were enlightened, but it had a number of bad effects. It encouraged low wage rates; it was resented as charity by the better workers and the weaker came to rely upon it; it encouraged large families which could not be adequately provided for; it increased the burden of rates from £2,000,000 in 1796 to over £8,000,000 by 1830; and it was particularly resented by those middle-class ratepayers who were not employers of labour. All these faults had been pointed out in a study made by Bentham, and most radicals, such as Cobbett, had nothing good to say of it.

Lord Grey appointed a special commission to inquire into the Poor Law, and its members contained a number of Utilitarians. Its proposals were accepted and incorporated in the **Poor Law Amendment Act, 1834**. No able-bodied man was to receive assistance except in the workhouse, where conditions were to be sufficiently unattractive to discourage applicants. Low diet and the minimum of comfort was to be the rule.

The Act laid down a new administrative structure. *Parishes were to be grouped into 'unions'* for the purpose of building and maintaining workhouses. This would also make for a fairer distribution of rates over poorer and wealthier parishes. **Boards of Guardians**, elected by those paying the poor rate, were to have general oversight of the paid officials such as the workhouse masters. A general policy for the whole country was to be laid down by a central **Poor Law Board**, consisting of three Commissioners and their secretary, the fanatical Utilitarian, **Edwin Chadwick**, with their headquarters at Somerset House, London.

The changes were welcomed by the middle and upper classes, especially when rates were halved within two years, but the workhouses became hated and feared by the working class. 'Bastilles' was the name widely applied to them. The proposals of the first commission of inquiry to educate pauper children in separate workhouses and to set up others for the aged and infirm were not applied by the Unions. Often the paupers, the insane and the genuinely unemployed men and women were herded in the same workhouses. Both the food and the work given were repellent. Families were separated; and inmates were seldom allowed outside, making it difficult for an able-bodied man, once inside, to get out again. Chadwick and the Commissioners (the 'three Pashas of Somerset House') had a fanatical belief in the rightness of the Act of 1834, and by 1836 had achieved its application in the whole of southern England. In the north, however, they failed to break down the system of using the poor rates for unemployment relief, and the violent resistance was led by John Fielden of Todmorden, Richard Oastler of Leeds (both factory owners) and a Methodist minister, **J. R. Stephens**, whose agitation led to the burning down of a number of northern workhouses. William Cobbett and many radicals opposed the law and its operation from the start, and to them it was proof of the uselessness of the Reform Bill of 1832 from a working-class point of view. It was this feeling which led on to the formation of the **Chartist Movement** in **1836**.

(5) *The Municipal Corporations Act, 1835*

In 1833 Grey appointed another commission to inquire into the state of English local government. Their report showed a state of chaos and corruption. *Some big towns which had developed fast with the Industrial Revolution*, such as Birmingham and Manchester, *had no Mayor and Corporation but were still under the control of a lord of the manor.* In most of the 246 chartered towns there was no system of election and seats on the Corporation were passed down in families. Other members were co-opted. Town affairs were neglected and, in the absence of any public control, town funds were being wasted and misapplied. These towns often had no responsibility for such things as refuse collection, lighting, paving etc., which were in the very inefficient hands of numerous local committees whose boundaries did not coincide with those of the town. Thus there was overlapping of authorities, waste and inefficiency, which horrified the Utilitarian members of the commission of inquiry.

The **Municipal Corporations Act, 1835 (Lord Melbourne** was now Prime Minister) was the real beginning of present-day English local government. The main changes made were as follows: (1) All male ratepayers were to vote for town councillors who held their representation for three years. (2) The council elected a mayor and aldermen, the latter comprising one quarter of the council and sitting for six years. (3) The council's accounts were to be audited and published annually. (4) The councils, by agreement with the old local Improvement Committees, were to take over their duties.

The Act gave control of the towns to the middle class, and it paved the way for future improvements. But it was not until Parliament itself took more interest in matters of health that the new local authorities took much action, and this was in the second half of the century.

The Whigs and the Working Class: Robert Owen

The Whigs adopted a repressive policy towards working-class discontent without attacking the problem at its roots—low wages and unemployment. In 1830 the labourers of the southern counties rose in revolt against the lowering of wages by the farmers, which had been done to meet the cost of the Speenhamland system on the rates, and also as a protest against an agricultural decline which had occurred despite the Corn Laws. Although there was rick-burning and destruction of machinery, no one was killed, yet the Government of Lord Grey set up a special court of judges who hanged nine labourers and imprisoned or transported hundreds of others. The government also came to the wrong conclusion that this discontent was purely the result of the demoralizing effect of the Speenhamland system—hence the Poor Law Amendment Act.

Working-class discontent took the form of increasing trade union activity, which both Grey and Melbourne regarded with animosity. Since their legalization in 1824, the trade unions had developed rapidly in the industrial districts; and the first attempt to unite all unions into one national movement was made under the leadership of **Robert Owen** (1771–1858).

Owen was born at Newtown, Montgomeryshire and worked as a draper's assistant, but by 1800 had become the owner of large cotton mills on the Clyde at New Lanark. Here he produced almost ideal working conditions for these years—good houses, no children under ten years employed, a school for the children of his employees, and ample recreation. He toured Britain and explained his ideas on factory reform and the importance of environment on the formation of character. In 1813 he published his important work, *A New View of Society*, in which he stressed the basic importance of education and environment. Owen, however, failed to persuade his fellow manufacturers to follow his example. He then turned to the advocacy of **'Villages of Co-operation'** throughout Britain, by which capitalist competition would be replaced by the workers producing their own needs on a profit-sharing basis and exchanging any surpluses with other co-operative villages. He was advocating an English co-operative commonwealth on socialist lines. Making little headway in Britain he established, at **New Harmony** in the **United States**, a communistic society organized by a group of his supporters, where profit-sharing and human brotherhood were to replace competition. This community failed, but in Britain Owen's influence was felt in the establishment of co-operative societies for trading purposes by groups of working people. Owen turned his appeals from his fellow capitalists to the working class, and his influence with the trade unions grew rapidly. Disillusion with the Reform Bill of 1832 intensified this development, and in October **1833**, Owen launched the **Grand National Consolidated Trades Union**, which was to comprise a union of all trade unions in the country. By this means Owen, who had no faith in the mere extension of the vote as a reforming measure, hoped to bring about the co-operative commonwealth in which the workers would take over and run the national industries. Soon branches of the G.N.C.T.U. existed throughout Britain.

The Whig government's alarm led on to the persecution of the trade unions, and a harsh example was made in the notorious case of the **Tolpuddle Martyrs**: six labourers of Tolpuddle in Dorset were sentenced to seven years' transportation for having sworn an illegal oath of loyalty and secrecy in forming a branch of the G.N.C.T.U. Owen raised a national campaign of protest which had very wide support, and they were released after four years. But the charges of 'illegal conspiracy' or 'molesting' other workers were used to imprison local leaders of Owen's union. A national strike was organized, and large areas of industry came to a standstill. But Owen then began to face the financial difficulties of maintaining thousands of unemployed workers; the magistrates imprisoned the local leaders, and soldiers were used to suppress meetings—all very reminiscent of 1815–1821. Against these pressures the movement failed and men returning to work were forced to sign the 'Document' which pledged them to abandon the G.N.C.T.U. The Whig anti-trade union activity only further embittered sections of the working class and led on to the formation of the Chartist Movement, which we will consider separately (p. 177). During the years 1830–1834, Lord Melbourne was Lord Grey's Home Secretary and was principally responsible for the repressive measures taken during that period. This did not endear him to the working class when he became Prime Minister in **1835**.

Other Whig Reforms

In **1836** compulsory **Registration of Births, Marriages and Deaths** was introduced. This enabled more accurate statistics of population to be kept and also enabled the factory acts and others involving age-limits to be more efficiently administered. Also in 1837, the **Limited Liability Act** was passed which freed the promoters of a company from the necessity of paying all liabilities in case of failure. This was an aid to industrial expansion and 'free enterprise'. This especially encouraged railway construction, which advanced considerably in the next four years. In 1840 followed the **Penny Post**, the origin of our present-day postal system. This change was mainly due to the social reformer and inventor, **Rowland Hill**. In a special study of the old system of payment according to distance, he proved that the Post Office was losing revenue. The government accepted his conclusions and in 1840 the adhesive penny stamp for a weight of half an ounce was introduced. *The result was the increase of Post Office business by ten times in the next twenty years*, especially as the new system was not only a great aid to private correspondence but to the Victorian business world as well. In **1836** the **Marriage Act** permitted marriage in church, chapel or before a registrar, of persons who objected to the publication of banns. The Nonconformists had particularly suffered by the old restrictions, and the Act was an advance in religious toleration. In **1836** also the **Tithe Commutation Bill** gave relief to farmers by replacing the old Tithe payment by a rent charge based on the average price of corn for the previous seven years. Another improvement was the *lowering of the Stamp Duty on newspapers* from fourpence to one penny. For the business men it lowered the cost of advertising and increased the circulation of newspapers of all shades of opinion. It was a drastic reduction of the heavy duty imposed after 1815 which had been aimed chiefly against the radical press.

Summary

The Whig reforms of 1832–1841 were very important and were the forerunners of much nineteenth-century legislation. They were the direct results of the combined pressures of utilitarian and humanitarian thought, which had greater weight both inside and outside Parliament after the Reform Bill of 1832. The most controversial reform was the Poor Law Amendment Act and its administration, producing as it did widespread working-class opposition which expressed itself most strongly in the Chartist Movement after 1836. After 1835 the pace of reform slackened under Melbourne, and the Whigs were dogged by agricultural and industrial crises after 1837, as well as an unbalanced budget.

Important Dates

1833   **Factory Act.**
      Abolition of Slavery.
1834   **Poor Law Amendment Act.**
      The Tolpuddle Martyrs.
1835   **Municipal Corporations Act.**

1836 Registration of Births, Marriages and Deaths.
      The Marriage Act.
      Tithe Commutation Act. Stamp Duty lowered.
1837 Limited Liability Act.
1839 Increased grant to elementary education (see Ch. 45).
      Durham Report (see Ch. 40).
1840 Penny Post.

QUESTIONS

(*1*) *Describe the changes made by the Poor Law Amendment Act and explain the opposition to it.*

(*2*) *Why was reform of local government urgently necessary?*

(*3*) *In which of the Whig reforms can the influence of utilitarianism and humanitarianism be seen?*

(*4*) *Write notes on the importance of the following:* (a) *the case of the Tolpuddle Martyrs;* (b) *Registration of Births, Marriages and Deaths;* (c) *the Tithe Commutation Act;* (d) *the Penny Post.*

(*5*) *In what connection are the following important in this period:* (a) *Edwin Chadwick;* (b) *Lord Ashley;* (c) *Robert Owen;* (d) *William Wilberforce?*

CHAPTER SIXTEEN

SIR ROBERT PEEL IN THE YEARS 1832–1846

The Tamworth Manifesto, 1834

IN November 1834, Lord Melbourne resigned when complications arose for the Whigs over the Irish question, and William IV asked **Sir Robert Peel** to form a government. 'Peel's hundred days' cover the period of his first administration to April 1835, when Melbourne returned to power. In his election address to his constituents at Tamworth in the Midlands he defined the purposes of the **Conservative Party**, as it now began to be called. This statement, although cautious, was a clear break from the old unchanging Toryism of the past and made it clear that the Conservative Party would reform 'proved abuses' and would undertake the 'redress of real grievances'. At the same time his statement described the Reform Bill of 1832 as 'a final and irrevocable settlement'.

Peel lacked a Commons' majority and could not maintain his government. In 1839 he again attempted to form a government, but Queen Victoria resisted his efforts to replace her Whig ladies-in-waiting—the so-called **'Bedchamber Question'**—and he refused to accept her claim to overrule him. In 1841, the Conservatives gained a clear majority in the election and Peel formed his second administration, which proved to be an extremely important one for the history of Britain.

Britain in 1841 and the 'Hungry Forties'

The condition of Britain in 1841 was bad. The middle classes were discontented through trade stagnation and the working classes were suffering heavily. Bad harvests since 1837 had made things worse for farmers and workers, and the workhouses were full under the regulations of the 1834 Poor Law Amendment Act. *It is estimated that about ten per cent of the population were at the subsistence or pauper level.* In Manchester alone 50,000 workers were receiving Poor Relief. Working-class discontent, which now had the backing of the Chartist Movement, was widespread. Manufacturers were discontented also over heavy import duties on raw materials, and the cost of living for the wage earners was heightened by import duties on grain, butter, tea, sugar and other foods.

Peel and Free Trade

Peel declared his aim to be to 'make this country a cheap country for living'. His famous budget of 1842 set the tone for future trading and financial policy. He reduced import duties on 750 articles, especially reducing to a very low level the duties on imported raw materials needed for industry. His aim was to stimulate trade and to lower prices. The Exchequer lost about £20,000,000 in revenue; but *Peel reintroduced the very unpopular Income Tax*, which the wealthier classes had managed to remove in 1815. This imposed a tax of 7d. in the pound on incomes over £150 per annum (mainly a middle- and upper-class tax), and by 1844 the government had a revenue surplus of over £2,000,000. The importance of income tax was that it was a *direct* tax on the better-off sections of the community, whereas *indirect* taxation by import duties affected the wage-earners disproportionately. The budget of 1844 removed more duties, but with the increase of trade Peel was able to go even further towards free trade in the budget of 1845, when *he abolished all duties on raw materials except two*—450 duties were removed—sugar duties were also reduced and all duties on exports abolished. By 1846, about three quarters of the 1,000 duties of 1841 had been removed; but, despite this, the government's revenue had risen substantially. This resulted from a steady expansion of trade and the operation of income tax which, although imposed in 1842 for three years only, has remained ever since.

An important financial reform was the **Bank Charter Act** of **1844**. This was prompted by the amount of financial and industrial speculation in these years—especially the *'railway mania'*. The country banks were often in difficulties through having lent money to unsound enterprises, and this bred a lack of confidence in British credit at home and abroad. By the act of 1844 the Bank of England could only issue bank notes to the value of £14,000,000 without cover in the form of bullion. Above that figure all notes were to be covered in gold (75 per cent) and silver (25 per cent). This would check over-lending by the Bank to the country banks, which were now limited to £8,500,000 in their total issue. This was designed to lessen over-speculation and to prevent inflation. It worked reasonably well, although the Act had to be suspended on a few occasions. But it undoubtedly helped the process by which London became the financial centre of the world in the nineteenth century. In passing this act, Peel had had to resist speculative interests in the House of Commons and, as with free trade, he had to 'educate' his own party to accept it.

Peel and Ireland

The Irish problem presented another challenge to Peel's statesmanship. In Ireland itself **Daniel O'Connell** began a strong campaign for the repeal of the union between England and Ireland by Pitt's Act of 1801. This campaign began in 1842 when O'Connell organized a series of mass meetings in Ireland with the demand for independence as their main theme. He hoped that the pressure which had achieved his victory in connection with Catholic Emancipation would have a similar success by 1843, but *Peel was resolutely opposed to O'Connell's demands* and he sent 35,000 troops to Ireland in that year. O'Connell was himself opposed to the use of physical force and when the Lord Lieutenant banned an intended mass meeting at **Clontarf** in **1843** he refused the demands of his more extreme followers that it should nevertheless be held. This decision weakened his influence in Ireland, where the more extreme **Young Ireland Movement** (see also p. 208) took to more revolutionary policies. O'Connell was arrested and tried on a charge of sedition—a trial which was unfairly conducted and led to his imprisonment. The House of Lords, however, reversed the verdict against O'Connell in 1844.

Factory and Mines Reform

The leading factory reformers had been pressing since 1833 for laws to protect the adult worker. This campaign was undertaken by Lord Shaftesbury with the support of such leaders as John Fielden and Richard Oastler. They formed a special **'Ten Hours' Committee'** whose aim was to secure a ten-hour day for women and children in the first place. They felt confident that, owing to the dependence of men on the work of women and children, it would also lead to a ten-hour day for men. Shaftesbury secured the appointment of a Committee of the House of Commons to inquire into the working of the 1833 Factory Act, and another Committee to report on the working conditions of children in the mines. On these committees Edwin Chadwick, the ardent Benthamite (Utilitarian), served.

The report on the mines was issued in 1842. It disclosed shocking conditions for women and children. Young children of five or six years acted as trappers to open and shut the ventilating doors of the mines —dangerous and unhealthy—working for twelve hours without a break. Young persons who hauled the trucks of coal to the shaft bottom worked in low galleries on their hands and knees, chained to the trucks. Shaftesbury wished to stop the employment of young persons underground below the age of thirteen, but he was defeated on this in the Commons and was forced to accept the age of ten as the limit in the **Mines Act of 1842**. It also forbade the employment of women underground. Inspectors were also appointed to see that the law was enforced.

The Factory Act of 1844 was another result of Shaftesbury's activities and the 'Ten-hours' Committee'. Parliament was opposed to the ten-hour idea and the act did not meet all the reformers' demands. Peel himself was opposed to the ten-hour day campaign. However, the Act secured a day of six-and-a-half hours for children between eight and thirteen and a twelve-hour day for women workers and girls. Regulations for fencing factory machinery were introduced, especially to protect women and girls whose clothing was easily caught in unguarded machines. These rules applied to the textile factories, and in 1845 Shaftesbury secured their extension to calico-printing. However, in 1847, after the fall of Peel, a ten-hour act was passed. Social reforms under Peel, although not entirely satisfactory to Shaftesbury and his supporters, had moved definitely towards better industrial conditions. They were good though limited.

The Anti-Corn Law League

This League was formed in 1839 to secure the abolition of the Corn Laws of 1815. Its two greatest leaders were **Richard Cobden** and **John Bright**. Cobden was a calico manufacturer of Manchester and a propagandist for free trade, and Bright was a cotton manufacturer of Rochdale and a member of the Society of Friends (Quakers). Owing to the strength of the free trade movement in Manchester, the term **'Manchester School'** was used for the free trade movement in general. Manufacturers tended to support the League because lower bread prices would automatically increase real wages and thus reduce trade-union pressures and would also help the free trade movement in general. For cheaper raw materials and expanding markets abroad they now depended on the development of free trade.

The League was a most efficient organization. Manufacturers contributed heavily to its funds, as did a large section of the working class. The Whig reduction of paper duties aided the immense distribution of League pamphlets, and the League could afford to employ a large permanent staff. Its meetings were attended by vast audiences, spellbound by the powerful oratory of John Bright, *who was able to appeal to both the middle and working class and united them both against the landlord interests.* The latter depended mainly on the argument that the removal of the Corn Laws would flood Britain with cheap corn and ruin agriculture.

By 1845 Peel, especially influenced by the arguments of Richard Cobden, had decided that the Corn Laws must go, but he wanted a General Election on the issue. However, events in Ireland forced his hand. In that country the year 1845 was disastrous; an extremely wet summer ruined both the wheat and potato crops, and the workhouses were soon full of starving and dying Irish. To relieve this distress, **Peel knew that the free import of corn into the United Kingdom was**

PEEL'S SECOND GOVERNMENT

1841–1846

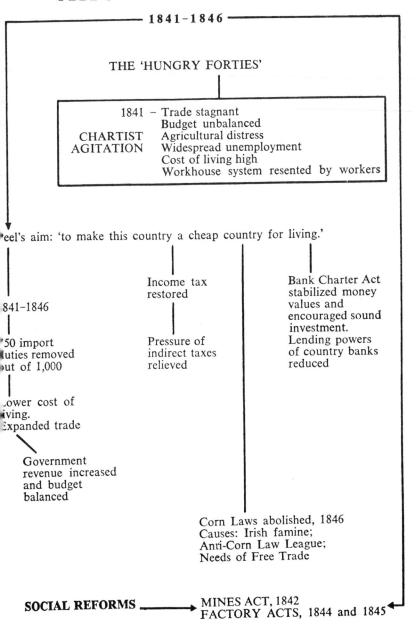

THE 'HUNGRY FORTIES'

CHARTIST
AGITATION

1841 – Trade stagnant
Budget unbalanced
Agricultural distress
Widespread unemployment
Cost of living high
Workhouse system resented by workers

Peel's aim: 'to make this country a cheap country for living.'

1841–1846

750 import
duties removed
out of 1,000

Lower cost of
living.
Expanded trade

Government
revenue increased
and budget
balanced

Income tax
restored

Pressure of
indirect taxes
relieved

Bank Charter Act
stabilized money
values and
encouraged sound
investment.
Lending powers
of country banks
reduced

Corn Laws abolished, 1846
Causes: Irish famine;
Anti-Corn Law League;
Needs of Free Trade

SOCIAL REFORMS ⟶ MINES ACT, 1842
FACTORY ACTS, 1844 and 1845

essential. Opposition within his own cabinet led him to resign; but when the Whig leader, **Lord John Russell**, failed to form a government, Peel returned. He was now supported by the Duke of Wellington, but was also dependent on the support of the free trade Whigs. While Ireland starved, the Commons and Lords debated the question for several months and not until June 1846 were the Corn Laws repealed —in fact, a very small duty (nominal duty) was to be retained for three years until a complete removal. Peel's triumph led, however, to a combination of the landlord interest in the Commons with his other political opponents. This movement was led by **Benjamin Disraeli**, who succeeded in combining Whigs, Radicals and Protectionists against Peel over the latter's proposals for maintaining law and order in Ireland. His defeat and resignation followed.

Benjamin Disraeli (1804–1881)

Disraeli was the son of a Christianized Jew, Isaac D'Israeli, a writer of some distinction. Disraeli entered Parliament as M.P. for Maidstone in 1837, and was howled down in his maiden speech. He dressed flashily and cut an extremely unorthodox figure in the House of Commons. His ideas were in the nature of 'Tory Radicalism'—that is, he wished to see the old aristocracy work in the interests of the mass of the people, although he opposed giving political power to the working class. He disliked the commercial middle class, and saw only in the culture and traditions of the aristocracy the real hope for the future. He was a novelist of some power, and his work *Sybil or The Two Nations* was a study of England at the time of the Chartists and had the underlying theme of aristocratic revival to solve the grave social problems of the times. Disraeli's hope of being included in Peel's administrations were frustrated, and he took up the cause of the landlord class against Peel and in support of the Corn Laws. He formed the **Young England Movement** in alliance with a number of young aristocrats, of whom the Tory M.P., **Lord George Bentinck**, was the most prominent. The tactics of Disraeli and his supporters were a major cause of the length of time it took to remove the Corn Laws.

Effects of the Corn Law Repeal

The opposition to Peel within the Tory Party led many free trade Tories, such as **Gladstone**, to move over to the Whig Party, which, in the late 1860s, became the Liberal Party with a clear free trade programme. Disraeli's opposition to Peel had, however, enabled him to move up in the Tory party to a position second only to the leader of the aristocratic Tories, the **Earl of Derby**. The repeal of the Corn Laws thus caused a new grouping of the parties and the rise of new forces in each.

On the economic side the Protectionist argument that repeal would ruin agriculture proved quite wrong, and Disraeli himself, when Chancellor of the Exchequer in 1852, did nothing to bring back protection. The possibility of foreign competition forced farmers and landlords to improve their agricultural methods, and they were directly assisted by the government in doing this. Better wages, the growth of population, the development of better distribution through the new railways, all helped to increase demand for corn and to keep up a reasonable price. In fact, the mid-Victorian period from 1846 to about 1870 was quite a good one for agriculture. Cobden and Bright had hoped for a big fall in wheat prices, which did not occur; but, on the other hand, improvements in wages and general conditions increased the purchasing power of the workers and thus increased the demand for agricultural produce. However, after 1870 the competition of imported American wheat did have serious effects on British agriculture (see Ch. 41).

Summary

In the Tamworth Manifesto of 1834 Peel accepted the Reform Bill of 1832 and stated the new Conservative policy of steady, progressive reforms which could be justified. Peel's second ministry of 1841 to 1846 saw the decisive breakthrough to Free Trade. The abolition of the Corn Laws was a victory for humanity and common sense against the landed interest. Peel also improved the position of the currency, cheapened foodstuffs and introduced a number of important social reforms in line with the avowed principles of the Tamworth Manifesto. The Protectionist argument of disaster for British agriculture put forward by Disraeli proved incorrect in the immediate future. The years 1846–1870 were years of 'high farming' in Britain. But after 1870 Free Trade did go against the interests of farming when American wheat came on to the home market.

Important Dates

1834 The Tamworth Manifesto.
1839 The Bedchamber Question.
1842 Free Trade budget.
       Income tax re-introduced.
1844 Bank Charter Act.
       Factory Act.
1845 Further budget instalment of Free Trade.
1846 Repeal of Corn Laws.
       Emergence of Disraeli.
       Defeat and resignation of Peel.

QUESTIONS

(1) *What was the general social condition of Britain in 1841 and how did Peel propose to meet the problems arising from it?*

(2) *What was the importance of the budgets of 1842 and 1845?*

(3) *Why did Peel decide on the repeal of the Corn Laws?*

(4) *What social reforms were introduced in Peel's second ministry?*

CHAPTER SEVENTEEN

THE CHARTIST MOVEMENT

THIS was an important labour movement of the nineteenth century, organized independently of the two main parties of the time. Its activities extended mainly over the years 1836 to 1848.

Causes of the Rise of Chartism

The main causes were: (1) the working classes were disappointed with the Reform Bill of 1832 and with the anti-working-class record of the Whigs as shown in their attitude to trade unionism; (2) the Poor Law Amendment Act of 1834 was a special grievance, particularly in the northern towns, where leading radicals and a number of manufacturers successfully resisted it; and (3) many radicals had campaigned against the limited Reform Bill of 1832 from the first, and radicalism gradually shaded over into the Chartist movement.

In 1836 a number of workers, among whom **William Lovett** was especially prominent, formed the **London Workingmen's Association,** which was the basis of the Chartist Movement, set up at a great inaugural meeting in Birmingham in 1838. The main points of the Charter were the demands for (1) universal male suffrage, (2) equal electoral districts, (3) annual parliaments—*i.e.* annual elections, (4) payment of M.P.s, (5) the secret ballot in elections, and (6) no property qualifications for candidates. These were the famous six points of the **'People's Charter'**.

Differing Views within the Movement

The Chartists never entirely agreed among themselves as to the *means* by which their aims were to be accomplished. The *'moral force' Chartists* are best represented by William Lovett, a skilled craftsman of London, who believed that persuasion and propaganda were the main means to be used, whereas the *'physical force' elements*, represented by **Feargus O'Connor**, editor of the Chartist newspaper *The Northern Star*, believed in revolutionary or near-revolutionary methods. Another leader, **Bronterre O'Brien**, advocated the nationalization of industry and its control by the workers, while the Birmingham banker, **Thomas Attwood** (see also p. 154) believed in the reform of the currency system. Thus they were not all convinced that the mere petitioning of Parliament was enough, although this was a major Chartist method in these years.

The First Chartist Petition, 1839

In 1839 a Chartist Convention of some fifty delegates met in London and organized a monster national petition, but before it was presented to Parliament they moved to Birmingham, where there was strong support and where monster meetings were addressed by the Chartist leaders in the Bull Ring. *The first petition of July 1839, to Parliament contained about a million and a quarter signatures.* It was sponsored by Attwood, who was an M.P. for Birmingham, but was overwhelmingly rejected by the Whig House of Commons.

The rejection of the petition led to the formulation of plans by the 'physical force elements' for a national rising, to be heralded by the capture of the town of Newport in Monmouthshire, where a number of Chartists were imprisoned. Under the leadership of **John Frost**, 4,000 men marched on the town on 3rd November, 1839; but they were beaten back by soldiers and police, twenty-four Chartists being killed. Frost was sentenced to death, but this was commuted to transportation for life. The would-be insurrection had been defeated. In 1840 the principal Chartist leaders were imprisoned for varying lengths of time.

The Second Chartist Petition, 1842

In 1842 O'Connor took a leading part in the organization of *the second national petition containing about three million signatures.* It was rejected in the House of Commons by 287 votes against and 49 in favour.

This second rejection led to the attempted organization of a general strike. In the northern towns the strike had widespread support and various disturbances occurred, known as the **'Plug Riots'**, when gangs of striking workers went round the factories knocking out the boiler-plugs to prevent non-strikers working. However, when O'Connor turned against the strike movement because he feared other leaders would attempt to turn it into a general insurrection, it petered out. The authorities arrested and transported a number of Chartist supporters.

In the period 1842–1846 there was trade expansion and a drop in unemployment. This lessened the Chartist appeal. At the same time other movements were claiming a good deal of working-class support—the new **Co-operative Movement**, the **Trade Unions**, the **Anti-Corn Law League** and the activities of the Ten Hours' Committee. The repeal of the Corn Laws in 1846 and the development of Free Trade by Peel improved the conditions of the workers. In these circumstances the Chartists, while clinging to the six points, began to experiment in other directions. The most important experiment was the formation of the **Land Co-operative Society** in 1845 and the setting up of **O'Connorsville** in Hertfordshire. Tenants were settled on the land purchased by the society, and from their rents it was planned to buy more land and create nationally small farms free from landlordism. This scheme failed.

The Third Chartist Petition, 1848

The last Chartist national effort was in 1848. In 1847 an economic depression created once again bad conditions in industry, and Chartism revived. O'Connor was elected M.P. for Nottingham. The revolutionary movements of 1848 abroad also encouraged the Chartists. The third national petition was organized, and a great rally was planned for 10th April on Kennington Common, after which the third petition was to be taken to Parliament. The government of **Lord John Russell** took strong measures. The Duke of Wellington was put in command of troops guarding London, and great numbers of special constables were enrolled. The meeting on Kennington Common took place against government orders, and was addressed by O'Connor who, however, was 'persuaded' by the police not to carry out the intended march to Westminster. The meeting had been attended by something over 25,000 people. *The third petition was taken in a cab to the House of Commons, with 2,000,000 signatures,* some of which were put on the petition to cast derision on the movement—a point quite understandable when such names as 'Queen Victoria' and the 'Duke of Wellington' appeared on it. Once again the petition was decisively rejected.

An attempt by an insurrectionary group to organize a popular rising in London was foiled by government spies, and in any case neither Lovett nor O'Connor supported their plans. The movement now lost its cohesion, and the leaders became drawn into other working-class movements which helped to achieve the Reform Bill of 1867 by which some working men, as distinct from the middle-class voters, gained the vote for the first time.

Reasons for the Chartist Failure

The following points should be considered: (1) It was most unlikely that the wealthier classes, who controlled Parliament, would have agreed to manhood suffrage, which could well have swept them from power. (2) The efforts at insurrection were doomed to failure, for the police and the army were under upper-class control, and the possibility of adequately arming any large sections of the workers was very small. (3) The socialist doctrines preached—sometimes very violently—by many Chartist leaders caused a widespread belief, which was shared by Queen Victoria herself, that the Chartists aimed at a 'Red Republic' which would nationalize all property. (This tended to consolidate the wealthier classes even more strongly, as the French Revolution of 1789 was still not far behind them.) (4) The differences between the 'physical force' and 'moral force' elements weakened the movement, but even more weakening to the national movement were the differences according to locality. (In some large industrial towns the local Chartists abandoned agitation for the Charter in favour of gaining control of the local councils.) (5) The new Co-operative Movement tended to draw support away from the Chartists. (6) When conditions improved the movement declined, for it was really based on 'bread and butter' discontent.

In the long-run, most of the Chartist demands became part of the English parliamentary system, but their immediate achievements were small. However, they showed the wealthier classes the need to reform social conditions if revolution was to be kept at bay, and in this respect they increased the tempo of reform movements. They were an important part of the labour and general reform movement of the nineteenth century.

Summary

The Chartist movement expressed widespread working-class dissatisfaction both with the Reform Bill of 1832 and with the resultant Poor Law Amendment Act of 1834. The fortunes of the movement fluctuated somewhat with the conditions of trade and employment. It opposed the Anti-Corn Law League and resisted attempts to reach common ground with middle-class organizations, and at the same time the divisions within its own ranks weakened its activities at critical points. These divisions were, however, more complicated than mere 'physical force' against 'moral force'; although this was a definite division. The movement failed because the whole weight of the 'Establishment' was against it, but most of its demands have since become an essential part of English political democracy. It was the first attempt to establish a 'labour' party independent of the traditional parties.

Important Dates

1836 London Workingmen's Association formed.
1838 Chartist movement, with its six main demands, inaugurated.

1839 **Chartist London Convention and the first petition.**
Newport rising.
1842 **Second Chartist petition.**
'Plug riots'.
1845 **'O'Connorsville' established.**
1848 **Meeting on Kennington Common.**
Wellington in charge of anti-Chartist preparations.
Third petition rejected.

QUESTIONS

(1) What were the main reasons for the rise of the Chartist movement?

(2) Mention four important Chartist leaders and state their points of view.

(3) How would you account for the fact that all three Chartist petitions received some support in the Commons?

(4) How would you account for the failure of the Chartists to achieve their aims?

CHAPTER EIGHTEEN

BRITISH FOREIGN POLICY UNDER PALMERSTON

Henry John Temple Palmerston (1784–1865) succeeded to his father's Irish peerage in 1802. As an Irish peer he was entitled, if elected, to sit in the House of Commons. He became Tory M.P. for the pocket borough of Newport, Isle of Wight, in 1806. Between 1809 and 1828 he was Secretary at War, and in the 1820s was a supporter of the 'enlightened Tory group'. In 1830 he joined Grey's Whig ministry as Foreign Secretary. He was one of the most colourful and powerful statesmen of the nineteenth century, a man of tireless energy, and an outspoken promoter of Britain's interests on every possible occasion. During his years as Foreign Secretary Britain was at the peak of her international influence in the nineteenth century and his policies directly aided the development of her Empire. Abroad he tended to support liberal and anti-despotic movements—a support which usually coincided with Britain's own interests. At home he opposed any further changes in the parliamentary system after 1832 and he seemed to think that British 'democracy' was the best form of government, which other countries would do well to imitate.

The Belgian Revolution, 1830

In 1830 the Belgians rose in revolt against the Vienna settlement of 1815 which had united them with Holland. Their grievances were religious, economic and political; and there was little doubt that they were justified. They hoped for the assistance of the new King of the French, **Louis Philippe**, who had replaced the despotic Charles X in the revolution of 1830. In fact, the Belgian rising had been inspired in part by events in France. Palmerston sympathized with the Belgians, but at the same time he feared that *France might revive the old policy of control of Belgium* to the political and commercial disadvantage of Britain. There was, however, the danger that the eastern powers of Russia, Prussia and Austria would intervene to help **William I** of the United Netherlands, against his rebellious subjects. From the time of the Troppau Protocol their aim had been to prevent liberal revolutions gaining control of any European state. *Palmerston therefore aimed to preserve a peaceful balance of power in Europe and to solve*

182

the Belgian question. Together with the French foreign minister, Talleyrand, he now persuaded the Dutch and Belgians to accept an armistice, but the Belgian people then decided to choose as King of the Belgians, the **Duc de Nemours**, second son of Louis Philippe. Palmerston voiced strong objections and secured the election of the more acceptable **Leopold of Saxe-Coburg**, the uncle of the future Queen Victoria. The Dutch then began military operations against Belgium, and Palmerston agreed to assistance being given by French forces to the Belgians; but, together with Austria and Prussia, he secured the withdrawal of these forces as soon as the Dutch were repelled. In France Louis depended very much on good relations with Britain, which his middle-class supporters wanted, and a combined French and British force defeated the last remnants of the Dutch forces at Antwerp. It was not until 1839 that the Dutch accepted the **Treaty of London** in which the Great Powers guaranteed the independence and neutrality of Belgium—the treaty torn up by Germany in 1914.

Palmerston had achieved his aims of preventing French expansion and at the same time had shown the eastern powers that any move by them would mean a clash between themselves and Britain and France. In any case, revolutionary movements in Poland, Italy and the German states had kept the eastern powers well occupied. Thus Palmerston had employed the *'balance of power'* principle, had aided the Belgian revolution and maintained what he considered to be Britain's interests.

Portugal and Spain

Traditional British policy since the Treaty of Utrecht, which had confirmed our possession of Gibraltar and greatly increased British power in the Mediterranean, had been to ensure the independence of Portugal and Spain from any French intervention—especially any union of the thrones. In 1833 Palmerston secured the support of Louis Philippe against the would-be despotic pretenders to the Portuguese and Spanish thrones, **Don Miguel** and **Don Carlos** respectively. British naval power was used to support the constitutional parties, although Don Carlos later returned and the Carlist wars resulted in Spain. However, Palmerston had prevented any unilateral action by Louis Philippe, had supported the anti-despotic parties and had safeguarded British interests.

Mehemet Ali and the Middle East

The Middle East presented Palmerston with more complicated matters to deal with. So far Palmerston had succeeded in working with Louis Philippe, thus presenting a united front to the eastern powers, but the affair of Mehemet Ali produced strong Anglo-French conflict.

Mehemet Ali, ruler of Egypt for the Sultan of Turkey, had assisted the latter in the Greek War of Independence on condition of receiving the Morea in southern Greece and the island of Crete. After the Turkish defeat Mehemet Ali demanded part of Syria and, when this was refused, he sent an army under his son **Ibrahim Pasha** into that country. Ibrahim defeated the Turks at the **Battle of Koniah**. The Sultan then appealed for help to **Nicholas I** of Russia, who sent Russian troops to protect Constantinople. This 'protection' alarmed Palmerston, who then persuaded Louis Philippe to agree to a joint Anglo-French naval force being dispatched to the Aegean Sea to help persuade the Sultan to make peace with Mehemet Ali, who gained control of Syria and Palestine. In this case he had supported outright aggression rather than see Russian intervention in Turkey. However, the Czar had made an important gain by the **Treaty of Unkiar Skelessi** of **1833** with the Sultan. By this secret treaty, the Sultan agreed to close the straits leading from the Aegean into the Black Sea to the warships of all nations except those of Russia. Palmerston's agents got to know of this agreement and he determined to undo it as soon as possible.

So far, Palmerston had maintained the working alliance with Louis Philippe, but the crisis of 1839–1841 brought this to breaking-point. In 1839 the Turks launched an invasion of Syria, but the army of Mehemet Ali, re-organized since 1833 mainly by French officers, inflicted a crushing defeat on the Turks, and the whole question was thus re-opened. Louis Philippe and his Prime Minister, **Thiers**, were hoping to gain part of Syria for France in reward for their services. Palmerston's aim was now to prevent French expansion into Syria and also to prevent Russia intervening alone on the side of the Turks. He summoned a meeting of the Great Powers in London, omitting France. **The Convention of London**, signed by Britain, Russia, Austria and Prussia, offered concessions to Mehemet Ali which he rejected. British forces captured Acre on the Syrian coast and Alexandria was bombarded. Against a combination of the Great Powers Mehemet Ali's position was hopeless. Syria and Crete were returned to Turkey, but Mehemet Ali was recognized as hereditary ruler of Egypt.

Palmerston had (1) strengthened the Turks, (2) prevented unilateral action by Russia, (3) thwarted the expansionist schemes of Thiers in the Middle East, and (4) safeguarded British trade in the Middle East and the overland route to India.

Palmerston, having supported the Turks, persuaded them to undo the Treaty of Unkiar Skelessi with Russia. By the **Straits Convention** of **1841**, (to which France was now a party) the Sultan agreed to close the entrance to the Black Sea to the warships of all nations in time of peace.

Palmerston's Policy in the Far East

In 1839 the Chinese government, in an effort to stop the opium trade, in which the East India Company had an interest, seized a number of cargoes at Canton and placed an embargo on British trade. Palmerston's reply was the bombardment of Canton by British warships. Although Palmerston was out of office during Peel's second ministry, the **Treaty of Nanking (1842)** was a direct result of his policies. **Hong Kong** *was leased to Great Britain and five* **'treaty ports'** *were opened to British traders.* The Chinese paid £6,000,000 compensation for British losses from the seizures and embargo. Despite attacks on him by Cobden, Bright and Gladstone in the Commons, Palmerston remained popular.

During his first period as Prime Minister (1855–1858), Palmerston's policies involved Britain in further conflict with China. The Chinese had refused to make the opium trade legal in 1842, and in 1856 they seized the opium-running vessel the *Arrow*, which had English registration and a Chinese crew. The French were also involved in conflict with China, and a joint Anglo-French naval force bombarded Tientsin in 1858. The Chinese were forced to legalize the opium trade by the **Treaty of Tientsin, 1858**, and more ports were opened to British and French traders. Russia at the same time seized all Chinese territory to the north of the Amur River. Despite fierce criticism of him by his opponents, Palmerston was popular with his middle-class supporters for his protection and promotion of British commercial interests, however ruthless the methods. In the General Election of 1858 Palmerston was delighted to see the pacifist Free Traders Cobden and Bright both lose their seats.

The Spanish Marriages

Towards the end of his reign Louis Philippe, under pressure from royalist interests in France, wished to marry one of his sons to Queen Isabella of Spain, but British opposition led to an agreement that the Queen should marry a Spanish cousin and, after she had had children, Louis Philippe's son would marry her sister. This would prevent the children of the second marriage succeeding to the throne. Palmerston became Foreign Secretary again in 1846 after the fall of Peel and was soon faced with another direct challenge to the traditional British policy over the union of France and Spain. Queen Isabella married a cousin who was unlikely to beget children and at the same time her sister married Louis Philippe's son, the **Duc de Montpensier**. Palmerston roused great opposition in Britain to this trickery of Louis Philippe, and the official friendship of Britain and France, on which the King had relied in his earlier years, was shaken. The King had much opposition in France itself over this episode and it added to those causes which were to bring his downfall in 1848.

Palmerston and the Year of Revolutions, 1848

The year 1848 was one of great importance in European history, when liberal revolutions broke out in France, in the Italian provinces of the Austrian Empire, as well as in Hungary and in Vienna itself. The Czechs also challenged their Austrian rulers by a revolution in Prague.

British foreign policy in 1848 under Palmerston's direction was a mixture of self-interest and genuine sympathy with the cause of continental liberalism. British assistance took rather indirect forms, for example, when British arms were allowed to reach the people of Sicily in their struggle against the tyrannical **King of Naples, Ferdinand II**. But, beyond protests, Palmerston did nothing when the Hungarian patriots were crushed by the invading armies of Nicholas I of Russia. Palmerston was not anxious to see the Austrian Empire break up, thus opening the Balkans to Russian influence. However, he had to take account of public opinion; and when **General Haynau**, who had been responsible for brutal reprisals against the Hungarians, was chased by the workers at Barclay and Perkins brewery in the Mile End Road (which he was visiting), Palmerston expressed sympathy with the chasers. This annoyed Queen Victoria—an annoyance further increased when Palmerston sent a report to the Austrian government on this incident without consulting her. At this time, also, Palmerston recognized the new French Republic, and this to a certain extent was a warning to the eastern powers not to intervene against France. *Palmerston was still concerned with the balance of power in Europe*, and for this purpose the friendship of France was necessary. Palmerston knew that any use of British land forces in Europe to support revolutionary régimes would lead to a general war, which he was anxious to avoid.

The Don Pacifico Case, 1850

For some years the Greek government had failed to meet its debts to British traders and relations between Britain and Greece were bad. **Don Pacifico** was a Portuguese Jew born in Gibraltar and thus a British citizen. His house in Athens was attacked and destroyed by a mob, and the Greek government refused to pay the £20,000 compensation which he demanded. Palmerston took up the case and, receiving no satisfaction from the Greek government, *he ordered a British naval force to bombard* **the Piraeus**, the port of Athens, and to seize some Greek vessels as a guarantee of payment. This high-handed action annoyed Russia and France, who were both guarantors, with Britain, of Greek independence but had not been consulted by Palmerston. In the House of Commons Palmerston's opponents, led by Gladstone, launched a fierce attack upon him, but the censure motion was defeated. In a five-hour speech Palmerston defended his whole policy since 1830 and, in regard to Don Pacifico, he made his famous comparison with the rights of the citizens of the ancient Roman Empire to protection and the similar rights of British subjects—'As the Roman in days of old held himself free from indignity when he could say *"Civis Romanus sum"* so also a British subject, in whatever land he may be, shall feel confident that the watchful eye and strong arm of England will protect him against injustice and wrong.' He then went on to coin the phrase *'Civis Britannicus sum'*.

Palmerston and France under Louis Napoleon

In December 1851 Louis Napoleon became President of France after a *coup d'état*. Palmerston congratulated the French Ambassador in London before consulting either the Queen or the Prime Minister, so Lord John Russell dismissed him. In 1852 Palmerston's supporters in the Commons defeated Russell, who was compelled to resign. In 1855, Palmerston became Prime Minister with the avowed purpose of retrieving the mismanagement of the Crimean War, which he did efficiently (see p. 194). The Queen had been offended over the recognition of Napoeon III without being consulted, for both she and Prince Albert thought correctly that the monarch had the constitutional right to be informed and consulted about foreign policy. Nevertheless, Palmerston, in his eagerness to maintain the friendship of France, had acted high-handedly.

Italy and Austria 1859–1865

In this period Palmerston was Prime Minister and Lord John Russell Foreign Secretary, but Palmerston's policies continued to be followed. in **1858**, by the **Compact of Plombières**, Napoleon had agreed to assist the Italian struggle for liberation from Austria, and in **1859** defeated the Austrians at the **Battles of Magenta and Solferino** in northern Italy. Then Napoleon suddenly retired by making the **Peace of Villafranca** with the Austrians, much to the disgust of the Italians. The Kingdom of Sardinia, whose Prime Minister, **Count Cavour**, had made the pact with Napoleon at Plombières, gained Lombardy, but not Venetia or the small states of Parma, Modena and Tuscany. However, the latter took matters into their own hands and by plebiscites decided on union with Sardinia. At this point Palmerston's Foreign Secretary made it clear that any Austrian armed intervention against

PALMERSTON

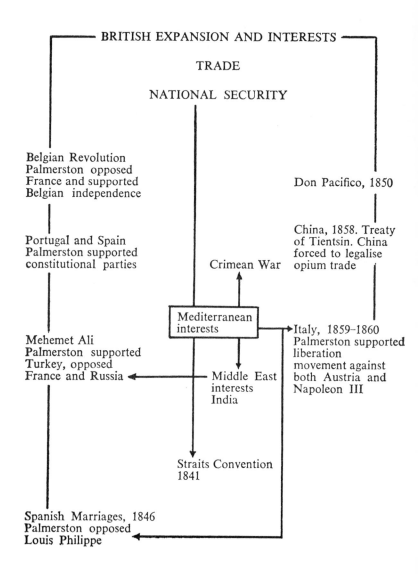

BRITISH EXPANSION AND INTERESTS

TRADE

NATIONAL SECURITY

Belgian Revolution
Palmerston opposed
France and supported
Belgian independence

Don Pacifico, 1850

China, 1858. Treaty
of Tientsin. China
forced to legalise
opium trade

Portugal and Spain
Palmerston supported
constitutional parties

Crimean War

Mediterranean
interests

Italy, 1859–1860
Palmerston supported
liberation
movement against
both Austria and
Napoleon III

Mehemet Ali
Palmerston supported
Turkey, opposed
France and Russia

Middle East
interests
India

Straits Convention
1841

Spanish Marriages, 1846
Palmerston opposed
Louis Philippe

them would be opposed by Britain. It was also a warning to Napoleon III to accept the situation in Italy; and, in view of the concern for Italian liberty which he had avowed, he dared not risk a clash with Britain. In this way Palmerston's policies directly aided the Italian cause.

Similarly, when **Garibaldi** and his **'Redshirts'** seized control of Sicily in 1860 and prepared to cross the Straits of Messina to the mainland, Napoleon III's desire to prevent them marching against the Pope in Rome was opposed by Palmerston, and Napoleon III gave up the idea. British warships had already been at Marsala in Sicily where Garibaldi's force made its first landing under their cover. The British navy in the Mediterranean was the decisive factor in Palmerston's diplomacy at this point. It was claimed for Palmerston that Britain had thus aided the cause of Italian freedom, but another important factor was that Palmerston saw a united Italy as a future ally of Britain and a counterweight to French power in the Mediterranean.

The American Civil War 1861–1865

In 1861 the American Civil War broke out between the northern states and the slave-holding south. Palmerston's official policy was neutrality, but in fact two breaches of this neutrality occurred, one by the Americans and one by Britain. In 1861 two southern agents travelling to Europe in the British ship the *Trent* were seized by Northerners. Palmerston protested at this action against a vessel of a neutral state, and troops were sent to Canada in preparation for action against the northern states. This brought an apology from **President Lincoln** and the two agents were released. Palmerston himself had definite sympathies with the southern cause, which his action in this case seemed to demonstrate, as it also did in the famous *Alabama* case. The southern states had ordered the building of this vessel at Birkenhead as an unarmed merchant ship, but it was so constructed that it could be rapidly converted into a warship. The Northerners got to know of this, but the ship had sailed before the order from the British government to stop building arrived. Both Palmerston and Russell were severely criticized in the Commons for their failure to act more promptly. Once again, Palmerston's liking for the Southerners caused suspicions to arise.

Palmerston and Prussia under Bismarck

In 1864 Prussia and Austria combined to force the Danes to give up the provinces of **Schleswig-Holstein,** despite the fact that Palmerston had previously assured the Danes of British support if attacked. No such support came and Schleswig went to Prussia and Holstein to Austria. In 1866 Prussia defeated Austria in the **Seven Weeks' War** and took over both territories. The Prussian **Chancellor Bismarck** had *'called Palmerston's bluff'*, for he had correctly estimated in 1864 that Britain would not intervene. Palmerston had chosen an unfortunate moment to encourage the Danes to resist. Bismarck had won the support of Russia in 1864 partly because he had helped to suppress the Polish revolt against Russian control in 1863. Austria was at that time his ally, while Napoleon III was involved in the effort to set up an Empire under his protection in Mexico. *Thus the Balance of Power in Europe had shifted decisively towards Prussia, and Palmerston could do nothing about it.* When he died in 1865 new conditions were developing in Europe which were to force Britain into isolation from the affairs of Europe.

Summary

Palmerston entered Parliament in 1806, the year after the battle of Trafalgar which ensured Britain's naval superiority during the remainder of Palmerston's career. Much of his effectiveness was based on British naval power in the Mediterranean, the Atlantic and the Far East, and we have seen instances of its employment in all these spheres —the Spanish and Portuguese question, the Mehemet Ali episodes, the Don Pacifico case, the opium wars against the Chinese. It was used as a threat at certain other junctures, especially during the period of Italian unification. He based his policies on Britain's power and commercial self-interest and used the balance of power principle to prevent a major war in Europe and to prevent the domination of Europe by any one power. This led him to support liberal movements abroad in so far as they did not lead to a failure in the balance of power or, as in the case of Belgium, actually served British political and commercial interests. His sympathy with liberal movements abroad was partly based on his conviction that the British limited monarchy and parliamentary system was the best ever devised, and any countries which overthrew despotism and established an elective parliamentary system must be friendly to Britain and must help Europe to resist the despotism and ambitions of the Russian Czars. On the other hand, if a form of dictatorship, such as that of Napoleon III, served British purposes as an ally, he was ready to support it. His policy was adaptable, forceful and ruthless; and it helped the expansion of British trade and commerce and of the Empire. This made him a popular figure in the early Victorian period. He was the incarnation of 'John Bull'.

Palmerston's foreign policy contained traditional eighteenth century elements of the balance of power, involved support for a number of national movements of liberation (especially when they were in line with British interests), and the support of British commercial and naval power at all costs and sometimes with injustice. He was high-handed, he failed to consult the Sovereign when he should have done, but he was immensely popular in Britain, especially with the middle class who benefited most from his policies. At the end of his career, however, new forces were arising abroad, especially in Germany, which he could not control and Britain was on the eve of her 'splendid isolation'.

Important Dates

1830	**Belgian Revolution.**
1833	**British intervention in Spain and Portugal.**
	Mehemet Ali gains control of Syria and Palestine.
	Treaty of Unkiar-Skelessi.
1830–1832	**Revolutionary movements in Germany, Italy and Poland.**
1839	**Turks defeated by Mehemet Ali.**
	Convention of London.
1841	**The Straits Convention.**
1846	**The Spanish Marriages.**
1848	**Revolutions in Europe.**
1850	**Don Pacifico case.**
1851	**Palmerston congratulated Napoleon on gaining power.**
	Dismissal of Palmerston.
1855	**Palmerston Prime Minister.**
	Crimean War in progress.
1856	**The 'Arrow' incident.**
1858	**Treaty of Tientsin.**
1860	**Garibaldi and the 'Redshirts'.**
1861	**American Civil War.**
	'Trent' case.
1863	**'Alabama' case.**
1864	**Prussia and Austria attack Denmark.**
1865	**Death of Palmerston.**

QUESTIONS

(1) Show how British interests were involved in Palmerston's policy towards (a) *the Belgian Revolution, 1830,* (b) *Mehemet Ali in 1833 and 1839,* (c) *Italian unification, 1860.*

(2) What were the causes of conflicts with Greece and China during Palmerston's time?

(3) Describe Palmerston's dealings with either France or Russia from 1830 to 1865.

(4) Why was Palmerston under constant attack by Gladstone and his supporters?

(5) How would you account for Palmerston's popularity in Britain?

CHAPTER NINETEEN

THE CRIMEAN WAR
1853–1856

HE **Crimean War** of **1853–1856** was the first major war since 1815, and it brought to an end nearly forty years of international peace between the great powers. The war fits into the pattern of British foreign policy in the nineteenth century and is part of its anti-Russian aspect. We have already seen how Palmerston did everything possible to prevent Russia having her own way in the Balkans and the Middle East. But Britain felt her interests were also threatened on the Indian frontier, especially in Afghanistan. General feeling was strongly anti-Russian in Britain in the early Victorian period, mainly because **Nicholas I** was regarded as the embodiment of tyranny and reaction, especially after his intervention in Hungary in 1849.

Immediate Causes of the Crimean War

Russian policy was looking towards the complete break-up of the Turkish (Ottoman) Empire, which Nicholas referred to as 'the sick man of Europe'. In 1844 he visited Britain and suggested that Britain and Russia should settle the question between them: Britain to take Egypt and Crete, and Russia Constantinople. He also proposed that Russia should assume the role of protector of Wallachia and Moldavia, Serbia and Bulgaria, when they were removed from Turkish control. Such proposals would have meant a great extension of Russian power —including the control of the Balkans and Constantinople and free access for her warships to the Mediterranean; and they were distrusted in official circles in Britain.

The Holy Places

France under Napoleon III was also drawn into the Eastern Question. In 1853 Napoleon III persuaded the Sultan of Turkey to recognize the claims of French Catholic monks to the guardianship of the Holy Places in Palestine which were associated with the life of Christ—a guardianship which they had been forced to abandon to the Greek Orthodox Church at the time of the French Revolution. The Czar Nicholas at once opposed the French and sent a demand to Constantinople that Russia should be recognized as the protector of all Orthodox

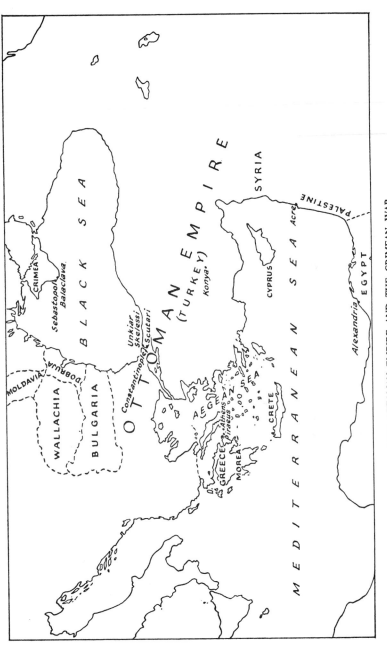

THE OTTOMAN EMPIRE AND THE CRIMEAN WAR

Christians in the Turkish Empire. In Constantinople itself the British Ambassador, **Lord Stratford de Redcliffe**, who in fact wanted a peaceful settlement, was opposed by the equally determined Russian Ambassador, **Prince Menschikoff**. The government at home under **Lord Aberdeen** was mild and peacefully-inclined, but de Redcliffe virtually took matters into his own hands and encouraged the Sultan to stand fast against the Russian demands, but urged them not to break off negotiations. In July 1853, the Russians moved troops into the Turkish provinces of Moldavia and Wallachia. A conference of Britain, Austria, France and Prussia in Vienna put forward proposals which the Turks, urged on by Stratford de Redcliffe, rejected; and *in October 1853, Turkey declared war against Russia*. The Russians then sank the Turkish fleet in the Black Sea and began a general invasion of the Balkans. *In March 1854, Britain and France declared war against Russia.*

The War

The Allied plan was to invade the Crimea and thus draw Russian forces from the Balkans. But things went badly wrong. Supplies to the troops broke down, there were disputes between the British and French commanders, and there was most inadequate provision for the troops against the rigours of a Crimean winter. Allied casualties were severe; and at the hospital at Scutari, across the Black Sea, the death-rate was enormous until **Florence Nightingale**, fully supported by Palmerston who became Prime Minister in 1855, broke through official obstruction and organized her band of nurses to care for the sick and wounded. *Within a short time she reduced the death-rate in the hospital by forty per cent.*

After landing in **September 1854**, the Allies (who included a contingent of Sardinian troops) won the **Battle of the Alma**, but failed to follow this with an attack on Sebastopol, now fortified by the Russian engineer, **Todleben**. The Russian counter-attacks were defeated at the battles of **Balaclava** and **Inkerman (both in 1854)**, despite the loss of six hundred men by the ill-fated charge of the **Light Brigade** at Balaclava under mistaken orders.

The war dispatches of *The Times* correspondent, **William Russell**, aroused indignation at home and resulted in Aberdeen being replaced by Palmerston in February 1855. Palmerston proceeded to clear up much of the mess of disorganization in the War Office and the supplies departments. In **September 1855**, the Allies captured the principal fort of **Sebastopol**, the Malakoff (Redoubt), and the Russians evacuated Sebastopol itself and capitulated. Nicholas I died in March 1855, and his successor **Alexander II**, anxious for reforms in serf-ridden Russia, accepted an armistice.

The Treaty of Paris, 30th March, 1856

(1) The Black Sea was prohibited to the warships of all nations and the Russians were not permitted to build any naval or military installations on its shores. (2) The Danube was made an international waterway and the Black Sea was also to be free to all merchant vessels. (3) The provinces of Moldavia and Wallachia were to have their own government while recognizing the suzerainty of Turkey. (4) Russia was to abandon her claims to protect the Orthodox Christians in the Turkish Empire, but Turkey was asked to give an undertaking of better treatment for her Christian subjects.

The allied aims had been achieved—*the Turkish Empire was intact and the Russians had been thrown back from the Balkans and the Mediterranean.* Napoleon III had avenged 1812 and was able to pose as the supporter of national independence for the Balkan territories of the Turks, to protect Catholic interests and to make Paris once again the diplomatic centre of Europe. Britain had resisted the Russian advance and protected the overland route through the Middle East to India (a route not now as important as it used to be) and had safeguarded her Mediterranean interests.

But the arrangements of Paris did not last long. In 1858 Moldavia and Wallachia formed the **Kingdom of Rumania**, and in 1871 Russia, with Prussian support, repudiated the Black Sea clauses. The Sultan continued to mis-rule his Christian subjects.

Summary

The Crimean War was one part of the whole Eastern Question during the nineteenth century. It involved the relationship and claims of Russia and her opposing powers with the weak Turkish (Ottoman) Empire at the centre of the problem. The traditional policy of Britain to safeguard the integrity of the Turkish Empire and the respective ambitions of Napoleon III and Czar Nicholas I were the basic causes of the conflict, to which there were other contributory factors. The war itself was wasteful of life and resources and produced shocking scandals of military and organizational incompetence. The results as seen in the Treaty of Paris, 1856, were only effective for a short time. Whether such a war had any real justification has always been a matter of dispute.

Important Dates

1853 July: Russians invaded Moldavia and Wallachia.
**   October: Turkey declared war on Russia.**
1854 March: Britain and France declared war against Russia.

September: Allies landed in the Crimea.
Battle of the Alma.
Battle of Inkerman.
Battle of Balaclava and the charge of the Light Brigade.

1855   March: death of Nicholas I.
September: Allies captured Sebastopol.

1856   March: Treaty of Paris.

QUESTIONS

(1) *What interests had Britain and France in entering the Crimean War?*

(2) *Why was it such an unsatisfactory campaign?*

(3) *What were the terms of the Treaty of Paris, 1856?*

CHAPTER TWENTY

INDIA FROM 1800 TO THE MUTINY, 1857

Pɪᴛᴛ's India Act of 1784 led to a more forward political policy in India. More men and money for expansion were put at the disposal of the Governors-General. In 1799 the **Marquess Wellesley** defeated Tipoo Sultan of Mysore at Seringapatam in reply to his efforts to restore French influence. Wellesley also gained control for Britain of the Carnatic and a part of Oudh. This annexationist policy was continued under the governorship of Lord Hastings when part of Nepal was annexed and the Mahrattas suffered defeat. Under **Lord William Bentinck (Governor-General 1828–1835)** important social reforms were introduced. He suppressed the practice of *suttee*, by which the widows of Hindus were burned on their husbands' funeral pyres. He also suppressed the *thugs*, a caste of religious assassins in the north-west territories. At the same time he greatly increased the use of the English language in both education and administration. **Lord Auckland (1836–1842)**, carrying out Palmerston's general line of foreign policy, had to deal with Russian pressures on Afghanistan. He deposed the pro-Russian ruler, **Dost Mohammed**, and a British force occupied the capital, Kabul. But a rising in favour of Dost Mohammed led to the retreat of the English forces, who were massacred as they attempted to retreat through the Khyber Pass. This was a serious setback for Britain in the **First Afghan War**.

British expansion within India continued with the annexation of Sind in 1843 and of the whole of the Punjab in 1849. In 1852 the whole of Southern Burma also came under British control. Thus the years 1800 to 1856 were a time of imperial expansion by Britain, and it was a period when commercial power was more forcefully, and at times ruthlessly, supported by arms. This was the background to the assumption of the Governor-Generalship by one of the most important British administrators of the nineteenth century, **Lord Dalhousie (1848–1856)**.

Dalhousie's Policies in India

Dalhousie's policies are closely related to the outbreak of the **Mutiny** in **1857**. There were two aspects of his policy: (1) to extend further

British political control wherever possible, and (2) to 'westernize' India. Both of these caused much opposition in India. Dalhousie revived the old native *'Doctrine of Lapse'* by which a state would come under the control of the ruling power if its own ruler died without natural heirs. A number of Indian states were thus taken over by Britain. In the case of Oudh, however, this was annexed in 1856 because of the brutality of its king. To Dalhousie, western education and science were absolutely essential for India, and he encouraged the introduction of schools run on western lines, of railways, telegraphs, roads and canals. He also encouraged the introduction of British industrial methods into India.

Causes of the Mutiny

(1) British expansion caused considerable discontent, especially among a number of the princes.

(2) Those princes remaining in power feared ultimate annexation. They also disliked the British policy of reducing taxation on the peasantry, for their power mainly depended on this. The native Indian landlords and tax-collectors were others who, for obvious reasons, disliked British rule.

(3) Economic opposition to Britain came from the old craft industries of India which were now feeling heavily the competition of British industrial wares, especially cotton cloth. The domestic spinning and weaving industries had been an additional source of income to the peasant, who was now becoming dependent solely on the land. This created a good deal of peasant opposition to Britain.

(4) The annexation of Oudh was a cause of discontent among the sepoys of the Bengal Army, many of whom came from Oudh.

(5) The mixing of castes, which the railway system entailed, was resented; as was also the abolition of certain religious customs, however cruel or superstitious in British eyes. The efforts of some officers of the Indian Army to convert their men to Christianity was deeply resented and caused a fear that this was to become general British policy.

(6) In 1856 there was much disaffection in the Bengal Army, in which Brahmin soldiers were expected to obey officers of a lower caste and also, if necessary, to serve overseas, which also entailed a loss of caste. The proportion of British to native officers was inadequate, and British officers frequently had no knowledge of the Bengali language.

(7) The sepoys learnt that the new cartridges for the Enfield rifles were greased with the mixed fat of the cow (sacred to the Hindus) and of the pig (unclean to the Moslems). This was the final religious spark which set alight the whole mutiny.

THE INDIAN MUTINY

CAUSES

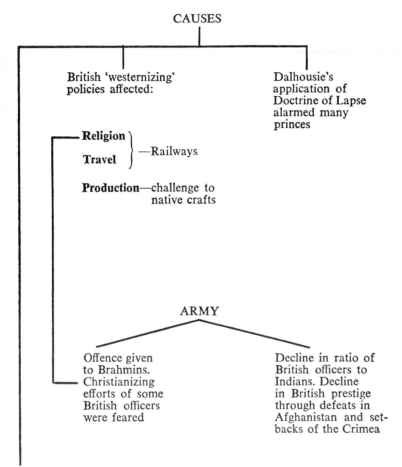

British 'westernizing'
policies affected:

Dalhousie's
application of
Doctrine of Lapse
alarmed many
princes

Religion
Travel
—Railways

Production—challenge to
native crafts

ARMY

Offence given
to Brahmins.
Christianizing
efforts of some
British officers
were feared

Decline in ratio of
British officers to
Indians. Decline
in British prestige
through defeats in
Afghanistan and set-
backs of the Crimea

GENERAL CHALLENGE BY WESTERN CIVILIZATION TO THE
LONG TRADITIONS AND PRACTICES OF INDIA

The Mutiny

The mutiny broke out at **Meerut** on **10th May, 1857,** when a number of Sepoys were imprisoned for refusing to use the greased cartridges, the heads of which had to be bitten off before use. The mutiny spread to **Delhi,** where the King of Delhi was proclaimed Emperor of India.

At Delhi the small British force held out for two months against superior numbers, but was eventually overcome. A relieving force from the Punjab under **John Nicholson** reached the city and attacked it. Nicholson was killed, but the city was taken after a week's fighting. Savage reprisals for the earlier massacre of British subjects followed, including the shooting without trial of the two sons of the proclaimed Emperor. At **Cawnpore** the whole of the British force was massacred by **Nana Sahib** after they had surrendered. Cawnpore was eventually re-taken by a force under **Sir Henry Havelock,** and savage reprisals followed. At **Lucknow** the besieged British force succeeded in holding out until relieved by Havelock. At home there were many who demanded wholesale revenge, but both the Queen and her Viceroy, **Lord Canning,** resisted these demands—hence his nickname of 'Clemency Canning'.

The mutiny had failed because the risings in different centres were unco-ordinated and no single national leader emerged. The heroic resistance of the British and the remarkable achievements of Nicholson and Havelock were of great importance. Lord Canning also succeeded in getting the timely help of British troops who were on their way to China. Britain was also aided by lack of unanimity among the princes. The Nizam of Hyderabad and the rulers of Nepal and Gwalior supported the British, as did the Sikhs of the Punjab.

Results of the Mutiny

By the **Government of India Act,** passed by **Lord Derby's** government in **1858**: (1) The Crown took over all the powers of the East India Company; (2) India was to be governed by a Secretary of State for India and a Council of fifteen members; (3) A Viceroy was to govern on instructions from home, with the aid of an Executive and Legislative Council.

Queen Victoria issued a proclamation in November 1858, which promised that India would be governed in the interests of all its peoples and an amnesty was granted to all rebels except those convicted of murder.

The lasting results of the Mutiny were bad. The abolition of the East India Company was inevitable, but the purpose was to make more sure than ever that Britain was in effective control of India. Few Indians gained responsible positions before 1914, when only one-twentieth of important civil service posts were occupied by Indians. In the Indian Army the proportion of British officers was increased to about one-third.

Summary

The Indian Mutiny was the first great challenge to British imperialism in modern times and was extremely dangerous to Britain's power. The causes were a number of national and religious grievances and, in some cases, the selfish interests of the Indian princes. British administration had, in its eagerness to 'westernize', given considerable offence to Indian traditions at the very time when the organization of the army in India was reducing the actual influence of British officers and soldiers. The Mutiny witnessed heroism and atrocity on both sides and was one of the most savage conflicts of the century. It left a permanent mark on Anglo-Indian relations. The reforms introduced after the Mutiny were long overdue.

Important Dates

1848–1856   **Administration of Lord Dalhousie.**
1856   **Annexation of Oudh.**
    Brahmin soldiers to serve overseas.
1857   **May: Mutiny broke out at Meerut.**
    Siege of Delhi.
    Massacre of Cawnpore.
    Siege of Lucknow.
1858   **Government of India Act.**

QUESTIONS

(1) What were the main causes of the Mutiny?

(2) Why was the Mutiny such a great shock to the British public, and why did it fail?

(3) What changes were made by the Government of India Act, 1858?

CHAPTER TWENTY-ONE

THE SECOND REFORM BILL, 1867

For thirty years after the 1832 Reform Bill, only the Radicals and the Chartists had demanded a further extension of the vote. The new middle class, enfranchised in 1832, were against further change. The Whig leader, Lord John Russell, was nicknamed 'Finality Jack' because of his declaration that the 1832 Act was final.

However, certain important party changes in the mid-century brought parliamentary reform once again to the fore. The old Whig Party gradually changed into the Liberal Party, the leadership of which fell to Gladstone in 1868. Among the Radical members of the Liberal Party were a number of industrialists, such as John Bright and Richard Cobden, who wished to see the vote further extended. *Another factor was the rapid growth of the industrial towns since 1832*, producing a great number of skilled workers whom the radicals, and Gladstone himself, regarded as entitled by their education to vote in elections. Further, *the trade unions took up the cause of electoral reform, led by* the **London Trades Council** in **1866**.

The aged Russell became Prime Minister after Palmerston's death in 1865, with Gladstone as Chancellor of the Exchequer. The latter introduced a Reform Bill which lowered the £10 qualification of 1832 to £7, but it was too little for the radicals and too much for the right-wing of the Liberals led by **Robert Lowe**, who thoroughly distrusted the idea of popular democracy. Russell was defeated and resigned. He was succeeded by the Conservative leader, Lord Derby, in whose cabinet one of the most important men was Benjamin Disraeli.

The popular campaign now intensified and a demonstration, planned to take place in Hyde Park, resulted in the government closing the gates, whereupon they were broken down and the reform meeting was held. John Bright and his supporters also conducted a nation-wide campaign. Within the Conservative Party, Disraeli represented the more progressive and democratic elements, although he was not in favour of political power falling completely into the hands of the working class. But he was determined to gain credit for his party as the party of parliamentary reform against such opponents as Lowe. In March 1867, he introduced a Reform Bill which would have given the vote to all rate-paying householders in the towns; but, to counterbalance this increase in the popular vote, he introduced a number of so-called *fancy franchises*, by which persons with certain educational qualifications were to receive the vote and those who had certain property qualifications as well were to receive *two* votes. These latter clauses were, however, defeated, and the Second Reform Bill of 1867 was then passed with important amendments. The vote was now given to all rate-paying householders and to lodgers paying a £10 rental. In the counties the vote went to the £12 leaseholders. Boroughs with less than 10,000 inhabitants lost one M.P. and the forty-five seats thus liberated were distributed to the larger towns and counties.

Results of the Second Reform Bill

The electorate was doubled, about one million new voters being added to the rolls. *The new voters were mainly the skilled workers of the towns,* but in the countryside the agricultural workers were still unable to vote in elections, where the better-off farmers and the landlords still dominated the political scene. A small town of 10,000 inhabitants could still send a member to Parliament. However, the Act was progressive, and Robert Lowe and his supporters described it as a *'leap in the dark'* from which the danger of revolution might arise.

In the election of December 1868, Gladstone and the Liberals (who claimed the credit for having defeated the *fancy franchise* suggested at first by Disraeli) won the day, despite the fact that it was a Conservative ministry which had introduced and passed the Second Reform Bill. This was a blow for Disraeli, who had become Prime Minister in February 1868, in place of Lord Derby.

The working class—or at least a section of it—gained the vote for the first time. In the towns they supported the new Liberal party led by Gladstone, who became Prime Minister later in 1868 and who was pledged to important social reforms.

Summary

The various pressures which produced the Second Reform Bill of 1867 were derived from the radical and working-class agitation in combination with the attempts of the two main parties to outpace one another. The death of Palmerston in 1865 and the accession of Russell to the leadership produced important changes in the Whig party—changes in a more democratic direction—which were accelerated by the succession of Gladstone to the leadership in 1868. A stiff political fight took place between the anti-democratic right wing of the party led by Robert Lowe and the sections favouring an extension of the franchise led by Gladstone, Bright, Cobden, and others. Disraeli succeeded in taking advantage of these divisions to bring in the Second Reform Bill from the Conservative side. The most important change under the Bill of 1867 was that for the first time the franchise went to a section of the working class.

Important Dates

1865 Death of Palmerston.
1866 Popular agitation by London Trades Council.
Hyde Park demonstration.
Derby became Prime Minister with Disraeli, Chancellor of the Exchequer.
1867 March: Second Reform Bill introduced by Disraeli.
'Fancy franchises' removed.
1868 Feb: Disraeli succeeded Lord Derby as Prime Minister.
Liberal victory at General Election in December.

QUESTIONS

(*1*) *What political circumstances brought about the Second Reform Act?*

(*2*) *What were the main changes under the Act?*

CHAPTER TWENTY-TWO

WILLIAM EWART GLADSTONE
CAREER TO 1868

Early Career

THE son of a Liverpool merchant and West Indian slaveowner, Gladstone was elected for Newark in 1832 under the reformed system. He served as Vice-President of the Board of Trade under Peel between 1841 and 1846 and was a fervent supporter of Peel's free-trade policies.

Gladstone's First Budget, 1853

He became Chancellor of the Exchequer in Lord Aberdeen's government of 1852–1855, a coalition between Whigs and Peelite Conservatives. Gladstone's grasp of finance was brilliant, and he could make financial matters interesting to his listeners, however detailed and difficult.

In his first budget he reduced or abolished import duties on more than two hundred trading items, mainly foodstuffs and partly-manufactured articles. *He also introduced higher duties on inherited land and fortunes*—this became, in fact, a stock-in-trade of Liberal finance during the nineteenth century. Income tax was extended to sections of the middle class so far unaffected by it; but at the same time he expressed the hope that, with the expansion of trade, income tax would be abolished. The costs of the Crimean War and of the Indian Mutiny were, however, to frustrate this aim. In 1854 he was compelled to double the rate of income tax to meet the costs of the Crimean War.

In Palmerston's second government, 1859–1865, Gladstone was again Chancellor of the Exchequer.

The Budget of 1860

This embodied all the main principles of Gladstonian financial and trading policies. Already in 1860, Richard Cobden had been sent to the France of Napoleon III to negotiate the **Cobden Treaty**, which provided for lowered duties by the French on imports from Britain in return for lower duties by Britain on French wines, and the actual abolition of almost all duties on French manufacturers coming into Britain. *Gladstone's budget went on to abolish import duties on 375 imports*, leaving only 48 on which duties were now charged. *Since Peel's first budget of 1841 over one thousand customs duties had been abolished.* In order to meet the loss of revenue, income tax was increased from 9d. to 10d. in the pound.

Gladstone determined to remove the remaining paper duties— 'taxes on knowledge' as he described them, which hampered the development of popular education and information. The House of Lords threw out the **Paper Duties Repeal Bill**, but Gladstone got round this by introducing one Finance Bill which included the Paper Duties Repeal Bill as well as the budget. If the Lords had rejected the whole budget they would have been challenging the right of the Commons to control financial affairs; and Gladstone would undoubtedly have taken measures to reduce the powers of the Lords. This they could not risk, and gave in. *The repeal of the paper duties greatly aided the development of popular newspapers and journals of all kinds.*

Gladstone's Economic Philosophy

He believed in liberating capitalist enterprise from as many restrictions as possible, and it was a great disappointment to him that he was not able to abolish income tax in the budget of 1860, as he had hoped and expected in 1853. He also opposed large government expenditures which would lead to government borrowing from the City of London—he disliked the idea of the 'City' having a financial stake in the government, thus depriving it of a healthy independence. For a nation to spend beyond its means was immoral. He also encouraged thrift in private life—the philosophy of 'self-help'—and in **1861** he established the **Post Office Savings Bank**. He also thought that wars should be paid for out of taxes, not by City borrowings, and this would make governments think twice before indulging in war. He wished to see the working class share in the general prosperity which he was sure would come with free trade and low taxation. Wages, he thought, would find their natural level in a free economic system.

Results of Gladstone's Policies

The results were for many years of great benefit to Britain. His policies aided enormously the expansion of trade and industry. Between 1850 and 1870 Britain's exports rose four times and imports three times. Exports of the great staple industries of iron and steel rose by 250 per cent. In the same period the purchasing power of the working class rose by one third. These developments were not purely the result of Gladstone's finance; but his great achievement was that he removed every possible obstacle to the expansion of Britain's industry and trade and estimated brilliantly the possibilities of mid-Victorian Britain.

Summary

Up to 1868 Gladstone was mainly concerned, as a member of various administrations, with the economic and financial affairs of the country. His budgets continued to develop the free trade principles begun by Sir Robert Peel in the government of 1841–1846, when he himself was at the Board of Trade. His principles of self-help, individualism and low taxation of earned incomes, pleased the rising manufacturers. His removal of the paper duties liberated the Press for popular publications and facilitated the extension of knowledge to wider sections of the people. The huge expansion of Britain's trade in the mid-Victorian period was greatly aided by his free trade measures.

Important Dates

1853 Gladstone's first budget abolished 100 import duties and increased inheritance duties.

1854 Crimean War. Income tax rate doubled.

1860 Budget leaves only 48 import duties.
Cobden Treaty with France.
Paper duties repealed.

1861 Post Office Savings Bank created.

1868 Gladstone becomes leader of Liberal Party.

QUESTIONS

(1) What were the main principles underlying Gladstone's financial policies?

(2) Why was Britain in a position to benefit from free trade in the mid-Victorian period?

CHAPTER TWENTY-THREE

GLADSTONE'S FIRST GOVERNMENT
1868–1874

THIS is the second great period of social reform in the nineteenth century after the Whig reforms of 1832–1841. Gladstone's attempts to solve the Irish question dominate the politics of the period 1870 to 1896, and it is convenient to give some attention to this. Although he never visited Ireland, he attempted to master the problem by assiduous study of every possible source, and he declared, *'My mission is to pacify Ireland.'*

Gladstone and Ireland

In **1848** the **Young Ireland Movement**, led by **John Mitchell** and **James Finlan Lalor**, had attempted to end the peasant-landlord system by a peasant rising and the seizure of the land on the classic model of 1789. Only sporadic risings occurred and these were suppressed by British troops and the leaders transported.

General conditions worsened. *Between 1848 and 1851 it is estimated that more than a million Irish died of starvation.* There was widespread creation of sheep-grazing farms on a large scale and reduction of corn land by half. Smallholders were turned off the land in thousands. This led to murder and arson directed against big farmers and landlords. These conditions led to the formation of the **Fenian Brotherhood,** dedicated to the gaining of Irish independence. This society was formed in **1852** with headquarters in New York. In 1866, a Fenian armed force invaded Canada, hoping for official American support because of American disputes with Britain arising from the Civil War, but it was quickly defeated. This was followed by a *campaign of terror by the Fenian movement in Britain.* In Manchester a prison van was attacked and some prisoners released. A policeman was killed in this affair and three Fenians were hanged—the **'Manchester Martyrs'** as they were called by the Brotherhood. In December, 1866, the wall of Clerkenwell prison was blown up in an effort to rescue some Fenian prisoners. Twelve persons were killed, and a hundred injured. All this prompted Gladstone to turn his urgent attention to Irish grievances.

Disestablishment of the Irish Church

Gladstone recognized the unjust position of the Anglican Church in Ireland, where four-fifths of the population were Catholic. The Church exacted tithe payments from its very widespread estates, and this was strongly resented by the preponderantly Catholic tenantry. The **Irish Church Bill** of **1869** removed state recognition from the Anglican Church in Ireland (*i.e.* it was disestablished). Its endowments were given to various charitable institutions such as hospitals and workhouses. Opposition to the Bill in the House of Lords was overcome by Queen Victoria's avowed support for it. This was the first of a number of piece-meal measures by which Gladstone at first hoped to remedy Irish grievances while maintaining the union with England.

The First Irish Land Act, 1870

Gladstone recognized the fundamental importance of the land question in Ireland. Some of the important features of the land system in Ireland were: (1) The existence of a large class of absentee Protestant landlords who lived in England and left their estates in the hands of agents or bailiffs—a very unpopular class in Ireland. (2) The absence of manufacturing industry made the Irish almost entirely dependent on the land; and this scramble for land led to subletting by tenants, which produced vast numbers of smallholdings of an uneconomic type, constant changes of tenure, and the shifting of tenants from one district to another in search of better land. (3) The landlords were not responsible for improving the land, which was left to the tenants, who promptly found their rents raised. (This discouraged improvement and led to the impoverishment of the soil.) (4) Eviction for non-payment of rent was widespread and the workhouses were full. (This led also to anti-landlord violence.) (5) A new type of speculative landlord began to appear in Ireland, whose eviction policies were more ruthless than those of the other landlords.

By the **Land Act** of **1870** Gladstone attempted to extend the 'Ulster custom' to the whole of Ireland. (1) A tenant was to be secure in his tenure while he paid his rent, and if removed for any other reason than non-payment, a scale of damages was to be established. (2) A tenant was to have the right to transfer his land to another tenant. (3) All rents should be 'fair'. A 'fair rent', however, was never clearly defined; and the Act, while bringing some improvement, was not really successful. (The bias of the courts towards the landlords was a hampering influence.) It was not successful in reducing violence, and Gladstone resorted to a **Coercion Act** in **1870** which gave special powers of arrest and trial to the authorities in Ireland.

The Home Rule Movement

In 1870 the **Irish Home Rule League** was formed to demand an end to the Union of 1801 and the setting up of an Irish Parliament to govern Irish affairs, but to leave trade and defence to Britain. In 1874, to the surprise and alarm of many supporters of the Union of 1801, *fifty-seven supporters of Home Rule were elected to Westminster* under their leader **Isaac Butt.**

Gladstone's Social Reforms

Between 1833 and 1858 the annual government grant to education had risen from £20,000 to £500,000; yet in 1861 the **Newcastle Commission** reported very unfavourably on the state of elementary education. The worst features of the situation were the absence of any effective education in the industrial areas and the appalling ignorance shown by otherwise intelligent children. This led to the introduction of the system of payment by results by the Secretary of Education, **Robert Lowe**, in 1861. Inspectors were to examine the children annually in a few basic subjects, and the school received its payments according to the number of its successes. This led to more efficiency, but much mechanical cramming. Yet the system lasted until 1897.

The government was concerned over elementary education for several reasons: (1) The Second Reform Bill of 1867 gave a section of the working class the franchise, and it was clear that further extension would come in the future. (Lowe's remark that it was necessary 'to compel our future masters to learn their letters' reflected the desire for a literate public.) (2) Continental education was in advance of Britain's, and Prussia's victory over France in 1870 was partly attributed to her highly organized elementary educational system. (3) Britain's industrial progress was seen to depend on the wider development of education, especially for the production of skilled workers. (4) Increasing interest was being shown in education; and before his death in **1861**, the **Prince Consort** had taken a leading part in the promotion of general and scientific education. Gladstone was influenced by all these factors.

The minister responsible for introducing the **Elementary Education Act, 1870** was **W. E. Forster.** The Act continued to give grants to the schools of the religious denominations, but also set up *School Boards* elected by the ratepayers. These boards were to levy rates and build schools where voluntary provision was insufficient. To meet religious objections, **Mr. Cowper-Temple** secured the passage of an amendment by which religious teaching in the board schools was to be restricted to the Bible and was to be free of any denominational instruction. Parents could withdraw their children from scripture lessons on religious grounds. The Boards fixed local school fees and could remit them altogether where they thought this necessary; and they also decided whether attendance should be compulsory in their districts. (It should be noted that in **1876** Disraeli's **Education Act** imposed fines for non-attendance without official consent. In 1880 the maximum age for compulsory attendance was fixed at thirteen years. In 1891 fees were abolished and, as we have seen, payment by results in 1897.)

Both Anglicans and Nonconformists showed varying degrees of opposition to the Act—they both distrusted the non-denominational state schools as breeders of 'paganism', while the Nonconformists were angered by Gladstone's strengthening of the position of the Anglican schools in areas where they were already dominant. The Act caused much religious controversy during the next fifty years, and at times both Nonconformists and Anglicans threatened to refuse to pay School Board rates.

The Endowed Schools Act and the Abolition of the University Test Act

In secondary education Gladstone also attempted to secure more efficiency and a wider grammar school curriculum. The **Endowed Schools Act** ensured the better use of funds left by former benefactors, and this was pleasing to the middle class which depended greatly on the public and grammar schools.

In the Universities, Gladstone brought about the abolition of the old University Test Act, affecting Oxford and Cambridge. Nonconformists had already been admitted to both universities, but they were still not allowed to take up scholarships, fellowships or other university posts. The **University Test Act** of **1871** allowed them to enter on the same terms as Anglicans—an example of Gladstone's belief in religious toleration.

Army Reforms

The Indian Mutiny, the Crimean War and the victory of Prussia over France in 1870 caused even the non-militaristic Gladstone to consider the state of the British forces, which had changed very little since Waterloo. Was the military system capable of the adequate defence of Britain, and could it carry the weight of British commitments all over the world? Investigation showed that it could not.

The man appointed by Gladstone as Secretary for War to carry through the army reforms was **Edward Cardwell**, who had had a long and distinguished political career. The main reforms were: (1) The Commander-in-Chief was put under the control of the Secretary for War and lost his over-independent position. (2) The Commander-in-Chief was now given command of all forces, regular and auxiliary, at home and abroad. (3) The Army's organization was now centralized at the War Office in order to produce a more efficient organization. (4) The private purchase and sale of commissions by officers was abolished, as it had retarded the recognition of merit and produced weaknesses in the army leadership. (5) The conditions of enlistment were greatly improved. (The period of twelve years service overseas was now reduced to six, with six in the home reserve.) Trades were also to be taught in the army. (6) Infantry regiments were re-organized into sixty-nine local districts and were to be known by local names and not just regimental numbers. In the same way the artillery regiments were localized.

To all these reforms there was much opposition by the old interests, strongly voiced in the House of Lords. Gladstone got round the Lords' opposition to the abolition of the purchase of Commissions by the issue of another Royal Warrant by Queen Victoria—the Royal Warrant having been the means by which the purchase system had been authorized. The reforms improved the efficiency of, and pride in, the armed forces, and attracted a better standard of recruit. Cardwell's work cost him much—his intense labours and the abuse he received undermined his health and he retired from politics in 1874.

The Trade Unions

Despite advances, the position of the trade unions before the law was still very weak; and the strike weapon could still lead to severe penalties being inflicted on the leaders because of the law against the 'coercion' of an employer or action 'in restraint of trade'. The unions had been forced to register themselves as Friendly Societies in order to allow their members sick benefits, which were also used to support members on strike. In 1867 a court ruling further weakened the trade unions' legal position. A trade union prosecuted its secretary for misappropriation of funds; but the judge ruled that, as the union was not a 'friendly society', its funds could not be protected by the law. *The unions now demanded full legal recognition as unions.* In 1867 another incident brought the trade union question to the fore, when action in Sheffield taken by strikers against non-strikers led to one man being killed. Other violent incidents caused the term *'Sheffield outrages'* to be used.

These events led Gladstone to appoint a commission of inquiry into the trade unions, and in **1871** the **Trade Union Act** and the **Criminal Law Amendment Act** were passed. By the first, the trade unions were given the clear legal right to own property and to have it protected by law, but the second angered trade unionists by making it illegal for strikers to 'obstruct', 'molest', 'intimidate' or even 'persistently follow' non-strikers. In other words, even 'peaceful picketing' was

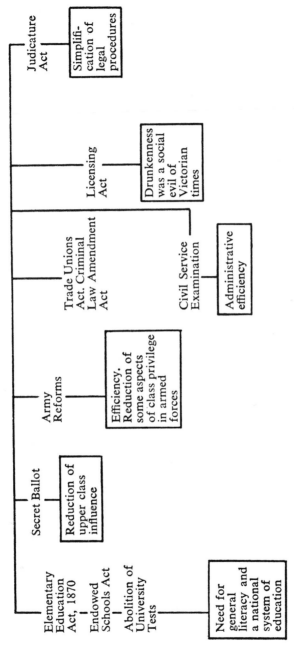

GLADSTONE'S FIRST GOVERNMENT
1868–1874

SOCIAL REFORM

Elementary Education Act, 1870 – Endowed Schools Act Abolition of University Tests
- Need for general literacy and a national system of education

Secret Ballot
- Reduction of upper class influence

Army Reforms
- Efficiency. Reduction of some aspects of class privilege in armed forces

Trade Unions Act. Criminal Law Amendment Act

Civil Service Examination
- Administrative efficiency

Licensing Act
- Drunkenness was a social evil of Victorian times

Judicature Act
- Simplification of legal procedures

IRELAND—Disestablishment of Irish Church
First Irish Land Act, 1870
1870, Home Rule League Formed

illegal. Thus Gladstone strengthened the trade unions in one direction, but weakened them in another.

Civil Service Reforms

With increasing legislation, government was becoming more complicated and required better administration, with many more civil servants. There was much admiration in Britain for the highly developed Prussian system of administration. *In Britain the old civil service was recruited almost entirely by family influence, and important posts were often held by semi-professionals who had other occupations as well.* The Utilitarians in Britain especially demanded less amateurism and more efficiency.

Gladstone's reforms aimed at reducing family influence by using the new techniques of the open competitive examination for posts in the Civil Service, except in the Foreign Office, where appointments were still made by recommendation. The result was an undoubted increase of efficiency and appointment by merit. The public schools supplied the main entrants for many years, but as the grammar schools developed in the twentieth century the way was open for wider recruitment from both the middle and working class.

The Secret Ballot, 1872

Gladstone was anxious to reduce bribery and intimidation in elections, which had continued after the two Reform Bills of 1832 and 1867. The new working-class voter of 1867 especially needed protection against the possibility of victimization by employers. Bribery would also be reduced in its more flagrant forms if the briber was not sure of the way the elector actually voted. The secret ballot already existed in Australia, with good results. Thus Gladstone advanced democracy by adopting one of the key demands of the earlier Chartists.

The Licensing Act, 1872

Gladstone was a preacher of thrifty and abstemious living, and the widespread drunkenness of mid-Victorian England horrified and alarmed him. The brewing interests were opposed to any regulation of the drink trade, and other opponents regarded any government regulation as a decrease of freedom. Even the Bishop of Peterborough preferred *'England free to England sober'*. However, Gladstone's Home Secretary, **Henry Bruce**, introduced legislation which fixed public-house closing times at twelve midnight in towns and eleven p.m. in the country. Regulations to prevent the adulteration of beer were introduced; and in areas where there were too many public houses, they were reduced.

The Supreme Court of Judicature Act, 1873

This act was designed to reduce the number of independent divisions of the high courts, which had made legal proceedings very expensive, long drawn-out and pettifogging. It established one Supreme Court of Judicature, divided into a Court of Appeal and a High Court of Justice. This consolidation led to greatly increased efficiency, which was the aim of so much of the other Gladstonian legislation we have noted.

Foreign Policy

Although Gladstone stressed in 1870 that Britain would defend Belgium if either Prussia or France broke the treaty of 1839, his foreign policy was widely attacked for apparent weakness. However, he was only recognizing that England could no longer play the role of a continental military power. Even in Palmerston's last years Britain's power in Europe had greatly diminished with the rise of Bismarck. Gladstone could only *protest* when Russia denounced the Black Sea clauses of the Treaty of Paris of 1856. Acting from a sincere wish for the peaceful settlement of international disputes, he agreed with the United States that an international commission should settle the dispute over the **Alabama**. The result was that Britain had to pay £3,250,000 in compensation to the U.S.A.

In 1873 Gladstone was defeated over an Irish Education bill, and in 1874 he resigned when differences developed in his own cabinet. In the election of 1874, Disraeli was returned to power, and the reasons for this are considered in the next chapter.

Summary

The period of Gladstone's first ministry was one of important social reform—probably the most important since the Whig reforms of 1832–1841. Gladstone's efforts to pacify Ireland were sincerely undertaken but bore little fruit. The education, civil service and army reforms were of exceptional importance; but the trade unions were not satisfied with Gladstone's approach to their problems. Their dissatisfaction partly accounts for his defeat in the towns in 1874. His reforms also aroused the widespread opposition of various 'vested interests', and his apparently tame foreign policy gave them a ready weapon of attack. Yet the period of his first government was one of considerable achievement in view of the weighty traditional interests which had to be overcome.

Important Dates

1868   **Gladstone Prime Minister.**

1869	Disestablishment of the English Church in Ireland.
1870	First Irish Land Act.
	Formation of the Irish Home Rule League.
	Elementary Education Act.
	Civil Service Reforms.
1870–1871	Army Reforms.
1871	The Trade Union Act.
	Criminal Law Amendment Act.
1872	Ballot Act.
	Licensing Act.
1873	Supreme Court of Judicature Act.

QUESTIONS

(*1*) *Why was reform in elementary education necessary?*

(*2*) *Describe Gladstone's Irish policy in this period.*

(*3*) *What was the nature of the land problem in Ireland?*

(*4*) *What were the conditions which made Cardwell's army reforms necessary?*

CHAPTER TWENTY-FOUR

DISRAELI'S SECOND GOVERNMENT
1874-1880

G LADSTONE'S defeat in 1874 could be attributed to the following factors: (1) The brewing interests, angered by the Licensing
Act, gave direct support to Conservative policy, even in the
public houses themselves. They denounced the attack on the working
man's beer. (2) The army reforms had exasperated the old army families, who had made great play of the dangers of Gladstone's methods
of using Royal Warrants and Orders in Council to get round the opposition to the House of Lords. Gladstone was represented as a danger
to democratic liberties. (3) The Education Act had annoyed the Nonconformists, many of whom had been loyal Whigs and Liberals up to
this time. (4) The trade unionists, many of whom had the vote under
the 1867 Reform Bill, were angered by Gladstone's Criminal Law
Amendment Act, which made peaceful persuasion of non-strikers
almost impossible. (5) Gladstone's foreign policy seemed to indicate
national weakness, and was resented in many quarters, especially by
those who had lived through the Palmerstonian era.

*Disraeli's aim was to show that progressive social reform was not
a monopoly of the Liberals and Radicals,* and in some ways his social
reforms were an advance on those of Gladstone. To Disraeli the new
'masses' were important and needed firmly anchoring to Conservatism.
His concern for social conditions, derived from his views of Tory
democracy, were sincere. At the same time he determined to strengthen
the power of the Empire wherever possible.

The new Home Secretary, **Richard Cross**, was the man relied upon
by Disraeli to bring about much-needed social reforms. He was in
many ways far ahead of the average member of the Conservative party
in his views of society. Above all, he understood the importance of
further undermining the old doctrine of *'laissez-faire'*.

The Artisans' Dwellings Act, 1875

This was the first direct government attack on bad housing, much
of which had arisen out of the Industrial Revolution. Cross was
anxious to carry through a determined attack on the worst aspects of
slum landlordism, but opposition in Parliament from both parties

forced him to modify his approach. He had wanted to *compel* local authorities to dispossess the worst landlords, but this was changed to the right of the local authorities to purchase and pull down insanitary dwellings, and build others. This right was exercised by an increasing number as time went on, and the Act was a clear indication that the government accepted the need for direct action.

The Public Health Act, 1875

Here more compulsion was employed. All previous regulations were codified and local authorities compelled to appoint Medical Officers of Health and Health Inspectors. They were also compelled to improve drainage, sewage-disposal, refuse collection and water-supply in their areas, and to destroy polluted foodstuffs. Infectious diseases were to be notified to the M.O.H.s, who were empowered to issue orders on how to deal with them. *This Act was the real beginning of the present-day local health services,* but even then many Conservatives and Liberals disliked this invasion of 'liberty' and referred to Disraeli's legislation as 'a policy of sewage'.

Conspiracy and Protection of Property Act, 1875

This replaced Gladstone's Criminal Law Amendment Act, and greatly improved the position of the trade unions. An action by a combination of workmen, such as withdrawing their labour, was legal if it were legal for an individual. Peaceful persuasion (picketing) of other workers to induce them to strike was now made legal.

The Trade Union Amendment Act, 1876

This was also an important gain for the trade unions, for a trade union was now clearly defined; and the old regulations of 1825, which had made strikes difficult on the grounds that they were 'in restraint of trade', were now removed.

Employers' and Workmen's Act, 1875

Under the old law, a worker who broke his contract with an employer was tried under criminal law and could be sentenced to a fine or imprisonment, whereas the employer had the civil law applied to him and had to pay damages. Under the new law they were both liable to civil penalties.

Factory Legislation

Disraeli's **Factory Act** of **1874** at last really limited the working day to ten hours as demanded by the earlier 'Ten-hours' Committee'. By the **Factory and Workshops Act** of **1878** workshops employing less than fifty workers, which had previously been left to rather unsatisfactory supervision by the local authorities, were now brought under inspection by government inspectors. As there were many thousands of such workshops in the country, this Act increased the protection given by factory legislation to the workers in them. At the same time all the laws relating to factories and workshops were now codified so that their application could be more efficient.

The Merchant Shipping Act, 1876

Samuel Plimsoll, M.P. for Derby took up the cause of the seamen who served in cramped and unhealthy conditions in overloaded ships—the 'coffin ships'. The insurance companies were also hit by extensive claims from shipowners whose vessels had sunk, often with the loss of entire crews. Despite opposition from the shipowners which nearly caused Disraeli to drop the proposed legislation, Plimsoll secured the acceptance of the load-line for ships—the **Plimsoll line**. Although its positioning on the vessel was left to the shipowner (the Board of Trade became responsible in 1890), this considerably lessened risks at sea. Plimsoll became president of the first seamen's trade union.

Enclosure of Commons Act, 1876

By this measure the enclosure of common land was prohibited unless it could be shown to be in the public interest. One famous result of this was *the saving of* **Epping Forest** *in 1878* as a recreation area for the people of London. The Act recognized the importance of recreation for the people, which the wide acceptance of the Saturday half-holiday and the great increase of cheap excursion trains had made possible.

The Education Act, 1876

This went further than the Act of 1870 and made parents, who kept their children away from school without official permission, liable to fines. This was a step towards compulsory elementary education.

Disraeli's Foreign and Imperial Policies

Disraeli was fascinated by the civilizations of the East, and he wished the destinies of the British Empire to be linked firmly with the East. In **1874** he acted in a completely unorthodox manner by borrowing £4,000,000 from the house of Rothschild to buy Britain a half-share in the **Suez Canal**, whose importance for trade and the Empire he clearly saw. He was severely criticized in Parliament for not having consulted his own Cabinet, but his action was popular in the country. In 1875-1876 he promoted the first royal visit to India—that of the **Prince of Wales**, and in **1877** he persuaded Queen Victoria to adopt the title **'Empress of India'**.

A cardinal point of his policies was to maintain the integrity of Turkey as a bolster (or buffer) against Russian ambitions in the Middle East and Mediterranean. It would also constitute a protection of Britain's imperial routes to India.

The Eastern Question, 1875–1878

In 1875, revolt against their Turkish overlords broke out in Bosnia and Herzegovina. The rebellion spread to Bulgaria and Macedonia, at which point Germany, Austria and Russia presented the **Berlin Memorandum** to Turkey demanding an armistice and certain reforms. When Disraeli, distrusting the Balkan aims of Austria and Russia, refused to support the Berlin Memorandum, it was withdrawn. In Turkey itself there was a revolution which placed Abdul Hamid, the 'Red Sultan', on the throne. He turned his bands of irregular troops, the *'Bashi-Bazouks'*, on the rebellious populations, who were subjected to murder and atrocity on a cruel scale.

Gladstone attacked Disraeli's Turkish policy vehemently and in his famous pamphlet *The Bulgarian Horrors and the Question of the East*, he demanded that the Turks be expelled from the Balkans 'bag and baggage'.

When Abdul Hamid, relying upon Disraeli's support for Turkish integrity against Russia in particular, rejected reforms in Turkey demanded by the Conference of the Great Powers at Constantinople, the Russians declared war (April **1877**). Despite the Turkish defence of **Plevna** for several months, Russia reached Adrianople, not far from Constantinople itself. Disraeli had kept Britain neutral so far, provided that Russia did not threaten the Suez Canal, Egypt or Constantinople; but now he sent the Mediterranean Fleet to Constantinople amidst an outbreak of 'jingoism' in Britain—the popular song declared:

'We don't want to fight; but, by jingo, if we do,
We've got the ships, we've got the men, we've got the money too.'

At this point the Russians accepted an armistice with the Turks, and by the **Treaty of San Stefano, 3rd March, 1878**, Rumania, Serbia and Montenegro became independent states and Russia gained Bessarabia from Rumania. Across the Balkan Peninsula was created the **'Big Bulgaria'**, and it was against this that both Britain and Austria protested. They saw in this a state which, under Russian influence, would dominate the whole of the Balkans. Disraeli sent Indian troops to Malta and prepared for war if Russia refused another conference. Russia, however, agreed to the **Congress of Berlin (13th June to 13th July, 1878)**. Disraeli himself attended and the chairman, Bismarck, regarded him as the dominating influence at the Congress. The Russians accepted the drastic reduction of Bulgaria. Bulgaria handed back to Turkey territory which enabled Turkey to protect Constantinople. The northern part of Bulgaria became a principality, but the southern part, Eastern Rumelia, remained under Turkey, with, however, a Christian governor. A secret agreement between Britain and Turkey gave Britain control of Cyprus in return for an undertaking to defend Turkey from any Russian attack. The Sultan gave promises of better treatment of his Christian subjects, but these proved as unreliable as those of 1856. Austria occupied Bosnia and Herzegovina, and Serbia and Montenegro lost some territory.

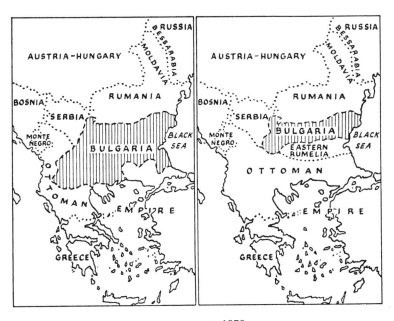

BULGARIA IN 1878

Comments on Disraeli's Policy

Disraeli's imperialist aims appeared successful. He had gained Cyprus as a valuable British base and had repelled Russia from the Balkans. He had defended Constantinople and maintained the integrity of the Turkish Empire. He had strengthened the anti-Slav or anti-Russian influences by strengthening Austria's power in the Balkans and reducing the small states of Montenegro and Serbia. To the disgust of Gladstone, Macedonians and Serbs in considerable numbers were returned to corrupt Turkish rule in the interests of anti-Russian policy. Queen Victoria invested Disraeli (or the **Earl of Beaconsfield** as he had been since 1876) with the Order of the Garter; but Gladstone, in his famous **Midlothian campaign** in Scotland, denounced Disraeli's imperialism and demanded a policy based on justice, national freedom for oppressed peoples, and the use of arbitration in international disputes. Gladstone had given up the Liberal leadership to **Lord Hartington** in **1875**, but now emerged again as the leader. Queen Victoria took great offence at Hartington's removal and her dislike of Gladstone, who (she said) 'always addressed her like a public meeting', increased.

Gladstone's campaign had much to do with Beaconsfield's defeat in 1880, but he had run into other difficulties also. In **Afghanistan** British forces had arrived at **Kabul** in **1879** to overthrow the pro-Russian ruler, and had then retired leaving a small British mission, which was soon afterwards massacred. This was followed by humiliating defeats for British forces before eventual success was gained by the defeat of the anti-British ruler at **Kandahar** in August **1880**, by **General Roberts**. British difficulties had told against Beaconsfield, whose 'forward' policy came under bitter attack from Gladstone. Trouble also arose with the Boers in South Africa, where the Boers had accepted British occupation of the Transvaal as protection against the Zulus. The British were defeated by the Zulus at **Isandhlwana** in **January 1879**. Although the Zulu chief, **Cetewayo**, was defeated at **Ulundi** in July 1879, Britain failed to give the promised independence to the Boers, and declared the Transvaal a Crown Colony. (Gladstone himself refused the Boers independence when he became Prime Minister in 1880; and, when British forces were defeated by the Boers at **Majuba Hill** in February **1881**, he withdrew all British forces from the Transvaal.)

At home Disraeli had to face the serious decline of agriculture, which was due to the competition of grain from the new lands of Canada, Australia and the American 'Middle West'. Men drifted to the towns, where unemployment grew fast.

Summary

Disraeli's second ministry of 1874–1880 was another period of important social reform. The stress on social welfare was becoming stronger than previously and a number of private property rights began to be invaded by the state. At home his policy—for which he owed much to Richard Cross—was one of 'Tory Democracy', while abroad his pro-Turkish and anti-Russian policies culminated in the

Congress of Berlin, 1878. His daring purchase of the Suez Canal shares was a piece of keen imperialist foresight. Another factor of importance was his consistent build-up of the image of monarchy and his drawing of Queen Victoria from her unpopular retirement, which she had imposed on herself since the death of the Prince Consort in 1861. In the later years of his ministry he had the frustrations of agricultural crisis at home and setbacks in imperial affairs.

Important Dates

1874 Purchase of Suez Canal shares.
   Factory Act.
1875 First royal visit to India (Prince of Wales).
   Artisans' Dwellings Act.
   Public Health Act.
   Conspiracy and Protection of Property Act.
   Employers and Workmen's Act.
1876 Merchant Shipping Act.
   Enclosure of Commons Act.
   Education Act.
   Trade Union Amendment Act.
1877 Queen Victoria 'Empress of India'.
1878 Congress of Berlin.
   Factory and Workshops Act.
1879 Kabul massacre.
   Zulu victory at Isandhlwana.
   Cetewayo defeated at Ulundi.
   Sharp decline in British agriculture.

QUESTIONS

(1) In what ways was Disraeli's legislation in the interests of the working class?

(2) What was Disraeli's imperial and foreign policy and why was it attacked by Gladstone?

(3) What did Disraeli achieve by the Congress of Berlin?

(4) For what reasons was Disraeli defeated in the election of 1880?

CHAPTER TWENTY-FIVE

GLADSTONE'S SECOND MINISTRY
1880–1885

ALTHOUGH Gladstone won the election of 1880, his party was itself divided between the Whig elements, representing the cautious, rather backward-looking groups, and the new Radicals, represented by the young **Joseph Chamberlain**. The Radicals denounced Disraeli's imperialism, but the Whig element in the party was certainly pro-Empire. Gladstone himself had denounced Disraeli's foreign and imperial policy, and his own government was about to be faced by serious imperial problems.

The Irish Nationalists now numbered eighty M.P.s and were strong enough to make the Irish question dominant for many years to come. They could decide the fate of Gladstone's government. A group of M.P.s in the Conservative Party, led by **Lord Randolph Churchill,** came to be known as the **'Fourth Party'**; and in 1885 they actually brought Gladstone down by a temporary alliance with the Irish party. Thus Gladstone was without the clear-cut political power which he had enjoyed in 1868 to 1874.

Ireland

In 1879 there was another famine in Ireland which aggravated the old causes of discontent. Many landlords evicted their tenants in order to create larger holdings, but even in 1881 the average holding was still only about thirty acres. In Ireland it *'rained outrages'* against landlords and their property, and this discontent developed into the organized agitation of the **Irish Land League** founded by **Michael Davitt**, but the leadership of it soon fell to **Charles Stuart Parnell (1846–1891)**. Although a Protestant and an Irish landlord, Parnell became the dominating figure of Irish politics between 1880 and 1891. From his mother, who was an American, he inherited a hatred of Britain and a genuine concern for the Irish. The case of the 'Manchester Martyrs' particularly roused him, and he became a member of Isaac Butt's Home Rule League. He was elected M.P. for County Meath in 1875.

Parnell wished to turn the peasantry from outrage into organized action for Irish independence, and when the House of Lords rejected a Bill introduced by Gladstone in the Commons to give compensation to evicted tenants, Parnell organized the boycott. This was named after the agent for the estates of the Earl of Erne, a certain **Captain Boycott**, who refused to accept the rents demanded by the local organization of the Land League in County Mayo. His estates were put under a kind of siege, his property attacked and destroyed and his servants compelled to leave him. His estates were given military protection by the British forces. Parnell also caused any farmer taking over the land of an evicted tenant to be isolated 'like a leper of old'. Although Parnell disapproved of outrages, they increased, and **'Moonlighters'** set fire at night to the property of those who would not accept the policy of the Land League.

Gladstone and Irish Violence

In **1881** Gladstone brought in a **Coercion Bill** which suspended the Habeas Corpus Act in Ireland. At the same time he made a constructive move by introducing the **Second Irish Land Bill, 1881**, by which tenants were given the **'three F's'**—fair rent, fixity of tenure and free sale. Under this, land courts were set up to fix fair rents and a tenant who paid his rent could not be evicted. He could also sell his interest in the land to the highest bidder. This was a clear effort by Gladstone to meet part of the Land League's agitation, but the League refused to co-operate with the new courts, which made them unworkable in many parts of Ireland. Parnell had now clearly come out for Home Rule for Ireland, and he was also President of the **Irish Home Rule Confederation**. In the House of Commons he secured an iron discipline among the Irish members for the purpose of obstructing the work of the Commons, and succeeded, for example, in extending the debate on one clause of Gladstone's Coercion Bill for forty-one hours. Gladstone partly offset this by securing alterations to the rules of debate, particularly the right of the Speaker to fix a time for termination—the **'guillotine'** procedure, by which a debate could be cut short.

The Kilmainham Treaty, 1882, and the Phoenix Park Murders

Parnell and several other Irish leaders were now imprisoned in Kilmainham Gaol, Dublin and the Land League was declared a criminal association. However, Gladstone himself was moving towards Home Rule and he reached an agreement with Parnell, by which the latter would abandon the 'no-rent' campaign of the Land League and denounce violence and outrage in return for a cancellation of all arrears of rent of Irish tenants due to the campaign. This was the famous **'Kilmainham Treaty'**. Parnell was released in April 1882.

Gladstone's direct dealing with Parnell caused the resignation of the Viceroy and the Secretary for Ireland, who were replaced by **Lord Spencer** and **Lord Frederick Cavendish** respectively. On the evening of his arrival in Dublin, Lord Cavendish and the Irish Under-Secretary, **Burke**, were both murdered in **Phoenix Park** by a group of the extremist **'Invincibles'**. Parnell himself denounced this crime as 'cowardly and unprovoked', but English opinion hardened even further against the Irish and against Parnell in particular, who was regarded by many as having instigated the crime. When a campaign of dynamite outrages began in Britain, Gladstone passed a **Crimes Act** and a **Coercion Act** giving summary powers to the authorities in Ireland and abandoning trial by jury in serious political cases. Parnell himself refused to appear before a tribunal to denounce outrages, declaring himself answerable only to the Irish people, who in 1883 subscribed £37,000— the 'Parnell tribute'—to pay off his debts. In 1885, when Gladstone proposed to renew the Crimes Act of 1882, Parnell's followers voted with the Conservative opposition to reject the budget, and Gladstone resigned.

Gladstone and the Empire, 1880–1885

South Africa presented Gladstone with an immediate problem. Despite his denunciation of Disraeli's policies, Gladstone hesitated to meet the Boer demands for the recognition of the Transvaal as an independent South African Republic. This was partly due to the fact that the government was considering other plans for South Africa, but the Boers declared their own independence and inflicted a disastrous defeat on the British force sent against them at **Majuba Hill** in **1881**. Gladstone was not prepared to continue the conflict and he recognized the Transvaal's independence under British suzerainty by the **Pretoria Convention** of **1881**.

The next problem arose in Egypt, where things had gone from bad to worse. The Khedive was utterly failing to meet his huge commitments to foreign lenders; and Britain and France, the chief creditors, set up their **Dual Control** in Egypt and deposed the defaulting Khedive in favour of his son. However, in 1882, an army officer, **Arabi Pasha**, seized control and adopted a policy of anti-foreign nationalism. An Anglo-French fleet arrived at Alexandria to protect foreign interests, and this was followed by riots in the city in which some Europeans were murdered. At this point the French, afraid of Germany in Europe and not wishing to be embroiled in Egypt, withdrew their fleet. The British then bombarded Alexandria and Arabi Pasha withdrew to Cairo. Then a British force under **Sir Garnet Wolseley** landed at Port Said and defeated and captured Arabi Pasha at the **Battle of Tel-el-Kebir**. Gladstone's Egyptian policy showed divisions in his govern-

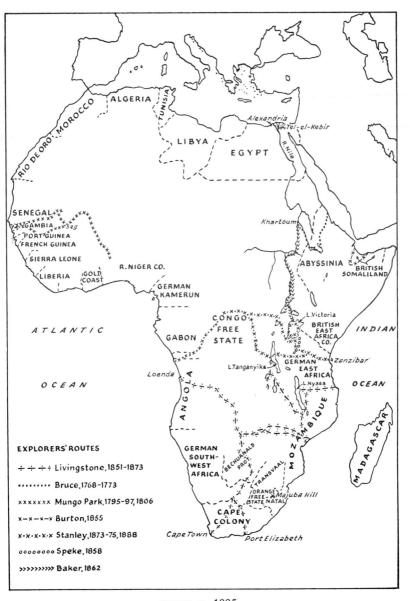

MOROCCO
RIO DE ORO
ALGERIA
TUNISIA
LIBYA
EGYPT
Alexandria
Tel-el-Kebir
R. Nile

SENEGAL
GAMBIA
xxSeg
PORT. GUINEA
FRENCH GUINEA
SIERRA LEONE
LIBERIA
GOLD COAST
R. NIGER CO.
GERMAN KAMERUN

Khartoum
ABYSSINIA
BRITISH SOMALILAND

ATLANTIC

OCEAN

CONGO
FREE
STATE
GABON
Loanda
ANGOLA

L. Victoria
BRITISH EAST AFRICA CO.
GERMAN EAST AFRICA
L. Tanganyika
Zanzibar
L. Nyasa

INDIAN

OCEAN

MOZAMBIQUE

MADAGASCAR

GERMAN
SOUTH-
WEST
AFRICA
BECHUANALD PROT.
TRANSVAAL
ORANGE FREE STATE
NATAL
Majuba Hill
CAPE COLONY
Cape Town
Port Elizabeth

EXPLORERS' ROUTES

÷ ÷ ÷ ÷ Livingstone, 1851–1873

••••••• Bruce, 1768–1773

xxxxxxx Mungo Park, 1795–97, 1806

x–x–x–x Burton, 1855

x·x·x·x·x Stanley, 1873–75, 1888

ooooooooo Speke, 1858

>>>>>>>>> Baker, 1862

AFRICA C. 1885

ment, for the Radical, John Bright, resigned after the bombardment of Alexandria. Other members of the cabinet considered Gladstone to be inadequately protecting British interests, which centred upon the cotton crop and the Suez Canal. Gladstone now left sufficient forces in Egypt to guarantee stable government until Britain could withdraw altogether at a later stage. In the meantime **Sir Evelyn Baring**, later **Lord Cromer** (see p. 358), was appointed Consul-General in Egypt.

Gladstone's handling of the Sudanese problem also caused division in his own ranks. In the Sudan the Moslem religious leader, **Mohammed Ahmed, the Mahdi**, led a revolt against the occupying Egyptian forces, and also annihilated a force sent from Egypt under a British officer, **Hicks Pasha**, at the **Battle of Shekan**. The Egyptian garrisons in the Sudan, many under British officers, were now in peril. Gladstone hesitated. Once again, the Radical members of his cabinet wanted complete withdrawal. At last he decided to send out **General Gordon** *to evacuate the garrison*. The choice was strange, for the General was noted for his obstinate character and militant Christianity. When Gordon arrived at **Khartoum** in February **1884**, he decided that the positions could and must be held against the Mahdi. Gladstone, loth to act against the Sudanese and angered by Gordon's attitude, again hesitated; but public pressure, and an urgent demand from Baring in Egypt, caused him to send a force under Sir Garnet Wolseley. When the latter reached Khartoum, Gordon had been murdered by the Mahdi's followers. Gladstone's reputation at home sank heavily, especially when he decided that the only course was to withdraw entirely from the Sudan.

On the Afghanistan frontier Russia made a number of moves culminating in the occupation of **Merv** in **1884**. Gladstone agreed to a boundary commission to investigate, but Russian forces then occupied **Penjdeh** on the Afghan frontier. Gladstone made preparations for military action, but the Russians agreed to international arbitration. This resulted in Penjdeh being awarded to them, and this did not increase Gladstone's popularity at home.

Summary of Gladstone's Policies

Gladstone had preached fervently the right of national independence of subject peoples, especially in his attacks on Disraeli's 'forward' policy. This caused him to hesitate to take military action, even where vital British imperial interests were at stake, as in the case of the Boers of the Transvaal, the Sudanese revolt, and Arabi's nationalist movement in Egypt—all of which Gladstone regarded as legitimate national movements. This led to divisions in his cabinet and, as in the case of Gordon, the appearance of hesitation and muddle. His belief in international arbitration led to Russian advances on the Afghan frontier. Thus in an imperialist age, when forces of economic

PROBLEMS OF GLADSTONE'S SECOND MINISTRY
1880–1885

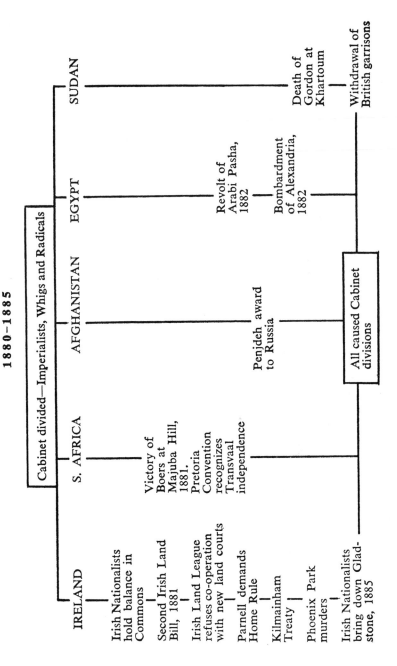

Cabinet divided—Imperialists, Whigs and Radicals

IRELAND

Irish Nationalists hold balance in Commons

Second Irish Land Bill, 1881

Irish Land League refuses co-operation with new land courts

Parnell demands Home Rule

Kilmainham Treaty

Phoenix Park murders

Irish Nationalists bring down Gladstone, 1885

S. AFRICA

Victory of Boers at Majuba Hill, 1881.

Pretoria Convention recognizes Transvaal independence

AFGHANISTAN

Penjdeh award to Russia

EGYPT

Revolt of Arabi Pasha, 1882

Bombardment of Alexandria, 1882

SUDAN

Death of Gordon at Khartoum

Withdrawal of British garrisons

All caused Cabinet divisions

competition were dictating the policies of Britain's rivals, such as Russia, Germany and France, *Gladstone's policies appeared weak to the imperialists in his cabinet, while the Radicals, such as John Bright, thought he was not sufficiently anti-Imperialist.* His dealings with Parnell over the Irish question became extremely unpopular after the Phoenix Park murders. It was also well known that the Queen herself was opposed to Gladstone's approach to imperial problems. Moreover, in forming his cabinet Gladstone had given the key posts to the aristocratic Whigs represented by Lord Hartington, who also disliked his policies over Ireland and the Empire, while the younger Radicals held minor posts only.

Domestic Policy. The Third Reform Bill, 1884

Gladstone had moved further away from the landed interests during the past twenty years, and he was determined to remedy the fault of the 1867 Reform Bill which failed to give any workers in the country-side the vote. In this he was supported strongly by the young Radical Joseph Chamberlain, who at this time was denouncing the privileges of inherited wealth and demanding an extension of democracy. The **Third Reform Bill** was really made up of two Acts which comple-mented each other—the **Reform Act** and the **Redistribution Act**. The Reform Act gave the vote in the counties to all householders and £10 lodgers, as for the towns in 1867, and was to apply also to Scotland and Ireland. This added about two million voters to the roll. The Redistribution Act deprived seventy-nine towns of less than 15,000 population of their representation in Parliament, and towns between 15,000 and 50,000 were to have one M.P. only. This meant that the great majority of constituencies were now single-member. The House of Lords had at first thrown out the Reform Act, and this led to demands by many leading Liberals to *'end or mend'* the House of Lords. Queen Victoria, however, intervened, and the Redistribution Act was the result of agreement between the Liberal and Conservative parties. The opposition of the House of Lords ceased.

An important result of the Third Reform Act was to give Parnell more support than ever from the new voters in Ireland, and in England many of the new working-class voters supported the Radicals.

The Bradlaugh Case

Considerable embarrassment arose for the government from the claim of the atheist and radical M.P. for Northampton, **Charles Bradlaugh** to the right to make an affirmation of allegiance rather than take the parliamentary oath, which went contrary to his anti-religious views. Gladstone pleaded strongly for toleration of Bradlaugh's viewpoint, but prejudice against him was so strong, even among members of Gladstone's cabinet, that the House of Commons refused to allow him to take the usual oath when he attempted to do so. He was re-elected three times by his constituents, but forcibly expelled from the House until later, in 1886, a new and more competent Speaker ruled in his favour. The Bradlaugh case was exploited by Gladstone's opponents in the Commons to weaken his government's position, but the outcome of the case was most important for the rights of M.P.s and their constituents as well as for the development of religious toleration. Gladstone himself emerges from this case with great credit in view of his own strong religious convictions.

Gladstone had continued to negotiate with Parnell, but without success. At this point Joseph Chamberlain, with Gladstone's support, produced a scheme for elected county councils in Ireland, which would have given at least local 'Home Rule'. Parnell's dissatisfaction with this led him to vote in conjunction with the 'Fourth Party' against the budget in 1885. *Gladstone was defeated and resigned.*

Lord Salisbury now became Prime Minister for the next seven months until an election could be held under the new arrangements of the Third Reform Act. His Conservative ministry was a 'Caretaker' one, with no parliamentary majority. Joseph Chamberlain now produced a challenging Radical programme including such demands as free education and the graduated taxation of the returns from capital investment by the wealthy. In the election the Liberals gained a majority of 86, but this was the exact number of Parnell's Nationalists in the House of Commons. *Parnell therefore controlled the parliamentary situation.* Parnell had been given to understand by some Conservatives that they would introduce Home Rule for Ireland; but when it became known that Gladstone now definitely favoured Home Rule, the possibility was entirely abandoned by the Conservatives and Parnell brought the Irish votes over to Gladstone, who now formed his third ministry (February 1886 to June 1886).

The First Home Rule Bill, 1886

Gladstone immediately had trouble with his own party. The Hartington section refused to join the government, as also did the Radical Chamberlain, who wanted a scheme of Home Rule with Irish representation at Westminster. Gladstone's proposals made no provision for Irish presence at Westminster, but proposed to keep control of the armed forces, foreign policy and trade in the hands of the British Parliament, leaving all other matters to an Irish Parliament at Dublin. When the Bill was introduced in April 1886, it was attacked not only by the Conservatives, but by the Chamberlain Radicals and the Hartington Whigs. It was defeated on the Second Reading on June 8 1886 by a vote of 343 to 313—the biggest attendance at a division ever recorded up to that time. *Gladstone resigned in June 1886.*

Summary

Gladstone's second ministry was fraught with difficulties arising from imperial problems. Despite the Second Land Act, little progress was made with the Irish problem, and Parnell's strong position in the House of Commons lessened Gladstone's independence. The Phoenix Park murders in particular made it difficult for Gladstone to continue negotiations with Parnell. Within his cabinet, divisions arose over Ireland, Egypt and the Sudan, South Africa and Afghanistan. In domestic policies, the Third Reform Bill further widened the franchise, but this also had the effect of further strengthening the Irish party. The Home Rule Bill of 1886 was strongly attacked by Radicals, Whigs and Conservatives, and the opposition within Gladstone's own party led to his defeat. The Bradlaugh case also presented Gladstone's opponents with an opportunity to embarrass the government.

Important Dates

1881 Coercion Bill, Ireland.
Second Irish Land Act.
Boers' victory at Majuba Hill.
Pretoria Convention.
1882 Kilmainham Treaty.
Phoenix Park murders.
Arabi Pasha's revolt in Egypt suppressed.
1884 British withdrawal from the Sudan.
Penjdeh dispute, Afghanistan.
Third Reform Bill.
1885 Murder of Gordon at Khartoum.
Parnell and the 'Fourth Party' bring about Gladstone's defeat.
1886 February-June: Gladstone's third ministry.
First Home Rule Bill defeated.

QUESTIONS

(1) Why did unrest and violence continue in Ireland during Gladstone's second ministry?

(2) What problems faced Gladstone in (a) *the Empire;* (b) *the Liberal party itself;* (c) *The House of Commons?*

(3) Describe the changes brought about by the Third Reform Bill and estimate its importance.

(4) Write notes on (a) *the 'Fourth Party';* (b) *Captain Boycott;* (c) *the Mahdi.*

CHAPTER TWENTY-SIX

LORD SALISBURY'S SECOND (CONSERVATIVE) GOVERNMENT 1886-1892

THERE now followed one of the most important periods of Conservative rule during the nineteenth century, involving further stages of the Irish problem, of reforms at home and of important decisions affecting foreign policy and the Empire.

The Irish Problem under Salisbury

Salisbury was opposed to Irish Nationalism and in favour of firm government in Ireland, combined with a policy of gradual reform of grievances.

A new **Crimes Act** was now passed which was the work of the new Secretary for Ireland, **Arthur James Balfour**. This Act further extended trial without jury to all offences against law and order. Parallel with this he introduced a **Land Act** which increased the amount of assistance to tenants wishing to purchase their farms. But Irish discontent increased, and the Land League now started the **'Plan of Campaign'** by which tenants joined together to offer the landlord a fair rent which, if he refused, was paid into the League's funds. Balfour's answer was a rigid application of the Crimes Act and the sending of police and military support to landlords evicting tenants. The term *'Bloody Balfour'* became common among the discontented Irish.

Parnell and Crime

In April 1887 *The Times* published an apparent facsimile reproduction of a letter Parnell was supposed to have written in which he declared that Burke, murdered in Phoenix Park, 'got no more than his deserts'. Parnell denounced this letter as a 'barefaced forgery'. Further letters were published, and in 1888 the Government was compelled by public pressure to appoint the **Parnell Commission** of inquiry. This inquiry proved that the letters were forgeries by an unscrupulous journalist, **Richard Pigott**, who fled to Madrid and committed suicide after leaving a full confession of his crime. Both in Ireland and England Parnell's prestige rose high, but soon afterwards he was cited as co-respondent in a divorce suit brought by one of his principal supporters, **Captain O'Shea**, against his wife **Katharine O'Shea**. At once Victorian England, and in Ireland the Catholic Church, turned against him. Gladstone, who had hoped to win the next election and bring in Home Rule with Parnell's support, advised him to give up his leadership of the Irish movement, but Parnell refused. The efforts to maintain his leadership told heavily against his health and he died in October 1891 aged forty-five.

Parnell's death weakened the Irish movement and correspondingly strengthened Britain's control of Ireland. Balfour introduced further reform measures. The most important of these were: (1) the **Land Purchase Act, 1890**, which enabled the peasant purchaser of land to receive the full price from the government with repayment spread over forty-nine years; and (2) the **Congested Districts Board**, which was to promote industry in districts too poor to warrant peasant-proprietorship, and also to assist emigration and the combining of smallholdings into larger units.

Domestic Reforms under Salisbury

Since the **Municipal Corporations Act of 1835**, no great changes had occurred in methods of local government, despite the great increase in population and especially in the size of towns. In 1888 more than 27,000 committees or boards throughout the country were controlling such things as lighting and sanitation, but none of these boards was elected in the same way as the members of the town councils. In the countryside, the J.P.s not only carried out their judicial functions, but were also administrators. By the County Councils Act, 1888, the J.P.s lost their administrative powers, which were taken over by elected county councils, as were also the functions of the various boards referred to above. The **London County Council** was also set up, comprising parts of Middlesex, Surrey and Kent. The Corporation of the City of London remained, however, independent.

An important **Factory Act of 1891** raised the minimum age for employment of children in factories to eleven years, and in the same year *fees in elementary schools were abolished.*

Foreign and Imperial Affairs under Salisbury, 1886–1892

Towards the end of the nineteenth century, a Canadian politician described Britain's foreign policy as one of *'splendid isolation'*. Salisbury had to take into account the fact that Britain had ceased to be a power capable of employing a large regular army in Europe, and that our power depended on the navy and the Empire. But Britain's political isolation was brought about by the bad relations with France since our take-over in Egypt and the ending of Dual Control. Russia was also regarded as a menace to Britain's imperial power, while it was clear that Bismarck wished to see Anglo-French relations remain in this unsatisfactory state. However, Salisbury made a number of important agreements which reduced Britain's isolation rather than increased it. In 1887, a secret treaty was made with Italy and Austria, by which Italy would support Britain in Egypt in return for Britain's support of Italy against any naval attack by France; and both Austria and Italy agreed to resist any forward moves by Russia in the Balkans. When Bismarck suggested an Anglo-German alliance in 1889, Salisbury refused this because Germany was not prepared to resist Russia in Britain's interests. *To Salisbury, as to Palmerston and Disraeli, Russia was the main menace.* Thus, while some agreements were reached with foreign powers, they were limited. Under Salisbury Britain could make little useful contact with the three Great Powers: Germany, Russia and France.

The Bulgarian Question

In 1885 Eastern Rumelia rose in revolt against the Turks and demanded union with Bulgaria, *thus defying the settlement of the Congress of Berlin, 1878.* Both Austria and Germany resisted Russian attempts to secure the throne of Bulgaria for a Russian nominee, and Salisbury made his agreement clear, but the effective resistance, which suited British anti-Russian policy, was really made by Germany and Austria—a situation which would not have been pleasing to Disraeli.

In Africa, however, Salisbury's policies secured considerable advance for British interests. In general he was ready to support British commercial undertakings if called upon, but otherwise left the penetration of Africa to 'private enterprise', such as the exploitation of Nigeria by the **Royal Niger Company** and of Uganda and Kenya by the **British East Africa Company**. At the same time **Cecil Rhodes** and the **British South Africa Company** were establishing themselves in what was to become Rhodesia. However, direct agreements were made between Britain and Portugal, France and Germany. In 1890 Portugal acknowledged British control of Nyasaland, while France recognized British control of Zanzibar in exchange for British recognition of French dominion in Madagascar. With Germany Salisbury agreed to recognize German control of German East Africa, the Cameroons and South-west Africa in return for German recognition of British rights in Uganda, Kenya and Zanzibar. Britain also handed over Heligoland in the North Sea to Germany.

Salisbury advanced British imperial interests and at the same time his policy in Europe was not altogether one of 'splendid isolation'. But his policies were unspectacular, and Balfour's rather ruthless policies in Ireland also lost Salisbury some support in the election of 1892, when Gladstone returned to power, still relying upon Irish support in the Commons.

Gladstone's Fourth and Last Government, 1892–1894

In February 1893, Gladstone introduced the Second Home Rule Bill. This was similar in most details to the first, but it now included arrangements for the representation of Ireland at Westminster. The Irish members of the Commons were to have the right to vote only on Irish and Imperial matters. The Bill passed the Commons with a majority of thirty-four, but the overwhelmingly Conservative House of Lords rejected it by 378 votes. Gladstone resigned in 1894 and was succeeded by Lord Rosebery, really the choice of Queen Victoria and not of the Liberal Party. Rosebery found the opposition of the Lords to various progressive measures so constant that his position was hopeless. He resigned in 1895 and Lord Salisbury formed a Conservative government. A general election followed, and Salisbury received a majority of 152—a decisive swing to the Conservatives. This majority included the Liberal-Unionists such as Chamberlain, who had now moved over to the Conservative position on Ireland. *The Conservatives were destined to be in power for the next ten years.*

Summary

Under Salisbury the Irish problem eased somewhat in Britain's favour. At home important changes were also made in local government. Despite the idea of 'splendid isolation' Salisbury played an important role in foreign affairs and encouraged successfully imperialist advance in Africa through trading concessions and a number of important agreements with other states. Gladstone's fourth and last ministry saw the passage of the Second Home Rule Bill by the Commons but its rejection by the Lords.

Important Dates

1886   Balfour's Irish Land Act.
   The Irish 'plan of campaign'.
1887   The 'Times' letter identifying Parnell with crime.
1888   The Parnell Commission.
   Suicide of Pigott.
   Divorce scandal undermines Parnell's influence.
   County Councils Act.
1890   Land Purchase Act.
   Congested Districts Boards established for Ireland.

1891 **Factory Act.**
Elementary school fees abolished.
1893 **Gladstone's Second Home Rule Bill rejected by Lords.**

QUESTIONS

(*1*) *What was Balfour's policy for Ireland?*
(*2*) *Why did the Irish nationalist movement weaken in this period?*
(*3*) *Describe Salisbury's foreign and imperial policies.*
(*4*) *What domestic reforms were introduced by Salisbury's administration?*

CHAPTER TWENTY-SEVEN

CONSERVATIVE RULE, 1895-1905: SOUTH AFRICA

AMONG the members of Salisbury's new government was **Joseph Chamberlain** as Colonial Secretary. His influence on politics in the late nineteenth and early twentieth century is sufficient to warrant a brief summary of his career. Through his successful work with the firm of *Nettlefold and Chamberlain* in Birmingham, he had become a millionaire by the age of thirty-eight. He retired from industry in 1874 to take up politics. At that time his views were extremely radical, and he expressed his belief that Britain would become a republic. He was also a keen supporter of state elementary education and became chairman of the influential **National Education League**. In 1873 he was elected Mayor of Birmingham after the Liberals had gained control of the city council.

As Mayor of Birmingham he encouraged forms of municipal socialism, by which essential services such as gas and water came under the control of the Corporation. He initiated a vast programme of slum clearance and was the national pioneer of good working-class housing and improved sanitation. His enthusiasm for popular education was seen in the establishment of the **Birmingham Free Library and Art Gallery**, and in 1900 was the founder of the **University of Birmingham**.

Chamberlain was elected as Liberal Member of Parliament in 1876, and his influence soon began to be felt in the Liberal party. In the government of 1880–1885, Gladstone made him President of the Board of Trade. Gladstone was too distracted by Ireland to bring in measures of social reform, except the Third Reform Bill, and Chamberlain became critical of the party leadership. Gladstone gave him the task of negotiating the 'Kilmainham Treaty' with Parnell, but this was ruined by the Phoenix Park murders. In 1885 Gladstone's cabinet rejected Chamberlain's plan of an elected council for Ireland; and, as a result, Chamberlain and his supporters opposed the Home Rule Bill of 1886, because it made no provision for Irish representation at Westminster and threatened to break completely the imperial connection between Ireland and England. Chamberlain wished to support some form of union between Ireland and England, while giving the Irish more local control. Chamberlain and his supporters were known as the *Liberal-Unionists*.

During the years 1886 to 1895, Chamberlain developed a Radical programme which was not accepted by Gladstone and the leading members of the Liberal party and was therefore known as the *'unauthorized programme'*. This programme demanded free elementary education, smallholdings for agricultural workers (called the *'three acres and a cow'* programme), the graduated taxation of the wealthy to pay for social improvements, and the right of local authorities to compulsorily purchase land for building houses. To this he added demands for compensation to workers injured in industry, old age pensions and sickness insurance.

Chamberlain gradually became a fanatical supporter of the Empire. After a visit to the U.S.A. in 1889 he became even more convinced that Britain should increase her imperial power. He saw in the U.S.A. a powerful competitor and a great example of economic enterprise. In Salisbury's government of 1895 he became Colonial Secretary, having now moved over to the Conservatives. He was almost immediately involved in the South African question, which became one of the most important issues of the day.

Main Developments in South Africa, 1815–1899

In 1814 Britain gained permanent control of the Cape of Good Hope by a payment of £6,000,000 to the Dutch government, and from that moment serious difficulties developed between the British and the Dutch farmers or Boers living in South Africa. British policy under the Governor-General, **Sir Benjamin D'Urban**, annoyed the Dutch. Both the British administration and the missionaries appeared ready to make concessions to the coloured peoples, an attitude annoying to the slave-owning Dutch farmers who justified slavery by reference to the Bible. In 1828 the right of coloured people to possess land was recognized and then, in 1833, the British Parliament abolished slavery in the Empire. The Boers declared the compensation paid to be insufficient, and they were further annoyed by the refusal of the home government to allow Kaffir territory to be seized. In 1836 the **Great Trek** took them out of the Cape altogether, some moving into Natal, another group beyond the Orange River and others beyond the River Vaal. In all directions they had to fight their way against native resistance.

The Boers had fought against the Zulus in Natal, and the latter were certain to attempt a counter-attack both against the Boers and the British in the eastern parts of Cape Province. This danger led the British to declare **Natal** a British colony in **1843**. In **1848** the **Orange Free State** established by the Boers was also annexed. However, in **1852** the **Sand River Convention** recognized the independence of the **Transvaal** under its leader, **Pretorius**, and in **1854** the **Bloemfontein**

Convention also recognized the independence of the Orange Free State.

British policy at the Cape continued to favour the natives as against the Dutch. The Orange Free State was particularly annoyed by the British support of the Griqua tribe's claim to a diamond-mining area, which they soon afterwards ceded to the British—the real origin of British claims to the Kimberley diamond fields.

A much greater cause of trouble arose from the determination of the Zulus under **Cetewayo** to drive the whites from South Africa. In 1877 the Afrikaners under their President, **Burgers**, agreed to accept British annexation as a protection against the Zulus on condition that, after the defeat of the Zulus, self-government would be restored. At this time the Transvaal government was bankrupt and quite willing to accept British aid. However, the Vice-President, **Paul Kruger**, disagreed with the British occupation. After a difficult struggle against the Zulus, the British finally defeated Cetewayo at **Ulundi**, but British forces did not withdraw nor was the Transvaal's independence restored. This led to the **First Boer War**, the defeat of the British at **Majuba Hill, 1881** and the restoration of Transvaal independence by Gladstone under the **Pretoria Convention** of **1881**. Even more important was the **Convention of London, 1884**, by which the Transvaal became the **South African Republic** and agreed to accept free trade and not to impose any taxation on foreigners which was not imposed on its own people. It was also prohibited from making foreign treaties or treaties with native tribes without the agreement of the British government. The President of the South African Republic who agreed to these terms was **Paul Kruger**.

Despite the London Convention, Kruger attempted to extend the frontiers of the Transvaal, but the British forced him to give up control of Bechuanaland. The British were unwilling to see Boer territory to the north of the British diamond area of Griqualand West. **Cecil Rhodes** and the British South Africa Company were now given a charter to develop what later became Rhodesia, thus preventing the northward expansion of the South African Republic. Kruger was also prevented from gaining a seaport when the British annexed Tongoland and Kosi Bay. *Thus the Republic was hemmed in on all sides.*

The 'Uitlanders'

In **1884** the **Witwatersrand** gold-field discoveries brought prospectors pouring into the area—British, Dutch, Germans and Americans came. Kruger's Republic became the richest country in Africa whereas before it had been one of the poorest. Kruger saw the means of solving his government's financial difficulties by the taxation of these foreigners or *'Uitlanders'*. He also sold monopolies in essential supplies for the goldfields, such as dynamite and iron, and this raised costs for the prospectors. The mining town of Johannesburg became the centre of opposition to Kruger, especially when severe restrictions were also placed on the political rights of the *Uitlanders*. Although nine-tenths of the taxes going to the government were derived from the *Uitlanders*, in 1894 a new law prevented any foreigner under forty having the vote and only those over that age who had lived fourteen years in the South African Republic had this right. It must also be remembered that the *Uitlander* population was greater than that of the whole Boer population.

Cecil Rhodes (1853–1902) and Paul Kruger

Intended by his parents for the Church, Rhodes was destined to play a very different role. On account of poor health he joined his brother on a farm in Natal in 1870, the year in which diamonds were found at Kimberley. His own diamond prospecting gave him a fortune by the age of 19, and he then undertook an eight-months journey north of the Vaal and Orange Rivers. He rapidly developed the ambition to make Britain the dominant power in Africa and he advocated the construction of *a great railway from Cairo to the Cape*. In 1881 he became a controlling influence in the **de Beers Mining Corporation** formed on his initiative by amalgamation with the Kimberley mines. He was also elected a member of the Cape Assembly.

To Rhodes' ideal of a British dominated Africa, Kruger was violently opposed, while Rhodes actively opposed every effort of Kruger to expand the territory of the South African Republic. *At the same time Rhodes advocated a federation of the African states within the Empire*, but Kruger, who at this time cultivated political relations with the Kaiser's Germany, refused to consider it. In 1884 Rhodes, as deputy commissioner in Bechuanaland, forced Kruger to withdraw Boer settlers from the territory. Southern Bechuanaland came directly under British control and a protectorate was established over the north up to the 22nd parallel. The Cape colonists now had a clear route to the north. But both Germans and Portuguese were attempting to gain trading concessions in the remainder of the territory, and Rhodes established a **Chartered Company** to promote British interests. In 1893, the British campaign against the **Matabele** under their chieftain **Lobengula** was Rhodes' proposal, and with its success half a million square miles were gained for the Empire and *the territory became* **Rhodesia** *with 12,000 white settlers in* **1895**. In 1890 Rhodes had become Prime Minister of the Cape, a powerful position which he used for a determined promotion of his imperial policies. These British advances had increased the tension between the British and Kruger's Republic.

The Closing of the Drifts

Relations between British and Boer deteriorated rapidly. Kruger refused concessions to the *Uitlanders*, while the British occupation of **Tongoland** was another cause of friction. In 1894 Kruger began to impose heavy rates on the Transvaal section of the Cape railway, but the Cape traders now unloaded their goods at the drifts or fords on the Vaal River, from which they went to Johannesburg by wagon. Kruger's reply was to close the drifts—a situation in which the British government, with Chamberlain now Colonial Secretary, threatened to use force. Kruger grudgingly re-opened the drifts.

The Jameson Raid

Rhodes concluded that the only way to defeat Kruger's anti-British policy was a planned rising of the *Uitlanders*, to be supported by an invading force from Bechuanaland under the command of **Dr. Starr Jameson**, one of the directors of Rhodes' British South Africa Company. The leaders of the *Uitlanders* hesitated at the last moment when they learnt that the movement was to be under the British flag, for they had always supported the idea of an independent Transvaal. They decided to postpone their rising; but Jameson, apparently against the wishes of Rhodes, invaded the Transvaal on 29th December, 1895 with four hundred and seventy men. There was, however, no rising in Johannesburg, and Jameson's force was surrounded at **Doornkop** and forced to surrender. Jameson was later handed over to the Cape government. This dismal failure of Rhodes' conspiracy made relations between the British and Boers even worse. Rhodes himself lost the support of the Boers in the Cape and was forced to resign his premiership. Kruger's position in the Transvaal was strengthened. Negotiations undertaken at Bloemfontein in 1899 by **Sir Alfred Milner**, Governor of the Cape, and Kruger completely failed to gain concessions for the *Uitlanders*. Milner, supported by the Colonial Secretary, Chamberlain, kept rigidly to the demand for a five-year qualification for the franchise, although Kruger had now offered seven. A petition from the *Uitlanders* to Queen Victoria complained of the intolerable burdens imposed on them, and this roused anti-Boer hysteria in Britain. British forces were sent to the Transvaal frontiers, and the Boers also made military preparations. In October 1899, Kruger proposed the settlement of all disputes by arbitration, but at the same time demanded the removal of all British forces from the frontier and the turning back of those already dispatched from Britain. When this ultimatum was rejected by the British government, war broke out between the combined forces of the South African Republic and Orange Free State on the one side and Britain on the other.

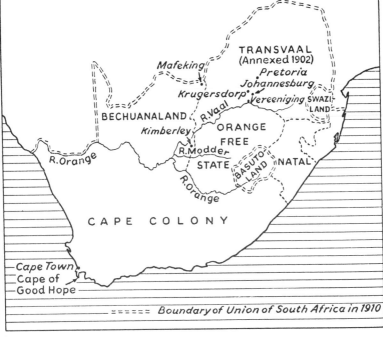

SOUTH AFRICA 1900–1910

The South African War or 'Boer War', 1899–1902

The Boers, strengthened by up-to-date arms supplied by Germany, went immediately on the offensive, laying siege to Kimberley, Mafeking and Ladysmith. The British were defeated in December 1899 at Stormberg, Magersfontein and the Tugela River. These reverses led to the appointment of **Lord Roberts** as Commander-in-Chief, with **Lord Kitchener** as his Chief-of-Staff. By using 250,000 men in wide enveloping movements, Roberts relieved both Ladysmith and Kimberley early in 1900 and Mafeking in May. The latter place had held out for seven months under **Lord Baden-Powell**.

Roberts also occupied Bloemfontein, Johannesburg and Pretoria, but the Boers continued vigorous guerrilla warfare for another eighteen months under their leaders **Botha, De Wet** and **Jan Christian Smuts**. To meet these tactics Kitchener established concentration camps into which civilians were moved in their thousands, and he also laid waste large areas. The camps were so appallingly run and the death-rate was so high that opposition at home under the young Radical, **David**

Lloyd George, who had denounced the war policy of Chamberlain grew intense, and drastic reforms were made in the camps. But Britain's unpopularity in Europe was great and the government's unpopularity at home increased. However, the Boers were overwhelmed by superior numbers and concluded the **Treaty of Vereeniging** in **May 1902**. By this treaty the Transvaal (South African Republic) and the Orange Free State came under the British Crown, but were promised self-government and the use of Afrikaans as their official language. Britain made a grant of £3,000,000 to compensate for the 'scorched earth' policy of Kitchener. Kruger had fled to Holland in 1900 and died there in 1904, and Rhodes died two months before the Treaty of Vereeniging, which achieved his principal aim, the incorporation of the South African Republic and the Orange Free State into the Empire.

The Union of South Africa

The Union of South Africa was created during the period of Liberal rule between 1906 and 1916. In 1906, the two Boer states were accorded their own parliaments and governments, and in **1910** the **Union of South Africa** was finally set up. The separate parliaments were then abolished and one parliament established at Cape Town. A Governor-General represented the Crown; and an elected Assembly was created, together with an upper house or Senate. In each of the four great 'provinces' locally-elected councils dealt with purely local matters. The extent to which the old conflicts had toned down was shown by the election of General Botha as the first Prime Minister. Beyond the Union, Rhodesia, Bechuanaland, Basutoland and Swaziland remained under British administration.

In 1961, the Union of South Africa left the British Commonwealth because of the general condemnation by other Commonwealth states of the policy of 'apartheid' pursued by the South African government. This meant the creation of separate territories and townships for the coloured and Bantu population, and restrictions on education, employment and movement in public places for them. In both World Wars, South Africa supported Great Britain; but in the Second World War there were some forces favourable to the Nazi creed who wished to keep South Africa apart.

Summary

New social and political forces developed during the period of Conservative rule from 1895 to 1905. Imperial policy became more dynamic under the influence of Joseph Chamberlain and his supporters. His earlier career had important results on the policies of both major parties and he played a leading part in imperial, foreign and domestic policies. The Salisbury and Balfour governments supported, both directly and indirectly, British expansion and influence in Africa. This in itself brought on conflict with France, which was quickly settled; but a more serious conflict with the Boers later culminated in the South African War. The apparently irreconcilable aims of British and Boer are seen most clearly in the differing aims of Kruger and Rhodes.

Important Dates

1814   Britain gained Cape Colony.
1836   The Great Trek.
1852   The Sand River Convention.
1854   The Bloemfontein Convention.
1884   Convention of London—Transvaal became the South African Republic.
   Gold discovered on the Witwatersrand.
   'Uitlander' problem arose.
   Rhodes, deputy commissioner in Bechuanaland.
1893   Matabele defeated and Rhodesia established.
1895   29th December: Jameson Raid.
1899   Outbreak of South African War.
1900   Relief of Ladysmith, Kimberley and Mafeking.
1902   Treaty of Vereeniging.
1910   Union of South Africa established.

QUESTIONS

(1) Discuss the importance of Joseph Chamberlain as a social reformer.

(2) What causes of conflict between British and Boer developed after 1884?

(3) Discuss the career and explain the importance of Cecil Rhodes.

(4) Why were the Boers finally defeated?

(5) Describe the constitution of the Union of South Africa, 1910.

CHAPTER TWENTY-EIGHT

FOREIGN POLICY UNDER SALISBURY (1895-1902) AND BALFOUR (1902-1905)

Reconquest of the Sudan

SALISBURY was forced to take account of the advances of other imperial powers, such as Germany and France, in Africa. He was particularly concerned with the possibility of further French advance from Morocco and the Sahara, and he decided to attempt the reconquest of the Sudan ruled by the **Mahdi** since the murder of Gordon. In 1898 Kitchener overwhelmingly defeated the Mahdi's forces at **Omdurman**, only to learn that a French force under Major Marchand had already reached the Upper Nile at **Fashoda** and raised the French flag. If the French achieved their aim of controlling the Southern Sudan this would also give them control of part of the River Nile itself. At Fashoda, Marchand's and Kitchener's forces faced each other and at home both France and Britain prepared for war. When France failed to gain support from Russia and Germany, Marchand withdrew. In any case, France was alarmed by the growing power of Germany. This was a decisive moment, and it led on to the signing of the Anglo-French Convention of 1899, which defined their respective spheres of influence and ensured British control of both Egypt and the Sudan. It was a victory for the policies of Salisbury and his Colonial Secretary, Chamberlain.

Britain and Turkey, 1896

The Sultan's promises of better treatment for his Christian subjects, made by Abdul Hamid in 1878 at the Congress of Berlin, proved useless. When, in 1896, his Armenian subjects attempted to gain a measure of self-government, his answer was a ruthless massacre and general persecution. In Britain, Gladstone emerged once more to denounce the Turkish atrocities. But Salisbury appeared unable to assist the Armenians, except to protest. However, in 1897 the fact that Britain deployed her fleet in the Eastern Mediterranean enabled Crete to gain her independence from the Turks. The Greeks, who had supported the Cretans, were defeated by the Turks in 1897, but Salisbury here intervened with effect to prevent any loss of territory by Greece. In general, Salisbury was still pursuing the traditional British policy of restraining Turkey, but not sufficiently to weaken her as a counter to Russia.

Salisbury and Germany

British policy-makers had to take into account the growing power of Germany. Bismarck had abandoned his earlier policy of restricting German ambitions to Europe only, and Germany entered the 'scramble for Africa'. After the fall of Bismarck in 1890, German policy became even more ambitious. The **German Naval Programme** of **1898** was the beginning of a programme which aimed at rivalling Britain on the seas, as Germany was already rivalling her in commerce and colonization. The German plan of a **Berlin-Baghdad Railway** was a challenge to the influence of Britain in the Middle East and the Mediterranean.

Salisbury's first efforts to counteract German influence were directed to France and Russia. The Fashoda incident made temporary difficulties with France, and Russia showed no immediate interest—the old antagonisms were still strong. Chamberlain favoured an Anglo-German alliance, but when Salisbury sent him to Germany the Kaiser showed no real interest. In any case, the support given by the Kaiser to the Boers under Kruger was a clear indication of his anti-British attitudes at that time. The years 1898–1900 stressed the real diplomatic isolation of Great Britain, when no accord was reached with Germany, France or Russia.

Under the Foreign Secretary, **Lord Lansdowne**, Britain now began to seek other directions in which to strengthen her international position. In **1902** he reached an understanding with Japan through the **Anglo-Japanese Treaty**, by which Britain and Japan promised mutual support if one of them were attacked by two powers and neutrality if attacked by one. Thus Britain deterred a possible combination of Germany and Russia in the Far East, which at that time was feared. The effect of the alliance was partly seen in the defeat of Russia by Japan in 1905, for it helped to ensure that Russia was without an ally, and, of course, the defeat of Russia *seemed* to serve traditional British interests.

In 1902 a general election once again returned a Conservative government. Salisbury retired (he died in 1903) and was succeeded as Prime Minister by **Arthur James Balfour**, the main architect of Conservative policy towards Ireland since 1886. In January 1901, Queen Victoria died after a reign of sixty-four years and was succeeded by her son **Edward VII**. The Queen had been strongly pro-German, but her son now openly supported the attempts of Balfour and Lansdowne to bring France and Britain together against the power of Germany and her allies.

The Entente Cordiale, 1904

As we have seen, the Fashoda incident had shown the French that Britain was determined to strengthen her interests in Africa, but at the same time the danger of war between Britain and France with a rapidly re-arming Germany on the French frontiers had caused considerable misgivings in France. Official French policy, represented by the Foreign Minister, **Delcassé**, was beginning to change. Visits by Edward VII to France helped to produce a new political atmosphere, and Lansdowne was able to negotiate what was known as the **'Entente Cordiale'** with France in **1904**. Britain agreed to support French claims in Morocco, while France fully recognized Britain's control of Egypt. Britain had relied on German support for her policies in North Africa, but Delcassé seized the opportunity of removing the need for any such German influence. This was the beginning of the trend which was to bring France and Britain much closer in the next few years. It was not, however, an alliance, but an 'understanding'.

Salisbury's policies in his last few years, and later Balfour's, were beginning to reduce the so-called isolation of Britain. There was a distinct change occurring in international affairs, which was to culminate in the Great War of 1914–1918. But British and French and, later on, Russian policy was to re-affirm the *Balance of Power* principle.

Summary

During this period France finally accepted Britain's position in Egypt and the Sudan, and in 1904 the *Entente Cordiale* was established. Britain had failed to reach any satisfactory agreement with Germany, whose naval building programme and schemes for the Berlin-Baghdad Railway got under way during this period. The important Anglo-Japanese Treaty of 1902 gave Britain an ally in the Far East, while Russia's defeat by Japan in 1905 had the indirect effect of lessening Britain's fear of, and hostility towards, Russia. Salisbury followed the traditional British policy of bolstering the Turkish Empire, but he effectively supported the independence of Crete and the integrity of Greece in 1898. Gladstone's attacks on Turkey in his last years had some effect both on the British public and on official policy.

Important Dates

1896	Armenian massacres.
1897	Cretan independence supported by Britain.
1898	German naval programme.
	Attempted British-German alliance fails.

1901	**Death of Queen Victoria.**
1902	**Balfour becomes Prime Minister.**
	Anglo-Japanese Treaty.
1904	**Entente Cordiale.**
1904–1905	**Russo-Japanese War.**

QUESTIONS

(*1*) *Explain the foreign policy of Salisbury and Balfour as it affected Turkey, Germany, and Japan.*

(*2*) *What circumstances brought about the 'Entente Cordiale' in 1904?*

SALISBURY AND BALFOUR
1895–1902   1902–1905

S. AFRICA	SUDAN	GERMANY	TURKEY	IRELAND	DOMESTIC
British policy to encircle S. African Republic	Omdurman, 1898	Berlin-Baghdad Railway plan	Armenian Massacres, 1896	County Councils 1898	Workman's Compensation Act, 1897
Rhodes' aim of S. African Federation opposed by Kruger	Fashoda, 1898 French withdraw	German naval programme, 1898 Chamberlain fails to secure Anglo-German alliance	Salisbury protests Supports independence of Crete	Wyndham's Land Purchase Act, 1903	Chamberlain fails to get scheme for Old Age Pensions
Uitlander problem		Anglo-Japanese alliance, 1902 aimed against both Germany and Russia	Supports Greece and Turkey		Education Act, 1902. School Boards of 1870 abolished. Education Committees established
British occupy Tongoland, 1890					
Jameson Raid, 1895		Growing French fears of Germany			
S. African War, 1899 and Peace of Vereeniging, 1902		Entente Cordiale, 1904			

CHAPTER TWENTY-NINE

DOMESTIC AFFAIRS UNDER SALISBURY AND BALFOUR

Ireland

BALFOUR'S general policy continued as before—the introduction of reforms which would 'kill Home Rule by kindness'. Conservative policy had progressed almost towards some of the old Radical proposals put forward by John Bright twenty years before—the creation of a landowning peasantry in Ireland as a modification of the landlord system. The main protagonist of this policy under Balfour was one of the young and more progressive Tories, **George Wyndham**, Secretary for Ireland. By Wyndham's **Land Purchase Act, 1903**, the government would loan purchase money to the peasantry where the landlord had agreed on a fair price. Annual repayments would make the borrower the owner of the land after sixty-eight years. This Act proved a considerable success, for by 1910 over a quarter of a million tenants had taken advantage of it.

In 1898, under Salisbury, County Councils had been established for Ireland—a scheme originally advocated by Joseph Chamberlain for according more self-government to the Irish.

Workmen's Compensation Act, 1897

This was promoted by Joseph Chamberlain, and altered the law governing relations between employer and employee. It enabled workers in certain trades to claim compensation for injury sustained at work. Chamberlain hoped that it would apply to all industries eventually, but it did not apply to merchant shipping, agriculture, domestic service, nor to workshops and buildings in which steam power was *not* used. Thus the reform was very limited from the worker's point of view, but its significance as a new departure was that *it recognized the rights of some workers to a form of insurance*. Chamberlain also produced a scheme for Old Age Pensions, but there was great opposition to it, and it was abandoned on the outbreak of the Boer War.

The Education Act, 1902

A Royal Commission of 1895 had reported very unfavourably on education, both general and technical, in England; and adverse comparisons were made with the highly centralized and efficient German system. Salisbury established the **Board of Education** in 1899 to bring more cohesion into the whole system. In 1902, Balfour, with the strong support of Chamberlain, introduced the Education Bill, *which laid the foundations for education in Britain during the twentieth century.* Its main points were that the School Boards of 1870 were abolished, and the new Borough and County Councils now appointed **Education Committees** to control elementary education and a considerable part of secondary education as well. The Catholic and Anglican schools retained their own religious teaching, appointed their teachers and met the costs of building, and they were compelled to bring their schools up to a certain standard of efficiency to qualify for rate support. The Committees were also to build new secondary schools where needed and to assist the older grammar schools. The Nonconformists disliked the abolition of the School Boards and the giving of further assistance to the church schools, and many refused to pay rates. In Parliament, the Liberals opposed the bill strongly in the Nonconformist interest. However, this campaign died down, and the new system had come to stay.

Chamberlain and Tariff Reform

Chamberlain had become convinced, especially by his study of German and United States tariff systems, that Britain's traditional free trade policy should be drastically modified. German and American trade had expanded in recent years at a far greater rate than Britain's from a much smaller initial figure. In 1903, Chamberlain resigned his post as Colonial Secretary in order to give his time to his newly-formed **Tariff Reform League**. His main proposals were: (1) a small duty on foreign imported food in order to favour imports from the Empire; (2) an import duty of ten per cent on all imported manufactures in order to lessen foreign competition and increase wages and employment at home, which, in its turn, with higher wages made possible, would reduce the effects of a slight rise in prices which the duties would produce; (3) to meet any rise in the cost of living, all duties on tea, sugar and many other articles of common consumption should go. By these means Chamberlain hoped to further his dream of Empire by greater trade within it. He also wanted the income from import duties to be used by the government for social reform of all kinds. But the Conservative Party was divided on the issue. The industrialists, who were doing quite well under free trade, feared that any increase in the cost of living would lead to demands for higher wages and to industrial disputes. The Liberals, the new Labour Party and the trade unions all denounced the scheme as leading to a higher cost of living. The

Liberals' propaganda used the idea of the 'big loaf' under free trade and the 'little loaf' under Conservatism. In the General Election of 1906 the Conservatives returned only 157 members; the Liberals numbered 377; the Labour Party and allies 53; and Irish Nationalists 83.

Reasons for the Liberal Victory of 1906

The following points should be considered: (1) Chamberlain's tariff reform proposals had divided the Conservatives. (The young Winston Churchill left the Conservatives over this issue and joined the Liberals in 1904.) (2) There was reaction against the imperialism which had led to the Boer War, and this issue was raised again by the Radicals in 1906. This reaction was also aided by the growth of the Labour Party and of the trade unions. (3) From the workers' point of view, Salisbury's and Balfour's social legislation had been weak, (e.g. the Workmen's Compensation Act, 1897). Indeed, Chamberlain's radical social proposals had been whittled down and amended out of recognition. (4) In South Africa the government had allowed the importation of Chinese coolie labour to work in the Transvaal mines, where their low wages meant severe discrimination against other workers, including British immigrants. There was also a great outcry on humanitarian grounds. (5) Balfour had done nothing to reverse the Taff Vale decision of 1902, which was a threat to trade unionism (for details see p. 379). The Liberals made it clear that they would amend the law; and, of course, the Labour Party took up this matter in the election with great vigour.

Summary

New constructive policies for Ireland brought on an easing of the Anglo-Irish conflict, especially during George Wyndham's office as Secretary for Ireland.

A number of social reforms were introduced during this period, but they were not very extensive. The Education Act (Balfour's) of 1902 was probably the most important. Chamberlain's tariff reform campaign divided the Conservative Party and allied against it the combined forces of the new Labour Party and of the Liberals. This led to the overwhelming defeat of the Conservatives in 1906. The Conservatives had also aroused the opposition of both Labour and Liberal parties by their acceptance of the Taff Vale decision of 1902 against the trade unions. The South African War had told against them and there was a public reaction against some aspects of British imperialism.

Important Dates

1897   **Workmen's Compensation Act.**
1898   **County Councils for Ireland.**
1902   **Education Act.**
1903   **Wyndham's Land Purchase Act.**
        Chamberlain's tariff reform campaign began.
1906   **Liberal election victory.**
        Growth of the Labour Party.

QUESTIONS

(*1*) *Give an account of Conservative policy in this period towards* (a) *Ireland;* (b) *education;* (c) *Protection of the worker.*

(*2*) *What were Chamberlain's tariff reform proposals and why did he put them forward?*

(*3*) *What were the reasons for the Liberal victory of 1906?*

CHAPTER THIRTY

THE LIBERAL REFORMS OF 1906-1914

Introduction

NEW forces were now developing in British politics. The Labour Party was now a factor in Parliament. Within the government of **Henry Campbell-Bannerman**, the Radical element was represented by **David Lloyd George** as President of the Board of Trade. **John Burns**, one of the leaders of the Dockers' Strike (see p. 379), was President of the Local Government Board. The government also included **Winston S. Churchill, Sir Edward Grey** (Foreign Secretary) and **R. B. Haldane**. Most members of the government had no connection with the old aristocracy but were connected with business—the first time this had happened in British history. The progressive measures of this government were achieved against the constant opposition and delaying tactics of the House of Lords, which fought a rear-guard action in the interests of the old system and old privileges, especially those of the landed class.

South Africa

One of the first actions of Campbell-Bannerman was to ban the importation of Chinese coolie Labour into South Africa, and also to give the Transvaal and Orange Free State full self-government. This paved the way for the creation of the **Union of South Africa** in 1910 and wisely helped to reduce friction between the Afrikaners and the British.

The Trade Disputes Act, 1906

The government brought in an early Bill to *reverse the Taff Vale decision* (see p. 380) which had made trade unions liable to pay damages for losses caused by a strike. Here the growing influence of the Labour Party and the trade unions was clearly shown, as was also the influence of the Radical sections of the Liberal Party.

Lloyd George

As President of the Board of Trade, Lloyd George established the **Port of London Authority** and generally improved the conditions of the dock workers. New regulations were introduced which improved the conditions of British merchant seamen. But Lloyd George's main work arose from his appointment as Chancellor of the Exchequer in 1908. During this year Campbell-Bannerman retired and was replaced by **H. H. Asquith**, who remained Prime Minister until 1916.

The People's Budget, 1909

In 1905 a Royal Commission had been set up to report on the Poor Law. This report was very critical of the whole Poor Law system, and a minority of the Commission wanted the Poor Law and workhouse system abolished entirely. Partly as a result of this report, and partly as a result of its own Radical tendencies, the government was determined to spend more on social benefits, and the **'Welfare State'** is regarded as having had its origins at this time. *In 1909 the first Old Age Pensions were introduced.* It was hoped that they would reduce the dependence of the aged poor on the old Poor Law and the workhouse. At the age of 70 the pension was to be 5/- weekly, provided other earnings were not more than 10/- a week.

Lloyd George made it perfectly clear as to where the money (estimated at £15 million) was to come from to pay for pensions and for the increases planned in the navy to meet the threat from Germany. *'Make the rich pay'* was Lloyd George's slogan—an approach made many years before by Chamberlain and other early Radicals in the Liberal Party.

The famous Budget of 1909 *increased Death Duties* and added 2d. to the rate of income tax. A *super tax* was levied on incomes over £3,000. Lloyd George also proposed a *land tax* on increases in land values because of development. The House of Lords, with its heavy representation of the land, rejected the budget by 350 votes to 75. The Commons had passed it by 379 to 149. This raised in acute form the question of *where the real control of the nation's finances should rest*, and Asquith declared the action of the Lords to be against the constitution. The question was put to the test of a general election, the result of which was the return of 275 Liberals, 273 Conservatives 40 Labour Party and allies, and 82 Irish Nationalists. This meant that the Irish under their leader **John Redmond** were able to gain a Liberal undertaking to introduce Home Rule in return for Irish support in the Commons' struggle against the Lords.

The Parliament Bill, 1911

The rejection of the budget by the House of Lords led to the introduction of the **Parliament Bill** in the House of Commons. *It aimed at preventing the House of Lords rejecting or amending 'money bills' and* *to give the Speaker of the House of Commons the power to decide which were 'money bills'* under the terms of the proposed Act. It also declared that *any bill passed by three successive sessions in the Commons was to become law even if it had been rejected by the Lords on the three occasions.* Finally, the maximum period between elections was to be five years instead of seven as hitherto.

Edward VII died in May 1910, and his son, **George V**, eventually agreed to create enough Liberal peers so that the bill could be passed in the Lords. Another general election in December 1910, left the representation of the parties almost as before. The Lords still attempted to amend the bill, but the Commons refused to accept the proposed changes; and eventually enough Conservatives in the Lords, rather than see their control of the House swamped by 250 Liberal peers, agreed to the bill and allowed it to pass by the narrow majority of 131 to 114.

Thus the powers of the House of Lords were greatly reduced, but they could still hold up legislation for two years until the further changes made by the Labour government of 1945–1950 (see p. 327). However, the Act was a victory for parliamentary democracy against the old nineteenth-century privileges of the Lords, and was a sign of more democratic times.

Haldane's Army Reforms

The Secretary of State for War, **R. B. Haldane**, aimed to create a British army capable of continental warfare, for by 1906 it was becoming clear that Europe was dividing into two armed camps. He replaced the old 'Volunteers' by the new *Territorial Force* (later to be called the *Territorial Army*) of 300,000 men with up-to-date training. A special *Expeditionary Force* was formed from the regular army consisting of six infantry divisions and one cavalry division, with special reserves. The Officers Training Corps of the Public Schools were also brought under the supervision of the War Office. Haldane greatly improved the War Office organization; and the *War Book* of 1911 was the official guide to government action if war broke out. Although Haldane failed to create the very large army he advocated, his reforms were to prove their value in 1914.

Social Reforms in the Years 1906–1914

The years 1908–9 saw the passing of the **Old Age Pensions Act**, and at the same time the government sponsored the **Coal Mines Act** which introduced the *eight-hour day in the mines.* Unrest among the railwaymen also led Lloyd George, then President of the Board of Trade, to set up **Conciliation Boards** for the railways to secure peaceful agreements between workers and the railway companies. New committees known as **Trade Boards** were set up for those industries in which conditions were very bad—the *'sweated industries'*. These boards, containing representatives of workers and employers, established minimum wages for a number of industries, and the trade board system was gradually extended to more industries. Thus Lloyd George hoped to replace outright conflict between capital and labour, by a system of peaceful negotiation the results of which would be satisfactory to both sides of industry. This was his answer to the very 'militant' tendencies of the big trade unions in these years (see also Ch. 42). **Labour Exchanges** (later called **Employment Exchanges**) were set up in **1909**, with the purpose of enabling workers to register, and so reduce the waiting-time between one job and another.

In 1907 the government introduced *school medical inspection* and also *school meals* for those in need, although the latter was not compulsory on local authorities. The **Education Act** of **1907** was also important; for it introduced the 'scholarship' system, by which secondary schools, receiving assistance from the rates, were compelled to reserve 25 per cent of their places free for pupils from the elementary schools who reached the required examination standard. The age of transfer was usually eleven, and was the origin of the *'11 plus'* system, which **Comprehensive** schools are now designed to replace. The act of 1907 greatly widened the scope for pupils from the elementary schools whose parents could not afford to pay fees.

The **National Insurance Act** of **1911** requires special mention. In these years there was much discussion of the old Poor Law which originated in 1834, and especially when a government Poor Law Commission reported on the Poor Law in 1909. An increasing number of people wished to see the end of the Poor Law and the establishment of an insurance system covering all workers, both for health and unemployment.

Lloyd George was responsible for introducing the first National Insurance system. The Insurance Act provided sickness and unemployment insurance. The sickness contributions were paid by the worker, the employer and the state—fourpence, threepence and twopence respectively. Maternity benefits were also introduced. Special Insurance Committees were set up to administer the Act and the trade unions and Friendly Societies were also recognized as *'approved societies'* for administering the Act. The unemployment scheme applied to workers in a number of trades, but *not* to *all* workers. In this case, also, contributions were paid by worker, employer and the state and an unemployed worker could receive up to 7/- a week for not more than fifteen weeks in the year.

The Act also set up the *panel system* for doctors, who received annual payments for each patient on their national insurance panel.

There was opposition from the doctors to this element of state control, but the system greatly improved the national health.

Payment of M.P.s, 1911

In 1909 the **Osborne judgment** of the House of Lords made it impossible for a trade union to use its funds to finance parliamentary candidates or pay salaries to M.P.s. There was widespread labour agitation against this ruling, and Asquith's government introduced the *payment of M.P.s in 1911*, at a salary of £400 per annum. In 1913 the Osborne judgment itself was amended by the **Trade Union Act**, which enabled a trade union to use part of its funds for political purposes if a secret ballot of the members approved this. In addition, any trade unionist not wishing to pay the 'political levy' could *'contract out'* of such payment without losing his trade union rights.

The Suffragettes

Besides being a period of increasing conflict between workers and employers, the years 1900 to 1914 witnessed the rise of the suffragette movement demanding votes for women on an equality with men. In **1903** the **Women's Social and Political Union** was formed by **Mrs. Emmeline Pankhurst**. In 1906 the movement had been led to expect sympathy from the government of Campbell-Bannerman. In 1907 he introduced the **Qualification of Women Act**, which enabled women to become councillors and chairmen or mayors of county and borough councils. But this small measure did not satisfy the suffragettes, who now took to more vigorous, often illegal, action, such as chaining themselves to the railings of Buckingham Palace, setting fire to pillar-boxes, and slashing pictures in the National Gallery. The police and some of the public treated them very roughly in return, and in prison they were forcibly fed when on hunger-strike. Parliament passed the so-called **'Cat and Mouse Act'**, by which they were released when in danger of dying from starvation in prison and then re-arrested after recovery. On Derby Day, 1913, the suffragette **Emily Davidson** threw herself under the King's horse and was killed. By 1914 the suffragettes had not achieved their aims.

Ireland, 1906–1914

The Irish M.P.s under John Redmond had enabled the Parliament Act of 1911 to be passed, and in 1912 Asquith introduced the **Third Home Rule Bill**, which proposed an Irish parliament, which would control all Irish affairs except those relating to defence, war and peace, and foreign treaties. Taxation was also left in the hands of the British parliament, for the most part. Forty-two Irish members were also to sit at Westminster. The bill was passed by the Commons in April, 1912, but rejected by the Lords—which meant that it could not become law until 1914. These two years were now used by the **Conservative Protestants of Ulster** to rouse northern opposition to proposals which they feared would lead to complete Catholic domination. The principal figure in this movement was the Protestant lawyer and M.P., **Sir Edward Carson**, who formed and armed the **Ulster Volunteers**. He took up the cause of Protestantism and British industry in Northern Ireland. The southern answer was to form their own force, the **Irish Volunteers**. In the meantime Carson had gone to the length of forming a *Provisional Government in Ulster*, which was to take over the government of Ulster on the day that Asquith's Bill became law. The next stage was the intention of the government to suppress the northern revolt by force, but at this point the British officers stationed at the Curragh Camp near Dublin declared that they would not lead any forces against the north. This, the famous **'Curragh Mutiny'**, led Asquith to assure the officers that they would not be asked to use force against Ulster. The outbreak of the Great War in 1914 led to the suspension of the Home Rule Bill for the duration of the war. Asquith, however, was severely criticized for having apparently given in to the officers' 'rebellion'.

Summary

The election of 1906 expressed the play of the new forces of the twentieth century. There was dissatisfaction with the slowness of social reform and a general desire to see it speeded up. Among the new forces was the Labour Party, while Liberalism itself was now much more under the influence of its radical wing, represented by such personalities as Lloyd George. The Liberal record in social affairs from 1906 to 1914 was outstanding. The reduction in the powers of the House of Lords and the payment of M.P.s were considerable advances in parliamentary democracy and of special advantage to Labour. The period was by no means placid, however. There was much labour unrest; there were widespread strikes, as the cost of living rose; the suffragette movement was extremely active; and serious conflict arose in Ulster over the Third Home Rule Bill.

Important Dates

1906 **Trade Disputes Act.**
        Haldane's army reforms begun.
1907 **Qualification of Women Act.**
        Education Act.
        School meals and medical inspection.

1908 **Old Age Pensions.**
        Coal Mines Act.
1909 **Trade Boards Act.**
        Labour Exchanges set up.
        The People's Budget.
        General Election—Irish M.P.s hold the balance.
        The Osborne Case.
1910 **Death of Edward VII and accession of George V.**
1911 **Parliament Bill passed.**
        National Insurance Act.
1912 **Third Home Rule Bill.**
        Carson and the Ulster Volunteers.
1913 **Trade Union Act.**
        The 'Cat and Mouse Act'.
1914 **The Curragh incident.**

QUESTIONS

(1) What action was taken by the Liberal governments in this period to support the trade unions?

(2) Examine the importance of the work of Lloyd George in this period.

(3) What was the importance of the Parliament Act of 1911?

(4) Describe and explain Haldane's army reforms.

(5) What were the main social reforms of this period?

CHAPTER THIRTY-ONE

ORIGINS OF THE FIRST WORLD WAR

Introduction

DURING the years of Liberal administration, between 1906 and the outbreak of the war in 1914, British foreign policy was conducted by **Sir Edward Grey**, who made frequent efforts to reach agreement with Germany. But increasing tension developed, not only between Britain and Germany, but also between Germany and Russia, and between France and Germany. The *Entente Cordiale* between Britain and France in' 1904 was not a pledge of British support of France against Germany, but was really the end of old antagonisms between French and British policies. Britain had previously looked to German support against France in Africa, but now Britain was being drawn away from Germany, to the considerable satisfaction of the French. We must now consider the importance of certain issues which led up to 1914.

The Moroccan Question and the Algeciras Conference, 1905–1906

Britain supported French policies in Morocco, much to the annoyance of Kaiser William II, who demanded an international conference on Morocco. When Delcassé, the French foreign minister, opposed this, he lost his position through pressure from Germany on the French government. The **Conference of Algeciras** in Spain, **January 1906**, increased, rather than lessened, Franco-German antagonism. France and Spain were given control of Moroccan ports while France alone controlled customs and arms supplies. Germany gained an equal share of control of the Bank of Morocco with Britain and France. The Germans also managed to negotiate a concession for the building of the port of Tangier, which the French had also aimed to secure and which had been promised to them.

The Formation of the Triple Entente, 1907

Russia had supported Britain and France at Algeciras, and the French wished to bring Russia and Britain closer in order to add strength to the Franco-Russian alliance formed in 1893. At this time conditions were favourable for an Anglo-Russian agreement. The old anti-Russian policy of the time of Palmerston and Disraeli was less urgent. The defeat of Russia by Japan in 1905 showed Britain that her ally, Japan, could hold back Russian expansion in the Far East; while nearer home, in the Balkan Peninsula, the new nations were far more independent of Russia than Disraeli had anticipated in 1878. In fact, *German influence, particularly in Turkey, was greatly increasing.* The Kaiser's project of the Berlin-Baghdad Railway, was a threat to the interests of both Russia and Britain in the Middle East. All these considerations led to the *Anglo-Russian agreement* brought about by Sir Edward Grey in 1907. Britain gained control of the foreign policy of Afghanistan and equality of trading rights with Russia was recognized. In the Middle East, Russia gained control of northern Persia and Britain of the southern half. Thus the **'Triple Entente'** (not an alliance) of France, Russia and Britain was brought about.

Germany and Britain

Under the inspiration of **Sir John Fisher**, First Sea Lord and **Lord Cawdor**, First Lord of the Admiralty, a new and more powerful battleship, *H.M.S. Dreadnought* was built in 1906. Both Fisher and Cawdor were convinced that the German navy programme, inspired by the head of the German Navy League, **Admiral von Tirpitz**, was designed to destroy Britain's naval supremacy. The Liberal government of Campbell-Bannerman supported Fisher and Cawdor, although the number of 'Dreadnoughts' demanded by Fisher was somewhat reduced. The Germans also began to build similar vessels in 1907. Thus *a naval competition between Germany and Britain developed.* Fisher was the advocate of a 'preventive war' against Germany. The Kaiser's statement that 'the trident must be in our hands' seemed to justify British fears.

The Agadir Incident, 1911

In 1911 French forces occupied Fez, the capital of Morocco, in order to defeat a rising against the Sultan, who was an ally of the French. *The Kaiser's answer was to send the German gunboat, Panther, to Agadir* to protect, as he declared, German interests. In France, Germany and Britain preparations for war were made, such was the tension created. Britain was particularly concerned to prevent the Kaiser from obtaining a naval base in or near the Mediterranean. Eventually, when the French agreed to concede part of the Congo to Germany, the Kaiser withdrew his Moroccan claims. Lloyd George had also warned the Germans that war with France would mean war with Britain.

The Balkan Wars, 1912–1913

The immediate cause of the outbreak of war in 1914 was the explosive situation in the Balkans. The **First Balkan War** of **1912** saw a general attack on Turkey by Bulgaria, Serbia, Greece and Montenegro. As a result, Turkey lost nearly all her territory in Europe, but the **Second Balkan War** of **1913** enabled her to regain much of this lost territory owing to quarrels between her former enemies. In the second war, Serbia, Greece and Rumania were aligned against the Bulgarians who had refused to give Serbia part of Macedonia. The Bulgarians were defeated and the position of Serbia was strengthened, much to the annoyance of the Austrians. To thwart the Serbian propaganda for an outlet to the sea and for the union of the Slav peoples of the Balkans in one state—a propaganda strongly directed by the Serbian secret society of the *'Black Hand'*—*Austria in 1908 had taken complete control of Bosnia and Herzegovina*, over which she had been accorded a protectorate in 1878. Tension between Austria and Serbia increased daily.

On 28th June, 1914, the heir to the Austrian throne, the **Archduke Ferdinand** and his wife were murdered by a student, a member of the Black Hand Society, at **Sarajevo**. On 23rd July the Austrian government's ultimatum demanded that Serbia should suppress all anti-Austrian societies, dismiss officials hostile to Austria, and allow Austrian officials to enter Serbia to ensure the carrying out of these demands. The Serbs refused the latter demand, although they offered to refer the main points in dispute to the Hague International Tribunal. With the agreement of Germany, Austria declared war on Serbia on 28th July. Russia now mobilized and, after a Russian rejection of a German ultimatum to demobilize, Germany declared war on Russia on 1st August. France having mobilized on 31st July, Germany declared war on France on 3rd August. On 2nd August, the Germans demanded free passage for their troops through Belgium, which was refused. *On 4th August, 1914, Germany invaded Belgium*, thus dishonouring the treaty of Belgian neutrality of 1839.

British policy was hesitant to the last moment. Sir Edward Grey had suggested a London conference to settle the Serbian question, but Germany rejected this proposal. The British people were reluctant to enter the war, but the invasion of Belgium was used to bring over several of the doubters in the cabinet, and Lloyd George himself, as well as most of the Labour Party except a small group led by **Ramsay MacDonald**, supported the war. *Britain declared war on Germany on 4th August* when no reply was received to her demand that Germany should respect the neutrality of Belgium.

Reasons for the Outbreak of the Great War of 1914–1918

In considering this question the following points should be taken into account, though they are not necessarily listed in order of importance:

(1) The Prussian domination of Germany achieved by Bismarck led to Prussian values dominating German thought. This thought was aggressive and demanded a *'place in the sun'* for Germany. This brought Germany into conflict with Britain and France through her naval programme and intervention in Africa, as in the case of Morocco.

(2) *The Prussian spirit led to the cultivation of the idea of German superiority.* The glories of war were preached, and the idea of the right of the superman to control the world by superior force was the stock-in-trade of many writers, the most prominent of whom was the German philosopher, **Nietzsche**. The schools and universities were widely permeated by this spirit.

(3) *Austria was determined to wipe Serbia off the map*, and this anti-Slav policy brought Austria directly into conflict with Russia, who was the principal supporter of the idea of a united Slav state under Serbian control. Such a state would also weaken Austria to the advantage of Russia. This struggle of Austrian imperialism against Serbian ambitions was a very definite cause of the Great War.

(4) In itself the invasion of Belgium was not a cause of the war— both France and Britain had already themselves made plans to use Belgium as a base in case of war. However, the ruthlessness of the German action strengthened the arguments of those in Britain and France who wished to fight Germany. It seemed to bear out the views of German aims expressed by strong anti-Germans such as Lord Fisher. Those elements in France who had for long wished for a war of revenge to regain Alsace-Lorraine were also strengthened.

(5) *The weakening of Turkey led to the Balkan wars and general unrest in the Balkans*, and the determination of Germany and Austria to play a strong part there.

(6) In recent years the economic causes of the war have received more emphasis. German industry, trade and shipping had greatly extended since 1870 and were serious rivals to both France and Britain by 1914. *This economic competition of the rival imperialist camps seemed to thrust the Great Powers towards conflict*—especially when Africa had been completely colonized and any further gains by one or more powers could only be at the expense of others. Britain, France and Russia all had strong economic reasons to hold together in the **Triple Entente** as a counter to the **Triple Alliance** of Germany, Austria and Italy. But the question still remains today—was war *inevitable* on economic grounds? The Entente powers undoubtedly feared for their economic interests when faced by the aggressive attitudes of the Kaiser,

who himself brought an element of instability into the international situation. He was described by one statesman as like a cat in a cupboard—when the door was opened you never knew where he would jump. From all this developed the armaments race between the two camps, and the Kaiser's cynical attitude towards the Hague Peace conferences roused further fears.

(7) The overriding *immediate* cause was the Serbian problem and the opposing great power alliances which were drawn into the struggle.

Summary

The period 1906–1914 was one of growing antagonism between Britain, France and Russia on the one hand and Germany and her allies on the other. This was especially seen over the Moroccan question and Serbia. Attempts at disarmament failed, and the British 'Dreadnought' policy was followed by a similar one in Germany. An arms race developed, including a German naval challenge to Britain. In 1907 the Triple Entente ended the old disputes between Britain and Russia as those with France had been ended in 1904.

Important Dates

1906   January: first 'Dreadnought' built.
          Conference of Algeciras.
1907   Triple Entente.
          Anglo-Russian agreement.
          Germany begins 'Dreadnought' building.
1908   Austria took over Bosnia and Herzegovina.
1911   The Agadir incident.
          Danger of War.
1912   First Balkan War.
1913   Second Balkan War.
1914   28th June: murder of Archduke Ferdinand.

QUESTIONS

(1) *What difficulties arose between the great powers over Morocco in this period?*

(2) *Why was there growing antagonism between* (a) *Britain and Germany;* (b) *Austria and Russia?*

(3) *Discuss the possible causes of the Great War.*

CHAPTER THIRTY-TWO

THE FIRST WORLD WAR
1914-1918

The War in Europe

THE German attack, based on the *Schlieffen Plan*, was aimed at a rapid defeat of France and then concentration on the defeat of Russia. **Moltke**, the German commander, launched his forces through Belgium with the aim of seizing the Channel ports, surrounding Paris from the north and then turning against the French forces isolated on the frontier of Alsace-Lorraine. The Belgians at **Liège** and the British Expeditionary Force at **Mons** delayed the German advance and assisted a French withdrawal. The German attack reached the Marne and the Germans began the shelling of Paris. Moltke now changed the direction of the German advance in order to encircle the French armies in the centre, and thus abandoned the attempted encirclement of Paris. A reserve French army under **General Joffre** was brought up from Paris and the British also re-inforced the Marne front. The Germans were then pressed back over the River Aisne. *The German hope of a quick victory was frustrated by the* **Battle of the Marne**.

Trench warfare now developed, with neither side able to break through. The trench system eventually extended from the Belgian frontier to Switzerland, and for four years the armies faced one another within this system. Attempts to break through were immensely wasteful of human life; and neither poison gas, nor aircraft, nor tanks made any effective difference to the ghastly stalemate which developed. This led on to efforts by the Allies to open other fronts.

The Eastern Front, 1914

The Russians invaded East Prussia in August, but were defeated by the German armies of **Hindenburg** and **Ludendorff** at **Tannenberg**. The Russian armies were successful, however, against the Austrians in Galicia, and the Serbs regained Belgrade. However, the entry of Turkey on the side of Germany in November 1914 and that of Bulgaria in the following year, made the Allied position on the Balkan front very difficult. On the other hand, Italy entered the war on the Allied side in May 1915. (Under the terms of the Triple Alliance she had agreed that she would not enter a war *against* Britain.) *The Turkish armies were a great asset to the Germans,* whose officers had for some years been in charge of their training. The Turks controlled great areas of the Middle East, and Russian ports in the Black Sea were now open to attack.

The naval side of the war is dealt with separately but it is appropriate to mention here that the **Battle of the Falkland Islands** in **1914** saw the defeat of one of the principal German naval forces, and the British navy soon gained control of the main sea routes. The transport of Allied troops and materials went on with little hindrance at this stage of the war.

The Western Front, 1915

This year witnessed futile and expensive attacks both from the Allied and German side. A British offensive at **Neuve Chapelle** resulted in heavy casualties and no gains. A German offensive at **Ypres** (April), in which poison gas was used, broke through the French lines but was held by the Canadians. By mid-summer there were twenty-one British divisions in France, and in September a British offensive was launched at **Loos**, with terrible casualties and no progress. **Sir John French**, who had been severely criticized for the tactics he employed, was replaced as British Commander-in-Chief in December 1915, by **Sir Douglas Haig**. At home **Lord Kitchener**, as Secretary of State for War, energetically built up a new British army. A **Ministry of Munitions** was set up and the organization of labour greatly improved by the **National Registration Act** of **July 1915**.

The Eastern Front in 1915

During 1915 the Germans under **Hindenburg** and **Mackensen** inflicted serious defeats on the Russians, and captured Warsaw in August. Although the Germans failed to knock Russia out of the war, the immense Russian casualties (nearly 2,000,000 men killed, wounded or captured) were a serious setback for the Allies. The Austrians were helped by the Russian reverses, and were able, with the aid of Bulgaria who now entered the war, to recapture Belgrade.

Gallipoli

The stalemate in the west and the difficulties of Russia strengthened the demand of those in the British Cabinet, led by **Lloyd George** and **Winston Churchill**, for the opening of a new front against Turkey, forcing a way through the Dardanelles, capturing Constantinople and linking up with Russia through the Black Sea. It was also hoped to bring the Balkan states on to the Allied side.

In March 1915, the efforts of the British navy to force a way through the Straits into the Black Sea proved a failure, and the Turks then strengthened their shore defences for the next six weeks before an Allied force of 75,000 under **General Sir Ian Hamilton** landed on Gallipoli. This force, known as the **'Anzacs'**, contained a large contingent of Australians and New Zealanders. The British positions could only just be held against Turkish attack, and a landing at **Suvla Bay** was also bogged down. Casualties mounted and general conditions became so appalling that the whole force was evacuated between 19th December, 1915, and 9th January, 1916. This was a very serious failure for the Allies.

The Siege of Verdun and the First Battle of the Somme, 1916

In February 1916, the Germans began their attack on the key French fortress of **Verdun**, with the object of drawing in and destroying as many as possible of the French forces—'to bleed the French army to death.' After which, an all-out German offensive (it was thought) would bring victory. For six months the French under **Marshal Pétain** held out with the rallying slogan, *'They shall not pass!'* and the German offensive was broken off. This great French defensive victory was followed by Sir Douglas Haig's British offensive on the **River Somme**, commencing on 1st July, 1916. With the use of tanks, Haig continued the offensive during the autumn. British casualties were over 450,000, the French 340,000 and the Germans 530,000, with a gain of about seven miles to the Allies. The Germans now withdrew into their defence system which was known as the **Hindenburg Line**. The only compensation for the Allies in 1916 was the naval **Battle of Jutland**, which saw the German navy driven back to their Kiel base, where they remained for the rest of the war. (See section on the war at sea.) But even Jutland was a controversial victory and British naval losses were heavy. Lord Kitchener was drowned at sea while on a mission to Russia. At home Lloyd George now replaced Asquith as Prime Minister.

The War on the Western Front, 1917

In April 1917, Haig's offensive at the **Battle of Arras** gained only a few miles, although **Vimy Ridge**, part of the Hindenburg Line, was captured. An attempt by the French under **Nivelle** to break through the Hindenburg Line failed disastrously, and Nivelle was replaced by Pétain. Between July and November the British under Haig conducted the offensive of **Passchendaele**, but this also failed disastrously, with over 300,000 British casualties. Unrest in both the British and French armies (mutinies occurred in the latter) was a characteristic of 1917—

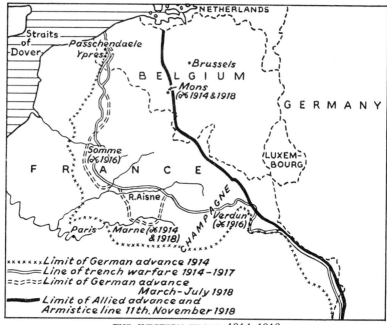

THE WESTERN FRONT 1914–1918

the horrors and frustrations of trench warfare were proving almost unbearable.

The **Russian Revolution** broke out in **March 1917** and *after the Bolshevik victory of October, Russia went completely out of the war.* A British offensive at **Cambrai** made some headway with the use of tanks, but in the **third battle of Ypres** the British offensives again broke down. In Italy, the serious defeat of the Italians by the Austrians at **Caporetto** led to a weakening of the western front through the urgent transfer of troops to aid the Italians. On the positive side, **the U.S.A.,** provoked by unrestricted submarine warfare by the Germans, entered the war. In April 1917 came a change of great importance for the Allies. (See section on war at sea.) There were also important British successes in the Middle East (see p. 272).

[A] The Year 1918 and the End of the War

At the beginning of 1918 Germany's allies were in a poor state, especially Austria-Hungary, whose food supplies had gone in great quantities to Germany. The Turks were also doing badly in the Middle East. If the Germans were to have any hope of winning the war it was important to strike as soon as possible. The collapse of the Russian front gave Ludendorff another half million troops for the western front. Ludendorff's first aim was to strike at the junction of the British and French at **Arras**, an attack which began in March and spread along the whole allied front. The British suffered heavily on the **Somme**, but the Germans failed to capture Arras. In April came the daring British attack on the German naval base at **Zeebrugge**. However, the German offensive reached the Marne and Paris was shelled from a distance of seventy miles. **Marshal Foch**, who was now *Supreme Commander of the Allied Forces* on the western front, launched the allied counter-offensive on 21st August. The German offensive had already cost the Germans 500,000 casualties, and their food supplies were so poor that they had been unable to exploit any advantages gained. Nowhere had they succeeded in breaking through. Thus the Allies were in a strong position, and *700,000 American troops had arrived in France*. British forces under Haig, using masses of tanks, broke through at **Amiens** and penetrated the Hindenburg Line. In September the counter-offensive became general, and the British were successful at **Cambrai**, and the Americans were now taking an active part in the **Argonne** Forest and at **Verdun**. In the Balkans, the Bulgarians capitulated after an offensive by the British forces from Salonika; and the Turks also surrendered in October after their defeat in the Middle East. The Austrians also surrendered after defeats by the Italians, and mutinies broke out in the German army and navy. German resistance crumbled under the weight of the great French, British and American offensives. The Kaiser fled to Holland and an *armistice was signed on 11th November, 1918*.

[B] The War in the Middle East

In the Middle East the Turks aimed to reconquer Egypt and hoped for Moslem aid against the British. Their object was in the first place the Suez Canal, so important for Britain in her communications with India, Australia and New Zealand.

The attacks on the Canal failed, the Turks being defeated at **Ismailia** and **El Kantara**, and hindered in their total strategy by a *revolt against their rule in Arabia*. In the following year they were defeated by the British at **Romani**, and the Canal itself could be used for war vessels and troop transport. The Turks had to cross the extremely difficult Sinai desert.

The early setbacks for the Turks encouraged the British commander, **Sir Archibald Murray** to assume the offensive into Palestine. With Egypt safe and a valuable base, the British lines of communication were assured. In December 1916, the British captured **El Arish**. It was now decided to invade Palestine by the coast route which would have the support of the navy. However, the British under Murray failed to capture **Gaza**, on which the Turks had fallen back, and Murray was replaced by **General Allenby**.

After receiving further reinforcements, Allenby moved his main forces along the coast road and inwards towards Beersheba and succeeded in turning both the right and left flanks of the Turkish army by his victories at **Beersheba, Gaza, Askalon** and **Jaffa**, and on **9th December, 1917**, he entered **Jerusalem**. However, early in 1918, some of Allenby's British troops were withdrawn to strengthen the western front against the great German offensive, and it was not until he had received large reinforcements of Indian troops that he was able to resume full-scale operations in September 1918. By a rapid cavalry movement Allenby succeeded in blocking the Turkish line of retreat northwards. This was a major defeat for the Turks, aided by the support of the pro-British **Emir Feisal** of Arabia. This led to the encirclement of **Damascus**, which surrendered on **1st October, 1918**, and **Aleppo** was captured in the same month. The Turks had been utterly defeated by brilliant generalship, and the control of Palestine and Syria was firmly in British hands.

The work of **T. E. Lawrence** ('Lawrence of Arabia') had been of vital importance in securing Arab support against the Turks. Promises of Arab post-war independence were also important, and Lawrence's success in gaining the support of the Emir Feisal added considerably to the success of Allenby's campaign. The early repulse of the Turkish drive towards the Suez Canal contributed much to later successes. *It ensured the passage to Egypt of Indian reinforcements and was the base from which British engineers organized railway and road construction for the movement of troops and supplies.* Allenby's strategy was brilliant and, unlike the western front, the terrain was almost ideal for the use of cavalry.

Mesopotamia

The *Euphrates and Tigris valleys* offered the most likely approach for the Turks and Germans towards India, and the defence of Mesopotamia (*now* Iraq) was undertaken by the Indian government. British operations began very successfully and by December 1914, the control of the delta had been achieved by the capture of **Basra** and **Kurna**; and the defeat of the Turks in April 1915, at **Shaiba** strengthened still further the British control. The British campaign now took the form of an advance along the Tigris in very difficult conditions of flooding and of great heat. However, in September the key position of **Kut-el-Amara** was taken by **General Townshend's forces**. Against Townshend's advice that his forces were insufficient the high command insisted on an advance towards Baghdad. The British forces were repulsed by the Turks at **Ctesiphon** and had to fall back on Kut, which now suffered a

THE MIDDLE EAST AND THE EASTERN FRONT 1914–1918

five months' siege by the Turks in appalling conditions. Food and medical supplies were quite inadequate and soldiers were dying at such a rate from starvation that Townshend could do nothing but surrender in April 1916. *The heroic resistance of five months had, however, saved the British from complete defeat in Mesopotamia,* and with the subsequent reorganization of food, general supplies and transport, Kut was recaptured by **General Maude** in December 1916. **Baghdad** also fell to the British in **March 1917**—a most important achievement after the early setbacks. This also meant that the southern end of the incomplete Berlin-Baghdad Railway was now in British hands. It led on to the defeat of the Turks in **Persia** (*now* **Iran**). At the beginning of **November 1918,** British forces captured **Mosul,** about 250 miles north of Baghdad. By that time Turkey had already capitulated.

Much of the later success was due to the initiative of General Maude, who insisted on the improvement of the lines of communication by engineering work before embarking on his campaign. He avoided the bad mistakes which had earlier led to the loss of Kut. The successful British campaigns in the Middle East were a great contribution to the defeat not only of Turkey but also of Germany.

[C] The War at Sea

British naval superiority at the beginning of the war was considerable—for example, she had seventy-three battleships to Germany's forty-six. *British strategy was to close the exits from the North Sea at the Dover straits and in the north,* where the main battleships were stationed at **Scapa Flow.** Britain's naval superiority enabled her to capture very quickly the German colonies in Africa and to drive German merchant vessels off the high seas. The first naval success was by **Admiral Beatty** at the **Heligoland Bight** on 28th August, **1914,** when the Germans lost three cruisers and one destroyer—after which they concentrated on the use of submarines, mines and sudden raids. These tactics led to the loss by Britain of three cruisers, a super-Dreadnought and one battleship between September and January. The **Battle of the Dogger Bank** in **January 1915,** saw another success for Beatty when the German battleship *Blucher* was sunk.

In the Far East *the Japanese seized the German naval base of* **Kiaochow,** and the German **Admiral von Spee** moved his ships into the South Pacific where he defeated a very inferior British squadron at the **Battle of Coronel,** but this was avenged in December 1914 in the **Battle of the Falkland Islands** when von Spee's force of five vessels was sunk with the exception of only one which escaped. The German raider, *Emden,* which had escaped from Kiaochow and done much damage to British shipping, was sunk by the Australian cruiser *Sydney* in November 1914.

The Battle of Jutland, 31st May, 1916

The German battle fleet emerged into the North Sea in May 1916, and the British Grand Fleet came into action against it. The British Fleet under **Admiral Jellicoe** lost fourteen vessels (comprising 113,000 tons) and over 6,000 men, while the Germans under **Admiral von Scheer** lost eleven ships (seven of them of small tonnage but a total of about 120,000 tons) and 2,500 men. The German navy retreated to its base at Kiel, from which it only emerged once more during the war, and then to no effect. *British command of the seas was maintained, but the battle itself was inconclusive and disappointed the British public who expected a Trafalgar-like achievement.* The battle showed defects in British naval design and armament, for the German ships proved to be better protected than the British. *This battle was the only battle beween two modern fleets ever fought in northern waters, 250 ships being involved and 25 admirals.* The German achievement was considerable, and British naval and public complacency were shaken, but the details of the battle show that both Beatty and Jellicoe conducted a brilliant engagement and criticism of them was not justified. The battle ensured against any invasion of Britain, and kept British command of the North Sea; but the escape of the German fleet enabled it to protect German bases from which submarine warfare was intensified.

German Submarine Warfare

In February 1915, the Germans declared a submarine blockade and attacked Allied and neutral shipping without warning. Britain replied by a counter-blockade, under which the navy could take neutral ships suspected of trading with Germany to a British port for examination. On 7th May, 1915, the Cunard liner *Lusitania* (with some Americans on board) was torpedoed; in December 1916, the passenger vessel the *Sussex* was torpedoed in the Channel; and in November 1916, the hospital ship *Britannic* was sunk. In 1917 there were more sinkings of American vessels, and the *United States entered the war on 6th April, 1917.* Over 17,000 persons (civilians) had been drowned, and losses of British, Allied and neutral shipping in 1917 were over 6,000,000 tons. The German aim of crippling Britain's food supplies was coming perilously near to achievement.

The British government now created a special *anti-submarine division of the navy* under Sir John Jellicoe as First Sea Lord. The *convoy system* was adopted and was in full operation by September 1917. A special campaign of mine-laying in enemy harbours and in the Straits of Dover was undertaken, while a great increase in mine-sweepers helped to reduce the German mine-laying menace. Merchant ships

FACTORS AND EVENTS IN FAVOUR OF THE ALLIES

NAVAL POWER

BLOCKADE OF GERMANY

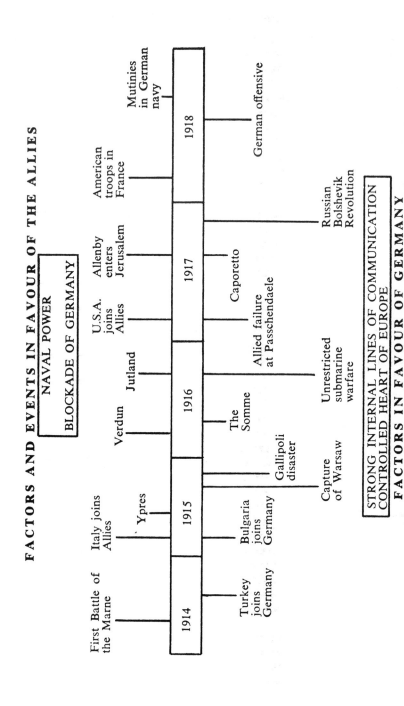

STRONG INTERNAL LINES OF COMMUNICATION
CONTROLLED HEART OF EUROPE

FACTORS IN FAVOUR OF GERMANY

were increasingly armed and camouflaged, and Q-boats (disguised naval vessels) took an increasing toll of German submarines. *Aircraft were also used for this purpose.* The convoy system and other measures proved most effective, and only a very small number of the million American soldiers brought over under convoy were lost. **The Harwich and Dover patrols** were established to meet raids by German vessels on British shipping and coastal towns, and at the same time to convoy troops and supplies across the Channel. These forces also attacked German-held ports and did important mine-sweeping work. These special measures were extremely effective, and in almost three years more than 5,000,000 troops were convoyed across the Straits of Dover without any loss of life whatever.

On 23rd April, 1918, occurred the famous attacks on **Zeebrugge** and **Ostend**—both successful—under the command of **Vice-Admiral Sir Roger Keyes**. These made useless the two most dangerous bases of the German U-boats, and the shock to German naval morale undoubtedly contributed to the surrender of the German Fleet in November after the outbreak of mutiny.

[D] The Home Front During the War

Many thought that the war would end in a quick Allied victory, but **Lord Kitchener**, Secretary of State for War, made plans for a long struggle. *By his recruiting drive he enrolled over a million men by the end of 1914.* Winston Churchill was First Lord of the Admiralty and Lloyd George, Chancellor of the Exchequer. An early financial result of the war was the doubling of Income Tax from 9d. to 1/6 in the pound. Early political crises came when the casualties at the front rose, involving the almost entire destruction, by 1916, of the British armies which were then in being or had been created by Kitchener in 1914. *Bad management of production and supply at home resulted in a shortage of shells at the front and unnecessary casualties.* At the time of Gallipoli, Lord Fisher, the First Sea Lord, resigned as a result of his disagreement with the Gallipoli plans. In 1914 Asquith formed a *coalition government* containing 12 Liberals, 8 Conservatives and 1 Labour member. *Lloyd George was then appointed Minister of Munitions*—a post created to overcome the weaknesses which the shell-shortage scandal had shown. Lloyd George put zest and initiative into the industrial drive—making employers speed up their efforts and persuading the trade unions to accept women workers in the munitions factories.

The problem of conscription came to the forefront as casualties on the western front mounted. There was division in the cabinet, but under pressure from Lloyd George and the Chief of the Imperial General Staff, **Sir William Robertson**, *conscription was introduced in*

January 1916. On the death of Lord Kitchener at sea, *Lloyd George became Secretary of State for War.*

Lloyd George Becomes Prime Minister, 1916

Asquith was increasingly criticized for lack of drive and for clinging to old governmental methods in a totally new situation. The press was influential here—the *Daily Express, The Times* and the *Daily Mail* all expressed criticism of Asquith, and the Conservative leader, **Bonar Law**, also supported them. These pressures led to the assumption of the premiership by Lloyd George. He immediately created a small **War Cabinet** to conduct the war in place of the full cabinet meetings which resulted in much delay of business under Asquith. This cabinet consisted of himself, Bonar Law, **Lords Milner** and **Curzon** and, as representative of Labour, **Arthur Henderson**. He also appointed leading business men to deal with food supplies and the problems arising from the German submarine blockade—all this brought fresh initiative and success into the government's work. He took unpopular measures such as restricting licensing hours of public houses, limiting restaurant meals and, in 1918, introducing complete rationing. Taxation on the wealthier classes became heavy—*he increased Super Tax and introduced an Excess Profits tax.* New ministries were created, the most important being the **Ministries of Pensions**, of **Labour** and of **Food**, and the **Air Ministry in 1918**.

On the military side of the war, Lloyd George was frequently in conflict with Haig and Robertson, who were mainly in charge of grand strategy. They believed in victory on the western front, but Lloyd George wanted other fronts to be developed, and had been an ardent supporter of the Gallipoli effort. Lloyd George also pressed for the creation of one *Supreme Commander* for the western front, especially as he often disagreed with Haig and Robertson. This was not achieved until the *appointment of Marshal Foch in 1918*, and was then shown to be a wise move.

Lloyd George's work in the war was outstanding—he was ruthless, could cut through 'red tape', and introduced unpopular but necessary measures such as price control, rationing and conscription. In introducing the naval convoy system he had to overcome much opposition from the Admiralty itself. He maintained the general support of Labour during the war, and in 1918 recognized the great work of women during the war by giving the vote to women over thirty who were ratepayers or the wives of ratepayers, and to all men over twenty-one **(Representation of the People Act, 1918)**. He was a forceful, convincing and extremely witty orator and took the people very much into his confidence. He made large promises, especially before the 'Khaki election' at the end of the war—*'a land fit for heroes to live in.'*

The Treaty of Versailles

The war resulted in the *complete collapse of the old empires of Germany, Russia and Austria-Hungary.* Revolution and chaos were the results. In Russia the **Communists** had gained power, in Germany revolts had broken out in the German army and navy and in Berlin itself, and Austria-Hungary had broken into its component parts. *The old Turkish Empire had disappeared with the rest* and a new nationalist movement was about to dethrone the Sultan. Complete devastation afflicted large areas of France and Belgium, and in Germany outright famine prevailed in many districts. *The total death-roll in the war had been not less than 13,000,000 men.*

The **Versailles Peace Conference** met on 18th January, **1919**. The important **Council of Four**, who decided the main terms of the settlement, were **Lloyd George** (Britain), **Georges Clemenceau** (France), **Woodrow Wilson** (U.S.A.) and **Orlando** (Italy). Wilson, in his famous *'fourteen points'* had laid great stress on the need for the self-determination of peoples and the establishing of natural frontiers accepted by the peoples. *Clemenceau had little time for Wilson's democratic sentiments* and was mainly concerned to see that Germany paid the full price for the war and could never again threaten French security. He was aptly named 'The Tiger'. Lloyd George had the task of attempting to reconcile such differences and he exercised a moderating influence.

The Settlements

Clemenceau wished to deprive Germany of the sources of coal and iron, including Alsace-Lorraine, the Rhineland, the Saar, Upper Silesia as well as Danzig and East Prussia, but Lloyd George and Wilson succeeded in moderating these demands. *The Saar was put under international control for fifteen years*, after which a plebiscite was to decide its future; meanwhile the Saar mines came under French control. *Danzig became a Free City under the League of Nations*, while about *one-third of Upper Silesia went to Poland*, who now had a 'corridor' running to the sea and dividing East Prussia from the remainder of Germany.

The *'guilt clause'* of the Treaty declared Germany the provoker of the war. She lost all her colonies, which were handed over to the League of Nations for control by other states as *'mandatory' powers* under the League. Germany was disarmed, except for a small force of 100,000 men without heavy armament. Germany had to pay the Allies reparations in the form of coal, iron, chemicals, ships etc.; and in 1921 her total reparations were fixed at the prodigious (and as it proved unpayable) total of £6,500,000,000.

In Eastern Europe, *Austria was reduced to a small state, with its capital Vienna, and only 6,600,000 inhabitants.* Out of the old Austro-Hungarian Empire arose the new states of **Hungary, Czechoslovakia** and **Yugoslavia.** In these countries new governments had taken matters into their own hands and the statesmen at Versailles accepted, through other treaties, the settlements already decided by revolution. Turkey retained Constantinople, but in the main her territory was confined to Asia Minor. There the Allied powers maintained troops until 1923, when the Turks under **Mustapha Kemal** amended much of the earlier settlement. Greece was given the old Turkish territory of Thrace, and Rumania gained Bukovina and Bessarabia. In the Baltic, new independent states were formed of **Esthonia, Latvia** and **Lithuania**—breakaways from Czarist Russia. **Finland** gained complete independence. The new Communist government in Russia under **Lenin** had accepted peace at any price from the Germans at **Brest-Litovsk** in **March 1918,** and were in no shape to resist these changes had they wished to do so.

EUROPE 1919–1923

Many of these arrangements gave better and more natural frontiers to old states and sound ones to new states, but they also created some *difficult economic and minority problems* which were to cause trouble in the future. There were 300,000 Germans in the Italian Tyrol and 360,000 Yugoslavs in the Istrian Peninsula, and the settlement left over 2,000,000 Germans in the new Poland. The port of Fiume, claimed by both Italy and Yugoslavia, was placed under the League of Nations, as also were the Dardanelles, a centre of so much dispute in the past. In the Middle East Britain was given the Palestine Mandate and also that for Mesopotamia.

The League of Nations

The League of Nations was formed as an integral part of the Treaty of Versailles. Its headquarters were at Geneva in Switzerland and its first Secretary-General was an Englishman, **Sir Eric Drummond**. This had been one of President Wilson's most cherished ideals, and the *Covenant of the League* pledged its members to settlement of international disputes by peaceful means or, if any state fell from this standard, to apply 'sanctions' of various kinds, including military if need be, against the offending state or states. Various important agencies were established to carry out important international social work—such as the **International Labour Office**, whose task was to achieve international agreements on labour conditions in the member states. Another purpose of the League of Nations was to promote international disarmament. Unfortunately, *the United States refused to join the League* and dropped back to an isolationist policy in respect of Europe; and Wilson's policy, despite great efforts on his part which brought about his death, was repudiated.

Summary

The first German onslaught was frustrated and the war became a trench war on the western front. British naval power was shown early on, and even Jutland maintained it. Attempts to open new fronts against Germany proved very difficult and Gallipoli was a disastrous failure. Gradually British superiority in the Middle East asserted itself and Turkey was unable to keep the allegiance of the Arabs. In the west, the German failure at Verdun was crucial for the outcome of the war, but even more important was the involvement of the United States in 1917. Germany was unable to sustain a long war and was also unable to meet the superiority of the Allies in manpower and material resources. Naval power also defeated the U-boat campaign and ensured not only the blockade of Germany but the survival of Britain and the effective supply of overseas forces. The home front saw complete government control of the British people for the first time in their history, and the idea of complete individual economic freedom was never to revive. The Treaty of Versailles was a complicated but reasonable settlement in most ways, but a number of serious problems were created. The wisdom of its treatment of Germany has always been a matter of dispute.

Important Dates

1914 First Battle of the Marne.
Russians defeated at Tannenberg.
Turkey joined Germany.
Battle of the Falkland Islands.

1915 Italy joined the Allies.
Battle of Ypres.
Battle of Loos.
Germans captured Warsaw.
Gallipoli.
'Lusitania' sunk.

1916 Siege of Verdun.
First Battle of the Somme.
Germans withdrew to Hindenburg Line.
Battle of Jutland.
April: British surrendered at Kut (Mesopotamia).

1917 Battle of Arras.
Passchendaele.
Mutinies in French army.
Russian Revolution.
Battle of Cambrai.
Italians defeated at Caporetto.
Unrestricted German submarine warfare.
U.S.A. enters war.
9th December: Allenby entered Jerusalem.

1918 Zeebrugge raid.
Ludendorff's offensive.
Marshal Foch Allied Commander-in-Chief.
21st August: Allied counter-offensive began.
British penetrated Hindenburg Line.
Battle of Cambrai.
Allenby captures Damascus.
Capitulation of Bulgaria, Turkey and Austro-Hungarian Empire.
11th November: Armistice.

QUESTIONS

(1) Why had Germany failed to win the war by 1916?

(2) What circumstances favoured the Allies in 1917?

(3) Describe the main achievements of British forces in the Middle East.

(4) Explain the organization and importance of British naval power during the war.

(5) What was the importance of Lloyd George as a war leader?

(6) Give the arguments for and against the Treaty of Versailles.

CHAPTER THIRTY-THREE

THE POST-WAR PERIOD TO 1929

(1) The Post-War Coalition, 1918–1922

THE war had serious effects on Britain. Her losses in men and material were very heavy. Nearly a million men were killed. About 40 per cent of British shipping was lost. Housing needs after the war were at least half a million. A huge National Debt had accumulated, the interest-payments on which accounted for about half the government's revenue from taxation, and *the very size of this debt made expenditure on social services after the war far smaller than they should have been.*

In the 'khaki' election of November 1918, the Labour Party officially broke away from the war-time coalition and put up candidates independently. The situation for Lloyd George was propitious, for he was widely regarded as the 'man who won the war' and he expressed his determination to 'make Germany pay' and to make Britain *'a land fit for heroes to live in'*. He also reached an agreement with Bonar Law by which 150 Liberal candidates would be unopposed by Conservatives. The result was *the return of 484 Coalition M.P.s, of whom 338 were Conservatives.* Among the remainder were 59 Labour M.P.s (an increase of twenty on the previous representation), 73 Sinn Fein (Irish) M.P.s who refused to sit at Westminster and set up their own parliament in Dublin, a few Asquith Liberals, and others. *The important fact was that the Conservatives had a clear majority, and Lloyd George's position depended on them.*

Lloyd George and Foreign Policy

We have seen the moderating influence exercised by Lloyd George in the Versailles settlement, and he was now faced with the existence of the new communist state of Soviet Russia. *The policy of France, the U.S.A. and Japan was to attempt the crushing of Soviet Communism before it could consolidate itself.* The Secretary of State for War, Winston Churchill, was strongly in favour of such intervention, and Lloyd George, although not as strongly anti-communist as the Conservative members of his government, supplied over £100 million of arms to the White Russians and sent military expeditions to

Archangel, Murmansk and **Baku**. Labour unrest at home, and the defeat of the interventionist forces in Russia led to the withdrawal of all British forces by the end of 1919—a very quick failure, with much money wasted and nothing to show. The Labour Party carried on a vigorous campaign against Lloyd George's policy, and won thirteen more seats in Parliament at by-elections between 1918 and 1922.

Social Unrest after the War

The government's first scheme of demobilization involved priority for the release of skilled men who, however, had been the last called up. When mutinies occurred in the British forces, the government changed its policy to *'first in, first out'*. Within seven months four million men were demobilized and at first readily found work.

Further trouble arose for Lloyd George when the war-time controls on prices, profits and wages were removed, with consequent inflation and a drastic lowering of living standards. *This produced much industrial unrest.* When a miners' strike threatened, Lloyd George appointed a commission under **Lord Sankey** to report on the mines, but its members could not agree on whether the mines should be nationalized (as demanded by the miners and the Labour Party) or return to private enterprise. Lloyd George then maintained government control of the mines established during the war and guaranteed the miners a seven and a half hour day by Act of Parliament. Again, after a national railway strike in 1919, Lloyd George ensured that most of the railwaymen's demands were met. In the same way the dockers' wages and conditions were improved as the result of another government commission.

Up to this point Lloyd George had met many of the workers' demands, but in 1920 the collapse of the post-war 'boom' produced a *million unemployed by the beginning of 1921 and two million by the summer.* Lloyd George now returned the mines and railways to private control. A threatened strike by the 'triple alliance' of the miners, railwaymen and transport workers failed, and wages were considerably reduced by the employers. These developments lost Lloyd George much support which he had hitherto enjoyed from the organized workers.

Lloyd George's government had a number of important social achievements to its credit. *Over 200,000 new houses were built in three years*—a considerable achievement for those times. But unfortunately the high marriage rate after the war meant that demand for houses outpaced the supply; and in 1922 there was, in fact, a greater shortage than in 1918. **The National Insurance Act** of **1920** was of great importance, for it increased from three million to twelve million the

number of workers entitled to sickness and unemployment benefit. The
Act also introduced a period of benefit for which no contributions had
been paid and the benefits now included wives and families. After
1921 the problem of widespread unemployment in Britain was a very
pressing one, and Lloyd George was anxious to see a full trade
recovery in Europe, for this would benefit Britain as well. *Reparations
from Germany in the form of coal and other goods were already doing
some harm to British industry*, but Lloyd George failed to persuade
the French to reduce their reparations demands on Germany at an
important *conference at Genoa in 1922*. He also wished to see the
revival of trade between Britain and Russia, but he failed to secure
the general recognition of Soviet Russia, which thereupon came to
an agreement with Germany by the **Treaty of Rapallo**. These failures
told against Lloyd George at home and tended to increase the influence
of the Labour Party which continued to win by-elections. The Conservatives in his coalition government did not like the Rapallo Treaty,
for it strengthened the position of Soviet Russia.

Lloyd George also had to deal with the post-war problem of Ireland,
and this caused him difficulties with members of his government. In

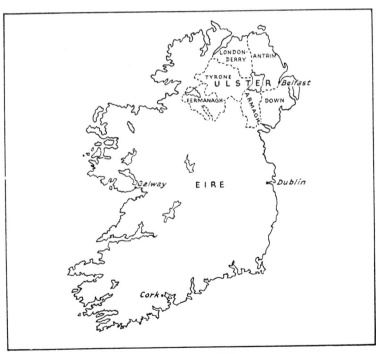

IRELAND IN 1923

1918 an Irish parliament, the *'Dail'*, was set up in Dublin and **Mr. De Valera** became the first President of the Irish Republic. The Irish now set up their own courts and general administration with the idea of replacing the British control still centred in the Castle at Dublin. This, however, was not satisfactory to the **Irish Republican Army** under **Michael Collins**, and they now repeated the tactics attempted during the war when the **Easter Rebellion of 1916** occurred, but was squashed by the English. British police, soldiers and officials were attacked, and in reply the British government now formed the special force of the **'Black and Tans'**—soldiers wearing khaki uniforms and black belts. This force, together with another special force of **Auxiliaries** (ex-officers), carried out reprisals for I.R.A. activities. These reprisals were savage and involved the burning of farms and the murder of civilians. At home, much opposition, strongly led by the Labour Party, was raised against Lloyd George's Irish policy. In 1921 he negotiated a treaty with the new Irish President, **Arthur Griffith**, by which the counties of Ulster remained under the British Crown, but the remainder formed an independent Ireland. Britain also kept three ports in Ireland for her navy. Ireland remained a member of the British Commonwealth and even a Governor-General was appointed by the King. This angered the I.R.A. which once again took up arms against both its British and its Irish opponents, but it was defeated by 1923. During this struggle Michael Collins was killed.

Lloyd George lost political ground over Ireland from both the Labour Left and the Conservative Right. The Left denounced the 'Black and Tan' episode and the Right felt that he had made too many concessions to the Irish. This produced strains within the Coalition Government.

Further complications arose over the economic state of the country in 1922, with widespread unemployment. In order to see where savings could be made in public expenditure, Lloyd George appointed a special economy committee under **Sir Eric Geddes**. Their report led to considerable cuts in the social services, and especially in education. This situation again strengthened the Labour Party in the country, for it led the opposition to Geddes. Then a curious incident abroad made matters even worse for Lloyd George. In Turkey the new national leader **Mustapha Kemal** was leading an armed revolt against the peace settlements as they affected Turkey. His campaign, especially directed against the Greeks who had been given control of **Smyrna**, brought him face to face with British forces at **Chanak** in a neutral zone. The British forces under **General Harrington** stood firm, but the situation could have led to war with the Turks. The final outcome was the removal of British troops and the establishment of modern Turkey by the **Treaty of Lausanne** in **1923**. The Chanak incident had told against Lloyd George in two ways—he was criticized in England for having almost brought us into another war; while others, particularly in the Conservative party, thought we had suffered a severe blow to our prestige in the Moslem world, especially in the Middle East, where Lawrence of Arabia had done so much to build up our prestige and influence during the war.

Thus the Lloyd George Coalition was losing ground both with the working class, which had expected much more of Lloyd George after the war, and with the Conservative members of his government. At a meeting at the *Carlton Club on* 19th October, 1922, the Conservatives decided to leave the Coalition, and Lloyd George resigned.

The General Election which followed showed a division between the Asquith Liberals (60) and the Lloyd George Liberals (57), and a great increase in Labour representation—142. The Conservatives with 345 M.P.s had a clear majority over all others, and Bonar Law now formed a Conservative government. *The Labour Party now became the official Opposition and* **James Ramsay MacDonald** *was elected leader of the Parliamentary Labour Party.* Discontent in the industrial areas had accounted for much Labour support, and at the same time two Communists were elected.

Bonar Law was Prime Minister for only a brief time, for he died in 1923 and was succeeded by **Stanley Baldwin**, who was to play an important part in the development of Conservative policy. As an industrialist, he sympathized with the idea of protective tariffs on imports in order to favour British industry and check foreign competition in the home market. He appointed **Neville Chamberlain**, son of the Protectionist, Joseph Chamberlain, as Chancellor of the Exchequer. The General Election of December 1923, was fought mainly on the Protectionist issue; and, as in 1905, the Labour and Liberal parties fought to maintain free trade as a means of keeping prices of home products from rising and thus lowering real wages. At this time there was much industrial working-class discontent owing to unemployment and recent reductions in wages. The result was the loss by the Conservatives of their over-all majority—the Labour Party increased its representation to 191, the Liberals to 159, and the Conservatives dropped to 258.

The First Labour Government, January–November 1924

Ramsay MacDonald now became the first Labour Prime Minister, with **Philip Snowden**, Chancellor of the Exchequer, **Arthur Henderson**, Home Secretary and **J. H. Thomas**, Colonial Secretary—three men who played a significant part in the development of the Labour Party in these years. MacDonald was dependent on Liberal support in the Commons and programmes of nationalization were therefore impossible. Snowden's financial policies were scarcely revolutionary—the maintenance of free trade, the removal of a number of war-time import duties and the balancing of the budget—all combined with very cautious government and local-government expenditure. This policy had the general support of the Liberals. However, the problem of unemployment remained, and MacDonald came into conflict with the trade unions through his opposition to the strike weapon. The most successful minister was **John Wheatley**, the Minister of Health, whose **Housing Act** speeded up slum clearance and greatly increased the amount of money available to local authorities for the building of new houses. This act produced a great housing drive, which set the pace for some years to come. The Minister of Education, **C. P. Trevelyan**, also secured the repeal of the 'Geddes axe' economies at the expense of education and appointed the important **Hadow Committee**, which, in 1926, decided on the age of eleven as the dividing age between primary and secondary education—a system which has continued into the 1960s.

Ramsay MacDonald was both Prime Minister and Foreign Secretary, and he played an important part in the affairs of Europe. He believed ardently in the League of Nations and in the reconciliation of former enemies. He was a prime mover in getting agreement between France and Germany in 1924 by which the former accepted the **Dawes Plan** for reparation payments by Germany. This was the beginning of better relations between France and Germany for several years and resulted also in Germany entering the League of Nations.

The 'Red Letter' and the Fall of the Labour Government

MacDonald was a strong advocate of better relations with Russia, and he quickly gave Russia full diplomatic recognition and brought about important trading agreements with her. But complications now arose over the *Campbell case*. **J. R. Campbell**, editor of the *Workers' Weekly*, was charged in the courts with inciting British troops to mutiny, but during the parliamentary recess the Labour Attorney-General dropped the prosecution, and the Conservatives declared this to be a purely political move. The Liberals supported this criticism and the government was defeated in the Commons, whereupon MacDonald resigned and another election was called. Four days before polling day the *Daily Mail* published what purported to be a letter from the president of the Third (Communist) International, **Zinoviev**, to the British Communist Party. This letter contained instructions for armed rebellion. The original of this letter—which has now been proved to have been a forgery—was never found, but it had a prejudicial effect against the Labour Party and MacDonald's efforts to improve relations with Russia. The Labour Party representation sank to 151 seats, the Liberals to 42, and the Conservatives rose to 419.

Baldwin had now promised to maintain free trade, and he formed his second government in November 1924.

Baldwin's Second Government, 1924–1929

Baldwin's approach to politics was one of 'safety first'. He wished for cautious social improvements through steering a middle course— he was anxious to avoid exasperating the trade unions and at the same time he wished to restrain the 'right wing' of his own party. With his pipe and bowler hat, he created the image of the steady, careful, tolerant Englishman, anxious to avoid extremes of any kind. As a financier and industrialist his qualifications for the post of Prime Minister were high. Three important members of his government were Winston Churchill, Chancellor of the Exchequer, **Austen Chamberlain**, Foreign Secretary and Neville Chamberlain (Austen's half-brother), Minister of Health.

In foreign policy Austen Chamberlain negotiated the **Locarno Pact, December 1925**, by which Germany's western frontiers were guaranteed and the Rhineland was demilitarized—both points showing the anxiety of Britain to reduce German opposition to Versailles by gradual stages and to ease the old French and German antagonism. The Locarno Pact also achieved a non-aggression agreement between France and Germany, and Germany agreed to arbitration in disputes between herself, France, Belgium, Poland and Czechoslovakia. By another clause of the Pact, Germany, France, Great Britain, Belgium and Italy guaranteed the peace of Europe. This was an important treaty, greatly strengthening the work of the League of Nations. *The entry of Germany into the League of Nations in the following year (1926) was a consequence of this agreement.*

The results of Locarno were seen in better relations between France and Germany in the period 1925–1929. Indeed, these years became the 'golden age' of post-war optimism when it appeared that international goodwill would triumph. In 1928 the **Kellogg Pact** saw the signing of an agreement by sixty-five nations to renounce war as an instrument of policy.

The results of the better international climate on Britain herself were seen in the *Baldwin government's reduction in arms expenditure* —the Army and the Royal Air Force were most affected, but under the **Washington Naval Treaty**, negotiated by Lloyd George in **1921**, Britain's navy had to be kept on a par with that of the U.S.A. Arms expenditure in the early 1930s was less than in 1913. Japan, who had also signed the Washington Naval agreement, was not yet regarded as a menace to Britain in the Far East, and improvements to the naval base at **Singapore** went on very slowly—and were stopped altogether by the Labour Government in 1929.

Industrial Problems and the General Strike, 1926

In his April budget of 1925, Winston Churchill announced *Britain's return to the gold standard*, by which English currency was tied to the international value of gold. Since 1918 prices had fallen, and this helped the wage-earners to meet wage-reductions to a certain extent. The effect of returning to the gold standard (a return wanted by the City of London to strengthen Britain as a financial centre) was to raise the prices of imports, and also to raise costs thus making export rather more difficult. To meet increased costs, employers began to demand wage-reductions, and this particularly affected the miners. A special commission under **Sir Herbert Samuel**, among other recommendations, advised the reduction of miners' wages or the increase of hours. The miners were further exasperated by the Commission's rejection of the nationalization of the mines. The miners, under the militant leadership of **A. J. Cook**, refused to accept reductions, and the **Trades Union Congress** now made preparations for a **General Strike** in support of the miners. Difficulties spread to the newspaper world when the printers of the *Daily Mail* refused to print a leading article which criticized the trade unions. The government demanded that the T.U.C. withdraw its instructions for a national strike, but they refused, and on *3rd May, 1926, the General Strike began*, and all major industries came to a virtual stop. Volunteers attempted to run trains and buses, but with limited effect. The strike committees allowed the transport of food supplies. The government then declared the strike illegal and increasingly used troops to keep essential services in being. On 12th May, the T.U.C. called off the strike, amidst bitter recriminations against the union leaders by the rank and file and especially by the miners, who continued their own strike until December, when they returned on the mine-owners' terms. The reasons for the T.U.C.'s decisions are controversial, but a section of their members were becoming increasingly militant, and the leadership was certainly not prepared for revolution.

After the strike, Baldwin himself adopted a moderate line and urged the employers to avoid any victimization of workers, but his request was not always carried out. The effect of the failure of the General Strike on the trade union movement was to strengthen the moderate leadership who believed in a non-militant and non-revolutionary development of the British trade unions.

The Trade Disputes Act, 1927

This Act was the direct result of the General Strike. By its terms any strike was illegal which aimed to coerce the government or to threaten the community. The *'contracting-in'* system was enforced—

BALDWIN AND CONSERVATIVE RULE
1924–1929

Return to the Gold Standard—raised costs of production

Samuel Commission—reduction of miners'
wages advised

GENERAL STRIKE FAILURE

Trade Disputes Act, 1927	Weakened trade union and labour movement	Mond-Turner policies
		Co-operation of labour and capital

FOREIGN POLICY

Locarno Pact, 1925
Germany enters League, 1926
Low arms expenditure.
General policy of
conciliation of Germany

SOCIAL POLICIES

Widows, Orphans and Old
Age Contributory Pensions Act

Local Government Act, 1929

Reduction of rates on
agriculture and industry

The People (Equal Franchise)
Act, 1928

Central Electricity Board and
BBC

that is, any trade union member who wished any part of his contribution to be used for political purposes (the *political levy*) was to give notice in writing to his trade union to this effect. Established Civil Servants were prohibited from belonging to any trade union affiliated to the T.U.C. The general result of this act was to reduce trade union payments to the Labour Party.

Baldwin's Social Policies

A number of important social advances were made by the Baldwin government. The **Widows, Orphans and Old Age Contributory Pensions Act** gave 10/- a week to widows and allowances for dependent children of widows, and a grant of 7/6 a week for orphan children.

Neville Chamberlain introduced the important **Local Government Act of 1929**. By this act the Boards of Guardians created under the Poor Law Amendment Act of 1834 were abolished and their work dealt with by **Public Assistance Committees** of county and borough councils. This was a further change away from the old Victorian Poor Law.

Agriculture was assisted by the de-rating of agricultural land and buildings, and industry was also helped by a three-quarters reduction of rates on industrial buildings and on railways.

The People (Equal Franchise) Act of **1928** at last brought about the change demanded by the suffragette movement. Women over twenty-one years of age were given the same voting rights as men.

Forms of nationalization were introduced by the setting up of the **Central Electricity Board** to control the whole distribution of electricity, and the **B.B.C.** *was established as a public corporation.*

The General Election of 1929

Despite the fact that Baldwin's government had a good record in the international field and had introduced a number of progressive measures, the General Election of 30th May, 1929, resulted in considerable losses to the Conservatives and the return of the second Labour government.

The reasons for this defeat can be attributed to the unadventurousness of Baldwin's policies—a slowness which was strongly criticized in the Conservative Party itself by its younger members, among whom **Mr. Harold Macmillan** was prominent. Insufficient was being done for the mass of the people, and a particularly unpopular action of the government had been the removal of special government assistance to local authorities for the building of houses. In 1927, also, relations between Russia and Britain had been broken by a *police raid on the premises of the Russian Trade Delegation, 'Arcos',* on the grounds that it was an espionage centre. As nothing incriminating was found, this raid was the subject of much criticism in the country. The Labour Party issued an effective programme statement entitled 'Labour and the Nation' and was in better organizational shape than in 1925. This was partly due to the fact that the General Strike's failure had caused the trade unions to concentrate more than previously on gaining parliamentary influence, and their support was strong. The Labour Party won 287 seats, the Conservatives 251 and the Liberals 59. The Conservatives thus lost their over-all majority, but the second Labour government was still dependent on Liberal support.

Summary

Lloyd George experienced increasing difficulty in holding the coalition together and his earlier popularity with the trade unions slowly declined. The economic recession from 1921 onwards created special labour difficulties and his Russian policy quickly proved an expensive failure. In the same way the Irish problem earned him opposition from numerous quarters, including a section of his own government. The first Labour government of 1924 was dependent on Liberal support. It was, however, able to achieve some progress, especially in housing and foreign affairs. After Labour's defeat, Baldwin continued the policy of international co-operation and efforts to ease German reparation burdens. The years 1925 to 1929 saw an all-round improvement in international relations. At home, Baldwin was faced by the General Strike, the failure of which produced a new period of co-operation between labour and capital. A number of important improvements in social benefits were brought about.

Important Dates

1918	**The 'khaki election'.**
1920	**Collapse of the post-war boom.**
1921	**Unemployment rises sharply.**
	'Black and Tans' in Ireland.
1922	**Irish Free State established.**
	Genoa Conference.
	Treaty of Rapallo.
	The 'Geddes Axe'.
	The Chanak incident.
	End of Coalition.
	Bonar Law became Prime Minister.
1923	**Baldwin became Prime Minister.**
	Protectionist idea revived.
	Defeat of Baldwin.

1924	First Labour government.
	Zinoviev letter.
1925–1929	Baldwin's second government.
1925	Britain returned to the Gold Standard.
	Locarno Pact.
1926	The General Strike.
	Germany entered League of Nations.
1927	Trade Disputes Act.
1928	Kellogg Pact.
	The People (Equality of Representation) Act.
1929	Local Government Act.
	Second Labour government returned.

QUESTIONS

(1) *What immediate problems faced the country at the end of the war?*

(2) *What problems made it impossible for Lloyd George to maintain the Coalition?*

(3) *Why did the Baldwin government fall in the election of December 1923?*

(4) *Examine the work of the first Labour government and explain its defeat in 1924.*

(5) *Why did the General Strike occur and why did it fail?*

(6) *Discuss Baldwin's foreign and defence policy, 1925–1929.*

(7) *Write notes on* (a) *Trade Disputes Act, 1927;* (b) *Representation of the People* (*Equal Franchise*) *Act, 1928;* (c) *Local Government Act, 1929.*

(8) *Why did the Conservatives lose the election of 1929?*

CHAPTER THIRTY-FOUR

THE CRISIS: 1929-1931

R AMSAY MACDONALD'S second Labour government contained the first woman minister—**Miss Margaret Bondfield,** Minister of Labour, with Philip Snowden as Chancellor of the Exchequer, J. H. Thomas as Lord Privy Seal, and J. R. Clynes as Home Secretary.

Home Policies

Being dependent on Liberal support, the government was unable to introduce measures of nationalization. As a partial substitute, the government encouraged a kind of self-regulated capitalism. An important example of this was the **Agricultural Marketing Act, 1931,** by which farmers could fix prices and organize marketing schemes for a number of products. **The Housing Act, 1930,** introduced by the Minister of Health, **Arthur Greenwood,** renewed the subsidies to local authorities and made special provision for slum clearance. The results of this act were seen during the next ten years, when more slums were cleared than ever before.

Efforts to reduce unemployment were unsuccessful, despite the schemes of J. H. Thomas (the minister responsible) in developing road works, in railway development and in the transfer of industries to distressed areas. To ease the burdens on the unemployed, the **Unemployment Insurance Act** of **1930** extended the 'transitional benefits' to people who were not already entitled to them by the number of their contributions to the fund. But *attempts to repeal the Trade Disputes Act of 1927 failed,* as did Sir C. Trevelyan's efforts to raise the school leaving age to 15.

Discontent with the slowness of social reform under Labour showed itself in the party, and in 1930 **Sir Oswald Mosley** resigned from his post as Chancellor of the Duchy of Lancaster to form the *New Party* with its journal *Action.* This was the path which was to lead to his formation of the **British Union of Fascists.** The Independent Labour Party M.P.s, led by **James Maxton,** were also critical of their government's record.

Foreign and Imperial Policy

The Labour Foreign Secretary, **Arthur Henderson,** one of the pioneers of the Labour Party, was an ardent supporter of the League of Nations. He helped to secure Germany's acceptance of the American **Young Plan** for reduced reparations in 1929. He aimed to continue the reductions of the post-war burdens placed on Germany by Versailles. He secured the withdrawal of Allied troops from the Rhineland five years ahead of schedule. He also took a leading part in preparations for the **World Disarmament Conference** of **1932**. By the **London Naval Agreement of 1930**, a ratio of 5:5:3 was fixed for the navies of U.S.A., Britain and Japan respectively, and no capital ships were to be built for five years. Britain also agreed to limit to fifty the number of her cruisers. This was a constructive agreement which limited naval ship-building, and was popular. In 1929 Henderson achieved *the resumption of diplomatic relations with Soviet Russia.* Labour's policy of all-round conciliation seemed to be working well.

Labour's policies for the Empire promised considerable progress, but here the government came up against intractable problems. Mr. MacDonald called a Round Table Conference on India in 1931, which was eventually attended by **Mr. Gandhi**, who demanded independence and self-government, whereas the farthest Britain would go was a scheme of 'Dominion Status'; to be followed by responsible government in the provinces and consultation with Britain in the central government. Henderson promised Egypt that Britain would give Egypt control of her internal affairs and withdraw from the Canal Zone, but negotiations failed when the Egyptian negotiators demanded joint control with Britain over the Sudan. The government faced a difficult problem in Palestine, where the Arab-Jewish conflict became severe. The Colonial Secretary, **Lord Passfield**, took measures to prevent the illegal entry of Jews into Palestine, but was severely criticized in Britain. The **Statute of Westminster, 1931**, recognized the right of any Dominion of the Commonwealth to complete independence. This was the end of the old basis of Empire, and enabled Pakistan and India to remain in the Commonwealth in 1947.

The World Economic Crisis, 1929–1931

The optimistic 'jazz' age of the 1920s was suddenly shaken by economic disaster. In 1929 a slump in commodity prices on the *New York Stock Exchange* ('Wall Street') led to a drastic fall in world prices of basic commodities. Producers and manufacturers found their profits disappearing overnight, and the slump spread to Europe and other parts of the world. Workers were laid off and unemployment soared to unprecedented heights. The sudden failure of a number of important banks in Europe, especially the *Credit-Anstalt* in Vienna, caused the foreign holders of funds in Britain to withdraw their money, and this caused an immediate drain of gold from Britain, whose gold reserve dwindled fast and whose pound sterling was in danger of complete collapse. *By July 1931, unemployment in Britain reached the total of 2,700,000.*

In the Commons the Labour government was now attacked for wasteful expenditure, and demands were made for economies at the expense of the social services. The government responded by setting up the **May Committee** (named after its chairman), which reported that if government expenditure continued at its present rate, it would lead to a budget deficit of £120 million. It recommended cuts in the salaries of Civil Servants, teachers and the armed forces as well as in rates of unemployment benefit. If this were not done, the pound's value would collapse. MacDonald was prepared to make every effort to save the pound from collapse but there was division in the government—especially over the proposed reduction in benefits to the unemployed. In August 1931, MacDonald resigned and agreed to form a **National Government** in which Baldwin and **Herbert Samuel** (Liberal leader) agreed to serve. Thus a crisis originating in Wall Street had resulted in the destruction of the Second Labour government. The government had no united answer to the problems of the crisis. The Labour Party now officially repudiated MacDonald, and **George Lansbury**, the socialist pioneer and pacifist, assumed the leadership.

The First National Government and the Election of 1931

The National Government's first action was to impose, with the majority agreement of the House of Commons, a general reduction of 10 per cent in the salaries of Civil Servants, teachers, and members of the armed forces and in the insurance benefits of the unemployed. Despite an American loan of £80 million, confidence in the pound sterling abroad continued to decline, and a mutiny in the navy at Invergordon, in protest against the pay cuts, had an alarmist effect out of all proportion to its real seriousness. The government attempted to stem the decline by taking Britain off the gold standard, and we were once again back to a paper currency.

In the General Election of October 1931, the government and its supporters won an overwhelming majority with 521 seats. The Labour Party sank to 52 and the Liberals 33. MacDonald now made Neville Chamberlain Chancellor of the Exchequer in place of Philip Snowden. This was a sign that the government were about to move Britain away from free trade to Protection. In February 1932, a general tariff of 10 per cent was imposed on imports, except foodstuffs and raw materials needed for industry. This wisely avoided any tax on food, for it was precisely this which had defeated Joseph Chamberlain in 1906. Goods from the British Dominions were exempt from the import charge under

THE SECOND LABOUR GOVERNMENT
1929-1931

HOME POLICY

Marketing schemes
encouraged.
Housing Act, 1930
Unemployment Insurance
Act, 1930
Failure to reduce
unemployment.
Failure to repeal
Trade Disputes Act

Dependent on Liberal
support.
Labour discontent
with slowness of
reform

Mosley forms New Party.
I.L.P. members critical
of government record

Difficulties of a
minority government

FOREIGN AND IMPERIAL

Henderson secures German
acceptance of *Young Plan.*
London Naval Agreement, 1930
Diplomatic relations resumed
with Russia, 1929
Statute of Westminster, 1931
Henderson fails in negotiations
over India and Egypt.
Prepares for World
Disarmament Conference

Principles: Conciliation of
Germany
Strengthen the
League
Disarmament
Co-operation with
Soviet Russia

WORLD ECONOMIC CRISIS, 1929-1931
MAY COMMITTEE REPORT
MacDONALD FORMS NATIONAL GOVERNMENT
OVERWHELMING DEFEAT OF LABOUR, 1931

the terms of **Imperial Preference**. Neville Chamberlain wished to see complete Empire free trade, and the important **Ottawa Imperial Conference** of **July-August 1932**, was called to consider this, but the Dominions themselves were now imposing protective duties, except that British goods were favoured by lower tariffs. The Dominions were not prepared to abandon their own protectionist policies, and the Conference failed to produce Empire free trade. Then again, at the **World Economic Conference** of **1933**, over which MacDonald presided, there was failure to reduce tariffs and other trade barriers—in fact, all the great nations were becoming more protectionist in an attempt to put their own interests first.

The Problem of Unemployment and the Means Test

Chamberlain was faced by the terrible unemployment problem in Scotland, South Wales, West Cumberland and Tyneside. All these were denominated first as **'Depressed Areas'**, then as **'Special Areas'** in 1934; and they received special grants of about £2 million. In 1937 efforts were made by the government to create new industries in these areas, but this produced only a small response and decreased unemployment by only a few thousand.

Men were now unemployed for such long periods that they exhausted their benefits based on actual insurance contributions. They were then accorded relief from **National Assistance** funds, but in 1931 the *'means test'* was introduced by which an unemployed man's savings and other income were taken into account before relief was granted. The objection to this was that it penalized those who had managed to save anything, and in any case the whole principle of the 'means test' was resented as an imposition. There were violent protests, and 'hunger marches' by the unemployed to London were organized on a large scale. Many Labour councils refused to operate the 'means test'. Partly in order to meet this type of opposition, Chamberlain, by his **Unemployment Insurance Act** of **1934**, removed the payment of relief from the Public Assistance Committees of the local councils to the new national **Unemployment Assistance Board**. However, the 'means test' system was not renewed.

The National Government of MacDonald took credit for the fact that *in 1933 unemployment fell by more than a million.* In 1934 Chamberlain reduced Income tax. He also restored the 10 per cent economy cuts in unemployment insurance and in 1935 the various salary cuts. The years 1935–1939 were good years for those employed —especially in the expanding areas of London and the south-east, but the Special Areas remained. *In 1939 Britain still had more than one million unemployed.*

Summary

The second Labour government was also a minority government. It achieved a certain amount of important legislation involving unemployment insurance and housing. In foreign affairs Henderson continued the post-war British policy of reducing the pressure of the Versailles Treaty on Germany and resumed diplomatic relations with Russia. The government also had to deal with problems arising from both Indian and Egyptian claims to complete independence and with illegal Jewish immigration into Palestine. The world economic crisis of 1929–1931 destroyed the second Labour government and weakened the Labour Party itself through the divisions caused by the varying attitudes to the 'May' economy proposals. The first National government under MacDonald took drastic economy measures and won the election of 1931 with an overwhelming majority. In economic affairs Britain now moved rapidly away from free trade towards Protection. A cause of extreme discontent, especially in the Special Areas, was the Means Test. The economic state of the country gradually improved, but in 1939 there were still a million unemployed of which a large part was accounted for by the Special Areas, where the National governments had failed to achieve any substantial improvement.

Important Dates

1929 Diplomatic relations between Russia and Britain resumed.
Young Plan of reduced German reparations.
British troops withdrawn from Rhineland.
Wall Street slump.

1930 Housing Act.
Unemployment Insurance Act.

1931 Agricultural Marketing Act.
Indian Round Table Conference.
Statute of Westminster.
July: unemployment in Britain reaches two million.
May Committee's report.
Invergordon mutiny.
Formation of National government.
Means Test introduced.

1932 General tariff of 10 per cent.
Ottawa Imperial Conference.

1933 World Economic Conference.

1934 Unemployment Insurance Act.

1935 'May' economy cuts restored.

QUESTIONS

(1) *Give an account of the second Labour government's main work in the period 1929–1931.*

(2) *How would you account for the overwhelming National victory in the election of 1931?*

(3) *Examine the policies of the National governments towards the problem of unemployment.*

CHAPTER THIRTY-FIVE

FOREIGN AND IMPERIAL POLICIES
1931–1939

Public Opinion

BRITISH public opinion in these years was strongly anti-war and firmly in favour of efforts to secure general disarmament through the League of Nations. Memories of 1914–1918 still dominated all thought on international questions, and many fondly hoped that even **Hitler** could be brought to peaceful agreements through the League. In 1933 the famous resolution of the Oxford Union Debating Society was passed which declared *'that this House will not fight for King and Country'*. There was widespread distrust of many politicians, big armament firms, and other vested interests which were widely held to have caused World War I.

World Disarmament Conference, February 1932–April 1934

MacDonald sympathized with, and his policies had helped to fortify, this pacific climate of opinion. (In any case, it must be borne in mind that the English people had never been militaristic.) Even after Japan's attack on China in 1931 and Hitler's rise to power in Germany in 1933, Chamberlain's budget of 1934 showed the lowest expenditure on armaments since 1914. By that time, however, the World Disarmament Conference was failing. This failure was due to sharp differences among the Great Powers. Britain, wishing to remain uninvolved in European conflicts, refused to guarantee France against German attack, while Germany demanded military equality with France. *There was much sympathy in Britain for Germany's denunciation of the Versailles Treaty as unjust.* This did not imply sympathy for Hitler and the Nazis, but it made the Nazi aims easier to achieve. Hitler now withdrew Germany from the League, and MacDonald saw his aims of a great disarmament agreement shattered. The National government lost some ground with public opinion and this in part accounted for a considerable recovery by the Labour Party in the election of 1935. MacDonald's health, and influence in political life, declined rapidly.

Japan and Manchuria, 1931

In September 1931, Japan invaded and seized control of Manchuria. **Sir John Simon**, pursuing the usual post-war British policy of conciliation, attempted to get agreement between Japan and China. A special *Commission under Lord Lytton* condemned Japan's methods, but had some criticism to make of China. No sanctions were imposed by the League against Japan—possibly because sanctions would have led to war against Japan with the non-League power of the U.S.A. standing aside. Thus aggression had won the day. At home the National government was criticized by the Left for not having taken a more effective line against Japan.

The Rise of Hitler

With Hitler's rise to power in 1933 the British Chiefs of Staff demanded a considerable increase in Britain's defence forces. They particularly demanded an increase in the R.A.F. to bring it to equality with the German air force (*Luftwaffe*). Their demands were not immediately heeded, but by 1935 even MacDonald realized that Britain had decreasing hopes of reliance on collective security through the League, and Hitler's introduction of conscription (a further defiance of Versailles) made this even clearer. MacDonald's policy now became one of exploiting **Mussolini**'s dislike of the rise of a fellow dictator, and at Stresa in Switzerland in 1935 he formed the **Stresa Front** of Britain, France and Italy, who together condemned the 'unilateral repudiation of treaties which may endanger the peace of Europe.' But also in 1935 MacDonald brought about the **Anglo-German Naval Agreement** by which Hitler agreed to a German navy which was to be no more than 35 per cent of Britain's. This very agreement was a breach of the Versailles Treaty.

In June 1935, MacDonald resigned the premiership in favour of Stanley Baldwin. **Sir Samuel Hoare** became Foreign Secretary and **Anthony Eden**, Minister concerned with League of Nations affairs.

Mussolini and Abyssinia

A new test for collective security and the League of Nations now occurred. It was also a test for the policies of the British government. Attempts were made in 1935 by Anthony Eden to meet some of Mussolini's claims in regard to Abyssinia, but these efforts were rejected by Mussolini. In October 1935, Italy launched an attack on Abyssinia. *This time economic sanctions were quickly applied against Italy by most members of the League, including Britain.* This was in accord with public opinion in Britain which, in the *League of Nations*

Union Peace Ballot of June 1935, had declared emphatically in support of sanctions against an aggressor. Again, in the general election of November 1935, Baldwin had promised Britain's support for collective security and had emphasized that no great rearmament was necessary. Once again, the Conservatives had an overwhelming majority with 432 seats, but the Labour Party recovered somewhat with 154 seats. The Liberals fell to 20.

Despite financial and trade sanctions, Mussolini's advance in Abyssinia continued, and now a widespread demand arose for the imposition of vital oil sanctions against Italy. Baldwin, however, refrained from a measure which might lead to war against Italy and destroy the Stresa Front against Hitler. The Foreign Secretary, Sir Samuel Hoare, now produced, in conjunction with the French premier, **Pierre Laval**, the **Hoare-Laval Plan**, by which Abyssinia would be partitioned between the Italians and the Abyssinians. Such was the public indignation, when this scheme became known in Britain and France, that Sir Samuel Hoare resigned and *Mr. Anthony Eden became Foreign Secretary*. Yet oil sanctions were still not imposed by the League and by May 1936, Mussolini was victorious and the **Emperor Haile Selassie** in exile. Earlier, in March, *Hitler had reoccupied the Rhineland unopposed*. Thus unilateral action and aggression continued to triumph.

The Spanish Civil War, 1936–1939

In July 1936, General Franco began a revolt from Morocco against the Spanish Republican Government. With the aid of Moorish troops he hoped to capture Madrid quickly and overwhelm Republican resistance, but in this he failed, and he was not victorious until 1939.

The Spanish Civil War presented a grave problem for Britain, especially when, despite a **Non-intervention Agreement** signed between the European powers and strongly sponsored by Mr. Eden, Italian and German troops (so-called 'volunteers') continued to reach Spain to assist Franco. Soviet Russia similarly assisted the Republicans. In Britain demands arose from the Left for the formation of a **Popular Front** government consisting of representatives of most parties which would give direct economic and military aid to the Republicans. *But the official Labour Party line continued to support non-intervention as did that of the Baldwin and Chamberlain governments.* For his continued support of the Popular Front campaign, **Sir Stafford Cripps** was expelled from the Labour Party. However, many Republican supporters from Britain, mainly recruited by the British Communist Party, fought against Franco in the **International Brigade**. Eventually, the weight of Italian and German aid to Franco, and serious divisions within the Republican movement, proved too much for the Republicans; and in 1939 Franco was victorious—another victory for Fascism against legally constituted authority.

The Abdication of Edward VIII, 1936

King George V died on 20th January, 1935, and was succeeded by his son Edward VIII. The new king had formed a strong attachment to an American divorcee, **Mrs. Simpson**, and wished to marry her. This was strongly opposed in high quarters, especially by Baldwin, by the Archbishop of Canterbury, **Dr. Lang**, and by a number of leading newspapers, notably *The Times*. But the King was supported by two great newspaper proprietors, **Lords Rothermere** and **Beaverbrook**, and there were suggestions of forming a 'King's Party'. The King, however, eventually accepted the necessity of his abdication if he was to remain determined to marry Mrs. Simpson; and he announced this in a radio broadcast on 11th December, 1936. The abdication caused much public stir, especially as the King was young and popular, and had shown conscientious interest in the people of the Special Areas. He was succeeded by his brother, the Duke of York, as **King George VI**. After the Coronation, Baldwin resigned and was followed by Neville Chamberlain as Prime Minister—a post he retained till 1940.

Rearmament

Hitler's successes began to have some effect on British armament policy, especially when Hitler boasted in 1935 that Germany's air force was equal to Britain's. *In Parliament Winston Churchill continued to demand British rearmament* and warned the nation continually about Hitler's aggressive intentions. From 1937, Chamberlain increased British armaments considerably; and by 1939, British aircraft production was greater than that of Germany. The army, however, was not increased in the same proportion, for the theory in favour at this time was that air power alone could be decisive in war. In 1938, Britain was spending about one quarter of her national output on armaments. Even the Labour Party in Parliament, while demanding a policy of collective security through the League, ceased to vote against the armaments estimates, and merely abstained. But Chamberlain continued to hope for a lasting settlement with Hitler without war.

Chamberlain's Foreign Policy, 1937-1939

Chamberlain's policy was based on continued attempts to reach agreement with Hitler. Churchill, a rather isolated figure in the Commons in these years, took the consistent line that Hitler intended aggression if he could get away with it, and that Britain must rearm.

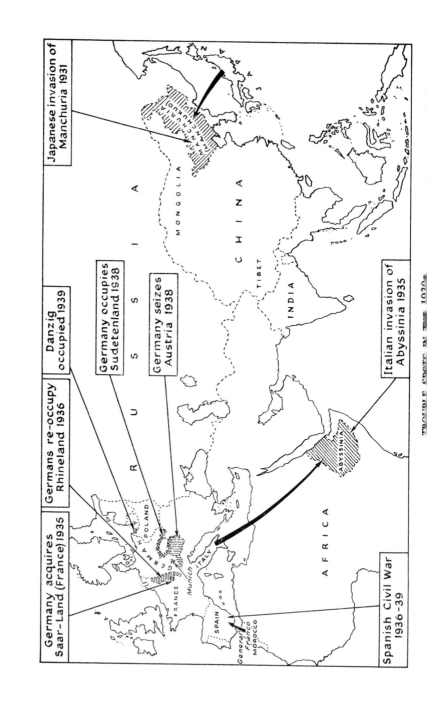

Japanese invasion of
Manchuria 1931

Danzig
occupied 1939

Germany occupies
Sudetenland 1938

Germany seizes
Austria 1938

Germans re-occupy
Rhineland 1936

Germany acquires
Saar-Land (France) 1935

Italian invasion of
Abyssinia 1935

Spanish Civil War
1936–39

TROUBLE SPOTS IN THE 1930s

The Foreign Secretary himself, Anthony Eden, had a number of differences in his views from those of the Prime Minister. Above all, he was in favour of a show of resistance to Hitler and Mussolini. He believed that such a show of real resistance would decisively check the ambitions of the dictators. In 1937 Eden succeeded in securing an agreement between the European powers at **Nyon** which put a stop to Italian submarine attacks on food vessels trading with Republican Spain. Again, at the **Brussels Nine-power Conference** of **1937** to consider Japanese aggression in the Far East, he accepted on behalf of Britain any action against Japan which would have American support. But the U.S.A. was unwilling to act and British naval power in the Far East was not strong enough for action against Japan. In February 1938 Eden resigned and was followed as Foreign Secretary by **Lord Halifax**. Chamberlain and Halifax both considered that the Stresa policy of alignment with Mussolini against Hitler could be successful in preventing Hitler's securing the **Sudeten** areas of Czechoslovakia and the union of Austria with Germany. Eden disagreed with this approach. Eden also resigned because of Chamberlain's wish to bring about the recognition of the Italian control of Abyssinia, and Halifax undertook negotiations which resulted in this recognition. *During these negotiations, Hitler had occupied Austria on 13th March, 1938.*

Czechoslovakia

Despite the seizure of Austria by Hitler, Chamberlain and Halifax continued their attempts to reach agreement with Hitler and to resolve the remaining German grievances arising from Versailles. Negotiations effecting Czechoslovakia resulted in Chamberlain accepting the arguments of Hitler for the union of the Sudeten areas with Germany; and the British Ambassador in Berlin, **Neville Henderson**, was an ardent promoter of this policy. The Czechs under their President **Eduard Benesh**, were determined to resist demands which would have meant the loss to Czechoslovakia of her strong Sudeten Mountain defences. In September 1938, the Sudeten Germans attempted a rising which the Czechs suppressed. There was some danger that Hitler would now march in, and Chamberlain decided to meet Hitler personally. *On 18th September, 1938, he flew to Germany and met Hitler in his Bavarian redoubt at* **Berchtesgaden**. He accepted Hitler's demands for the separation of the Sudeten area from Czechoslovakia and Dr. Benesh was forced to accept these decisions when both Britain and France made it clear that they could not support him if he refused. At Berchtesgaden it had been agreed that negotiations would take place with the Czechs and other powers concerned, but when Chamberlain met Hitler again at **Godesberg** on the Rhine, Hitler made it clear that he wanted immediate occupation of the Sudeten areas. Chamberlain rejected this and succeeded in delaying it until 21st October. Clearly Hitler had no real intention of negotiating as agreed upon at Berchtesgaden.

Hitler's Godesberg demands not only led to criticism of Chamberlain by the Left in Britain, but leading members of his own government and party also became critical—including Sir John Simon, Sir Samuel Hoare, and even Halifax himself. Chamberlain now ordered preparations for war, and air-raid shelters were dug, gas-masks distributed and preparations made for evacuating school-children to country areas. The Fleet was also mobilized.

Munich, 29th September, 1938

On 28th September, Chamberlain suddenly announced in the House of Commons that Mussolini, at Chamberlain's request, had persuaded Hitler to agree to a *Four Power meeting at Munich*. All M.P.s (with the exception of four, including Churchill) greeted this news with relief and excitement. On 29th September, Chamberlain, Daladier, Mussolini and Hitler met at Munich, and Hitler agreed that after the occupation of the Sudetenland, Czechoslovakia should be guaranteed by the four powers. Chamberlain took back to Britain with him a sheet of paper signed by himself and Hitler which declared that Britain and Germany would adopt this method of consultation to settle all future problems affecting them. *This, declared Chamberlain, meant 'peace for our time'*.

During 1938 and 1939, British rearmament was speeded up and **Sir John Anderson** was given charge of **Air Raid Precautions (ARP)**. More detailed plans for civilian evacuation were worked out.

With the German occupation of the Sudeten areas, the pro-German **Hacha** succeeded Dr. Benesh as President. Soon afterward Hacha declared the heart of the country, **Bohemia**, a German protectorate and on *11th March, 1939 German forces entered Prague*. The Skoda armament works now fell into Nazi hands.

Chamberlain's previous policies culminating in Munich were now seen to be a complete failure. In Britain compulsory military service for men over twenty was now introduced. Chamberlain offered the Poles an alliance, as also did France; for Hitler had stepped up his campaign for the return to Germany of Danzig and the Polish Corridor. Poland accepted the offered alliance, which was finally signed on 25th August. In the meantime Hitler repudiated the 1934 non-aggression pact with Poland, and also the Anglo-German Naval Agreement of 1935.

British-Soviet Negotiations

There was strong pressure on Chamberlain from many quarters for

Britain to form an alliance with Soviet Russia. Minor diplomatic officials were sent to Moscow to negotiate, but difficulties arose. Britain feared that **Stalin** intended to occupy the Baltic States of Estonia and Latvia, where Hitler had many sympathizers. Moreover, to the alarm of Russia, Hitler had already forced the Lithuanians to cede to Germany the port of Memel. Stalin also wanted the right to move Russian forces through northern Poland in the event of a Nazi attack on Poland, whether the Poles requested this aid or not. The negotiations dragged on to a complete impasse.

The Nazi-Soviet Pact, 23rd August, 1939

On 23rd August, **Ribbentrop** for Germany and **Molotov** for Russia signed the **German-Soviet Pact** which guaranteed Russia's neutrality if Germany were involved in war. The limits for the Nazi control of Poland were also agreed upon in a secret clause. The news of this pact shook the whole world, for Russia had been one of the principal denouncers of the Nazis and had been foremost under **Litvinoff** in the League of Nations in denouncing the compromise policies of Chamberlain. Munich had been a specially bitter target for Russian denunciation.

At this point Chamberlain and Halifax attempted to persuade the Poles to negotiate with Hitler over his demands, but they refused. On 1st September, a German land attack on Poland began, and Warsaw was bombed from the air. Chamberlain even now hoped that Hitler could be prevailed upon to stop hostilities and submit all disputed matters to a conference of the powers. Great uneasiness existed in Britain and, under heavy pressure from the House of Commons and his own cabinet, *Chamberlain sent Hitler, on 3rd September, an ultimatum demanding his withdrawal from Poland.* No answer being received by 11 a.m., Chamberlain announced that Britain was at war with Germany. Thus began the Second World War, which ultimately led to the alliance of Britain, the U.S.A. and Soviet Russia and the defeat of Hitlerism in 1945.

Some Causes of the Second World War

The following points should be considered, though they are not necessarily listed in order of importance.

(1) Fascism was a creed of aggression with the end justifying the means. In Fascist propaganda the principle of the greater the lie the greater its effect, was very common. Fascism was essentially expansionist and could not be satisfied with a purely internal consolidation of power. War was glorified and the very young indoctrinated accordingly.

(2) The very weaknesses of the non-fascist powers, especially their failure to utilize all the powers of the League of Nations against aggressors, was an indirect cause of the Second World War. The position was, however, complicated by the fact that the three main aggressor powers were members themselves of the League.

(3) The Versailles Treaty gave Hitler ready-made excuses for unilateral action and there was a good deal of 'guilty conscience' in Europe over Versailles, which Hitler was able to exploit. The feeling in Europe that Germany may, after all, have been treated with undue harshness in 1919, weakened the will to resist the Nazi advance.

(4) The absence of the U.S.A. from the League of Nations and her unwillingness to be involved in sanctions against aggressors (especially Japan) further weakened resistance to fascist expansion.

(5) The economic collapse of 1929–1931 was another basic factor contributing to Hitler's success in Germany and was another indirect cause of the Second World War.

(6) Hitler's role of 'protector' of Western Europe against Russian Communism found a good deal of sympathy in Europe. Chamberlain himself was strongly influenced by this consideration, as were many of his supporters.

(7) Europe failed to understand early enough the true ruthlessness of Hitler's aims and methods. His work *Mein Kampf* ('My Struggle'), in which he preached anti-semitism and the myth of Aryan (that is, German) superiority, was regarded with half-amusement rather than real concern.

(8) There were those in France, Britain and elsewhere who thought that a future war could be confined to Germany and Russia, and there was considerable sympathy with Chamberlain's view that German control of the Balkans was inevitable. This control in itself would constitute an anti-Russian barrier.

(9) The mistake of so many western statesmen was to think that Hitler could ever be 'satisfied'. Their diplomacy, and particularly that of Chamberlain, seems to have been old-fashioned—more 'nineteenth century' than a diplomacy capable of meeting the pressures of the most ruthless tyranny the world has ever seen.

The Second World War was caused by a combination of two factors —ruthless Fascist aggression on the one hand and division and weakness among its opponents on the other.

Summary

The general anti-war feeling of the British people was strong in this period and for many years there existed a generous attitude towards avowed German grievances. Arms expenditure continued to be low for several years. British efforts to bring about better relations between

France and Germany had no success, however, and their relationship worsened. Various forms of Fascist aggression proved highly successful and culminated in the formation of the Rome-Berlin-Tokio axis. The League of Nations proved weak and ineffective in the face of these developments. The British policy of the 'Stresa Front' proved ineffective in dividing Hitler and Mussolini. Chamberlain continued right up to September 1939 to make efforts to reach agreement with Hitler—efforts which resulted in the Munich agreement and the fall of Czechoslovakia. The results of the Spanish Civil War also encouraged the Fascist powers, who had been able to flaunt with impunity the Non-intervention agreement to which they were parties. The failure of the Russo-British negotiations in 1939 was the result of long-standing difficulties between the two countries which could not be rapidly overcome, and this failure was the prelude to the Nazi-Soviet pact which cleared Hitler from any immediate embarrassment from an eastern front.

Important Dates

1931   **Japanese attack on China.**
1932   **World Disarmament Conference began.**
1933   **'King and Country' resolution at the Oxford Union Society.**
1934   **World Disarmament Conference failed.**
        Germany left the League of Nations.
1935   **Stresa Front formed.**
        Anglo-German Naval Agreement.
        League of Nations Union Peace Ballot.
        Italy attacked Abyssinia.
1936   **Hitler reoccupied the Rhineland.**
        Outbreak of the Spanish Civil War.
        Popular Front agitation in Britain.
        Abdication of Edward VIII.
1937   **Chamberlain succeeded Baldwin as Prime Minister.**
        Nyon Agreement.
        Brussels Nine-power Conference failed to act against renewed Japanese aggression.
1938   **Eden resigned as Foreign Secretary—succeeded by Lord Halifax.**
        March: Hitler occupied Austria.
        September: Berchtesgaden meeting of Chamberlain and Hitler.
        Godesberg meeting of Chamberlain and Hitler.
        29th September: Munich Conference of Chamberlain, Daladier, Hitler and Mussolini.
1939   **March: Hitler occupied Czechoslovakia.**
        British-Soviet negotiations fail.

British-Polish alliance finalised.
Soviet-Nazi Pact.
1st September: Warsaw bombed.
3rd September: Britain at war with Germany.

QUESTIONS

(1) What was the general attitude of British opinion on the question of peace and war in this period?

(2) Trace the stages of aggression, with special reference to Manchuria, Abyssinia, Austria and Czechoslovakia.

(3) What parts were played in international affairs by Sir Samuel Hoare, Anthony Eden and Lord Halifax?

(4) Examine developments of the year 1939 which led on to the outbreak of war.

(5) Attempt a justification of Chamberlain's policies.

(6) What is the argument against Chamberlain's policies?

CHAPTER THIRTY-SIX

THE SECOND WORLD WAR
1939–1945

FOR the convenience of study this chapter is divided into the following sections:

    A. An outline account of the war.
    B. The part played by the fighting services.
    C. Conditions at home during the war.

[A] An Outline Account of the War

Poland had succumbed to Hitler's attack by 27th September and at the same time Russian forces occupied eastern Poland. The period from October 1939 to April 1940 is known as the period of the *'phoney war'*. Little fighting occurred on the main front, *e.g.* between France and Germany. The Home Guard drilled in Britain, often with no weapons or only useless substitutes, the French remained inactive in the **Maginot Line**. There were numerous rumours of an attempted negotiated peace by Hitler and some western statesmen. In November *Russia attacked Finland* after failing to gain from Finland territory which would have given better protection to Leningrad. After an heroic resistance, the Finns gave in and Russia gained what she wanted. Both Chamberlain and the French were preparing to send armed help to the Finns, but Russia's victory anticipated this move. The extremely bad winter of 1939–1940 appears to have delayed Hitler's plan of attack, but in April, German airborne troops seized strategic points in **Norway**, and **Denmark** was also overrun with little resistance. *The Chamberlain government sent a British force to* **northern Norway,** *but it was forced to withdraw,* mainly owing to lack of air cover. *This led to the fall of Chamberlain and his replacement by Churchill. In May 1940 the German panzer forces invaded* **Belgium** and **Holland** and, in a campaign of only five days, Holland came under German control. Hitler had by this means also by-passed the Maginot Line. *The Germans now attacked through the* **Ardennes**, broke through the French defences and moved towards the Channel coast. The northern armies were thus isolated—these armies were the British Expeditionary Force under **Lord Gort**, the French First Army and the Belgians. The

EUROPE DURING THE SECOND WORLD WAR

Key

Neutral Countries

German Occupied Countries

卐 Germany and Allies

Britain Russia & Allies

Belgian King now capitulated to the Germans, and the British and French fought a delaying retreat to reach **Dunkirk**, from which 320,000 troops were evacuated to Britain by vessels of every description. The men were saved, but all equipment was lost. A vital part was played in saving these armies by the Royal Air Force, the Navy and numerous small craft which came over from England.

Soon after the German occupation of Paris, **Marshal Pétain** became French Prime Minister and capitulated to Germany. *Mussolini now entered the war as the ally of Hitler.* When the French Fleet at **Oran** in North Africa refused to hand itself over to Britain, it was bombarded and put out of action to prevent it falling into Nazi hands.

The Battle of Britain, 1940

Hitler now planned to invade Britain, but a prerequisite was the destruction of the Royal Air Force. From August to September 1940, Hitler launched his air attack on British airfields and coastal defences. London was also attacked. However, such were the losses of Goering's *Luftwaffe* by September, that daylight attacks were abandoned and invasion plans suspended. **The Battle of Britain** had been won. It was a great defensive achievement which kept Britain in the war at a vital time. The *Luftwaffe* now developed the *night-blitz* which continued from September 1940 until May 1941. **London** was heavily attacked; and other great cities, especially **Coventry**, suffered enormous losses of life and damage. *The R.A.F. began reprisal raids on German industrial towns.*

The American **Lend-Lease Act** of **1941**, strongly urged by President **Franklin D. Roosevelt**, meant the increased supply to Britain of necessary food and much armament. German U-boats now concentrated on sinking British trans-Atlantic shipping; Roosevelt aided Britain by extending American anti-submarine patrols further into the Atlantic and by selling fifty destroyers to Britain for convoy work.

In Europe, Mussolini became a liability to Hitler. *Italian forces were driven out of Cyrenaica, Egypt, Kenya, British Somaliland and the Sudan.* The Greeks defeated the Italian invading forces and the British naval air-arm destroyed a great part of the Italian fleet at **Taranto**. Hitler now retrieved the position for Mussolini by invading Greece and Yugoslavia and forcing British forces out of Greece into Crete, which the Germans later captured by mass parachute attacks. In Africa the German General, **Rommel**, also drove the British forces back to the frontier of Egypt.

Hitler Attacks Russia

On 22nd June, 1941, Hitler suddenly launched his forces against

Russia. In all directions the German advance continued, and many Russian aircraft were destroyed on the ground by surprise attacks. The German advance took them to the outskirts of Leningrad, and within 100 miles of Moscow. In the south they captured **Kiev** and overran the Ukraine as a preliminary to an advance towards the Caucasian oil-fields. However, by 1942 the German advance had been held, and Hitler's aim of a quick victory was forestalled. Churchill formed the **Anglo-Russian Alliance** and convoys of war materials were sent to Russia by the northern route, where German submarines and surface raiders did great damage.

In the Far East, the Japanese launched their treacherous air attack on the United States Navy at **Pearl Harbor** on **7th December, 1941,** and destroyed the greater part of it. **Roosevelt** *immediately brought America into the war against the Axis powers.* The Japanese general campaign took them from Indo-China into Malaya and Siam. They captured Singapore and Hong Kong, drove the Americans from the Philippines and were soon masters of the Pacific.

The year 1942 was one of significant successes for the Allies, despite the early successes of Rommel and his *Afrika Korps* and the Italians against the British in North Africa and the initial success of German forces in Southern Russia. In Russia the Germans were not destined to reach the Caucasus, for at **Stalingrad** the Russians made the heroic stand which was one of the great turning-points of the war. Over 300,000 Germans under **General von Paulus** were surrounded and forced to capitulate. Hitler had refused all suggestions of a strategic retreat. In October, **General Montgomery** launched the British Eighth Army against Rommel at **El Alamein** and drove the Axis forces back into Tunisia, where they were also subjected to pressure from **General Eisenhower's** forces which had landed further west. The whole army capitulated, and the Axis campaign in North Africa was utterly defeated. *El Alamein and Stalingrad destroyed the myth of Nazi invincibility.*

In July, 1943 Hitler ordered another massive attempt to break through the Russian defences—this time on the Orel-Kursk-Bielgorod salient. For this purpose he employed seventeen armoured divisions. This enormous drive was defeated by the Russians. The **Battle of Kursk** ranked with Stalingrad and El Alamein as a turning-point in the war. The year 1943 saw further reverses for Hitler and Mussolini. *The Germans were compelled to raise the siege of* **Leningrad**. The intensity of Allied bombing of Germany greatly increased; and *in July, English and American forces landed in* **Sicily** *in preparation for the invasion of the Italian mainland, which they carried out across the Straits of Messina on 3rd September.* Mussolini's position in Italy became un-tenable and he was imprisoned and replaced by **Marshal Badoglio,** who took Italy out of the war. A daring German rescue of Mussolini

THE FAR EAST DURING THE SECOND WORLD WAR

enabled him, however, to form another government in northern Italy under German protection. The Allied campaign up the Italian peninsula proceeded slowly and with heavy casualties, for the Germans fought a determined and skilful defensive operation. Their defence of **Monte Cassino** was typical of this determination.

The Second Front, 6th June, 1944

The next step was to attack the German armies in France. The organization of D-day, 6th June, 1944, was conducted by General Eisenhower, with General Montgomery in command of land forces for the invasion of occupied France. *'Pluto'*, a special pipe-line was laid across the Channel for petrol supplies, and two artificial harbours were constructed for towing across the Channel. The Royal Air Force carried out intense bombardment of enemy emplacements and supply lines, while the Navy had complete command of the Channel. This enabled the successful landings in Normandy to take place. After consolidating their bridgehead, the Americans broke through the German defences to the right of the British and Canadians, and in the **Battle of the Falaise Gap** large German forces were encircled and destroyed. Northern and western France were overrun and Paris liberated, **General de Gaulle** being accorded the honour of being the first to enter the city. The Allies then fought on towards Holland and Belgium, *thus ending the flying-bomb* (**V-1**) *attacks on Britain*. However, the **V-2 rockets**, with their sites in the Low Countries, continued to fall on London. At this point Montgomery attempted to gain a bridgehead over the Rhine by the capture of **Arnhem** and the use of parachute troops. This, however, failed, and the Allies then concentrated on the capture of **Antwerp**, which fell in November. This enabled Allied supplies to reach the new fronts more rapidly and at the same time put *an end to the V-2 attacks on Britain*.

In July an attempt by members of the German forces to assassinate Hitler failed. A bomb had been planted at his headquarters but although it exploded, it did not succeed in killing Hitler. This was, however, a sign of the rapidly worsening position for Germany and Hitler. *The Russians had now defeated Bulgaria, Finland and Rumania and were rapidly advancing westward.* The Allied air bombardment of Germany (especially the Ruhr industrial district) was now enormous and devastating. In December 1944, the Germans under **Rundstedt** made their last powerful counter-attack through the Ardennes in the **'Battle of the Bulge'**. After some initial progress, the offensive failed. *In March 1945, Allied forces crossed the Rhine, the Ruhr was captured, and Russian and American forces met on the Elbe on 28th April.* Within a few days the Russians had occupied Berlin, which was largely destroyed, and Hitler had committed suicide in the bunker of the Chancellery. In Italy Mussolini had been captured and shot by Italian partisans. Hitler's successor, **Admiral Doenitz**, accepted unconditional surrender and an armistice was signed, at the instigation of General Montgomery, on **Luneberg Heath** on 7th May, 1945.

In the Far East, the American offensives had recaptured the Japanese-occupied islands, and Allied forces had thrown back the Japanese from India. *On 6th August the first atomic bomb was dropped on* **Hiroshima**, which was totally destroyed, and **Nagasaki** *suffered the same fate on 9th August.* The Japanese government capitulated on 14th August.

One of the immediate tasks of the Allied forces was to liberate those who still remained alive in the Nazi concentration camps, such as Dachau, Auschwitz, Belsen and Mauthausen. Sights of horror and human suffering such as the world had never seen, testified to the greatest crime in human history. The gas-chambers and the crematoria, besides thousands of corpses and skeleton-like survivors, revealed Hitler's efforts to exterminate the Jewish people and many other opponents.

[B] The Armed Forces during the War

The Royal Air Force. As we have seen, **Goering**'s aim in 1940 was to reduce British air power to a point where German air superiority would enable an invasion of Britain to succeed. **Fighter Command** was under **Air Marshal Dowding**, who had fifty-five squadrons—about the same as the Germans. *The use of radar* to give warning of enemy approach meant that long-range patrols were not necessary; and this, by saving pilot casualties, made up to a certain extent for the lack of adequate trained reserves. The Royal Air Force were fortunate that **Lord Beaverbrook** was Minister for Aircraft Production, for, under his direction, the efforts of the factories were enormous. The German pilots at first attacked convoys in the Dover Straits, and then turned to south-eastern England, but their losses were almost twice those of the R.A.F. They were more successful when they switched their attacks to airfields in Kent. In September, the German attack turned against London; but German losses continued to be so severe that daylight attack was broken off after the middle of September. It is now known that Hitler suspended his plans for the invasion of Britain as a result of the Battle of Britain. *'Never in the field of human conflict,'* said Mr. Churchill, *'was so much owed by so many to so few.'*

The R.A.F. played a key role in the North African campaigns and in Europe before and after D-day, and its effectiveness contributed greatly to victory.

Bomber Command, under its Commander-in-Chief, **Sir Arthur Harris** (appointed in 1942), also played a vitally important part in the air war. Harris was a propounder of the theory that air power, by destroying enemy production and enemy morale, could win the war. The British reply to the Nazi night-blitz of 1940–1941, was to reply in kind on German industrial centres. In 1941 large-scale bombing of the industrial Ruhr was conducted, but the effects of this policy had been greatly over-estimated and the great majority of planes on night-flights failed to get anywhere near their targets. (The Germans had made miscalculations as well.) In the autumn of 1941 the air offensive against Germany was halted, but when Harris took over in 1942 his avowed policy was to increase the weight of attack and overcome the deficiencies shown. *On 30th May, 1942, the first thousand-bomber raid took place on Cologne,* but it is now known that German industrial production was reduced by very little. In the following year the policy of mass bombing attacks was carried out on the Ruhr and large industrial centres, including Hamburg and Berlin. In reply to this, the Germans developed a long-range night-fighter which inflicted heavy casualties on the British and American bomber force. The whole policy has been much debated and it has been asked *whether the bombing of Germany should have absorbed nearly one quarter of all British war production.* Its effectiveness was much reduced by the German fighters and by the German removal of their factories to the outskirts of the big towns. However, it also became an avowed purpose of Bomber Command to shake German morale, and German civilians suffered increasingly as the war went on. Under the direction of **Air Marshal Tedder,** Bomber Command played a key role in the D-day landings of 6th June, 1944. Precision bombing was carried to its highest point—for example, most of the bridges over the River Seine were destroyed and railway centres devastated. This drastically hindered German troop movements at the most vital point.

By 1944 the Allied air forces had already established superiority, and the drain of German aircraft towards the Russian front had weakened their effectiveness in western Europe. The increasing effectiveness of the Red Air Force as the war continued, was an important contribution to the general air superiority of the Allies.

The Royal Navy

The war at sea quickly showed the danger arising from Germany's submarine superiority. The defences of the British naval base at Scapa Flow were penetrated by a German U-boat which sank the battleship *Royal Oak* in October 1939. However, the German battleship *Graf Spee* was compelled to take refuge from a British force in Montevideo harbour, where she was scuttled on Hitler's orders. *During the ill-fated Norwegian campaign the Royal Navy put sixteen German fighting ships out of action,* and this greatly weakened the German fleet and indirectly made the Dunkirk evacuation more effective than it would have been. It also reduced Hitler's chances of a successful invasion of Britain.

In May 1941, the two German pocket battleships, *Bismarck* and *Prince Eugen*, managed to reach the Atlantic and began attacks on British shipping. The Home Fleet at last managed to find the *Bismarck*, which escaped after sinking two British battleships. She was found again soon after this engagement by planes of the aircraft-carrier *Ark Royal* and was sunk.

In the Mediterranean, **Admiral Sir James Somerville** destroyed the French fleet at Oran and **Admiral Sir Andrew Cunningham**, commander of the Mediterranean Fleet based on Alexandria, put about half the Italian fleet out of action on 11th November, 1940, at **Taranto** by the use of planes from the aircraft carrier *Illustrious*. In March 1941, the Italian fleet was so damaged at the **Battle of Cape Matapan** that British control of the Mediterranean was assured. This enabled Britain to get supplies through to Malta during the later German aerial bombardment of the island and also to the forces in North Africa. *Fortunately the French sank their fleet at Toulon when Germany took over all Vichy France*, and thus prevented these ships falling into Nazi hands.

In the Far East, British naval fortunes were depressing. In December 1942, the *Prince of Wales* and the *Repulse* moved from Singapore to intercept Japanese shipping heading for Malaya, but on 10th December both ships were sunk by Japanese planes. Lack of air cover had led to this disaster.

The year 1943 was important for developments in the Atlantic. U-boat attacks on trans-Atlantic convoys intensified and British shipping suffered severely in the early part of the year. Here *the U.S.A. proved of great help, for she provided 260 destroyers for convoy protection*. Before the end of 1943, U-boat losses had increased at least five times. Another success for Britain in the sea war was the damaging by a British midget submarine of the battleship *Tirpitz* in Alten Fjord, Norway. This was an important achievement, for the *Tirpitz* had done great damage to Britain's northern convoys to Russia. In December 1943 the German battle cruiser *Scharnhorst* was sunk by the *Duke of York*.

On D-day, 1944, the Navy's command of the Channel enabled her not only to protect the crossing, but to put in a powerful bombardment of Nazi coastal positions. This, in conjunction with attacks by the R.A.F., was a most effective contribution to the successful landings, which could well have failed without it.

Britain and the U.S.A. established naval supremacy as the war went on, but British and U.S. disasters in the Far East left the Pacific under Japanese control for a long period until the U.S.A. had recovered from Pearl Harbor. *After the war Britain no longer possessed the economic strength to keep her old naval power*, which was far surpassed by that of the U.S.A.; but during the war she secured control of the Mediterranean very early and, together with the U.S.A., gained eventual control in the Atlantic. This enabled supplies of all kinds to reach the vital centres of the war.

[C] Britain during the War

It was not until *Winston Churchill became Prime Minister* in 1940 that a sense of real urgency began to develop at home. This urgency was underlined by the introduction of *food rationing, compulsory military service*, with exemption for certain key ('reserved') occupations, and the **Emergency Powers Act** of **May 1940**, which gave the government almost complete control over the lives and property of every citizen. Systematic evacuation to the countryside now took place and the **Local Defence Volunteers (Home Guard)** were increased and more efficiently trained. Churchill improved the organization at the top by setting up a *small War Cabinet* and creating essential ministries such as Shipping, Economic Warfare, Food, Information, and Home Security. The Ministry of Labour became the Ministry of Labour and National Service under **Ernest Bevin**, who energetically re-deployed labour into essential war work—and also conscripted women for war work. **Sir John Anderson**, after whom the Anderson domestic air-raid shelter was named, was in charge of Home Security. *Churchill himself was also Minister of Defence* and was ultimately responsible for the military side of the war. **The Ministry of Aircraft Production** was under Lord Beaverbrook, whose drive and capacity to cut through 'red tape' enabled the workers in the factories to respond magnificently, especially at the time of the *Battle of Britain, at the end of which Britain had more fighter aircraft than when the battle against the Luftwaffe began.* The Home Secretary, **Herbert Morrison**, had the task of maintaining morale on the home front and of imposing penalties of fines or even imprisonment on those convicted of 'defeatist talk'. He also operated a press censorship and at one point both the *Daily Mirror* and the *Daily Worker* were suspended. The latter resumed publication after the entry of Russia into the war and the change of the Communist Party from its former anti-war line. Morrison also introduced *compulsory firewatching* for householders during the Nazi night-blitzes when masses of incendiary bombs were used. He also combined local fire brigades into the **National Fire Service** under government direction. Special Port Directors had complete control over ports and harbours, while the Board of Trade controlled all rationing of clothes and foodstuffs by the points (or coupon) system. The rationing system worked well and home food supplies were greatly increased when the *Ministry of Agriculture supervised the conversion of another four million acres to cereal production*, a task greatly aided by the work of the **Women's Land Army**. The general health of people actually improved during the course of the war.

The government's financial measures also worked well. Churchill's first Chancellor of the Exchequer, **Sir Kingsley Wood**, had the important task of preventing inflation. For this purpose he aimed to take as much money out of circulation as possible. *Everyone now paid Income Tax, which was stepped up to 10/- in the pound.* Great *National Savings* drives were organized and a system of deducting a proportion of wages and salaries was devised with the promise to pay later—the *Post-war Credit System*. The government paid food producers subsidies which enabled them to keep prices down, and in 1942 restaurant meals were limited to 5/- and all petrol for pleasure motoring was prohibited. The result of these policies was to keep prices down, while incomes rose 30 per cent more than the cost of living.

After the night-blitz period the worst ordeal suffered by civilians was from the *flying-bombs* (V.1's) which began to fall on London in the week after D-day, 1944, from launching sites in northern France. About a further million and a half Londoners were evacuated very quickly. About 10,000 flying-bombs were launched by the Nazis between June and September 1944, of which about 2,500 veered off course and another 3,000 were brought down by the R.A.F. Even so, more than 6,000 people were killed, mostly in London, and great damage was done to housing. No sooner had the V-1 sites been overrun by the Allies than the V-2 rockets, silent in approach, began to fall on London from sites in Belgium and Holland. Another 3,000 people were killed in London. With the advance of the Allied armies into the Low Countries and the capture of Antwerp, these attacks ceased by the end of 1944, except for one or two isolated incidents early in 1945. But great damage had been done, and *everyone now understood that neither the Navy nor the R.A.F. were alone sufficient to protect Britain in the future.*

Political and Social Developments

After D-day, people at home were confident that the end of the war was near, and party politics began to come to life once again. There were demands from the Labour Party and the trade unions for clear statements from the government about post-war aims and reconstruction. To this pressure, the government responded by appointing **Lord Woolton** (Food Minister during the war) to the post of **Minister of Reconstruction**. Between 1942 and 1945 a series of planning commissions reported their findings. The **Scott Report (1942)** advised the control of all development in the countryside, the **Uthwatt Report** (also **1942**) advised the nationalization of land values and control of all new building—a result of this was the **Town and Country Planning Act, 1944,** which gave these powers to the government and local authorities. Earlier, in **1940**, the **Barlow Report** had advocated government planning of new industries in the Special (Depressed) Areas and this was done by the **Location of Industry Act, 1945**. The most important was the **Beveridge Report** prepared by **Sir William Beveridge**, who proposed the setting up of a **Ministry of Social Security** (not done until 1966) and the unification of all social benefits to cover the whole population. Besides advocating a free **National Health Service** and increases in sickness and unemployment benefits, he proposed the introduction of children's allowances, which was done by the **Family Allowances Act, 1945**. Another very important act was the **Butler Education Act, 1944** (for details see Ch. 45).

Social reform was taking shape, therefore, before the end of the war. But economically and financially Britain was in a bad state. *American Lend-Lease was terminated in September 1945*. In Britain itself the destruction of houses, factories, etc. amounted to more than £1,700 million; and we owed other countries about £3,000 million. About a third of Britain's shipping had been lost and about 60 per cent of our export trade.

Against this background occurred the momentous General Election of 5th July, 1945. The popularity of Winston Churchill was not sufficient to give the Conservatives a victory. *The Labour Party for the first time had a clear majority*—393 seats against 213 Conservative, 12 Liberal and 22 others. The reasons for this victory, which took some of the Labour leaders themselves by surprise, are reasonably clear. The Labour Party's manifesto, 'Let us Face the Future', stressed the need for a thoroughly *planned and controlled transition to peace* —very attractive to those (and they were many) who recalled the chaos after 1918. The Labour Party appeared more wholeheartedly in favour of the Beveridge Report than the Conservatives, who also suffered from the fact that a number of their leaders and M.P.s had been in favour of appeasing Hitler before 1939. The Conservative Party became tarred with the Munich brush—not altogether fairly—owing to Conservative dominance in the years 1931–1939. Some of the most successful ministers of Churchill's wartime coalition were Labour men —**Clement Attlee** (Deputy Prime Minister from 1942), Morrison and Bevin especially, and there was popular confidence in Labour's administrative ability.

Summary

Within less than twelve months Britain was alone in the war against the Axis powers and had withdrawn her forces from the Continent in the Dunkirk evacuation. The war was widened in 1940 by the entry of Italy in alliance with Hitler, and in 1941 by German and Japanese aggression against Russia and the United States respectively, which brought both these countries into the war as allies of Britain. By the Battle of Britain the invasion plans of Hitler were frustrated. The involvement of the U.S.S.R. and the U.S.A. constituted a fundamental change in the war which was to lead to allied victory, for the combined military and economic power of the Allies, when fully mobilized, was far greater than that of the Axis powers. The development of 'Resistance' movements in the Nazi-occupied territories took on new strength from 1941 onwards. The R.A.F.'s part in the war was crucial for success, although much controversy raged over heavy-bomber policy. Britain's naval power helped to save her at the time of Dunkirk and later with the success of the R.A.F., during the Battle of Britain period. But heavy blows were suffered by the navy, especially in the Far East, and the American involvement in the war was to prove, in the naval sense as in others, an absolute essential for victory. At home a high degree of efficiency and social justice was achieved in the organization of food and military supplies. After D-day new political pressures emerged and the people pressed for adequate assurances concerning post-war domestic policies. The most important document was the Beveridge report, which the people expected to be implemented.

Important Dates

1939 **3rd September: Britain at war with Germany.**
November: Russian campaign against Finland.
1940 **April: Norway and Denmark invaded by Hitler.**
German forces invaded Holland and Belgium.
May: Winston Churchill became Prime Minister.
Dunkirk evacuation.
French capitulation.
Mussolini entered the war.
Battle of Britain.
1941 **American Lend-Lease Act.**
Italian fleet destroyed at Taranto.
Italian forces driven from Cyrenaica, Egypt, Kenya, British Somaliland and the Sudan.
Germans captured Crete.
22nd June: Hitler attacked Russia.
Anglo-Russian alliance formed.
7th December: Japanese attack on Pearl Harbor.
U.S.A. entered the war.

1942 Rommel drove British forces back to Egypt.
In southern Russia, German forces advanced towards the Caucasus.
Fall of Singapore to Japanese.
October: Montgomery's victory at El Alamein.
Stalingrad.
Anglo-American forces under Eisenhower landed in North Africa.

1943 May: siege of Leningrad raised by Germans.
May: capitulation of all German and Italian forces in North Africa.
July: Anglo-American forces landed in Sicily.
September: Anglo-American forces crossed into southern Italy.
Mussolini replaced by Badoglio.
Atlantic U-boat campaign defeated by Allies.
Allied air offensive against Germany intensified.

1944 6th June: D-day.
Battle of the Falaise gap and Allied breakthrough towards Paris.
Paris liberated—de Gaulle entered at head of liberating forces.
V-1 attacks on Britain cease, but V-2 rockets follow.
Allied setbacks at Arnhem.
November: Antwerp captured. V-2 bases out of action.
December: Rundstedt's attack in Ardennes. 'Battle of the Bulge'.

1945 March: Allies cross Rhine.
Russians advanced to Berlin. Hitler committed suicide.
7th May: Germany capitulated.

QUESTIONS

(1) Why were the Nazis unable to win the war in 1940?

(2) What measures were taken in 1939 and 1940 to organize Britain's home front?

(3) Why was 1941 an extremely difficult year for the Allies?

(4) Give an account of the main activities of the R.A.F. during the war.

(5) Show the importance of British naval power during the war.

(6) What domestic plans were produced between 1942 and 1945 which affected the future of Britain?

(7) What were the main reasons for Labour's victory in the election of 1945?

CHAPTER THIRTY-SEVEN

BRITAIN UNDER LABOUR GOVERNMENT, 1945-1951

M R. ATTLEE'S first post-war government included Herbert Morrison, in charge of nationalization plans, Aneurin Bevan, Minister of Health, Arthur Greenwood, in charge of Social Services, Hugh Dalton, Chancellor of the Exchequer, Sir Stafford Cripps, President of the Board of Trade and Ernest Bevin, Foreign Secretary.

The government's task was to revive the nation's economic life, and at the same time to implement as much as possible of the Beveridge Report. *Nationalization came high on the list.* In 1946, the Bank of England was nationalized, as also were the mines, now placed under the control of the newly-created **National Coal Board**. Two important public corporations were set up for civil aviation—BOAC (British Overseas Airways Corporation) and BEA (British European Airways). In 1947 the **British Transport Commission** was set up to take control of road haulage, canals and railways. For road haulage, **British Road Services** controlled road transport, with some exceptions. **Cable and Wireless** overseas services were also nationalized. In 1948, the **British Electricity Authority** and the **British Gas Council** were established. When it came to steel nationalization, the Conservative Opposition made a determined stand against it on the ground that it was an efficient industry and was already reviving fast. In order to overcome the opposition of the Conservative-dominated House of Lords, the government introduced and passed *a bill in the Commons in 1949 which limited the delaying powers of the House of Lords to one year.*

The Lords were still able to delay the implementation of the Iron and Steel Bill in 1949; but in February 1951, with a small majority after the 1950 election, the second post-war Labour government nationalized the steel industry. Despite this post-war spate of nationalization, over eighty per cent of British industry remained under private control.

Post-War Controls

To increase exports and keep down unnecessary imports, the government imposed tight controls. The government itself decided on

327

priorities—for example, the building of factories was given preference over cinemas. Licences were required for both imports and
exports. Basic imports were controlled by various commissions
which supervised the sale and distribution of imports to manufacturers. The Commissions, the Board of Trade and the Ministry
of Supply were the main controlling organizations. Britain had never
before in peace-time experienced such widespread government control,
but the public accepted the necessity, although, as was to be expected,
there was a good deal of grumbling, and a *'black market'* in foods and
other necessities developed, with the resultant crop of post-war
scandals. However, the results were promising. *Exports, particularly
of the newer industries such as chemicals, electrical goods and cars,
increased rapidly.* This was given a rather artificial boost in 1949 when
Sir Stafford Cripps devalued the pound, thus making our exports
cheaper. This devaluation was necessitated by the fact that great
financial post-war loans from the U.S.A. and Canada had been quickly
absorbed and Britain's dollar funds for meeting foreign creditors were
dwindling fast. We could only earn more dollars by increasing exports
still further and making dollars cheaper to purchase in terms of the
pound sterling. Besides financial difficulties, the very severe winter of
1947 brought large areas of industry to a standstill, and factories and
households were constantly blacked out. *In March 1947, there were
over 2,000,000 unemployed,* but with better conditions this fell to
about 400,000 by the end of the year. Nevertheless the severe conditions had retarded Britain's recovery.

Another form of control was *rationing,* supervised by the Board of
Trade. *The coupon system covered almost every item of consumption,
including clothing.* Some items of rationing remained until as late as
1954, and the post-war years saw the continuance of food-queues at
the shops. In various ways the *'black marketeers'* attempted to get
round rationing, and those who had money to buy on the black market
were fortunate. In general, however, the rationing system worked well
and fairly, special allowances being made for old-age pensioners, for
young children and expectant mothers. Holidays abroad and petrol
for pleasure-motoring were severely limited.

*The first Chancellor, Hugh Dalton, 1945-1947, continued the policy
of very high taxation on the wealthy, but taxation on the middle and
working classes was also higher than ever before.* Even with the help
of the U.S. and Canadian loans, however, the government's income
was insufficient to finance all their schemes, and recourse to further
loans had to be made in 1948. Under Dalton's policies of 'cheap
money' to local authorities, the tendency to inflation developed, but
his successor, Sir Stafford Cripps, restricted credit and also gained the
co-operation of the trade unions and business to operate a *wage and
profits 'freeze'* to prevent inflation. Between 1948 and 1950 this policy

worked reasonably well and exports increased in these two years by 25 per cent. By 1950 a good deal of rationing had also disappeared, such as petrol, furniture and clothing. The government's policy also succeeded in preventing too many imports, which only rose by 7 per cent. The devaluation of the pound had also, of course, aided exports.

Labour's Social Programme, 1945–1951

During this period the so-called **Welfare State** was created in Britain. The system of Family Allowances had been introduced in 1945 before Mr. Attlee succeeded Mr. Churchill, but other important additions to the social services were now made. The **National Health Service Act** was passed in **1946** and came into operation in 1948, under the enthusiastic guidance of **Aneurin Bevan**. The Act established a free national medical service with a system of capitation payments to doctors and dentists related to the number of patients on their lists. *This also meant the end of the old voluntary hospital system* and the hospital service was now organized in fourteen regions under the control of regional boards and hospital management committees. There was opposition from the British Medical Association to the scheme, for the doctor no longer had freedom to set up his own practice where he wished. Local Executive Committees were set up to administer the Act and these consisted of representatives of doctors, dentists and the general public. To the patients all services were now free, including hospital and specialist treatment.

The National Insurance Act, 1946 was introduced by **James Griffiths,** Minister of National Insurance. Everyone from school-leaving age to the end of his life was to be insured, and the money was raised by contributions from employers, employees and the State. Self-employed persons were now included. Maternity benefits, death grants, pensions for women at sixty and men at sixty-five were introduced. The Act consolidated and largely replaced all previous insurance legislation, and all unemployment and sickness benefit was dealt with under its terms.

A great improvement was made in the position of persons suffering injury at work by the **National Insurance (Industrial Injuries) Act, 1946**. In place of the old system, by which a claimant had to make application for compensation through the courts, an injured worker could now receive payment from a fund to which both employers and workers contributed. A permanent disablement pension could be recommended by a special medical board and, in case of later rehabilitation by which the worker could undertake some work in the future, this payment was not withdrawn. This was a great improvement on the insecurity and legal difficulties of the old system.

The **National Assistance Act, 1948**, created the **National Assistance Board**, whose duty it was to see that all those who, for various reasons, did not qualify for insurance benefits or were in danger of becoming destitute, were now cared for by the local authorities. Local advisory committees were set up consisting of persons having knowledge of local conditions. In 1966 the functioning of this service, which really *put an end to all remnants of the old Poor Law*, came under the direction of the new **Ministry of Social Security**, advocated twenty years before by Lord Beveridge.

Another important advance was the **Children's Act, 1948**, which enabled the local authorities greatly to improve their services for the care of children in special need. The Children's Officers now became a most important part of the welfare services conducted by the local authorities. **The Youth Employment Service** was now established on a national and compulsory basis. In education, the government established an **Emergency Training Scheme** to increase the recruitment of teachers and greatly extended school meals and medical and dental inspection. **The New Towns Act, 1946**, saw the commencement of the building of new towns, mainly to house Londoners outside the heavily-congested Greater London Area. **The Town and Country Planning Act, 1947**, gave financial assistance to local authorities for the re-planning and re-building of war-damaged towns and others on modern lines. To meet the immediate housing shortages, the government encouraged the building of temporary prefabricated houses (*'pre-fabs'*), some of which remained in occupation for the next twenty years, such were the difficulties encountered by successive governments in getting enough houses built. Immediately after the war, this was a cause of great discontent and there were numerous incidents in which *homeless people ('squatters') took over empty buildings until ejected by the police*. Another important act was the **Atomic Energy Act, 1946**, which gave the Ministry of Supply the task of supervising the development of atomic power in Britain—a development which was to make Britain the pioneer country in the building of atomic reactors.

Foreign Policy under the Labour Governments, 1945–1951

International affairs after 1945 were dominated by the development of the so-called **'Cold War'** between the countries of communist alignment led by Soviet Russia and those of anti-communist alignment led by the United States. The conflicts of the 'Cold War' entered into the new organization of the **United Nations** created by the **San Francisco Conference** of April to June **1945**. In 1946 Mr. Churchill used the term *'Iron Curtain'* to describe the division of Eastern from Western Europe which was taking place. At the **Yalta Conference** of **February 1945**, in the Crimea, the Allies had agreed on the setting up of Allied

POST-WAR LABOUR GOVERNMENTS
1945-1951

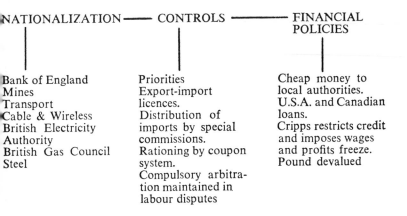

NATIONALIZATION —— CONTROLS ———— FINANCIAL POLICIES

Bank of England
Mines
Transport
Cable & Wireless
British Electricity
Authority
British Gas Council
Steel

Priorities
Export-import
licences.
Distribution of
imports by special
commissions.
Rationing by coupon
system.
Compulsory arbitra-
tion maintained in
labour disputes

Cheap money to
local authorities.
U.S.A. and Canadian
loans.
Cripps restricts credit
and imposes wages
and profits freeze.
Pound devalued

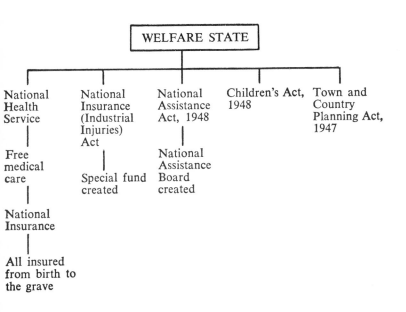

WELFARE STATE

National
Health
Service

Free
medical
care

National
Insurance

All insured
from birth to
the grave

National
Insurance
(Industrial
Injuries)
Act

Special fund
created

National
Assistance
Act, 1948

National
Assistance
Board
created

Children's Act,
1948

Town and
Country
Planning Act,
1947

occupation zones in Germany and in Berlin after Hitler's final defeat. At the **Potsdam Conference** of **July 1945**, Mr. Attlee replaced Mr. Churchill after Labour's election victory, President Truman represented the United States after the death of President Roosevelt in April, and Marshal Stalin represented Russia. It was decided to disband the German forces, to undertake the trials of German war criminals, to exact industrial reparations from Germany and to confirm the occupation zones decided upon at Yalta. Under this arrangement, Berlin was completely surrounded by the territory of East Germany under Russian control. The **Allied Control Council for Berlin**, representing the four allied powers, made arrangements for communications with Berlin through the Russian zone. The Conference also confirmed the Yalta decision to extend the frontiers of Poland to the **'Oder-Neisse line'**, thus giving Poland important German territory.

Growing Differences between East and West

During 1945 and 1946 several conferences of the Foreign Ministers were held, but increasing difficulties arose between East and West. The western powers had hoped for elections in all European states, both East and West, on liberal democratic lines; but with increasing communist control of the east European states the different interpretations of the word 'democracy' became evident. However, in 1947, the western powers gave full diplomatic recognition to Hungary, Rumania and Bulgaria, where communist control had either been achieved or was being prepared for.

Russia now began to put pressure upon Turkey for bases in the Dardanelles, but both Britain and the United States encouraged Turkey to resist and eventually the *U.S.A. installed rocket missile bases* on the frontier between Turkey and the Soviet Union. In Greece also, where a civil war between communist and anti-communist forces raged until 1949, *the U.S.A. gave direct financial aid to the Greek government.* In Germany the British and American zones were now unified in order to speed up industrial revival. *Thus Britain was dependent on American aid for her policies in Turkey, Greece and Western Germany; and Ernest Bevin (British Foreign Secretary) clearly accepted this fact.*

Bevin continued to stress the fact that Britain's own financial position was weak and that only the U.S.A. could defend the western world against Communism. He invited the U.S.A. to take a stronger part in the affairs of Europe and the world. The Americans were at first slow to respond and there was some tendency for old isolationist forces to come to the fore, but the question was settled in 1947 when President Truman announced that the U.S.A. must take a leading part in resistance to communist aggression—the **Truman Doctrine, 12th March, 1947**. This was followed by the **Marshall Plan**, announced by

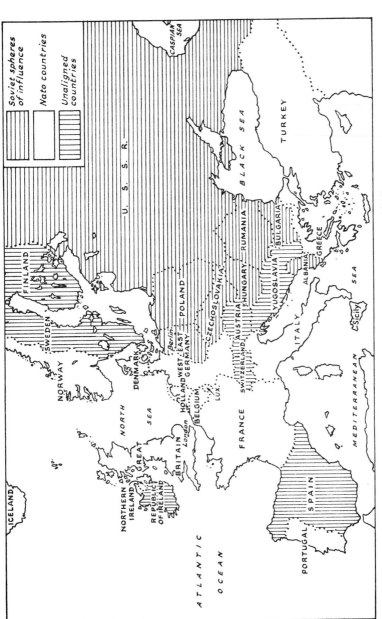

SPHERES OF INFLUENCE IN EUROPE AFTER 1945

the American Secretary of State, George Marshall, in **June 1947**. This was a vast plan for American financial assistance to help in the recovery of Europe. Ernest Bevin took a leading part in the creation of the **Organization for European Economic Co-operation (O.E.E.C.)** which was a representative organization of European states to administer Marshall aid. Although **Mr. Molotov**, Russian Foreign Minister, took part in preliminary discussions, he eventually withdrew, together with the other East European states. Thus the division between West and East was further increased.

The Formation of NATO and the Berlin Blockade

After the gaining of control of Czechoslovakia in 1948 by the Communists, measures were taken for the creation of a western defensive military alliance, and Bevin took a leading part in these moves. This led to the eventual creation of the **North Atlantic Treaty Organization (NATO)** in **April 1949**, when the U.S.A., Canada, Iceland, Denmark, Norway, Portugal and Italy joined Britain, France and the Benelux Countries (Belgium, Luxemburg and the Netherlands) in a defensive military alliance. Greece and Turkey became members of NATO in 1951. In reply the states of Eastern Europe formed their own defensive military alliance known as the **Warsaw Pact**.

The first great trial of strength in the 'Cold War' occurred in 1948–1949, during the period of the **Berlin blockade**. The apparent cause of the blockade was the Soviet Union's opposition to a new currency introduced for Western Germany and the western-controlled sectors of Berlin. But the conflict had deeper roots. Russia had disliked the western policy of the rapid revival of Germany. In 1946 Russia had demanded the removal of equipment from the Ruhr to Russia as part of German reparations, but the western powers had opposed this. Various other disputes had arisen. The Berlin blockade was seen in the West as an effort by the Soviet Union to gain complete control of the city. In July 1948, the Soviet Union closed all land and water routes into Berlin from the west and the blockade continued until May 1949. The western reply was to organize an air-lift of supplies which kept the city of Berlin alive and thus prevented capitulation. There was much tension and danger.

The Berlin blockade caused the movement towards the creation of NATO to be speeded up.

In the Far East the Communists under **Mao Tse-tung** had gained control of China and expelled the Nationalists under **Chiang Kai-shek** to Formosa, where they remained under American protection.

The Korean War

In June **1950**, war broke out between North and South Korea, and

North Korea was condemned by the United Nations as the aggressor. The United Nations commander was the American **General Mac-Arthur**. The main participants against North Korea were the Americans, who lost 60,000 killed. British and Turkish forces also participated. The entry of Chinese 'volunteers' on the side of North Korea and subsequent reverses for United Nations forces, led Mac-Arthur to demand the bombing of the industrial areas of Manchuria. But the danger of extending the war and the possible involvement of Russia, who had possessed the atomic bomb since 1949, led caution to prevail and President Truman dismissed MacArthur. The Labour Government had made clear its opposition to MacArthur's policies. In 1951 peace negotiations began and dragged on till 1953 when the 38th parallel was established as the frontier between North and South Korea, with a demilitarized zone separating the two countries.

The Korean War had increased the antagonism of the U.S.A. and the Soviet Union, as also had the achievement of power by the Communists in China. However, while the Labour Government gave recognition to Communist China and supported the plea for her admission to the United Nations, the U.S.A. did neither.

Palestine

Another area of dispute in which Britain was involved was Palestine, which had been the responsibility of Britain since the First World War. After 1945 Jewish families attempted to settle in Palestine in great numbers, especially as it had been declared a Jewish national home. Arab resistance led Britain to allow only very restricted entry. Eventually, in 1948, the Labour government handed the whole problem over to the United Nations and British forces, which had been subjected to both Jewish and Arab attack, left the country. The independent Jewish state of **Israel** was established, but this led to thousands of Arabs being forced out of Palestine as refugees. Twenty years later large numbers were still living in poverty in refugee camps which relief organizations under the United Nations and Red Cross have not been able to eliminate. This has further embittered Arab-Jewish relations, and resulted in the outbreak of war between Israel and the United Arab Republic in **June 1967**. The Israeli victory within six days and their occupation of Jerusalem, parts of Jordan, Syria and Egypt was a great set-back to Arab aims as expressed by President Nasser of Egypt. The Great Powers, especially the U.S.A. and Russia, have now become involved in efforts to bring a settlement to the Middle East. The Arabs continue to see Israel as the creation and agent of the western powers in the Middle East, while Soviet Russia supports the Arab cause.

During the years **1945-1951**, the Labour governments granted *independence to India, Pakistan, Burma, Ceylon and Transjordan*. The process of conversion of the old Empire into the Commonwealth of independent states was to continue until its completion in the 1960s.

The General Elections of 1950 and 1951

In the General Election of February 1950, the Labour Party's overall majority was reduced to six. This result was in part due to the continuance of many war-time restrictions, especially much rationing. But the failure of the governments to reach even an annual housebuilding rate of 200,000 told heavily against them. The unexpectedly high birth-rate after the war and the increase of early marriage had made the housing problem more severe than had been anticipated. The Conservatives also made much play of Labour's determination to nationalize the steel industry at all costs. Mr. Attlee's second government was soon faced with the Korean War and the costs of rearmament. These costs led to attempted economies in the National Health Service, and the Chancellor of the Exchequer, **Hugh Gaitskell**, introduced the unpopular 50 per cent charge on the costs of spectacles and dentures—a policy which resulted in the resignation from the government of **Aneurin Bevan** and **Harold Wilson**. The Korean war also caused inflation and a rise in world prices, which affected adversely the British standard of living. In October 1951, Mr. Attlee again went to the country, and the Conservatives were returned under Winston Churchill with an overall majority of seventeen, although Labour's total vote was still the largest. *The Labour Party was not destined to regain power until 1964.*

Summary

The problems facing the post-war Labour governments were formidable. The war had brought devastation and economic and financial loss to Britain on a vast scale. It was necessary to revive the economy and maintain essential controls for that purpose, thus preventing the post-1918 'free for all', and at the same time to implement the main recommendations of the Beveridge Report on social welfare. Great shortages and difficulties were faced for many years—not made easier by the very bad winter of 1947. Britain became very dependent on the support of American and Canadian finance. Nevertheless, the Welfare State was consolidated and food supplies gradually improved, though several articles were still rationed in 1951. Measures of nationalization figured in Labour's programme—mostly accepted by the Conservative opposition who, however, waged a constant campaign against steel nationalization. The problem of inflation was met with fair success by a policy of wages, prices and dividend restraint—a policy to become familiar in different circumstances in the 1960s. In foreign and imperial affairs, Mr. Attlee's governments were involved in the complications of the Cold War and Ernest Bevin is generally regarded as the strongest supporter of NATO. The Korean War produced political strains and a rise in prices, which had an adverse effect on Labour's position and partly accounted for her defeat in 1951. At the same time internal strains were developing within the Labour Party both over the Korean War and the question of Britain's nuclear armaments.

Important Dates

1946   National Health Service Act.
       National Insurance Act.
       National Insurance (Industrial Injuries) Act.
       New Towns Act.
       Atomic Energy Act.
       Bank of England nationalized.
       National Coal Board.
1947   British Transport Commission.
       Very severe winter—2,000,000 unemployed.
       Town and Country Planning Act.
       Truman Doctrine.
       Marshall Plan.
1948   British Electricity Authority.
       British Gas Council.
       National Health Service in operation.
       National Assistance Act.
       Children's Act.
       Palestine problem handed over to United Nations.
       Berlin Blockade begins.
1949   Powers of House of Lords reduced.
       NATO formed.
       May: Berlin Blockade ended.
       Sir Stafford Cripps devalued the pound.
1950   Labour majority reduced to 6 at General Election.
       July: Outbreak of Korean War.
1951   Steel nationalized.
       Some Health Service charges introduced.
       Conservative majority of 17 at General Election.

QUESTIONS

(1) *What was the economic condition of Britain at the end of the war?*

(2) *What measures of nationalization were introduced by the first post-war Labour government?*

(3) *Explain the nature of government controls after the war.*

(4) *Describe the organization and importance of the National Health Service.*

(5) *How was Britain involved in the 'Cold War'?*

(6) *What were the reasons for Labour's defeat in 1951?*

CHAPTER THIRTY-EIGHT

CONSERVATIVE GOVERNMENT, 1951–1964

Home Affairs

THE Conservatives had no intention of reversing the main social reforms of Labour, which had proved popular and effective. Between 1951 and 1954 Mr. Churchill's government did, however, denationalize steel and the road haulage system and remove the rationing system, which finally disappeared in 1954. The competitive principle was seen in the *creation of* **ITV**, which broke the monopoly of the **BBC**, and the introduction of *commercial advertising* on television.

Economic Condition of the Country, 1951

The Conservatives inherited an economic crisis of alarming proportions. The trade deficit—that is, the excess value of imports over exports—was £679 million for the first half of 1951, and gold and dollar reserves were draining away fast. The Chancellor of the Exchequer, **R. A. Butler**, was faced with the necessity of drastic measures. Imports to the value of £600 million were cut off, housing construction reduced, and further charges imposed for dental treatment and prescriptions. At the same time government subsidies to food producers were cut. The results of these measures were seen in rising prices; but, by 1952, the balance of overseas payments had been redressed, and the government then relaxed food rationing, denationalized steel, removed the remnants of war-time control of the trade unions, abolished the need for licences for private building and increased the pace of house-building. The rates of benefit for sickness, old age and unemployment were also improved. The general standard of living began once again to rise, and in 1955 Mr. Butler removed sixpence off the income tax. The government's housing policy, under the guidance of the Minister of Housing and Local Government, **Mr. Harold Macmillan**, produced *a million new houses in the period 1952–1955*. An important measure was the **Town Development Act of 1952** by which government financial assistance was given to towns willing to take newcomers from over-populated cities.

In June 1953, **Queen Elizabeth II** was crowned following upon the death of her father, George VI. The new *'Elizabethan Age'* was heralded by a great increase in national and personal expenditure. This was aided by a wide extension of 'hire-purchase'. Industrial production also rose in the period 1952–1955.

Sir Winston Churchill (knighted in 1953) retired in April 1955 and was succeeded as Prime Minister by **Sir Anthony Eden**. In the Opposition, **Hugh Gaitskell** replaced Mr. Attlee as *leader of the Labour Party*. The party was seriously divided between the Bevanites who wanted more nationalization and those, including Mr. Gaitskell himself, who wanted to slow down the pace of nationalization. These divisions affected the election of 1955 in favour of the Conservative Party, who increased their majority to sixty. The 'spending spree', rising employment and production, the ending of rationing, and a good housing record, were, however, the main reasons for their success.

The Suez Crisis, 1956

The Suez crisis was the most serious matter facing Sir Anthony Eden. Already in November 1955, Britain had attempted to strengthen herself and her allies in the Middle East by joining the **Baghdad Pact** (now CENTO) comprising Britain, Turkey, Iran, Iraq and Pakistan. In Egypt **Nasser**, now firmly in control, had been promised financial assistance by both Britain and America in the building of the **Aswan Dam**. When this promise was revoked in 1956, Nasser nationalized the Suez Canal and looked towards Russia for assistance with the dam. On 30th October, 1956, Israel attacked Egypt, soon followed by France and Britain, whose collusion with Israel in this attack is now reasonably certain. The United Nations, including both the U.S.A. and the U.S.S.R., condemned these actions and world opinion, voiced through the United Nations, compelled Israel, Britain and France to withdraw. A United Nations force was organized to control the border between Egypt and Israel. The Suez affair, which turned out to be a triumph for Nasser, told heavily against Sir Anthony Eden. He resigned in January 1957, on grounds of ill-health and was succeeded as Prime Minister by Mr. Harold Macmillan.

The Macmillan Governments, 1957–1963

Mr. Macmillan had the task of retrieving the government's fortunes after Suez; and the next election in 1959, which further increased the Conservative majority, showed that he was successful. The Conservatives were still indirectly aided by divisions in the Labour Party, in which the nationalization controversy now had added to it a division between those who wished to retain Britain's independent nuclear

CONSERVATIVE GOVERNMENTS, 1951–1964

MAIN FEATURES

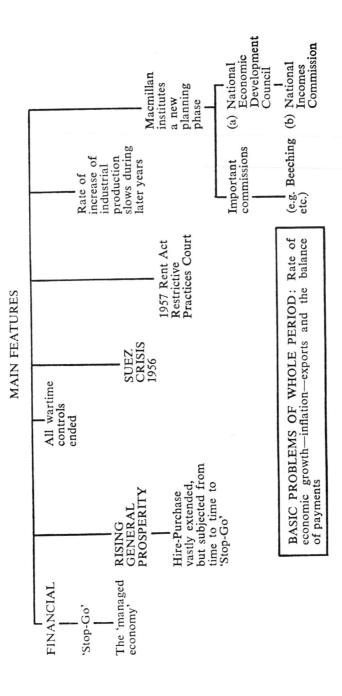

FINANCIAL

'Stop-Go'

The 'managed economy'

RISING GENERAL PROSPERITY

Hire-Purchase vastly extended, but subjected from time to time to 'Stop-Go'

All wartime controls ended

SUEZ CRISIS 1956

1957 Rent Act Restrictive Practices Court

Rate of increase of industrial production slows during later years

Macmillan institutes a new planning phase

Important commissions

(e.g. Beeching etc.)

(a) National Economic Development Council

(b) National Incomes Commission

BASIC PROBLEMS OF WHOLE PERIOD: Rate of economic growth—inflation—exports and the balance of payments deterrent and those who wished to give it up. Despite some hesitations, prosperity continued to develop between 1957 and 1959. In the latter year, industrial exports reached four times the 1946 figure. The new industries of machinery, chemicals, electrical goods and cars, were the main contributors to this. The Prime Minister himself built up the image of the *'affluent society'* typified by his later remark that *'you've never had it so good'*.

During the period 1957 to 1959, the battle against inflation and rising prices still had to be waged. In order to reduce expenditure, in 1957 the Chancellor of the Exchequer, **Mr. Thorneycroft**, raised the Bank Rate from 5 per cent to 7 per cent, reduced government expenditure and made hire-purchase more difficult. By the end of 1957, overseas trade had improved; but Mr. Thorneycroft resigned when the government decided to ease credit once again. His successor, **Mr. Heathcote Amory**, made money cheaper by lowering the bank rate to 4 per cent. Then in 1959–1960, another balance of payments crisis arose and prices were again rising; so **Mr. Selwyn Lloyd**, then Chancellor of the Exchequer, raised the bank rate to 6 per cent and instituted a pay-pause in trade union claims for higher wages, which checked inflation. These processes were given the epithet *'stop-go'* and were typical of Conservative efforts to 'manage' the economic life of the country by financial regulation through the bank rate. However, the really basic problem of Britain's production and export rate had not been solved.

In 1960 Mr. Macmillan was faced with a decline in popular support in the country and the opinion polls began to run against him. The 'stop-go' policies were unpopular, especially with the trade unions, and industrial disputes leading to strikes were on the increase. Mr. Macmillan now moved forward beyond mere financial regulation to measures of national planning. A special commission under **Dr. Beeching** inquired into British Railways and made drastic recommendations for modernization and closures, the **Buchanan Report** dealt with the road traffic problem, and the **Newsom** and **Robbins Reports** dealt with the future of education. Mr. Selwyn Lloyd set up the new **National Economic Development Council**, which had trade union support. **The National Incomes Commission** was set up to propose ways of keeping wages and salaries in line with production and thus reduce inflation. New plans for extensive hospital building were produced. In July 1962, in an effort to introduce new blood into the cabinet, *seven ministers were removed by Mr. Macmillan*—a very drastic change.

Earlier measures of the government were important. The **Restrictive Practices Court**, set up in 1957, was to inquire into cases of alleged monopoly and price fixing which was against the public interest. More controversial was the **Rent Act** of **1957**, which ended the war-time control of rents on more than five million houses. This was argued by the government as only fair to landlords, but many persons were forced to quit when rents were raised. However, many more houses now came on the market.

Summary

The period of Conservative rule was one of improving living standards for the vast majority of the people and was notable for a great outburst of personal expenditure aided by easy hire-purchase. However, the problems of inflation and the balance of payments remained critical and unsolved and were dealt with by alternating doses of deflation and reflation, manipulated mainly by the bank rate. The most serious international problem arose from the Suez campaign and its adverse effects on Britain's international standing. In the later years of 1961–1963, Mr. Macmillan moved towards a more fully planned system of economic growth and Mr. Selwyn Lloyd was responsible for the creation of the important National Development Council and the National Incomes Commission. The period from 1951 had been one of personal affluence, but the basic problems of low rates of increase of national production and the adverse balance of payments in our international trade still remained. During most of this period the Labour Party in opposition was torn by internal division, until Mr. Gaitskell achieved a high degree of party unity, and this had indirectly strengthened the Conservative position.

Important Dates

1951 Drastic reduction of imports.
      Mr. Butler Chancellor of the Exchequer.
1952 Balance of payments redressed.
      Food rationing relaxed further.
      Steel de-nationalized.
1953 Coronation of Elizabeth II.
      Churchill knighted.
      Gaitskell became leader of the Labour Party.
1955 Income tax reduced.
      Baghdad Pact.
1956 Suez Canal nationalized by Nasser.
      30th October: Israel attacked Egypt.
      British and French Suez expedition.
1957 Mr. Macmillan Prime Minister.
      Mr. Thorneycroft Chancellor of the Exchequer.
      Bank rate raised from 5 per cent to 7 per cent.
      Restrictive Practices Court set up.
      The Rent Act.

1959 Selwyn Lloyd's 'pay pause'.
1960 Long-term plans produced:
>   **The Beeching Report (Railways).**
>   **The Buchanan Report (Traffic).**
>   **Newsom Report (Education).**
>   **Robbins Report (Higher Education).**
1962 Drastic re-shaping of government by Mr. Macmillan.

QUESTIONS

(1) *What economic conditions faced the Conservative government in 1951 and how were they dealt with?*

(2) *How would you explain the long run of Conservative administration from 1951 to 1964?*

(3) *How did the Eden and Macmillan administrations attempt to meet* (a) *the problem of inflation;* (b) *the problem of the adverse balance of payments?*

CHAPTER THIRTY-NINE

DEFENCE AND FOREIGN POLICY
AND THE 1964 ELECTION

THE Labour government had decided that Britain should produce her own atomic bomb—the *'independent deterrent'*. This policy was developed further by Churchill, Eden and Macmillan.

Britain's first hydrogen bomb was tested in 1951 and thereafter efforts were concentrated on producing a nuclear deterrent. The first was **'Blue Streak'**, soon abandoned. Britain then adopted the American **'Skybolt'**, but the U.S.A. ceased to produce it in 1962. Mr. Macmillan then met **President Kennedy** at **Nassau** in the Bahamas, where it was decided that the U.S.A. would produce *'Polaris' missiles* to be installed in British-built submarines. Britain was also to support the formation of a *'multilateral nuclear force'* under NATO control.

The technological contest between East and West became intense. The Russians achieved a triumph by launching the first unmanned satellite, **Sputnik I**, in **1957**. They followed this by the *first manned satellite journey* by **Major Yuri Gagarin** in **April 1961**. This was a blow to American pride and was a warning that Russian missile power was now immense and in some respects ahead of the U.S.A. The space-race continued and it became, in the late 1960s, the *'race to the moon'*.

Mr. Macmillan was eager to solve the Berlin problem and other matters affecting the 'Cold War' by a 'Summit Conference'. Such a conference was due to meet in 1960 in Paris, but was brought to an abrupt end by **Mr. Krushchev** quitting the conference when the *American spy-plane, the U-2, was shot down over Russian territory.* Then in 1961 the **Berlin Wall** was built by the Communist authorities of East Berlin to prevent the exit of East Germans to the West. In October 1962 occurred the **Cuba crisis**, when President Kennedy announced that Russian rockets and missile bases were being installed in Cuba within seventy miles of the American mainland. The world came to the brink of nuclear war, but after the declaration of the blockade of Cuba by President Kennedy, Russian missile ships were turned back on orders of Mr. Krushchev, who agreed to the dismantling of these sites under international supervision. One good result of the crisis was the installation of the *'hot line' telephone* communication between the heads of state of Russia and America. Something for which Mr. Macmillan had worked hard was achieved in 1963 by the **Nuclear Test-ban Treaty**, signed in Moscow by all the Great Powers with the exception of France. This banned nuclear tests in the atmosphere, but not underground.

EFTA (1960) and the Common Market (1957)

On the economic side, Britain took a leading part in forming the **European Free Trade Association (EFTA)** in **1960**, comprising Britain, Austria, Denmark, Norway, Sweden, Portugal and Switzerland. In **1957** the **European Economic Community** (the **Common Market**) was established by the **Treaty of Rome** signed by France, West Germany, Italy, Holland, Belgium, Luxemburg. As a result these countries made great economic strides. In 1963 Britain's negotiator, **Mr. Edward Heath**, failed to gain entry for Britain to the Common Market; our exclusion was mainly due to the need to protect the interests of our Commonwealth trade and also partly due to the opposition of France.

Independence of Former British Colonies

Thus the Conservative Government was faced with many searching problems in both the home and the international field. *They also had the task of meeting the demands of the old colonies of the Empire for independence.* The Sudan gained independence in 1956, Malaya and Ghana in 1957, Cyprus and Nigeria in 1960, Sierra Leone and Tanganyika in 1961, Uganda in 1962 and Kenya and Zanzibar in 1963. The latter joined with Tanganyika to form the new state of 'Tanzania'. In 1963 the **Malaysian Federation** of Malaya, Singapore, British North Borneo (Sabah) and Sarawak was formed. Malta gained independence in 1964; and in Africa in the same year Zambia (Northern Rhodesia) and Malawi (Nyasaland) formed independent states with majority rule. Thus the party of nineteenth-century imperialism now presided over the end of the old Empire.

The General Election of October 1964

The election of October 1964, may well be regarded in the future as a real turning-point in British history, for thirteen years of Conservative rule came to an end and a re-vitalized Labour Party gained control. The reasons for this change can be summarized: (1) In 1962 industrial production rose only 1 per cent. (2) The trade unions were refusing to co-operate with Selwyn Lloyd's Incomes Commission. (3) In January 1963, Britain's efforts to enter the Common Market were rejected. (4) General de Gaulle was also refusing to co-operate in the formation of the NATO multilateral nuclear force which Mr. Macmillan had discussed with President Kennedy. (5) In 1963 unemployment began to reappear in one of the old pre-1939 depressed or 'special' areas, the North-east, where it rose to 7 per cent as compared with a national average of about 2 per cent. (6) The **Vassal** and **Profumo** cases told against the government. Vassal was an admiralty clerk convicted of spying, and an official inquiry showed weaknesses in national security. Mr. Profumo, Secretary of State for War, at first denied his association with a **Miss Christine Keeler**, but later confessed that he had lied to the House of Commons. This case also indirectly concerned national security, and the **Denning Inquiry** criticized Mr. Macmillan's supervision of national security. (7) In October 1963 Mr. Macmillan, who was in poor health, resigned. This led to a struggle for leadership in the Conservative Party. Mr. R. A. Butler, one of the prime architects of Conservative policy since the war, was passed over in favour of **Lord Home**, who resigned his peerage and became Prime Minister as **Sir Alec Douglas Home**. (8) **The Greater London Council** had replaced the old London County Council in 1963, and the Conservatives had confidently hoped that the change would favour them, but in the London elections of May 1964, every 'marginal seat' was won by the Labour Party. (9) *The divisions in the Labour Party had been largely healed by Mr. Gaitskell.* After his untimely death in February 1963, he was succeeded as leader by **Mr. Harold Wilson**. The latter now created the 'image' of the *Labour Party as the party of 'modernization', of efficiency, and of technological change.* He proposed to replace the Conservative 'stop-go' economics by better economic control and planning. He promised to improve the rate of house-building, to improve old-age pensions, to control the price of building land by a special **Land Commission** and to end the **Rent Act of 1957**.

The election of October 1964, gave the Labour Party an over-all majority of five, to be increased to 98 in the election of 1966. Since then the country has been faced with a balance of payments crisis. Despite large international loans the pound sterling had to be devalued in November 1967. *In July 1966, the government took compulsory powers to control wages, prices and dividends,* and *credit was restricted.* This resulted in large labour redundancy, especially in the Midlands car industry. This redundancy was a declared part of the government's policy of *re-deploying labour* into other essential industries even if the sales of cars in the home market were drastically reduced. A special **Selective Employment Tax** ('pay-roll tax') was particularly designed to reduce manpower in purely 'service' industries and cause its re-deployment in productive industry. Imports were restricted by the **Imports Surcharge** and restrictions were placed on the investment of money abroad. Exports were given special financial help and remained high. The government aimed to achieve a favourable balance of trade in 1967 and on this, future expansion was to depend, after the period of economic 'freeze'. The government has been compelled to suspend the great **National Plan** of increased production and social welfare published earlier in 1966.

Summary

Britain was now fully involved in the 'Cold War' and all efforts to bring about agreements with Russia and her allies failed. Britain's efforts to achieve an effective nuclear deterrent led to the expenditure of vast sums of money with little success. Russian missile-power was shown by the launching of Sputnik I in 1957 and the first manned space flight by Major Gagarin in April 1961. The failure of the Paris Summit Conference of 1960 led to further serious crises. In 1961 the Berlin Wall between East and West Berlin was built by the Communist authorities and the world reached the brink of atomic war in the Cuba crisis of the autumn of 1962. One bright development was the signing of the Nuclear Test-ban Treaty of 1963. The Common Market was created in 1957 through the Treaty of Rome, and Britain's later efforts to enter this trading system failed. Instead, Britain and her six trading partners formed the European Free Trade Association (EFTA). During this period a great number of former British imperial territories gained their independence. A number of special difficulties arose for the Conservative administration in the years 1962–1964 and these told against it, especially with the Labour Party having recovered its unity. Mr. Wilson created a new image for the Labour Party as the party of technological progress and modern efficiency and was at pains to erase the old 'cloth-cap' image.

Important Dates

1957 The Treaty of Rome (Common Market).
       Sputnik I.
1960 Failure of Paris Summit Conference.
       EFTA formed.
1961 April: Gagarin's space flight.
1962 October: Cuba Crisis.
       'Hot line' established.
1963 February: death of Mr. Gaitskell.
       Harold Wilson elected Labour leader.
       Sir Alec Douglas Home elected Conservative leader.
       Vassal and Profumo cases.
       Denning inquiry.
1964 Labour victory in G.L.C. elections.
       October: Labour won election with over-all majority of five.

1966 General Election gave Labour a majority of ninety-eight.
1966 July: Compulsory wages, prices and dividends 'freeze'.
Selective Employment Tax.

QUESTIONS

(*1*) *Trace the efforts made by Britain to produce an effective nuclear deterrent.*

(*2*) *Write notes on* (a) *the U-2 incident;* (b) *the Nuclear Test-ban Treaty;* (c) *the Common Market.*

(*3*) *Account for some of the factors leading to Labour's victory in the election of October 1964.*

CHAPTER FORTY

THE BRITISH EMPIRE AND COMMONWEALTH TO 1981

THE British Empire came into being in the eighteenth and nineteenth centuries. In the twentieth its progress to a system of independent states within the Commonwealth had been accomplished by 1965. This chapter will deal with the main developments in the more important centres of British power overseas.

Canada

After Britain's victory in the Seven Years' War (1756–1763), she was faced with the problem of how to deal with the French population in Canada. William Pitt the Younger's **Canada Act of 1791** created two provinces: Upper Canada (Ontario) and Lower Canada (Quebec), the latter being largely French in population. Each province had an elected assembly, but the Executive Council was nominated by a British governor. In Lower Canada, the Assembly was almost wholly French, but the Executive Council was predominantly British. To this French grievance was added another, when in 1833 the **British American Land Company** attempted to settle non-Catholics in Lower Canada. But grievances existed in Upper Canada also. Here the **United Empire Loyalists** who had fled from the U.S.A. after Britain's defeat in the American War of Independence were favoured in the distribution of land. There was also much discontent over the large areas of land in the possession of the English and Scottish Established Churches. It was also complained that Upper Canada had to bear an unfair proportion of taxation. General annoyance was caused when a special commission in 1834 advised the suspension of representative government in the provinces altogether.

In **1837** rebellions broke out under **Papineau** in Lower Canada and **Mackenzie** in Upper Canada. These rebellions were suppressed and Lord Melbourne sent the radical and utilitarian, **Lord Durham**, to Canada to report on its problems. His report had great influence on British imperial policy in the nineteenth century. He advised the reunion of Upper and Lower Canada with an assembly and a governor ruling with majority support in the assembly—that is, *he advocated representative government*. The assembly was to control all financial matters, but foreign affairs, external trade, defence and distribution of new land was reserved to the British government. Unfortunately Durham had dealt harshly with the rebels by deportations and executions, and had exceeded his powers. He was recalled, then resigned, but his Report, *the Durham Report, was issued in 1839.*

By the **Canada Act of 1840** Upper and Lower Canada were reunited. It created a Legislative Council of life members and a House of Assembly with equal numbers from each province. This still gave a British majority over the French, but Durham himself had favoured this. He had also advocated full responsible government, but the Act did not mention the responsibility of members of the government to the House of Assembly. However, **Lord Elgin** (Durham's son-in-law), who became Governor-General in 1847, ensured that the Prime Minister chose his government from the majority party in the Assembly; and *the principle of responsible government was gradually accepted.* Imperial interests, foreign policy, defence, etc., were still in the hands of the Governor-General as representative of the home government.

Relations between Canada and the United States affected the future of Canada and her form of government. Great economic competition developed between the two countries in the first half of the nineteenth century. The two great canals the Erie Canal (U.S.A.) and the Welland (Canada) competed for the trade of North America through New York and Montreal respectively. The 'forty-ninth parallel' (of latitude) had been fixed as the boundary westward from the Lake of the Woods to the Rockies, but this left the area between the Rockies and the Pacific open to rivalry between American and Canadian fur traders. In 1846 the whole of the 49th parallel westward, from the Lake of the Woods was fixed as the boundary after great tension between Britain and the U.S.A. *There were strong forces in the U.S.A. who hoped to absorb Canada* and this led to the Canadians demanding greater unity. The Canada Act of 1840 had also left other problems. Upper Canada became dissatisfied with its representation when its numbers came to be greater than those of Lower Canada through immigration. Immigration from Britain also led to increase of population in areas not included in the 1840 Act—such as Nova Scotia, New Brunswick and Prince Edward Island. The Canadians came to realize that they must strengthen their common links through their common needs—in particular defence against powerful neighbours and the need for *national railways* to improve their international markets, especially as Gladstone's free trade policies for Britain meant the loss of preference for Canadian timber. *The American Civil War had also interrupted much trade with the U.S.A.* and had shaken those Canadians who had formerly supported union with the U.S.A. For all these reasons, a new system of government was needed and in **1867** the **North America**

Act was passed. This produced a federal system for Canada, *and it was of Canadian origin and not imposed by Britain.* (1) Ontario and Quebec were again separated and the other two provinces of the federation were Nova Scotia and New Brunswick. (2) The Parliament in the new capital of Ottawa consisted of a Senate of life members nominated by the Governor-General and an elected House of Commons. Representation of the provinces was to be proportional to population. (3) Each of the four provinces had a parliament of its own which dealt with all matters not assigned to the Federal Parliament, which, for instance, had control of external trade, postal services, taxation and defence. (4) *New provinces could be added*—and in 1870 Manitoba joined the federation, in 1871 British Columbia, in 1873 Prince Edward Island, and in 1905 Alberta and Saskatchewan. Newfoundland, which in 1934 was administered directly by Britain, entered the Dominion of Canada in 1949. The **Hudson Bay Company's** territories were bought out in 1869.

The Act of 1867 dealt directly with the railway problem and arranged for the linking of the provinces by the **Intercolonial Railway** completed in **1876**. When, however, British Columbia joined the federation in 1871 the federal government promoted another railway to link Columbia with the other provinces, involving construction across the Rockies from the Pacific Coast. In **1885** the **Canadian Pacific Railway** was completed, linking Montreal with the Pacific over 2,500 miles away. The later construction of the **Northern Canadian Pacific Railway** and the **Grand Trunk Railway** completed the economic union of Canada. This led on to the growth of great and important cities. Canada's internal trade, especially in wheat, was greatly increased; and her export trade similarly affected through coast-to-coast communication.

In the 1970s the most critical development in Canada was the emergence to power in Quebec Province of the 'Parti Quebecquois' under the leadership of **Réné Levesque**. The party sought the political separation of Quebec from the Federation but at the same time maintaining a close economic connection with Canada. In May 1981 a referendum in Quebec on this question resulted in defeat for the separatists who gained only approximately 40 per cent of the vote. Later in the year **Pierre Trudeau**, the Canadian Prime Minister, succeeded in gaining the support of the nine English provinces for a new constitution and the repatriation of the North America Act from Britain. Quebec opposed the new constitution on the grounds that several clauses implied the possibility of her losing a number of important rights which she had gained in the past. She had also wished to be clearly recognised as one of the founding peoples of Canada.

Australia

After the American War of Independence Britain lost her old convict settlements in her former colonies in North America and turned to Australia for substitutes. In 1788 the first batch of convicts arrived in Australia with **Captain Arthur Phillip** and settled at Port Jackson. In 1793 the first free settlers arrived and cultivated their land with the help of convict labour. But the free settlers disliked the unhealthy division of their society into two distinct classes, and the Whig government began to modify the system. After 1840 no more convicts were sent to New South Wales and this encouraged the immigration of settlers. Towards the end of the eighteenth century **Captain MacArthur** introduced sheep from the Cape of Good Hope, and the very fine pastures beyond the Blue Mountains soon produced a thriving industry which was able to drive the old wool-producing countries of Europe out of the field. Then *in 1851 the discovery of gold* at Bathurst led to a 'gold rush' which caused many sheep farmers to give up in favour of gold mining. *Sheep and gold were the basis of the early economic development of Australia*—new companies and banks were set up, credit became easier, and numerous capital goods were imported from Britain, who benefited from these developments both ways.

These developments led to changes in government. There were early demands for self-government; and in 1842, New South Wales, which had been a Crown Colony since 1826, was allowed to elect two-thirds of its governing Council. In 1852 Victoria separated from New South Wales and was given an elected Council of its own. Responsible government also developed in four states in 1855, where the government was directly responsible to an elected assembly; and the same development took place in Queensland in 1859, and in Western Australia in 1890.

The problem of federation in Australia was very different from that of Canada, owing to the immense distances and the great differences in economic life between the states. The industrial states wanted tariffs to protect their industries, and the agricultural states wanted free trade. Communications were very difficult in the first half of the century, but increasing immigration and economic development led to railway construction—over 3,000 miles were constructed in ten years (1870 to 1880) and the telegraph system was expanded. This made the possibility of central government easier, but external affairs played an important part. The scramble between the great European powers and Japan for the colonization of the Pacific stressed the importance of Australian defence. *The German Kaiser's policy after 1890 and Japan's war against China in 1894 high-lighted the dangers to Australia* of not having a central government. But it took ten years

(1890 to 1900) before federation was achieved. *The new Federal Constitution was adopted in 1901, with a newly-created capital at Canberra in 1910.* Powers not definitely allocated to the central government remained with the six separate states.

Edward Gibbon Wakefield (1796–1862)

One of the great influences on colonization during the nineteenth century was **Edward Gibbon Wakefield**. While serving a prison sentence of three years in Newgate for abducting an heiress, he wrote a powerful criticism of the system of settlement in Australia, especially the failure to grant smaller tracts of land and thus encourage wider immigration. These '*Letters from Sydney*' (he was still in Newgate Prison) had a strong effect on government policy when published. In 1839 he accompanied his friend Lord Durham to Canada and *the famous Durham Report contained many of Wakefield's ideas* for the future government of Canada. Before this, in 1837, he had established the **New Zealand Association** to aid emigration to, and land settlement in, New Zealand. He was later one of the founders of the Canterbury settlement and he was for a time a member of the first New Zealand parliament. In his work, *The Art of Colonisation*, he developed his main ideas and stressed the advantages to the home country of the planned approach to colonization—increase of trade and imperial power, and the relief of the pressures of population at home. Politically, he believed strongly in the importance of self-government for the colonies. He had a long struggle against those at home who were opposed to colonies altogether, which was the prevailing idea in the Whig party; but he laid the foundations of the Second British Empire—the first having disappeared with the loss of the American colonies. In 1839 he sent emigrants to New Zealand against the official Whig policy, thus saving the country from a possible French annexation.

New Zealand

By Wakefield's action in 1839, the Whig government was forced to take measures to safeguard the interests of the British settlers. There had been much difficulty between the Maoris and the early settlers who had attempted to break into the tribal ownership of land and secure possession of plots for their own use. In 1838 the New Zealand Company sent out the first organized batch of settlers, and in 1839 a Lieutenant-Governor was appointed for New Zealand. He proceeded to make the important **Treaty of Waitangi** with the Maoris, who accepted British sovereignty in return for a guarantee of protection, the recognition of their ownership of the land and agreement to a system by which a tribe selling its land to settlers would do it through the Lieutenant-Governor. *In 1840 the Whig government made New Zealand a Crown Colony with a Governor and a nominated Council.*

Unfortunately, the Treaty of Waitangi did not prevent serious injustice to the Maoris, whose land was often obtained by unscrupulous means. Officials of the New Zealand Company despised the Maoris as 'naked savages'. This produced further conflict and bloodshed, and in 1844 war between the whites and the Maoris was imminent. However, in 1846 **Sir George Grey** was appointed Governor, being transferred from his governorship of South Australia. He was a man of scrupulous character and he rigidly enforced the Waitangi treaty by punishing offenders against its terms. He thus gained the confidence of the Maoris, and this was increased when he secured the *dissolution of the New Zealand Company,* and gained control over all land matters for the Crown. He managed to purchase the whole of the South Island for the Crown.

Grey was successful in securing an Act of Parliament which set up a federation of the six main areas of settlement. A Council nominated for life and a representative Assembly were established. The Assembly included four Maori members elected by their own people. *In 1856 responsible government was introduced* when the ministers were made answerable to the Assembly. However, the Maoris were excluded from the franchise. In 1876 the provincial assemblies, which had existed since 1852, were abandoned and the country was ruled by a single Parliament and government at Wellington. *This final development of the constitution was due to the rapid development of population and transport.* Settlers had increased from 60,000 in 1856 to 350,000 in 1878. Thus New Zealand passed through the stages of Crown Colony, a representative federation under Crown control, then self-government and, lastly, unitary government.

After Grey's departure in 1853 there were renewed troubles between Maoris and settlers. Between 1860 and 1870 strife was continuous, but the superiority of European weapons and the ravages of European diseases reduced Maori resistance. In 1870 they were allocated half of the North Island; and during his second governorship (1861–1868), Grey gave the Maoris direct representation in the New Zealand Parliament. In his second governorship, Grey had not the same constitutional powers as before; for the ministers were now responsible to the Assembly only, and were determined to put an end to Maori resistance.

New Zealand's economic development largely hinged on sheep-rearing and her export of wool to Great Britain rose rapidly. In 1870 her total exports of all goods amounted to about £4,700,000. *In 1907 New Zealand became a 'Dominion'.*

India after the Mutiny

The westernizing of India went on apace after the suppression of the Mutiny. Railway development was particularly important, and was undertaken with British capital. Its purpose was to aid British business in India and to provide rapid transport for troops in case of further trouble, especially on the North-west Frontier. British money was also widely invested in irrigation, engineering, canals and other forms of modernization.

This use of British capital roused the opposition of Indian nationalists, especially when factory conditions arose in India as bad as those of a hundred years before in Britain. The employment of cheap factory labour particularly aroused the opposition of the **Indian National Congress**, established in **1885**. They supported the Indian craft industries and, above all, agitated for the increasing admission of Indians to the Civil Service. The educated Indians naturally supported this latter demand, but *as late as 1914 the Indian Civil Service was still 95 per cent British*. The Indian Congress movement, however, was advocating self-government for India on English parliamentary lines.

British Reforms in India

During his ministry of 1880 to 1885 Gladstone, who sympathized with the idea of ultimate self-government for India, took important measures. The Viceroy, **Lord Ripon**, set up municipal committees and district boards elected by the taxpayers. His successor, **Lord Dufferin**, by the **Indian Councils Act, 1892**, extended the electoral system to the provincial councils. These reforms encouraged the ideas of Indian self-government and gave increasing political experience to the educated Indian. But the Indian National Congress pointed out that Indians were still carefully excluded from every high executive post. The examinations for the Indian Civil Service continued to be held in London and the lowering of the age-limit for these examinations in 1879 made it even more difficult for Indians to compete.

The Indian National Congress was formed in 1885 and held annual representative meetings after that date. It had a number of British supporters from the start, and was later to be dominated by the great figure of **Mahatma Gandhi**.

The Morley-Minto Reforms, 1909

The Liberal government of 1909 introduced, through the Viceroy, **Lord Minto**, further measures of self-government for India. The

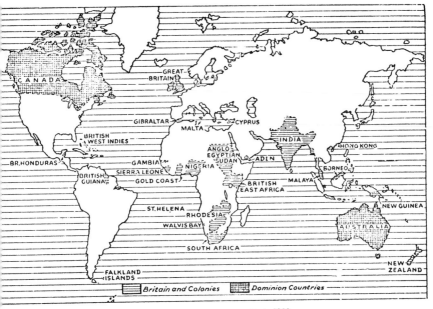

THE BRITISH EMPIRE AND DOMINIONS C. 1900

Secretary of State for India was **Lord Morley**. Their reforms gave the provincial councils of Bengal, Bombay and Madras elected Indian majorities. The Legislative Council for all India was to contain some Indian representatives as well as the Viceroy's Executive Council, and the Secretary of State's Council in London. However, *these councils could not pass legislation and were only advisory bodies to the Viceroy*, who still chose the actual government of India. *In 1917 Lloyd George declared democratic self-government for India to be the ultimate British aim*—a promise which the Indian National Congress kept before the eyes of successive British governments.

In 1917 the Secretary of State for India, **E. S. Montagu**, went to India to confer with the Viceroy, **Lord Chelmsford**. This resulted in Montagu's **Government of India Act, 1919**, which laid down that the Council of State was to consist of sixty members, only part of whom were elected, and that the Legislative Assembly was to contain 100 elected members out of a total of 140. The provincial assemblies were also to have elected majorities. Certain *'reserved'* matters were left with the Viceroy and his Executive Council, which was enlarged but not elected and was not answerable to the Legislative Assembly. These 'reserved' matters were the vitally important ones of foreign policy, law, the police, the armed forces and finance.

Thus over these very important matters there was no Indian control, and the *Indian National Congress, now beginning to be dominated by Gandhi, denounced these reforms as completely inadequate.*

National feeling against the British had been inflamed by the **Amritsar** massacre of **1919**, when the British commander, General Dyer, ordered his troops to fire upon a prohibited public meeting.

Mahatma Gandhi now gained a commanding position in the Indian National Congress movement. He lived the life of a saint, refusing all human luxury and advocating non-violent action—*'non-co-operation'*—against the British. He organized the boycott of British goods and the refusal of Indians in the Civil Service to work with the British. During **Lord Irwin's** period as Viceroy, 1926–1931, Gandhi undertook direct negotiations with the British at a **Round Table Conference** in London, but Britain's refusal to give self-government caused it to break down. However, the National Government's **India Act of 1935** made the provincial legislatures elective and Indian Ministers were to be responsible to them. The old system of the *'dyarchy'* (dual rule), by which the British had controlled the local law and police and the Indians other matters, was now abolished in eleven provinces. The central House of Assembly was now to consist of members elected by the provincial legislatures and the Council of State was broadened to represent various religions and interests. The actual central government of India, however, remained a dyarchy, with its members accountable for some matters to the Legislative Assembly, foreign affairs, finance and the armed forces being still 'reserved' to the control of the Viceroy. This, again, did not satisfy the Indian National Congress, although before 1939 there were Congress Party governments in a number of provinces. The **Moslem League** under **Mr. Jinnah**, demanded the protection of Moslem rights against the Hindu-dominated Congress Party, and the creation of a separate Moslem State. This latter was the solution accepted by the post-war Labour Government in 1947, with the creation of the separate states of India and Pakistan by the **India Independence Act**. This did not solve all problems, as the later strife between the two states over **Kashmir** was to demonstrate.

Egypt

We have already noted the main events in Egypt between the purchase of the Suez Canal shares and the reconquest of the Sudan by Kitchener in 1898.

The most important British administrator in the late nineteenth and early twentieth centuries was **Sir Evelyn Baring**, Consul-General from 1883 to 1907. (He was made **Lord Cromer** in 1892.) Although the Khedive was still ruler of Egypt for the Turkish Empire, Cromer came to be the decisive influence. Cromer and his advisers really controlled the Legislative Council. He stressed the importance to Britain of the Egyptian cotton crop and, by allocating over a million pounds to improved irrigation, *he helped to increase the Egyptian cotton yield from £8 million in 1883 to £30 million in 1907.* The great **Aswan Dam** which was a huge water reservoir to improve summer irrigation in the Nile Valley was completed, and the Egyptian government actually achieved a surplus of revenue over expenditure—all very satisfactory to foreign holders of Egyptian debt. Cromer also developed the railway system, improved the legal position of the peasant, and reduced both taxation and waste at the same time.

Cromer was completely opposed to Egyptian independence and was an avowed enemy of the developing Egyptian nationalist movement. He adopted a high-handed attitude to Egyptian officials and gave much offence by failing at times to consult the Khedive on important matters.

The Liberal governments of 1906 and 1914 increased the part played by Egyptians in the administration. (Cromer himself supported this.) More Egyptians entered the Civil Service and the Legislative Assembly was given the right to criticize government policies. However, the *Nationalist Party continued to press for independence;* and when he became Consul-General in 1911, **Lord Kitchener** took strongly repressive measures against the Nationalists. At the same time, however, he gave more powers to the Legislative Assembly (*e.g.* the right to debate the sacred topic of foreign affairs), and he increased the number of elected members as opposed to those nominated.

During the First World War, Britain took complete control of Egypt and discarded Turkish suzerainty altogether. After the war the Nationalist leader **Zaghlul Pasha**, organized a delegation, the **Wafd,** to the Peace Conference at Versailles. He made no headway towards Egyptian independence, and the British deported him to Malta. This led to anti-British rioting in Egypt and the High Commissioner, **Lord Allenby**, advised the release of Zaghlul for negotiations, which failed. In 1922 Britain proclaimed Egyptian independence while retaining troops there for the defence of the Canal. This was not regarded by Egyptians as real independence, and conflict continued. Tension was increased by the murder of the Governor-General of the Sudan, **Sir Lee Stack**, in 1924; and British forces occupied Alexandria when the Egyptians refused to withdraw their forces from the Sudan.

In the 1930s new developments prompted Zaghlul Pasha to accept new British offers which did not entirely meet the Nationalist aims. This compromise was partly dictated by the attack of Mussolini on Abyssinia. **The Anglo-Egyptian Treaty** of **1936** stipulated that British troops were to remain in Egypt for the next twenty years in the Canal

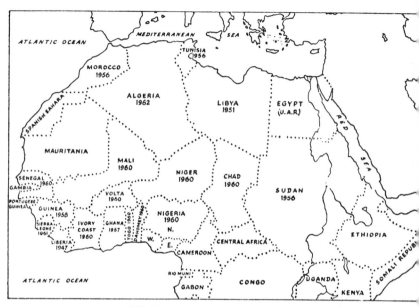

THE COUNTRIES OF NORTHERN AFRICA IN 1960

Zone. Egypt gained complete control of her own affairs, but the Sudan remained under British control.

During World War II, Egypt maintained an official neutrality, but after the war internal changes in Egypt rapidly followed. The rule of **King Farouk** was ended by an army revolt led by **General Neguib** in 1952 and the old Nationalist Party of the Wafd was dissolved, and replaced by the **National Liberal Rally**. In 1954 **Colonel Nasser** became Premier of the Egyptian Republic. Bad relations developed with Britain, especially when the Sudan declared for independence in 1956 rather than union with Egypt. The next crisis arose over the Suez Canal. Both Britain and America eventually refused to assist Nasser in the building of the new Aswan Dam. Nasser, who resented Britain's support of Israel, became the acknowledged leader of the Arab anti-Israel political forces. At the same time he nationalized the Suez Canal, thus expropriating both Britain and France. The result was a combined Israeli, British and French attack on Egypt in October 1956. This, the policy strongly advocated and adopted by Sir Anthony Eden (British Prime Minister), was denounced by the United Nations; and military operations were quickly brought to an end. This was a blow to the western powers and, although the Egyptians had done badly against Israel in the military sense, Nasser emerged in a strengthened position and British and French interests in the Suez Canal and Egypt were finally ended.

Nigeria

In Africa, a new British imperialism arose during the nineteenth century, strongly supported in the second half of the century by **Joseph Chamberlain** and **Lord Salisbury**, who gave particularly strong support to the work of Cecil Rhodes.

Other parts of Africa took on great importance for Britain. Nigeria had been an original centre for the slave traders, but after Britain's abolition of the slave trade in 1807 the country became important to British traders as a source of palm oil. The great explorer **Mungo Park** died in 1805 during his exploration of the Niger River, but other explorers followed. Here **Sir George Goldie** established the **United Africa Company**, which bought out French interests and became the **Royal Niger Company** in **1886**. The company negotiated important treaties with the Moslem rulers of the provinces and organized an army of the Hausa people trained by British officers. This strengthened British interests against the possible incursions of the French on the northern and western frontiers and of the Germans from the Cameroons. *Before 1914, the British government,* under the influence of Joseph Chamberlain, *had taken political control out of the hands of the Royal Niger Company.* This occurred in 1900, soon after the Fashoda incident with France had stressed, in Chamberlain's mind, the need for real British control. *The British Protectorates of Northern and Southern Nigeria were formed.*

The British control of Northern Nigeria was essentially the work of **Lord Lugard**, the first High Commissioner. He set up a capital under British control at **Zungeru**, and undertook military action against those native provincial rulers who were opposed to British control. A war against the Hausa people was fought in 1903–1904. He also replaced provincial rulers by those who accepted British control and were prepared to abolish the slave trade. He established English Residents in the provincial capitals, but left most local affairs in the hands of the Moslem emirs, half of whose revenue from taxation was allocated to the British for the development of transport, agriculture and public health. *In 1912–1914 he achieved the union of Northern and Southern Nigeria* against great opposition from the various tribes whose traditions were very different. He was given the title of first Governor-General, a post he held until 1918. The efforts of Nigeria towards true independence succeeded in 1960 with the ending of British rule and the creation of an independent Nigeria as part of the British Commonwealth.

East Africa and Central Africa

Britain's interest in East Africa arose from her trading agreements

with the **Sultans of Zanzibar**, and in 1887, anxious to counter the
German penetration of East Africa then occurring, the **Imperial British
East Africa Company** gained a lease from the Sultans of those areas
not occupied by the Germans, who were then strongly entrenched in
Tanganyika. In 1888 an official British expedition went to Lake Vic-
toria Nyanza, and in 1890 an agreement with Germany also gave
Britain trading rights in Uganda.

In 1893 the East Africa Company was bought out by the British
government and *in 1895 the British rights in East Africa were taken
over by the Foreign Office.* There soon followed further government
initiatives, sponsored by the Prime Minister, Lord Salisbury, and his
energetic Colonial Secretary, Joseph Chamberlain. *They decided to
finance the building of the railway from Mombasa to the Victoria
Nyanza, which was completed in 1903.* This had decisive results for
the future, for, besides giving access to the interior, the advantages of
the Kenya Highlands for British agricultural settlement were discovered during the construction of the railway.

From 1902 onwards applications for grants of land in Kenya poured
into the government, especially from South African settlers. The
government was pledged to reserve the best land to the Masai tribe,
and this at first limited development. The pioneer British settler was
Lord Delamere, and the policy was adopted of granting land to individual settlers and preventing the monopoly of land by powerful concerns for the purpose of re-sale or rental. This prevented unhealthy
land speculation. After the First World War, many ex-service men
settled in Kenya, where it had become the custom for the Kikuyu
tribe to undertake the basic labouring work. In 1919 the Europeans
gained elected representation for the first time on the Legislative
Council. *The original Protectorate became a Crown Colony in 1920,
while coastal regions remained the Kenya Protectorate.*

Considerable conflict of opinion arose between the home government and the Kenya settlers before 1939, mainly because the avowed
policy of the British government was to ensure that '*the interests of
the native peoples*', to quote an official statement, '*must be paramount.*'
Lord Delamere and his supporters wished to attain white supremacy.
The independence of Kenya, achieved in 1963, was the result of increasing local unrest and the emergence of very capable African
leaders. The **Mau-Mau** terrorist campaign, far from succeeding in its
aims, hardened the white settlers against concessions; and many of
them left Kenya when it became independent under **Jomo Kenyatta**.
However, a considerable portion have remained, and Kenya appears
to be developing on sound lines.

In East Africa the independence of Uganda, and of Tanganyika and
Zanzibar (now united as Tanzania) was achieved by 1966. In Central

Africa, however, things took a rather different course. The British government attempted to join in one federation the very different territories of Southern Rhodesia, Northern Rhodesia and Nyasaland—the **Central African Federation, 1953**, but this led to fears of white domination of the whole, and in *1963 the Federation was dissolved.* Northern Rhodesia then gained her independence as Zambia and Nyasaland as Malawi.

In Southern Rhodesia great difficulties now developed. It was still a colony of Britain and Britain refused to accord independence without guarantees of unretarded development for the Africans towards equality of political rights. The deadlock led on to the unilateral declaration of independence by Rhodesia under its Prime Minister, **Ian Smith**, in 1966, and to the subsequent failure of the direct negotiations between Mr. Wilson and Mr. Smith in the same year. This has resulted in the imposition of economic sanctions against Rhodesia through the United Nations.

The years from 1966 to 1978 saw further attempts to reach agreement between Britain and Rhodesia (Zimbabwe), but with no success. In 1977 Mr. Smith reversed his previous attitudes in an attempt to obtain an independent internal settlement by persuading the majority of his supporters to accept the principle of one man one vote in Rhodesian elections. He established the Executive Council consisting of himself and three leaders of the black community and proclaimed an election by 1 January 1979. However, the election had to be postponed on account of increased activity by guerrilla forces in Rhodesia operating from bases in Zambia and Mozambique. In the meantime the British and American governments refused to recognize the internal settlement and continued their efforts to secure a general conference to include the leaders of the externally-based guerrilla forces. They also refused to lift economic sanctions against Rhodesia.

However, in the autumn of 1979 Lord Carrington, British Foreign Secretary, succeeded in arranging a conference with the principal Rhodesian leaders at Lancaster House, London. After very difficult negotiations, agreement was reached on the need for elections to be supervised by a Commonwealth force, for the creation of a new parliament, which would also contain twenty white members, for a cease-fire in the guerrilla war against the whites and for a grouping of all guerrilla forces in agreed centres and their eventual absorption into a new national army. In the elections of February 1980 the party of Robert Mugabe gained a clear victory, and he became the first prime minister of the new state of Zimbabwe, which was proclaimed officially at Salisbury in April 1980. He allayed some of the fears of the whites by appointing four white members to his government, including one to the important post of Minister of Agriculture.

Summary

The development of the Empire and its transformation into the British Commonwealth is the main theme of this period. In the first stages the colonies of Australia, New Zealand and Canada developed forms of local government leading eventually to federation after much difficulty and internal conflict. During this process Britain relinquished much of her former authority until, by the Statute of Westminster, 1931, their right to full independence was recognized. In India, the expansion of British power culminated in the Mutiny and its after-effects. Indian nationalism grew rapidly in the twentieth century and achieved its main aim of independence in 1947. The development of Egypt was also towards the ending of all forms of military and political control by Britain, culminating in the final phase of Suez, 1956. Rhodesia also gained independence in 1980 and was renamed Zimbabwe. All these changes took more than a century of internal conflict, struggle with the ruling power, and unsuccessful efforts by Britain to make concessions while maintaining the substance of power.

Important Dates

1791	Pitt's Canada Act.
1837	Papineau and Mackenzie rebellions, Canada.
	New Zealand Association established.
1839	The Durham Report.
1840	Canada Act.
	Treaty of Waitangi (N.Z.).
1867	North America Act.
1883	Sir Evelyn Baring (Lord Cromer, 1892) becomes Egyptian Consul-General.
1885	Canadian Pacific Railway completed.
1892	Indian Councils Act.
1893	East Africa Company bought out by the British Government.
1898	Reconquest of the Sudan.
1900	British government took control of Nigeria from Royal Niger Company.
1909	Morley-Minto Reforms.
1912–1914	Lord Lugard united Northern and Southern Nigeria.
1919	Government of India Act.
	Amritsar Massacre.
1920	Kenya became a Crown Colony.
1922	Britain declared Egyptian independence.
1924	Sir Lee Stack murdered (Sudan).
1935	India Act.

1936	Anglo-Egyptian Treaty.
1947	Creation of India and Pakistan.
1952	General Neguib overthrew King Farouk.
1954	Colonel Nasser, Prime Minister of the Egyptian Republic.
1956	The Suez conflict.
1966	Unilateral declaration of independence by Rhodesia.
1978–1979	Attempted internal settlement in Rhodesia on basis of one man, one vote.
1979	Lancaster House Conference on Rhodesia.
1980	Independence of Rhodesia (Zimbabwe) proclaimed.

QUESTIONS

(*1*) *What was the importance of* (a) *the Durham Report;* (b) *the Canada Act, 1840?*

(*2*) *How and for what reasons did Canada become a federation?*

(*3*) *What circumstances led on to Australian federation?*

(*4*) *What was the importance of* (a) *Edward Gibbon Wakefield;* (b) *Sir George Grey?*

(*5*) *What reforms were made in the government of India between 1890 and 1935?*

(*6*) *Describe the relations between Britain and Egypt between 1919 and 1936.*

(*7*) *Describe the stages of development of Kenya up to 1920.*

(*8*) *Give an account of the policies and work of Lord Lugard in Nigeria.*

CHAPTER FORTY-ONE

TRADE AND INDUSTRY, 1815-1939

Britain in 1815

SOCIAL and economic conditions immediately after the Napoleonic wars were bad. Before the Corn Laws were passed, foreign corn came freely into Britain and reduced prices to such an extent that *many hundreds of farmers were bankrupted.* In agriculture, the old open-field system had largely disappeared owing to the war-time enclosures and many farmers unable to meet the expenses of enclosure became labourers or migrated to the towns. In the countryside, a new class of farmer and landlord was developing who farmed more consciously *for the market* than his eighteenth-century predecessors. In the towns, the old domestic industrial system was giving way to the factory system with increasing rapidity—very fast in the cotton industry and more slowly in the woollen industry. The new factories were already producing the social evils of long hours and the exploitation of very young children. The Napoleonic wars had saddled the government with a *National Debt of £700 million,* and taxation on ordinary articles of consumption was imposed in order partly to meet it. *This fell heavily on the working people,* and the *Corn Laws made things worse for them.*

Industrial towns were growing fast, and with them there developed very bad conditions of housing and sanitation. Speculative builders threw up thousands of *back-to-back dwellings* with no damp courses and very little light. Drinking water was obtained from pumps or bought from the water-sellers. These conditions gave rise to the appalling *cholera epidemics* of the times—as late as 1866 more than 10,000 people died in London through drinking polluted water.

At the same time Britain made enormous strides in invention. Steam power enabled the earlier inventions of Hargreaves, Arkwright and others to be more fully used. The patent on Watt's steam engine lapsed in 1800, and after that date many other firms built steam engines. Other important developments in electricity (summarized on p. 387) led on to the development of telegraphs and the trans-Atlantic and cross-Channel cables. Then the invention of the hot-blast furnace by **Nelson** in **1829** saved fuel costs and increased iron production from about 240,000 tons in 1806 to 2,700,000 tons in 1852.

In **1856, Henry Bessemer** invented the method of removing impurities from steel production and enabled more efficient steel to be produced for use in railways, shipping, etc. By 1879 **Gilchrist** and **Thomas** had gone further and removed, by this process, the phosphorous in steel, which had tended to make it brittle.

All these improvements mentioned above—the steam engine, electrical apparatus, the new steel production—had a more immediate effect on *railway development* than probably on any other industry. **George Stephenson**'s improvements to the locomotive and his great engineering enterprises led to the opening of the **Stockton to Darlington Railway** for goods traffic in **1825** and the **Manchester to Liverpool Railway** in **1830**. The canals were slow and expensive compared with the new railways, as also was the old road turnpike system. Gradually the railways took on passengers, and *between 1830 and 1850 over 6,000 miles of railway were built* with the money invested by the new middle class. Land, however, was costly; and small railway companies often amalgamated in order to reduce costs—in this way the **Midland Railway** and the **London and North Western Railway** were formed.

Enthusiasm for railway development had its greatest promoter in the *'Railway King'*, **George Hudson**, who did much to bring about the *'railway mania'* of the 1840s. Some of his speculations brought ruin to investors, but his enterprise gave him great popularity. He especially worked with George Stephenson to take the Midland Railway as far as Newcastle. Unfortunately, he was involved in fraudulent finance in connection with the Great Eastern Railway Company, and this led to his downfall. But Hudson's influence can be seen by the fact that *Parliament authorized in 1843 only 24 railways, whereas two years later 248 railway bills were passed.*

In **1844** Gladstone's **Railway Act** stated that each company was to run at least one train a day in each direction with third class accommodation at a penny per mile (the 'parliamentary train'). The social and economic effects of railways were enormous. They broke through the expensive monopoly of the canals and turnpikes and provided industrialists and passengers with cheaper services. Cheap excursions to the seaside developed in the 1850s; and this contributed to the health and relaxation of other sections of the population besides the upper classes, who had hitherto regarded places such as Brighton as their own preserve. The demands for rails and rolling stock helped to increase the output of the iron and steel industries. The speedier carriage of goods to the ports was a great factor in developing Britain's great export trade during the nineteenth century. Another important result was the breaking down of the old isolation of one part of the country from another—it speeded up mobility of labour, the postal system, the spread of national newspapers and news. *The railways* *brought about a total transformation of Britain in the nineteenth century.*

The development of shipping complemented the railways. New types of steamships were launched in the same period that the more powerful locomotives were built. By the year 1900 the Atlantic crossing was being done in five-and-a-half days, and the invention of the steam turbine by **Parsons** resulted in the *Mauretania* crossing the Atlantic in four-and-a-half days in 1909. These developments had been brought about by new and powerful engines and by the later use of oil-fired vessels. The compound engine invented by **Elder** in 1854 was a great advance on Watt's steam engine. This speeded up the change from sail to steam. *Steel ships launched on the Clyde in 1879 were only 10 per cent of the total tonnage, whereas in 1889 they were 97 per cent.*

Britain possessed numerous coaling stations throughout the world, and gained a monopoly of the shipping business in the nineteenth century. British industry was demanding products from the most distant parts of the world, and her shipping could bring them in, especially when refrigeration was added to sea transport in the last quarter of the century.

All these factors gave Britain economic superiority in the nineteenth century—great home resources of coal, an expanding Empire containing valuable raw materials, an engineering ability which enabled Britain to gain the lead in railways, shipping and industrial production. We must now consider the general economic growth of Britain since 1815.

From 1815 to the Great Exhibition, 1851

In this period, Britain's main industries increased their output enormously. For example, coal production rose from 10 million to 50 million tons, and by 1851 cotton cloth exports from Lancashire represented about 50 per cent of Britain's total exports. Both import and export were stimulated by the introduction of free trade, while very low rates of income tax meant maximum profits for business. Yet even in 1851, agriculture employed more men than all other industries put together. Britain was not yet completely dominated by industry, and there were, in fact, more domestic servants than workers in the combined woollen and cotton industries. The great increase of industrial production was to a large extent the result of the new machinery which enabled each worker to produce more.

The Great Exhibition held in Hyde Park in 1851 was intended to show Britain's progress to the world and to encourage foreign trade. The moving spirits of this exhibition were its President, the **Prince Consort** and its Secretary, **Joseph Paxton**, formerly the gardener to the Duke of Devonshire. The exhibition showed the exact stage reached by British industry—the advance of invention and the factory system; but still a great part of industry was organized on a craft basis or in small family concerns. 'Big business', with amalgamation of firms with great concentrations of finance, was to develop in the later part of the century. The profits from the Exhibition, to which there were over six million visitors, were used to further scientific education.

Mid-Victorian Prosperity, 1846–1873

The Great Exhibition was the expression of British confidence and developing prosperity after the difficult years since Waterloo. *Between 1846 and 1873 a great wave of industrial prosperity surged over Britain.* Exports rose three times and imports doubled. The output of coal doubled and the iron, steel, wool and cotton industries expanded at an even greater rate. The railway system grew rapidly and passenger traffic increased sevenfold. Even in farming, production increased owing to new methods and government assistance. This was regarded by many as the 'golden age' of Britain in the nineteenth century.

The reasons for mid-Victorian prosperity are many, but the following points are important: (1) by 1860 all the old *mercantile restrictions on trade had disappeared,* including the Navigation Acts. (2) The old *laws of settlement* which restricted the movement of labour had also gone, and this was essential for the growth of new industries. (3) By 1860 *free trade was almost complete.* (4) *Other countries needed trade with Britain,* whose industries were so far in advance of others at this period. Two important customers were the United States and Germany, as well as the developing countries of Australia and New Zealand. (5) *London became the world's money centre.* Through London much British money was invested abroad, and this investment was often used by foreign countries for the purchase of industrial equipment from Britain. (6) *Improved transport* enabled the farmer to sell his produce more widely, and he developed more varied production—meat as well as cereals. *The rising wages of the working class* also benefited agriculture by increasing demand for food. (7) In general, *the great lead which Britain had obtained over other countries* through the Industrial Revolution was now bearing its best fruit, and *severe competition from other countries had not yet developed.*

The working class appeared to have shared a good deal of this prosperity, except the agricultural workers. Other workers, apart from some sections of the unskilled, greatly improved their standards. The skilled workers' wage-rates rose steeply—the engineers by over 30 per cent. In general, wages outpaced prices, and between 1850 and 1873 the purchasing power of the working class rose by something like 30 per cent. Thus nearly all classes benefited, though factory and mine conditions and the state of housing and sanitation, as well as insufficient education, still told heavily against the working class.

The Economic Depression of 1873–1890

'Depression' for nearly thirty years followed the period of mid-Victorian prosperity. But it was not a general economic depression. General production in the basic industries continued to rise, as also did the standard of life, except in agriculture. There was, however, a considerable fall in prices and profits which affected the manufacturer. For example, the price obtained for iron fell by two-thirds in the ten years from 1873 to 1883, and the value of British exports fell sharply, producing an adverse balance of trade in which Britain was importing more than she was exporting. The working class benefited from the fall in prices, but the capitalist, uncertain over prices and profits, was more inclined to lay off labour, and thus unemployment became a more persistent occurrence in this period.

Britain's competitive position began to decline. Foreign governments subsidized ship-building, and foreign shipping began to compete with Britain through lower freight charges. Germany and the United States especially began to compete strongly with Britain. France and Germany were now producing their own steel in greater quantities, as also was the United States. All these countries, being newer in the field, were able to use the latest methods, whereas Britain was still basing her output on the technical advances of the first Industrial Revolution. Thus the demand both for British iron and steel, and for the coal to produce it, slackened in these years. *Germany now became protectionist* and this limited the German market for British goods. *The U.S.A. also became strongly protectionist* in the years after 1893. Both the U.S.A. and Germany went on to a gold standard and abandoned silver. The result was to restrict the amount of precious metals available as a basis for paper credit, and this tended to lower prices and slow down the rate of industrial advance.

The Royal Commission on Trade and Industry, 1886, dealt with weaknesses in British industry. It criticized the inadequacy of technical education in Britain as compared with that in Germany, who was also praised for her efforts to expand her trade with new territories. British efforts to expand were part of the *New Imperialism* encouraged by Salisbury and Chamberlain, which led to increasing trade with Africa, the Empire countries and South America especially. These efforts revived British trade to a great extent, but Germany and the U.S.A. continued to overtake Britain in coal and steel production. Britain was slow to employ new techniques, especially in the cotton industry and in the application of electrical power.

Higher prices after 1900 aided British producers, but by 1914 Britain was being rapidly overtaken by her main competitors.

British Agriculture—a Special Problem, 1873–1914

A severe decline struck British farming in this period. It was more severe than the crisis in trade and industry. Land went out of cultivation owing to low prices and profits and labour drifted to the towns. In 1875 wheat prices were 44/- a quarter—in 1894 they were 17/6.

Bad harvests in 1873, 1875, 1876 and 1879 and diseases among animals made things worse; but they were not fundamental causes of decline, for even in years of good weather, land cultivation remained unprofitable. *Competition in conditions of free trade was an important factor*, especially of grain imports from the newly-developing Middle West of America. Canned meat and refrigeration produced a flood of cheap meat imports into Britain from America, Australia and New Zealand. During the period of 'high farming' from 1848–1870, many farmers had turned to dairy farming and had done well during the period of mid-Victorian prosperity; but now dairy produce entered Britain in increasing quantities. An important factor was the *fall in the value of silver*, which meant that grain imports from India, for example, which had a silver currency, were very cheap.

Attempted Remedies

The **Eversley Commission** of **1892–1896** *set the general trend of agricultural policy for many years*. It advised a more diverse agriculture, including market-gardening and flower and fruit cultivation. The British fruit industry really dates from the late years of the nineteenth century. Prices recovered after 1900 and this also assisted farmers. It was also found that the wealthier classes preferred English meat to imported meat, and the latter was left mainly to the working classes. On the other hand, the agricultural worker suffered from low wages and unemployment and, if he did not drift to the towns, suffered again the rigours of the Poor Law. The weak position of the agricultural worker led to the failure of **Joseph Arch** to establish permanently his **Agricultural Workers' Union**.

Government policy was to attempt the creation of a new smallholder or peasant—the *'three acres and a cow'* policy, associated with the name of Joseph Chamberlain. In 1892 Gladstone introduced an act by which *County Councils could provide land to suitable applicants* who were to be assisted by government loans. This achieved very little, and the act was only permissive. In **1908** the Liberal **Smallholdings and Allotments Act** brought more compulsion on County Councils, but this was not successful and attracted the wrong type of applicant who had little experience of the land.

The war of 1914–1918 revived agriculture through the sheer necessity of the times. To meet the German submarine blockade, agriculture came under government control through **County War Agricultural Committees**, and these converted land to arable land and prohibited many of the crops which the Eversley Commission had advised during the depression. Minimum prices were fixed and through the **Wages Boards** the farm labourer for the first time had a guaranteed minimum wage. By 1918 Britain had increased her wheat production to 60 per cent more than immediately pre-war.

The Inter-War Years, 1918–1939

We have seen in Chapter 32 the complete government control of industry and trade during 1914–1918. The end of the war brought serious problems, which may be summarized:

(1) *Many of Britain's old export markets had been lost and other nations were taking her place.* Cotton is an example of this, for both China and Japan were now producing more than twice their pre-war production of cotton cloth. In 1935 the cotton-cloth exports of Lancashire had sunk to half those of 1914. Iron and steel suffered from similar competition in other countries.

(2) *The coal industry was the worst hit of all.* From the declining industries of iron, steel and cotton, as well as shipping, the demand for coal fell away drastically. The same applied to exports of coal, for Germany was paying war reparations in coal to some of Britain's biggest customers before the war. World shipping was turning to the use of fuel-oil in place of coal.

(3) *Britain had lost a considerable proportion of her carrying trade,* which created serious unemployment problems in the ship-building industry, especially on the Clyde. In 1890 Britain's share of the world's carrying trade had been 60 per cent, but in 1937 it was only 31 per cent.

(4) *Britain's return to the gold standard* hindered her export trade. In 1925 the value of Britain's currency in terms of gold was higher than that of other countries and this made her exports dearer.

Efforts to Improve the Economic Situation

Rationalization and the *gradual abandonment of free trade* were the main trends of the years 1919 to 1939. The first of these involved methods of reducing costs of production by improved machinery, amalgamation of small firms into larger units and by better use of labour. The cotton industry was in urgent need of these changes, but *unemployment was increased and the trade union movement was suspicious of rationalization.*

During the war import duties had been imposed (*the McKenna duties,* so named after the Chancellor of the Exchequer) upon such things as motor cars, watches and films in order to reduce their import and save shipping space for more essential supplies. After the war, these duties were maintained, with a reduction of one-third for Empire countries— **'Empire Preference'**. Then the economic collapse of 1929-1931 led to *more than 2,000,000 unemployed in Britain,* to the fall of the second Labour government in 1931 and to the formation of the National Government under Ramsay MacDonald. In order to lower prices and assist exports *the government took Britain off the gold standard* and, as a complementary action to this, an **Import Duties Advisory Committee** was set up to administer a tariff system. A 10 per cent duty was imposed on most imports and in some cases this rose to 20 per cent in the 1930s. These duties aimed to protect British manufacturers, reduce imports and achieve a favourable balance of trade, as well as to provide government revenue. The Empire countries could, however, send goods to Britain at lower tariffs. The **Imperial Economic Conference**, which met at Ottawa in 1932, endorsed the principle of Empire Preference. *Thus Britain, like other states since 1919, abandoned the free trade policy and entered upon Protection.*

The economic policies of the National Governments before 1939 did not succeed in securing full employment in Britain, and in 1939

YEAR	NO. OF UNEMPLOYED	OVER ONE MILLION
1912	1,050,000	
1917	160,000	
1921	1,500,000	
1929	1,250,000	
1930	1,750,000	
1931	2,900,000	
1937	1,450,000	
1943	81,600	
1954	284,800	
1961	350,000	

UNEMPLOYMENT FLUCTUATIONS BETWEEN 1912 AND 1961

there were still a million and a half unemployed, mainly in those areas where the old industries such as steel, iron, coal, shipping and cotton had been developed during the past century. These were the *'special'* (*or depressed*) *Areas.* However, in the South-east and in London, employment and incomes were far higher; for here new light industries were being developed, depending on the ready supply of electricity. For those employed, the standard of living rose between 1935 and 1939, when there was a fall in food prices. The economic problems of Britain during the Second World War and after are dealt with in Chapters 37 and 38.

British Agriculture, 1919–1939

In 1921, farm prices began to fall rapidly, and between 1920 and 1922, the price of wheat was halved. Many farmers now abandoned arable farming in favour of dairy farming. Farmers lost guaranteed prices and the workers saw the *Wages Boards abolished* by the Lloyd George Coalition Government. However, the first Labour Government of 1924 *re-established the Wages Boards* and the county minimum wage. Agricultural workers' wages had fallen from 42/- a week in 1920 to only 28/- in 1922, and many men were leaving the land. A considerable aid to the farmer was given by the **De-rating Act** of **1929**, which removed rates from farm land and buildings. The wartime policy of direct government aid by subsidies was also introduced before 1937 for important crops such as wheat, barley and oats. The new sugar-beet industry was financially aided by the government, which was represented on the **British Sugar Corporation**. The National Governments also passed **Agricultural Marketing Acts** in **1931** and **1933** which assisted producers of a number of commodities to combine for the purpose of economic marketing. However, further attempts to encourage smallholdings failed, and were not again to be revived. Conditions on the land were still not good enough to prevent increasing emigration and the drift to the towns. In 1931 the number of agricultural workers was half that of 1870 and the average yearly rate of drift from the land between the two wars was about 10,000. *It took another war and the maintenance of government subsidies to retrieve the situation for agriculture.*

Summary

Between 1815 and 1851 all Britain's economic resources developed at an increasing pace. Output was enormously aided by new methods and inventions in almost every industry, and the movement away from the domestic to the factory system was the main characteristic of the period, with the wider application to industry and transport of the new power of steam. The growth of towns and population was also striking. In transport the development of railways transformed the country, and the steamship also made its appearance. Mid-Victorian England was a period of unprecedented prosperity, aided by free trade and Britain's natural economic advantages over other states. This was succeeded by a long period of uneven development, with unemployment more frequent, low prices for basic commodities, and increasing foreign competition. Farming was in a desperate plight. During the First World War farming regained its former importance, only to find once again great difficulties in the post-war period. In regard to Britain's old basic industries, the post-war period was one of almost uninterrupted decline, with the growth of the Special (Depressed) Areas as its most distressing outcome. In the 1930s Britain abandoned her almost century-old system of free trade, but, although more diversified industry developed to compensate for the decline of the old, unemployment was still heavy at the outbreak of the Second World War.

Important Dates

1815	**The Corn Laws.**
1825	**Stockton to Darlington Railway.**
1830	**Manchester and Liverpool Railway.**
1830–1850	**6,000 miles of railway built.**
1844	**Gladstone's Railway Act ('Parliamentary trains').**
1845	**248 railways authorized by Parliament.**
1851	**The Great Exhibition.**
1854	**Elder's compound engine.**
1886	**Royal Commission on Industry and Trade.**
1892–1896	**Eversley Commission on Agriculture.**
1908	**Smallholdings and Allotments Act.**
1924	**Agricultural Wages Boards re-established.**
1925	**Britain returns to gold standard.**
1929	**De-rating Act.**
1931–1939	**Britain abandons free trade.**
1931	**Agricultural Marketing Act.**
1932	**Imperial Economic Conference.**

QUESTIONS

(1) Why was Britain able to make rapid industrial progress in the period 1815–1851?

(2) What were the important results of railway development in the nineteenth century?

(3) What were the main reasons for mid-Victorian prosperity?

(4) *What difficulties did Britain have to face in industry and agriculture after 1870?*

(5) *What efforts were made to reduce Britain's industrial and agricultural difficulties in the period 1870–1914?*

(6) *What were the causes of Britain's economic difficulties after the First World War?*

(7) *What measures were taken in the 1930s to overcome Britain's economic problems? With what success?*

CHAPTER FORTY-TWO

THE TRADE UNIONS AND THE LABOUR PARTY

THE later histories of the trade unions and of the Labour Party are naturally inter-related, but the summary at the end of the chapter gives a separate statement for convenience of revision.

After Chartism

After the failure of Owen's G.N.C.T.U. and the later decline of Chartism, trade union official policy became less militant and the strike weapon was even denounced by important trade unions. In the period of mid-Victorian prosperity the craft unions tended to set the general tone. These unions, composed of members of a single craft, such as the **Amalgamated Society of Engineers**, were known as the *'new model' unions*, having large funds and employing permanent officials. The leading officials of these unions met in London at intervals to discuss general problems, and they became known as the *Junta*. In the 1860s attempts were made to establish a Trade Union Labour Party, but this failed. However, in 1868 a national trade union meeting at Manchester resulted in the formation of the **Trades Union Congress (T.U.C.)**, supported by the powerful London 'Junta'. The London 'Junta' took a leading part in forming the **London Trades Council** in 1860 and this played an important part in the agitation for the **Second Reform Bill** of **1867**. Thus from early days the purely trade union aims and the political aims were intermingled.

The evidence given by the new unions of skilled workers helped to bring about Gladstone's Trade Union Act of 1871 and the improved Act passed by Disraeli in 1875 which legalized peaceful picketing. The votes of the skilled trade unionists helped to swing the election of 1874 in Disraeli's favour.

Thus for thirty years after 1848 the skilled trade unions strengthened their funds and organization and brought important political pressures to bear in Parliament. They were aided by the election of two independent 'labour' M.P.s in 1868. The strike was rare, but their funds were often used to assist workers 'locked out' by employers, or workers on strike in certain cases.

377

The New Unionism

The craft unions held the field during the period of mid-Victorian prosperity, but with the oncoming of economic depression and recurring unemployment *the unskilled workers began to emerge as a strong trade union force.* Their leaders were the younger men influenced by the Communist doctrines of **Karl Marx** and **Friedrich Engels.** The latter, who had textile interests in both Britain and Germany, issued the *'Communist Manifesto' of 1848* in conjunction with Marx. He had also written an important book on the state of the English worker —*The Condition of the English Working Class in 1844.* Marx was exiled from Germany in 1848 and lived the remainder of his life in England. In 1867 he published the first volume of *Das Kapital,* an analysis of capitalist society which greatly influenced the leaders of the new militant trade unions such as **Tom Mann, Will Thorne** and **Ben Tillett.** The *Communist Manifesto* had described the historical process by which eventually all power would be vested in the hands of the workers or proletariat. In 1864 Marx established the **International Workingmen's Association** (the **First International**). The London 'Junta' was at first represented, but as Marx's revolutionary views gained control they dropped away.

The most influential propounder of Marxism in Britain was **H. M. Hyndman,** author of *England for All.* In 1881 he established the **Social Democratic Federation,** among whose early members were **John Burns, Tom Mann, George Lansbury** and **Ernest Bevin.** Another influence from abroad in these years was that of the *American Knights of Labour,* who had ten thousand members in Britain in 1889. Two examples of the new unions of the unskilled men which developed in the 1880s were the **Seamen's Union** and the **Gas Workers' Union.** The latter, under the leadership of Will Thorne, won an eight-hour day in 1889. In 1889 also the **Miners' Federation of Great Britain** was formed. Another important influence towards socialism was that of the **Fabian Society,** established in 1884. This society demanded the local authority ownership of such social needs as gas, water and electricity—they preached 'municipal socialism' and 'socialism through parliament', in contrast with the more revolutionary approach of the Social Democratic Federation.

Although the S.D.F. and the Fabians were not as influential as they had hoped they would be, *the ideas of socialism were beginning to make an impact on the trade union movement and on a small section of the middle class.* A more influential development by far was the founding by the Scottish miner, **Keir Hardie,** of the **Scottish Labour Party** in **1888,** which demanded, besides improvements in working conditions, elements of nationalization. In 1892 Keir Hardie was elected M.P. for West Ham South, and in the same year **Robert**

Blatchford established the socialist newspaper *The Clarion*. In 1893 working-class delegates under the chairmanship of Kier Hardie, meeting at Bradford, established the **Independent Labour Party,** one of whose early members was the future Labour Prime Minister, J. Ramsay MacDonald.

These developments coincided with a further outburst of strong trade union action, of which the **Dockers' Strike** of **1889** was the most significant example. The **Dockers' Union,** newly formed under the leadership of Tom Mann and John Burns, brought their members out on strike in August 1889, with a demand for a rate of sixpence an hour—*the 'dockers' tanner'*. This movement of unskilled and heavily-exploited workers aroused more sympathy than the employers expected, and peaceful processions in London, drawing attention to low pay and very bad living conditions, led to support by **Cardinal Manning** and the **Lord Mayor**. Large strike funds were subscribed by other unions in Britain and the Empire. The main demands of the dockers were won.

Other unions of unskilled workers were now formed, stimulated by the success of the dockers. The **Agricultural Workers' Union** was re-formed, the **General Railway Workers' Union**, the **General Union of Textile Workers**, and others. Increasing membership of these unions was a feature of the years 1888–1890—the Miners' Federation quadrupled its membership in two years. The new union leaders were more militant than those of the craft unions—Tom Mann, John Burns and Ben Tillett—all pioneers of the early labour movement—were strongly influenced by the new socialist doctrines.

The Formation of the Labour Party

In 1899 the T.U.C. summoned a special conference consisting of representatives of the Fabian Society, the Independent Labour Party, the Social Democratic Federation, the trade unions and co-operative societies and others. From this was formed the **Labour Representation Committee**, whose first secretary was James Ramsay MacDonald. Its prime position was to put up Labour candidates for Parliament. The position of the new 'party' was strengthened by the *Taff Vale dispute*. In 1901 the House of Lords ruled that the **Amalgamated Society of Railway Servants** was to pay £23,000 damages as the result of a strike by its members on the Taff Vale Railway in South Wales. This so alarmed trade unionists that they saw the need of an independent force in Parliament; and, of course, the Labour Representation Committee waged an immediate campaign against the decision. One result was the *election of three Labour men to Parliament in 1902–1903*. In 1906 the Liberals were pledged to reverse the Taff Vale decision and, in the overwhelming defeat of the Conservatives in that year, the *Labour Party returned 29 members*. **The Trade Disputes Act of 1906** *cancelled the Taff Vale decision*. The growing strength and agitation of the new Labour movement had contributed strongly to this result.

Another case of vital importance to the trade union and Labour movement was the **Osborne Case** of **1909**, when a railway employee named Osborne secured a judgment by the House of Lords that a trade union was acting illegally in using funds for political purposes—for example, the payment of Labour M.P.s. Parliament's enactment in 1911 of payment of M.P.s relieved the position of Labour M.P.s somewhat, but the Labour Party continued to press for a new ruling, and in 1913 the **Trades Union Amendment Act** legalized this use of trade union political funds if a ballot of a majority of its members approved, but at the same time any trade unionist could '*contract out*' of paying the political levy.

In the years 1906-1914 *syndicalism*, led by some leaders of the new militant unions such as Tom Mann and A. J. Cook, attempted to change the aims and methods of the trade union and labour movement by advocating the formation of very large unions by amalgamation, with the purpose also of waging a stronger fight for socialism than the Labour Party in Parliament seemed to be doing. There was also opposition to the mild and partly liberal attitudes of the craft unions. Declining wages after 1900 also caused much discontent and there were national strikes of both the railwaymen and the miners. The struggle between the 'militants' and the 'reformists' or 'gradualists' took a sharp turn. The syndicalists were successful in forming the **National Union of Railwaymen** (uniting three unions) and the **Transport and General Workers' Union**. Then in 1913 was formed the '*triple alliance*' of the miners, railwaymen and transport workers to wage a united economic struggle for better conditions. The militants found a voice in the newly-formed *Daily Herald*, and the milder reformists in the *Daily Citizen*. The new *Labour College* (*1908*) was under Marxist direction. Thus the socialist movement, both the militant and more constitutional or parliamentary aspects of it, had grown considerably by the outbreak of war in 1914.

Labour and the Trade Unions, 1914-1918

During the war, the trade union movement supported the war effort, as did the Labour Party. However, the Independent Labour Party opposed it; and as Ramsay MacDonald was a member and supporter of the I.L.P., he was replaced as Chairman of the Labour Party by Arthur Henderson. **The Munitions of War Act, 1915**, *placed all armaments workers under government control, strikes were illegal* *and compulsory arbitration in disputes was imposed.* The trade unions accepted 'dilution' of labour by which women and unskilled workers entered trades, such as engineering, which the unions had jealously guarded in the past.

In 1916, when he became Prime Minister, Lloyd George brought into his cabinet Arthur Henderson (Minister for Education). **John Hodge**, a trade union leader in the steel industry, became Minister of Labour. They agreed to this on condition that the state should take over control of mines, shipping and food and should set up a **Ministry of Labour** as a permanent institution.

There was much unofficial opposition, however, among the trade unions—especially in South Wales where the miners were led by Arthur J. Cook. In 1915 they gained wage increases by using the illegal strike weapon. In the Clyde ship-building industry the unofficial **Workers' Committee Movement**, under Marxist control, was very strong. In 1917 Arthur Henderson supported a negotiated peace after the outbreak of the Russian revolution and both the Labour Party and the T.U.C. now took this line. Henderson resigned from the government. Thus, immediately before Allied victory, Labour policy changed considerably. Ramsay MacDonald had remained opposed to the war throughout and suffered a term of imprisonment.

The Post-War Period

In 1918 the Labour Party won fifty-seven seats in Parliament and became a stronger force to be reckoned with. On the trade union side, unrest among the miners resulted from the Coalition Government's refusal to increase wages and nationalize the mines despite the recommendations of the **Sankey Commission** which the government itself had appointed. This also strengthened the agitation of the Labour Party and the T.U.C. for the nationalization of the mines. The railwaymen successfully resisted an attempt to reduce their wages; and dockers, led by Ernest Bevin, refused to load a ship, called the *Jolly George*, whose cargo of ammunition was intended for use by the Poles against Soviet Russia. The Labour Party improved its position in Parliament by securing 142 seats in 1922 on the break-up of the Lloyd George Coalition. *Ramsay MacDonald*, re-elected party Chairman, *became the first Labour Leader of the Opposition.* The election of 1924 gave the party 191 seats and, with Liberal support, the *first Labour Government was formed.* The period was an unhappy one in the relations between the Labour Government and the trade unions; for MacDonald made arrangements to use troops to safeguard supplies in the face of a threatened dockers' strike, and the Labour Party in the country showed its disapproval of his action. The trade unions became convinced that their immediate aim should be to strengthen

TRADE UNION AND LABOUR PARTY GROWTH

TRADE UNIONS LEGALIZED, 1824 FAILURE OF OWEN'S POLICIES	Whig repression Tolpuddle Martyrs Chartism.
CRAFT UNIONS DOMINANCE, 1848–1880 CREATION OF T.U.C. 1868	Skilled workers opposed strike weapon. The 'Junta'
MILITANT TRADE UNIONISM AFTER 1880 UNSKILLED WORKERS ORGANIZE UNIONS INDEPENDENT LABOUR PARTY LABOUR REPRESENTATION COMMITTEE, 1899 LABOUR PARTY, 1906 LABOUR GOVERNMENTS IN TWENTIETH CENTURY	Influence of Marxism Dockers' Strike Keir Hardie Social Democratic Federation Fabian Society Substantial representation in Parliament Syndicalism Failure of General Strike, 1926

their own organization and not to rely upon Labour support in Parliament.

The pioneer of improved T.U.C. organization in particular was **Walter Citrine**, its secretary. He brought about the separation of the staffs of the Labour Party and the T.U.C. in the cause both of independence and efficiency. A special **Organization Department** was established to advise the trade unions on organizational methods. This was a further step towards 'professionalizing' the administration of the trade union movement.

The General Strike, 1926

The new strength of the T.U.C. was shown in the part it played in the developments leading to the General Strike of 1926. When the miners under A. J. Cook refused to accept wages' reductions advised by the Samuel Commission on the Mines, *the trade unions gave the T.U.C. General Council the power to negotiate directly with the Baldwin Government*. At the same time, the T.U.C. made elaborate preparations for the conduct of a general strike. When negotiations failed, the General Strike began on 3rd May, 1926. During the strike, the T.U.C. published the *British Worker* to counteract the government's *British Gazette*. The collapse of the strike has been referred to in Chapter 33. The miners were left, suffering from a bitter sense of betrayal, to continue the strike alone until forced by sheer hardship to return to work in December. The Negotiating Committee of the T.U.C. contained no miners' representative, and accepted the main proposals of the Samuel Commission which had caused the miners' strike in the first place. The General Strike, which was very solid, lasted nine days.

The failure of the General Strike was followed by the *Trade Disputes and Trade Union Act, 1927*, by which a sympathetic strike was illegal unless it took place in the same industry as the first strike. Any attempt to 'coerce the government' was illegal, and it imposed the *'contracting in'* regulation by which a trade unionist wishing to pay the political levy had to make a signed statement to that effect. Established Civil Servants were denied membership of any trade union affiliated to the T.U.C. The results of the failure of the General Strike and of this Act were seen in *a declining trade union membership for some years*, and a change of T.U.C. policy towards co-operation with the employers to improve industrial relations—a policy strongly sponsored by **Ben Turner**, Chairman of the T.U.C. in 1929 and, from the employers' side, by **Sir Alfred Mond**, Chairman of I.C.I. The Mond-Turner policies were also strongly supported by Ernest Bevin, to the disgust of the Marxist trade unionists such as A. J. Cook. Bevin now played an important part in the building of the new T.U.C. and Labour Party headquarters at **Transport House** and also in arranging the take-over of the *Daily Herald* by Odhams Press. In all this he had the support of Walter Citrine.

In the crisis, which overtook the second Labour Government in 1931, both Bevin and Citrine opposed vigorously the policy of economies at the expense of the workers and the unemployed; and they advocated, instead of economy and contraction, the expansion of investment, particularly in public concerns. They had also been annoyed with the failure of the government to include trade union representatives in the May Committee which advised the drastic economies that broke up the Labour Government and returned a National Government under MacDonald in 1931.

The T.U.C.'s energetic opposition to MacDonald's policies led it to play an increasing part in the formation of Labour Party policy in the 1930s, and a **National Council of Labour** was set up in **1934** composed of equal representation of the Labour Party and the T.U.C. As Fascism advanced in Italy and Germany and Mosley's British Union of Fascists became active in Britain, the Communist Party advocated the *Popular Front* of all anti-Fascist parties, and when Sir Stafford Cripps supported this, he was expelled from the Labour Party led by Mr. Attlee since 1935. Both the official trade union movement and the Labour Party resisted the Popular Front campaigns on the grounds that both Fascism and Communism were dictatorships. Both the T.U.C. and the Labour Party supported the demands for the use of sanctions against aggressors by the League of Nations, and *Bevin became a strong supporter of British rearmament and had much to do with the Labour Party's eventual acceptance of this principle in 1937.*

The part played by trade union and Labour Party leaders in the Second World War is dealt with in Chapter 36, and the work of the post-war Labour governments in Chapter 37.

Summary

After 1848 the trade union movement was dominated by the organizations of the skilled workers—the 'new model' unions who tended to frown on strike action. The formation of the T.U.C. in 1868 marks an important step forward, while the legislation passed by Gladstone and Disraeli strengthened the legal position of the unions. The period from 1880 saw the growth of the unions of un-skilled workers, and the Dockers' Strike of 1889 was a key point in this development. The leaders of these unions tended to be influenced by Marxism in one degree or another and urged a militant role for the unions in general. The formation of the Labour Representation Committee in 1899 was the origin of the Labour Party. The Taff Vale case placed restrictions on the unions, which were removed in 1906, and the Osborne case temporarily weakened the connection of the trade unions with the Labour Party—but this also was modified before 1914. During the First World War the trade union and Labour movements officially supported the war effort, but there were significant minority movements of opposition. The Labour Party itself developed rapidly after 1918, while on the trade union side the General Strike of 1926 had a profound effect on future union policy. The names of Ernest Bevin and Walter Citrine are closely bound up with the development of the organization and policy of the trade union movement from the General Strike to 1939.

Important Dates

1860 London Trades Council formed.
1864 International Workingmen's Association formed.
1867 Marx's 'Das Kapital' published.
1868 Trades Union Congress formed.
1871 Gladstone's Trade Union Act.
1875 Disraeli's Conspiracy and Protection of Property (Trade Unions) Act.
1884 Fabian Society formed.
1889 Dockers' Strike.
1892 Election of Keir Hardie for West Ham South.
1893 Independent Labour Party formed, Keir Hardie chairman.
1899 Labour Representation Committee formed, J. Ramsay MacDonald secretary.
1901 Taff Vale case.
1906 Trade Disputes Act.
1909 Osborne Case.
1913 Trades Union Amendment Act.
1918 Labour Party returns 57 M.P.s.
1922 Labour Party returns 142 M.P.s.
1924 First Labour government.
1926 General Strike.
1927 Trade Disputes and Trade Union Act.
1934 National Council of Labour established.
1935 Mr. Attlee becomes Labour Party leader.

QUESTIONS

(1) For what reasons was there a growth of the unskilled trade unions after 1880?

(2) What was the importance of the Taff Vale and Osborne cases?

(3) For what reasons did the Labour Party gain strength in the years 1918–1924?

(4) What were the effects of the failure of the General Strike (1926) on the trade union movement?

CHAPTER FORTY-THREE

SCIENCE, INVENTION AND TECHNOLOGY

THE following is a summary of the more important of the technical advances of the nineteenth and twentieth centuries.

The invention of basic importance for the Industrial Revolution was the *steam engine produced by James Watt* as an improvement on **Newcomen's** earlier machine. The later improvements by Stephenson and others led to its increasing application to industry and transport during the nineteenth century. The discovery of the latent heat of steam by **Joseph Black (1722–1799)** was the theoretical basis for improvement, and it is significant that James Watt attended his lectures at Edinburgh University. Another great theoretical advance which had profound effects in practice was that of the mechanical equivalent of heat and the conservation of energy by **James Prescott Joule (1818–1889)**. Joule's researches led on to the theory of thermodynamics and its application to machines, heating systems and to refrigeration.

On the practical side **William Rankin** and **J. Hornblower** invented greatly improved steam engines, and Hornblower produced the first compound steam engine which generated far greater steam pressure than Watt's engine. By 1850 the average horsepower of the steam engine had risen to 40 as compared with only 15 in 1800.

Another application of steam power was made in 1839 by **James Nasmyth** who invented the steam hammer which greatly improved and increased the production of iron and steel sheets as well as other equipment for industry. Mass production was further aided by **James Whitworth (1803–1887)**, the pioneer of standardized screws and machine parts. **Joseph Bramah (1748–1814)** invented patent locks and the hydraulic press, while mass production was further aided by **Henry Maudsley's** invention of the screw-cutting lathe. All these advances were of great importance for the progress of industry and for the great work of the famous bridge, steamship and railway pioneer, **I. K. Brunel**.

The early nineteenth century saw the foundations laid of the modern electrical industry. By his discovery of electro-magnetic induction in 1831, **Michael Faraday** laid the foundation of all later work on dynamos and electric motors. Electric generators for arc-lamps for street lighting were built in 1875, and *the first electric power station in Britain was opened at Deptford in 1890*. This led on to further developments of electric lighting and the use of electric transport before 1914.

The Nature of Man

The most startling challenge to the old ideas of the development and origins of man, plants and animals came as a result of the work of **Charles Darwin (1809–1882)**. In 1831 Darwin joined the government survey-ship the *Beagle*, and his voyage to South America gave him the material for his revolutionary work, *The Origin of Species*, first published in 1859. His studies of nature in South America showed him that new species of plants, birds and animals were formed and survived as they adapted themselves to changing physical conditions. Those that did not adapt, perished. Darwin went on to postulate in his *Descent of Man* (1871) that man had adapted himself for survival and progress from some ape-like ancestor. *The results of Darwin's theories were*: (1) A fierce attack on him by leaders of the Anglican Church—especially by **Bishop Wilberforce**, and by other religious denominations. Darwin's theories shook men's ideas of the creation of the world and of man himself. (2) To help create another reason for the immense self-confidence of the Victorians in *progress*; for if Darwin was right, then there was no limit, apparently, to man's continuing evolution to higher forms. (3) The use of Darwin's theory of the 'survival of the fittest' to justify ruthless empire-building and the necessity of war—an interpretation never intended by Darwin. In fact, in the first edition of *The Origin of Species* he did not use this phrase at all. (4) *To create a fierce division for many years between science and religion.*

Radioactivity

Radioactivity was first discovered by the French scientists **Becquerel** and **Madame Curie**. In 1898 Madame Curie discovered radium. This led to the later development of artificially radioactive substances and radioactive isotopes of great importance in medicine and chemistry. In **1895 Roentgen** discovered **X-rays**. In 1897 **Sir J. J. Thomson** discovered the electron, and from this the practical application of vacuum tubes for lighting soon followed, and at a later date the electronic tubes which are used in radio and television. **Lord Rutherford** discovered that *the structure of the atom* was a nucleus with electrons moving round it, and his successful experiments in splitting the nucleus in 1930 were a preliminary to the production of controlled atomic fission both for atomic reactors and for military purposes.

These discoveries in the field of radioactivity, of the atom and of electricity were the fundamental additions to forms of useful energy such as steam power. The use of petroleum and the development of the *petrol motor* towards the end of the century added another important dimension to power.

Another fundamental turning point in human development was the *theory of Relativity* as postulated by **Albert Einstein**. His theory, in effect, replaced, or refined upon, the old Newtonian theory of gravitation. He showed that space and time were not separate but one continuum, and that gravitation was a product of the geometry of space-time and not just the result of one mass being near another. His **Special Theory of Relativity** also showed that mass and energy are equivalent, and this is the theoretical basis of the explosion of the nuclei of atoms in the atomic bomb. It was Einstein himself who confirmed the theoretical correctness of the chain-reaction on which these explosions depend, although he was deeply distressed at the use to which his own and other researches were put in 1945.

Other Important Inventions of the Nineteenth Century

The following are a number of inventions which had a profound effect upon industry and everyday life in the late nineteenth century and in the present century.

In 1839 **Charles Goodyear** invented the process of vulcanizing rubber and later inventions enabled it to be moulded into tyres for cycles and motor vehicles.

In 1869 the beginning of 'plastics' is seen in the production by **John Hyatt** of the first *celluloid* by a combination of camphor and cellulose nitrate. In 1907 **Leo Baekeland** invented 'bakelite'. From these inventions synthetic fibres were produced using petroleum (first used in industry in 1860) and coal. *The first artificial silk or rayon was produced in France in 1884* and nylon had also been produced before 1914.

In 1850 a vacuum freezing machine was invented by the Frenchman **Carré** and all future developments of refrigeration followed from this. The most important English pioneer of refrigeration was **A. C. Kirk** of Bathgate, who produced very low temperature machines in 1862, and in the late 1870s the first refrigerated meat imports came into Britain from New Zealand and Australia.

Besides those inventions already mentioned the following also had great importance: **Perkin's** manufacture of the first aniline dye, 1856 (effects on clothing, fabrics, etc.); **Daimler's** *first internal-combustion engine, 1885*, which led to the development of the motor car and aeroplane. (**Henry Ford's** mass-production car plant began operating in 1909.) The **Remington** typewriter appeared in 1875. As early as

1815, came the first canned food production in France, but the canning of food only developed widely after 1870. In 1880, the first filament electric lamps were made by **Swan and Edison**; in 1884 came the invention of the steam turbine by **Parsons** and in 1897 the **Diesel** engine.

Thus, before the first World War, the great majority of discoveries and inventions on which progress in the twentieth century was to depend had been made. No other period in history—the 150 years since the beginning of the Industrial Revolution—had seen such immense scientific progress. It was greater than all the scientific progress made in previous historical time.

Summary

Britain's industrial and technical development depended greatly on the outstanding work of her scientists, engineers and inventors, among whom the names of Watt, Joule, I. K. Brunel and Faraday are some of the most prominent. Charles Darwin's work on evolution shook all previous ideas on the origins and development of man and nature. Later discoveries in the field of radioactivity are bearing their fullest fruit in the twentieth century. The discovery and manufacture of new materials was also a feature of the nineteenth century, especially in the field of artificial fibres. The basis of nearly every important scientific and technical development of the first half of the twentieth century was laid before 1914. Einstein's theories of Relativity also fundamentally altered the scientist's view of the universe.

Important Dates

1831 **Magnetic induction—Faraday.**
1839 **Vulcanization of rubber—Charles Goodyear.**
1850 **Carré's vacuum freezing machine.**
1856 **First aniline dye (Perkins).**
1859 **'Origin of Species' published.**
1862 **A. C. Kirk's low temperature refrigerator.**
1869 **Hyatt's first celluloid.**
1871 **'Descent of Man' published.**
1875 **Remington typewriter.**
1880 **First filament electric lamps by Swan and Edison.**
1884 **Rayon produced (France).**
          Parsons' steam turbine.
1885 **Daimler's first internal-combustion engine.**
1895 **Roentgen discovered X-rays.**
1897 **Sir J. J. Thomson discovered the electron.**
          First Diesel engine.

1898   **Radium discovered by Madame Curie.**
1909   **Ford began mass production of cars.**

QUESTIONS

(*1*) *What theoretical and practical work during the nineteenth century greatly increased the use of steam power?*

(*2*) *What were the results of the work of Charles Darwin?*

(*3*) *What was the importance of the work of the following inventors:* (a) *Charles Goodyear;* (b) *John Hyatt;* (c) *A. C. Kirk;* (d) *Swan and Edison;* (e) *Sir J. J. Thomson?*

CHAPTER FORTY-FOUR

COMMUNICATIONS

(1) Roads and Canals

DURING the eighteenth century the turnpike trusts had improved the roads and some of them employed the pioneers of modern road construction. Of these latter the most important were **Metcalf (1717–1810), Telford**, the great bridge builder and road engineer **(1757–1834)** (the Menai Bridge, the Caledonian Canal and the Holyhead Road were some of his achievements), and **MacAdam (1756–1836)**, to whom is owed the invention of a new and durable road surface and effective road drainage. However, with the opening of the first of the railways in 1825 and their rapid development afterwards, road improvements suffered a definite setback. *Attempts were made to establish steam-driven road vehicles*—the most celebrated being **Gurney's and Hancock's** steam coach service, opened between London and Birmingham in 1830. This proved too uncomfortable for the passengers to be a paying concern and the road tolls were too heavy. The railway interests secured the passage through Parliament of the **'Red Flag Act, 1865'**, which limited the road speeds of mechanically propelled vehicles to 5 m.p.h. in the countryside and 2 m.p.h. in the towns—a red flag having to be carried ahead of the vehicle.

However, after about 1840 road improvement revived; for, with the spread of private carriages owned by the newly-rich and with the development of industry, the roads became more important than ever, although the *mail-coach services, first established between London and Bristol by* **John Palmer** *in* **1784**, were now fast declining. Bituminous limestone now became popular for road surfacing, and in 1865 the first cement road was constructed in Scotland. After the spread of the motor-car in the early twentieth century the problem of dust became so great that new types of surfacing were developed to keep it down, the most effective being hot bitumen.

These road improvements were dictated by the rapid extension of travel by all classes. The first horse-drawn omnibus appeared in 1829 and the first open-topped omnibus in 1890—the same year in which the first electric trams were built in the Midlands. Then, in 1905, the first regular petrol-driven 'bus service began in London.

All these developments were aided by important technical advances.

The development of the petrol motor has already been mentioned, but an essential to easier travel on the new road surfaces was the production of adequate tyres for cycles, motor-cycles and cars, and *the first pneumatic tyre was produced by* **J. B. Dunlop** in **1888**. Old restrictions were gradually removed—in 1896 the speed limit was raised to 12 m.p.h. in 1903 to 20 m.p.h. and in 1934 it became 30 m.p.h. in built-up areas. Motor taxation began in 1910 and the Road Fund was set up in 1920. In 1948, long-distance transport was nationalized by the Labour government; but it was denationalized by the Churchill government in 1953.

Important developments since 1945 have been the immense spread of the motor-car and the increasing use of the Diesel engine for 'buses and heavy transport. The increasing number of cars has produced the most serious problems of air pollution and appalling road casualties. On the positive side, the post-war period has seen *the development of a new road network,* of which the pioneer was the 'M 1'. *The road traffic problem is a major problem of the twentieth century* and until solved it will constitute a serious handicap to Britain's social progress.

The canals of Britain had a brief career of usefulness, but were soon overshadowed and almost completely replaced by the railways as a means of transport. The great pioneer was **James Brindley**, who in 1761 completed the **Bridgewater Canal** between Worsley and Manchester. This canal was used mainly for coal transport, and it cheapened coal in Manchester. In 1777 he completed the **Grand Trunk** or **Trent and Mersey Canal**. In the 1790s there was a 'canal mania', when numerous canals were opened and much money invested in them; but most of them failed owing to financial stress during the Napoleonic Wars. In 1805 the **Grand Junction Canal** was opened. The last great canal construction was the **Manchester Ship Canal** in **1894**. The canals were nationalized after World War II at the same time as the railways.

(2) Railways

The first railways were used in the coalfields of the North-east and the Midlands, and they consisted of horse-drawn trucks on rails. The first public railway began in 1801 when the horse-drawn **Surrey Iron Railway** was opened between Wandsworth and Croydon. In the same year **Richard Trevithick** invented his *steam carriage*—the first steam locomotive, and in 1805 his first flanged-wheel locomotive ran at Newcastle. *The first passenger railway in Britain was opened in 1807*—the **Oystermouth Railway** at Swansea Bay. Great advances continued to be made; and, in 1814, George Stephenson built his first steam locomotive, the *'Blücher'*. The Stockton and Darlington Railway was opened in 1825 for goods traffic and the first large passenger steam railway, the Liverpool to Manchester, was opened in 1830. This latter was the work of George Stephenson and his associate engineers. The success of this railway led to a burst of railway building in the years 1833–1837—*a railway 'boom'*. The dominant figure on the promotion side in the years 1835–1852 was **George Hudson**, the 'Railway King'. On the engineering side the dominant figure in the later period of 1830 to 1860 was **I. K. Brunel**, the builder of the Great Western Railway and others.

The first excursion train was run in 1840 by the Eastern Counties Railway, and this development made great strides in the next ten years. During the Great Exhibition of 1851 the cheap excursion came into its own, with numerous excursions from various parts of the country to London. From this time the cheap excursion from London to the seaside became popular. *By the year 1852 all the main trunk lines were completed* and an average speed of 50 m.p.h. had been achieved.

The Railways Act of 1844, besides establishing the so-called 'parliamentary train' service, declared the right of the state to purchase the railways if it thought fit.

Other important developments were the building of *the first underground railway in London in 1863*—the Metropolitan, and the *first London tube in 1884*. In 1892 the old broad gauge was abandoned and a standardized gauge of 4 feet 8½ inches was introduced. The railways gradually became more concentrated on the management side— the First World War showed the value of a co-ordinated system, and in 1923 they were grouped into the four main lines which became nationalized as British Railways in 1947. Another important development initiated in the 1930s was railway electrification, and the 1960s has seen the replacement of the old steam locomotives for passenger traffic by the diesel-electric.

The important results of railway development are summarized on page 367.

(3) Sea Transport

The idea of applying the steam engine to ships was first seriously considered by the engineer **Symington** as early as 1787, but its first practical application was to the steamship *Charlotte Dundas* on the Forth-Clyde Canal in 1801–1802, when it operated large paddle wheels. In 1807 the *Clermont* was launched on the Hudson River in America. Bell's steamship the *Comet*, launched on the Firth of Clyde in 1812, was driven by a Watt's steam engine and had a sail attached to the funnel. It was from this pioneer effort that regular commercial services began between Belfast and Greenock and cross-Channel services between Dover and Calais.

As early as 1833 the *Royal William* made the *first all-steam crossing*

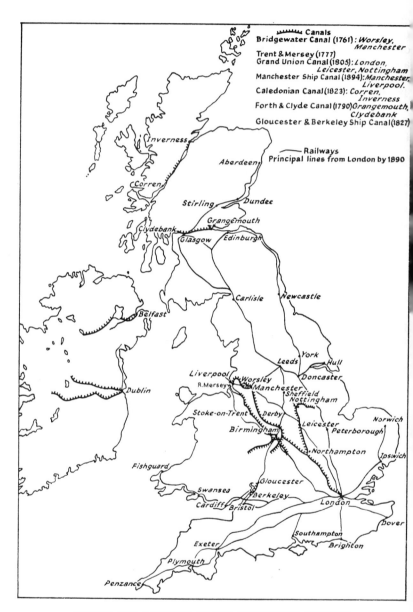

Canals

Bridgewater Canal (1761): *Worsley, Manchester*

Trent & Mersey (1777)
Grand Union Canal (1805): *London, Leicester, Nottingham*
Manchester Ship Canal (1894): *Manchester, Liverpool.*
Caledonian Canal (1823): *Corren, Inverness*
Forth & Clyde Canal (1790) *Grangemouth, Clydebank*
Gloucester & Berkeley Ship Canal (1827)

Railways
Principal lines from London by 1890

CANALS AND RAILWAYS IN THE NINETEENTH CENTURY

of the Atlantic—in 20 days. In 1838 this was followed by I. K. Brunel's *Great Western*, which was 212 feet long, 1,340 tons and had a speed of 8 knots. This was the beginning of regular trans-Atlantic crossings, and it took 13½ days. Both the *Great Western* and the *Sirius*, which also crossed the Atlantic in the same year, were paddle-steamers. In 1840 the first Cunarder, the *Britannia*, was launched, and was an entirely wooden vessel. The work of I. K. Brunel was seen again in the *Great Britain*, the first screw-driven steamer to cross the Atlantic (1843). Iron vessels now became more common, and Elder's compound engine gave much more power. In 1858 Brunel's *Great Eastern* was launched, it was 27,000 tons, carried 4,000 passengers and was powered by paddles, screw-propeller and sails. A new advance was made in 1894 when the *Turbinia*, driven by Parsons' steam turbine, was launched. In 1909 the Cunard liner, *Mauretania*, crossed the Atlantic in 4 days 11 hours—a record held for many years. This vessel was not broken up until 1935, when she was succeeded by the *Queen Mary* (1936) and the *Queen Elizabeth* (1940).

The replacement of wooden vessels by iron took place mainly after 1880. *In 1860 wooden sailing vessels were still twenty times more numerous than those made of iron.*

Together with these technical advances, efforts were made to improve the general conditions of seafaring during the nineteenth century. In **1824** the **National Lifeboat Institution** was founded, and in 1836 all lighthouses and lightships came under the control of **Trinity House**. A very important advance was introduced in 1850 when the Board of Trade undertook the issue of masters' and mates' certificates. The **Plimsoll Act** (the **Merchant Shipping Act**) of 1876 is referred to on p. 219, but an equally important development was the institution of **Lloyds' Register of Shipping** which enabled vessels to be examined and classified for insurance purposes. In 1908 the **Port of London Authority** was formed to control all the London docks. All Britain's great ports and docks of the twentieth century were developed in the nineteenth, and they are becoming increasingly in need of change and reconstruction. Britain's immense carrying trade in the nineteenth century was due to the brilliance of her marine engineers, which put her far ahead of other nations in speed and efficiency of transport—*even as late as 1914 Britain still had 47·7 per cent of the world's shipping tonnage—and the U.S.A. 4·3 per cent.*

The main technical changes in the twentieth century have been the replacement of coal-fuel by oil. Experiments in other forms of marine transport have resulted in the production of the *hovercraft*.

(4) Air Transport

For centuries men had been fascinated by the prospect of human flight and in the sixteenth century **Leonardo da Vinci** had studied the principles of flight, with at least one abortive practical effort. In **1783** the brothers **Montgolfier** flew their hot-air balloon from Versailles, and the British scientist **George Cayley** constructed a model of a helicopter in 1798. *But the basic problem was one of power.* In 1893, **Sir Hiram Maxim** built an aeroplane powered by steam which broke up on its first trial; but in 1896, a steam-driven model flew along the course of the Potomac River near Washington. The internal-combustion engine was, however, the answer to the problem. On 17th December, 1903, **Wilbur and Orville Wright** flew half a mile; and in September 1908, **Wilbur Wright** flew for thirty miles at Dayton, Ohio. This was the real break-through in modern aeronautics. In July 1909, **Blériot** flew the Channel. **Alcock and Brown** made the first trans-Atlantic flight in 1919, and in the same year the first flight to Australia was made by **Captain Ross Smith**. In 1927 **Charles Lindbergh** made the first solo Atlantic crossing.

During the Great War the use of the aeroplane and the Zeppelin for military purposes developed rapidly. By 1918 the Royal Air Force (formed during the war) had 20,000 aircraft at its command. In **1923 Imperial Airways** was formed, and from then on it gradually extended its range to cover the greater part of the Empire. The government subsidized the new corporation from the start and had representation on the corporation's controlling bodies. By 1929 Imperial Airways routes extended to India *via* Cairo and Baghdad. In 1931 **Amy Johnson** made the first solo flight by a woman and reached Australia, and this showed the feasibility of Imperial Airways extending its range to Australia, which it did by reaching Sydney in 1934, and in the same year Hong Kong. Two years previously, the African route had been extended from Nairobi to Cape Town. The first British trans-Atlantic service began in 1939, and in that year the two companies Imperial Airways and British Airways were merged to become the **British Overseas Airways Corporation (BOAC)**. On the technical side the most important advance was the production of **Sir Frank Whittle's** *first jet engines in 1937.*

The immense development of British airway enterprise between 1929 and 1939 is seen in the fact that between those dates the number of passengers carried rose from 5,000 to 95,000. The *Empire Air-Mail* service was also developed and, for a time, flying-boats were used. The great value of the air-mail scheme at that time was the fixing of $1\frac{1}{2}$d. an ounce as the charge—exactly the same as the home postal rates.

Developments during World War II were very great. In 1943 the *Gloster Meteor became the first jet-propelled aircraft in service* and in 1946 **Captain Donaldson** reached a speed of 616 m.p.h. in a Gloster Meteor IV, and in 1951 the first jet-propelled crossing of the Atlantic was achieved without re-fuelling. *Since the first flight at a speed greater than that of sound in 1947*, the development of larger and faster airliners has been achieved to the point at which the French and British aircraft industries, working in co-operation, expect to produce the first supersonic airliner, the *Concorde*, in 1968. Another dimension has been added by the pioneering successes of Russia and the U.S.A. in *the first manned satellite* operations leading to a landing on the moon, expected before 1970. *This is the beginning of a new age of interplanetary flight.*

(5) Telecommunications

In 1833 **Graus and Weber** in Germany invented the first electric telegraph, and in 1836 **Cooke and Wheatsone** in Britain invented the needle electric telegraph, operated by a needle pointing to letters of the alphabet, which was later replaced by the '**Morse Code**' invented by **Samuel Morse** in the U.S.A. The main users of these inventions were at first the railways. But the advantages of the telegraph to business, and especially the international stock exchange business, led to the laying of the first cross-Channel cable between London and Paris in 1851, and in the same year **Reuter's News Agency** was established. *In 1866 the first trans-Atlantic cable* was laid and the first cable to India by the **British India Telegraph Co.** in **1870**.

Alongside these developments numerous experiments continued to be made with the problem of relaying the human voice. As early as **1821 Wheatsone** had carried out experiments and was the first to use the term '*telephone*'. However, the great advance was made in 1875 by **Alexander Graham Bell** in America, when he succeeded in transmitting the first complete message. The speed of development is shown by the fact that only four years later, in 1879, *the first telephone exchange was opened in London* with about eight subscribers. At first the **National Telephone Co.** had control of the system in England, but in 1912 the Post Office took over. The National Telephone Co. had government assistance and direction from the start, but purely private companies were taken over by the Post Office in 1912. It had been ruled by the courts in 1880 that the telephone was legally a telegraphic system within the meaning of earlier acts which had placed the telegraph system under the Postmaster-General. Hence the telephone system had come under his control from the start and for many years he issued licences to private companies who paid royalties to the government.

Besides the later development of the automatic exchange, a development of the greatest importance took place in the autumn of 1966, with the opening of the *first electronic telephone exchange* in the world at the Derbyshire village of Ambergate. This is not subject to mechanical wear and is much smaller than the usual equipment. Besides doing all the work of selection, this exchange is self-correcting if a mistake occurs.

Wireless telegraphy dates from the end of the nineteenth century. Working from the theories of magnetic fields developed by **Clarke Maxwell, Guglielmo Marconi** succeeded in transmitting a message over one mile in Italy in **1895**. In 1896 he came to England and transmitted signals on Salisbury Plain and in the Bristol Channel. The critical break-through came in **1901** when he transmitted the first trans-Atlantic signal from Poldhu in Cornwall to Newfoundland—a distance of over 2,000 miles. By the **Wireless Telegraph Act** of **1904** a licence was required from the Post Office for transmissions in Great Britain. The importance of this great discovery for shipping and aircraft soon became evident, and by 1914 over 800 British vessels were equipped for wireless telegraphy. During the Great War *the wireless transmission of actual speech was first achieved*, and post-war developments saw the setting up of the **BBC** in **1922** as a public corporation with its transmission station at **Savoy Hill (2LO)**. In **1936** the pioneer work of **John Baird** on *television* in **1925** resulted in the first television broadcasts from **Alexandra Palace**, London. To all this was added television transmission by artificial satellite, of which the pioneer was the American, **'Early Bird'**.

The revolutionary effects of all these great developments of communication need to be considered: (1) They have affected the development of trade and industry—the rapidity with which both goods and advertisements can be spread to the far ends of the earth. They have created a world market for the export products of any nation and have intensified international competition for markets. (2) They have completely broken down the isolation of the old communities—especially does this apply to the relationship of Europe and America and to the remote regions of Africa and the Far East. (3) This creation of 'one world' has led to the powerful impact of European civilization on Africa and the Far East. (4) They have led to a vast extension of human knowledge. (5) The development of the cinematograph and the great cinema industry should also be considered in conjunction with these changes.

Summary

Communications in Britain were revolutionized between 1760 and the end of the nineteenth century. Roads were improved, canals served an important purpose for a brief time and finally a great network of railways transformed much of Britain's social and industrial life. By the end of the nineteenth century, the steamship had replaced sail; and after 1918 air transport developed rapidly. The motor-car had begun to be used widely by 1914. To all these vast changes was added the great expansion of telecommunications, covering the period from Cooke and Wheatsone to the first electronic telephone exchange in 1966. Both business and social communications have therefore developed from the narrow small-town and village limits of earlier centuries to a general world-wide system.

Important Dates

1761   Brindley completed Bridgewater Canal.
1777   Brindley completed the Grand Trunk Canal.
1784   Palmer's mail-coach service, London to Bristol.
1824   National Lifeboat Institution founded.
1825   Stockton to Darlington Railway.
1829   First horse-driven omnibus.
1830   Manchester to Liverpool Railway.
        Gurney & Hancock's steam coach service to Birmingham from London failed.
1833   'Royal William' crossed Atlantic in twenty days.
1836   Cooke and Wheatsone's needle electric telegraph.
1838   Brunel's 'Great Western'.
1840   First Cunarder, the 'Britannia'.
        First excursion train run by Eastern Railway.
1844   Railways Act.
1851   First cross-Channel cable.
1858   Brunel's 'Great Eastern', 27,000 tons.
1863   Metropolitan Railway.
1865   'Red Flag Act.'
1866   First trans-Atlantic cable.
1870   First London to India cable.
1875   Graham Bell's telephone.
1876   Plimsoll Act.
1884   First London tube railway.
1888   First pneumatic tyre (Dunlop).
1890   First open-topped 'bus.
1892   Railway gauges standardized.
1894   Manchester Ship Canal.
        'Turbinia'—first steam-turbine vessel.
1895   Marconi's first wireless transmission.
1901   First trans-Atlantic wireless signal by Marconi.
1903   17th December: Wilbur and Orville Wright flew half a mile.
1905   First regular petrol-driven 'bus service in London.
1908   Port of London Authority established.
1909   Blériot flew the Channel.
1910   Motor taxation began.

1919   **Alcock and Brown flew the Atlantic.**
1922   **BBC established at Savoy Hill (2LO).**
1923   **Imperial Airways.**
1927   **First solo flight of Atlantic by Charles Lindbergh.**
1930   **30 m.p.h. speed limit in built-up areas.**
1931   **Amy Johnson's solo flight to Australia.**
1936   **'Queen Mary' launched.**
         First television broadcast from Alexandra Palace, London.
1937   **Sir Frank Whittle's first jet engine produced.**
1939   **BOAC formed.**
1951   **First jet-propelled air-crossing of Atlantic without re-fuelling.**

QUESTIONS

(1) Why did canals develop in Britain and why did they eventually decline?

(2) Mention some important stages in railway development between 1820 and 1900.

(3) Write notes on (a) George Hudson; (b) I. K. Brunel; (c) C. A. Parsons; (d) G. Marconi.

(4) Why were steam vessels able to replace sail during the nineteenth century?

(5) Summarize the important social and economic effects of th development of communications to 1966.

*

CHAPTER FORTY-FIVE

EDUCATION, GENERAL AND TECHNICAL

THESE notes should be read in conjunction with those chapters which deal with reforms in the educational system brought about by the Acts of 1833, 1870, 1902, 1918 and 1944. Details of educational changes made between 1918 and 1965 will be found in the chapters dealing with that period.

The Elementary Curriculum

In general the curriculum remained narrow and the amount of money spent on elementary education in the first half of the nineteenth century was small. **The British and Foreign Schools Society** wished to restrict elementary education to the Bible and the three 'Rs'. In the schools of the British and Foreign Schools Society no other book than the Bible was read for thirty years. The aim was widely regarded as being the production of law-abiding citizens who kept their place in society and refrained from crime.

Following upon the appalling state of general ignorance existing among the young shown by the **Newcastle Commission** in **1861**, an attempt to improve the efficiency of elementary education was undertaken by **Robert Lowe's Revised Code** of **1862**. Lowe also believed that the working class should not be educated above its station in life, and the narrow curriculum already mentioned was maintained for the next thirty or forty years. Those schools which had introduced a little science were discouraged, and other subjects, such as history, were only introduced in the form of abbreviated readers for the reading examination which was given to each pupil under the new system of 'Payment by Results'. This latter entailed a yearly examination of each pupil by the inspectors and the payment of grants to schools in proportion to the number of children passing the examination. This system lasted for thirty years and had the effect of over-stressing the mechanical drilling and 'cramming' of pupils for the annual examination. This learning without understanding was condemned by **Matthew Arnold** as an Inspector of the Board of Education; but the Board, which even laid down the books to be read, ignored his enlightened advice for many years.

Secondary Education

During the nineteenth century, secondary education was confined to the middle- and upper-class children who attended the big public schools, the private schools or the old endowed grammar schools. *Their curricula were narrow, dominated by Greek and Latin studies* which their charters prevented them from changing. However, the **Grammar Schools Act** of **1840** at last permitted the law courts to re-interpret the charters to allow for curriculum changes, but change was very slow. In a number of important private schools the *Benthamite or utilitarian aims* of their founders encouraged commercial subjects for purely business aims, but decried subjects such as music, art, literature and history. The great public schools, such as Eton, Harrow and Rugby, were almost equally narrow in the first half of the century. All these criticisms were made by the **Clarendon Commission** of **1861**, which reported on the public schools; and this led to the better administration of a number of them by the **Public Schools Act** of **1864**. In the same year the **Schools Enquiry Commission** under **Lord Taunton** was appointed, mainly to consider the endowed grammar schools. This showed that the number of scholars receiving even the old classical education in the endowed schools was declining and that very little had been done to bring the curriculum more up to date. Following upon this report, the **Endowed Schools Act** of **1869** gave special commissioners wide powers of reorganizing the endowed schools, and this gradually improved both their organization and their curriculum as the century went on. Both *literature and science* began to figure more widely in the grammar school curriculum and in that of the public schools. This was helped by the inclusion of *English literature* as a subject in the Indian Civil Service examinations as well as the home Civil Service, the armed forces and entrance to the great universities.

The broadening of the secondary curriculum was especially stimulated by the pioneering work of a number of great headmasters. **Dr. Butler of Shrewsbury** introduced mathematics, science, history and literature and **Edward Thring at Uppingham** introduced craft subjects, music and art. Their influence was felt in the new public schools established during the second half of the century and in the endowed grammar schools.

What education existed for girls and women in the early nineteenth century was concerned mainly with social accomplishments, such as drawing, singing and playing the piano. For the middle class there were a number of boarding schools, but private governesses were mainly employed. In **1848, Queen's College** was established to train governesses and this was the beginning of more organized attention to the education of women. In the following year the first women's college was established—**Bedford College in the University of London,** and in **1850 Miss Buss** established the **North London Collegiate School for Girls**—the first day school for girls. **In 1853** the **Cheltenham Ladies' College**, the first public boarding school for girls, was opened and **Miss Beale** became its headmistress in 1858. In 1872 the first women's college, **Girton**, was established at Cambridge and **Lady Margaret Hall** at Oxford in 1879. London University also admitted women, beginning with the London School of Medicine in 1874. From these beginnings the secondary education of girls made great strides before 1914 and these pioneering efforts set the line for their general development. It must be emphasized, however, that these advances almost solely affected only girls of the middle class and, as in the case of boys, elementary education alone existed for those of the working class before the great reforms of the twentieth century.

The Balfour Education Act of 1902 abolished the old School Boards of 1870 and formed the new Education Committees of the Counties and County Boroughs. This led to the building of new grammar schools and to aid for the old ones out of the rates; but even more important was the Education Act of 1907, which established the *'scholarship system'* by which able pupils could gain free entry to the grammar schools, thus beginning to break down the idea that grammar schools existed for one class only in the community. This was greatly extended after 1918, and *state scholarships from the secondary schools to the universities* were established. It was an incursion on the virtual monopoly of university entrance enjoyed by the public schools up to 1918. Mr. R. A. Butler's Education Act of 1944 was a further advance of great importance. It abolished all fee-payment in state secondary schools and established a system of pupil selection at the age of 11 for grammar, technical or modern schools (*the 'eleven plus'*). This system has in the 1960s been radically altered by the Labour governments in power since 1964. Although several **Comprehensive Schools** were established before that date, the main national change has taken place since then. These schools will, in the main, take all pupils at 11 years of age and retain them until the statutory leaving age or until 18; though there are a number of variations from the 11 plus age. Any *'streaming'* or *selection* will be done within the schools, whose numbers range somewhere between 1,000 and 2,000. Another important change since 1945 has been the large number of Secondary Modern pupils taking the G.C.E. examinations at *'O' Level* and the establishment in 1964 of a new national examination of a different type from the 'O' Level, namely, the **Certificate of Secondary Education.**

The introduction of the Comprehensive system has been a matter of widespread national debate as to its value compared with the former independent position of the grammar schools, the great majority of which will be absorbed.

Technical Education

Very little technical education existed, outside the apprenticeship system, in the early nineteenth century. Even the apprenticeship system, derived from Elizabethan days, was falling to pieces under the impact of the factory system. A few **Schools of Industry** existed, but the pioneers of scientific and technical education for the working people were the **Mechanics' Institutes,** the first of which was founded by **Dr. Birkbeck** in London in 1824. By 1850 there were over 700 mechanics' institutes in Britain. Despite their early popularity they ran into difficulties—there was political opposition from those extreme Tories who feared the revolutionary effects of educating the workers, and at the other extreme from those radicals who feared that education would, in fact, tame the revolutionary spirit. The initiators of the movement, especially the radical **Lord Brougham** and Dr. Birkbeck, considered that the mechanics' institutes would have a 'civilizing' influence. Gradually, the labouring class dropped away in favour of trade unionism, of co-operation and of Chartism, especially when 'controversial' subjects were frowned upon. The lectures became dominated by the middle class.

The trade unions, who had become disillusioned by the mechanics' institutes, took up the question of technical and general education on their own. The **London Artisans' Club** was established in 1868 with trade union support. Then technical subjects began to figure in the **Royal Society of Arts** examinations, which were taken over by the **City and Guilds of London** in **1879.** In 1881 the first technical college in Britain was founded—the **Finsbury Technical College,** and in 1882 the **Regent Street Polytechnic.** The work of all these colleges was based on part-time study.

In 1882 Gladstone appointed the **Royal Commission on Technical Education.** The Commission stressed the absence of technical instruction in Britain compared with some foreign states, especially the new Germany under Bismarck. The Commission's report led on to the **Technical Education Act** of **1889,** which gave government aid to technical education and léd to the County Councils establishing technical classes. But grants were only for technical education of the *'industrial classes',* and this held back the wider development of technical education at a time when Germany was surpassing Britain in some important industries. However, in the early 1900s aid was given on a wider basis, and *by 1905 twelve polytechnics existed in London* where part-time scientific and technical education was given. *Six of these were giving degrees.* The period since 1918 has seen the development of Technical Schools as well as an increasing number of technical courses in both secondary modern and grammar schools. Since 1945 an important development has been the growth of **Colleges of Advanced Tech-**

nology with degree courses. The competition of Germany had big effects on Britain in the nineteenth century, and the technical advances of the U.S.A. and of the Soviet Union have constituted a great challenge in the twentieth. The problem of the *'brain-drain'* of scientists and technologists to the U.S.A. has presented Britain with a special problem of how to improve salaries and facilities for research. This 'brain-drain' has been partly compensated for by the numbers of science students and workers from the under-developed countries of the Commonwealth entering Britain and remaining there.

Summary

The development of the educational curriculum was a slow process during the nineteenth century. For elementary schools the Revised Code of 1862, introducing 'payment by results', tended to keep the curriculum narrow. The grammar and public schools were also hampered by old statutes which held them to a narrowly classical curriculum. The combined influences of parliamentary aid and the work of a number of outstanding headmasters gradually brought about a widening of the curriculum in respect of science and arts subjects as well as the practical subjects. The important Education Acts of 1902, 1907 and 1944 were great steps forward in widening the social field of education as well as the curriculum, and the claim of even wider scope is now made for the latest development of the Comprehensive schools system. Technical education fell behind that of a number of other countries in the nineteenth century, but began to develop before 1914 towards its present importance in Britain. The technological development of the U.S.A. and the U.S.S.R. represent, however, a great challenge to the technical and scientific position of Britain.

Important Dates

1824	**First Mechanics' Institute (Dr. Birkbeck).**
1840	**Grammar Schools Act.**
1850	**North London Collegiate School.**
1853	**Cheltenham Ladies' College.**
1861	**The Newcastle Commission.**
	Clarendon Commission.
1862	**Robert Lowe's Revised Code.**
1864	**Public Schools Act.**
1868	**London Artisans' Club.**
1869	**Endowed Schools Act.**
1874	**London School of Medicine admitted women members.**
1882	**Royal Commission on Technical Education.**
1889	**Technical Education Act.**

1902   Balfour Education Act.
1905   Twelve polytechnics in London.
1907   Education Act.
1944   Butler Education Act.
1964   Labour Government decided on Comprehensive schools system for whole country.

QUESTIONS

(*1*) *Why was the elementary school curriculum narrow during the nineteenth century?*

(*2*) *Show how the curriculum was widened in the grammar and public schools.*

(*3*) *Show the influences which brought about more education for women during the nineteenth century.*

(*4*) *Why did technical education become of more national concern before 1914?*

(*5*) *What was the importance of* (a) *the Grammar Schools Act, 1840;* (b) *the Revised Code, 1862;* (c) *the Endowed Schools Act, 1869;* (d) *the Technical Education Act, 1889;* (e) *the Balfour Education Act, 1902;* (f) *the Education Act of 1907?*

(*6*) *What was the educational importance of* (a) *Matthew Arnold;* (b) *Edward Thring;* (c) *Miss Buss;* (d) *Dr. Birkbeck?*

CHAPTER FORTY-SIX

HEALTH AND HOUSING

General Conditions in the Early Nineteenth Century

THE death-rate had declined in the late eighteenth century through improved drainage, better hospitals, the advance of medical knowledge and the elimination of smallpox through the new inoculation technique (vaccination). But the rising industrial towns and increasing population of the early nineteenth century produced new problems. *In 1840 one child in every six died before it was a year old and a third of all children died before the age of five.* The chief causes of this were bad sanitation which gave rise to typhoid fever, tuberculosis, cholera and scarlet fever. While the average death-rate was 23 per 1,000 (2·3 per cent) of the population, in the slum areas of industrial towns it rose to 40 per cent. London's population increased from 865,000 in 1800 to nearly 1,900,000 in 1841. This produced very bad housing conditions in London, *where only one-sixth of the working class had more than one room to live in.* In London and the industrial towns, the system of house-building tended to be in courts, with back-to-back houses with no yards, and wash-houses and closets grouped in the middle of the court, and the possible addition of a communal pump. Drinking water was mostly supplied in London by water-selling companies using *unfiltered and unpurified Thames water.* Until 1866 the London open drains ran into the Thames.

Wrong theories as to the cause of infectious diseases held back progress, and it was many years before bad water was even recognized as a cause of the deadly cholera epidemics.

The Utilitarians were particularly concerned about the problem of health and in 1844 a special commission of inquiry by the Poor Law Commissioners, set up under the Poor Law Amendment Act of 1834, issued a report entitled *'Report of the Commission of Inquiry into the State of Towns'.* This report saw the beginnings of health and town reform in the nineteenth century. It affected London and other towns, and in London especially reforms began to be made. In 1847 the **Metropolitan Commissioners of Sewers** took over complete control from the numerous local committees which were inefficient in their attention to health, and in **1848 the first Public Health Act** gave local authorities powers to improve sanitation, but they were not compelled to do so. Parliament itself continued to show increasing concern, and an Act of 1858 provided over £3,000,000 for removing sewage from the Thames. More important still was the **Metropolitan Water Act of 1870,** which compelled the water companies to provide a continuous supply through the pumps and to filter the water. In **1905** the **Metropolitan Water Board** was set up and it took over all private water companies. Other great cities, however, such as Birmingham (under the inspiration of Joseph Chamberlain), had established municipal water, gas and electricity supplies many years before.

The middle class had escaped the worst results of these early town conditions by building their houses outside the towns, and with railways developing fast the business man after 1850 began to '*commute*' between the suburbs and the centre of the towns. But even in middle-class homes the water-closet was not common until the late nineteenth century. **The Public Health Act** of **1875** gave local authorities the power to enforce building regulations, but they were still not compelled to do so. However, an increasing number of authorities took these powers, and the **Artisans' Dwellings Act** brought about further improvement. The first act to give local councils powers actually to build houses was the important **Housing of the Working Classes Act** of **1890,** from which all local authority housing is derived. In 1909 they were also given powers to control the density of housing and to impose planning. At the same time, a number of pioneers were building '*garden cities*', of which the most notable (primarily for the middle class) were Port Sunlight, Bournville and Letchworth Garden City.

Medical Science

Two great handicaps to medical progress were the high death-rate in hospitals due either to shock from operations or to blood poisoning. The patient, kept under the effects of opium or alcohol, had to be operated upon as quickly as possible, but with the discovery of chloroform as an effective anaesthetic by **J. Y. Simpson** of Edinburgh in **1847,** more time and care could be taken. With the discovery by **Louis Pasteur (1822–1895)** of the germ basis of disease, further progress was made. **Joseph Lister (1827–1912),** Professor of Surgery at Glasgow University, saw that Pasteur's use of carbolic acid to kill germs in the air could be used in operating theatres to dress wounds and to spray the air with diluted carbolic acid. In 1887 he discovered that blood serum would destroy microbes and keep them out of the human body, and he then abandoned his first methods. Lister's improvements brought about an immediate decline in deaths during operations and childbirth and were a major contribution to the advance of medicine. In the same years as Lister, the German bacteriologist, **Robert Koch (1843–1910)** studied the bacilli of numerous diseases and greatly extended the range of inoculation.

Another great pioneer of general health and hospital improvement was the heroine of the Crimea, **Florence Nightingale**. Long before Pasteur's discoveries, she had emphasized in all her work the need for scrupulous cleanliness and saw clearly the relationship of dirt to disease. She was the pioneer agitator for replacing the old, untrained hospital 'watchers' by trained nurses and her appeals for funds to build the **Nightingale School of Nursing** at **St. Thomas's Hospital** brought a successful response. Until her death in 1910, she continued to write and agitate for improved hospital services and improved health services for the people, and her influence was powerful.

Recent discoveries have greatly improved general conditions of health. The discovery and use of vitamins, the sulphonamide group of drugs and penicillin, the development of new machines, the use of artificial heart valves, skin-grafting and human organ grafting are developments of the utmost importance.

Parallel with all this has been the development of the **National Health Service** as described in the chapters dealing with the years since the Second World War.

Summary

Conditions of health in the early nineteenth century were very bad, especially in the growing industrial towns and in London, where adequate water supplies and sanitation were long in coming. The First Public Health Act of 1848 saw the influence of the utilitarians beginning to break through into the field of health and sanitation. Medical science, although greatly improved during the eighteenth century, was still hampered by traditional practices based on inadequate theory. The key discoveries of Simpson, Lister and Pasteur transformed medical practice in the second half of the nineteenth century, during which period the work of Florence Nightingale was also outstanding.

Important Dates

1840	**One child in every six died in first year of life.**
1844	**Report of the Commission of Inquiry into the State of Towns.**
1847	**Metropolitan Commissioners of Sewers took over control of London sanitation.**
	J. Y. Simpson used chloroform as an anaesthetic.
1848	**First Public Health Act.**
1869	**Lister developed carbolic antiseptic spray.**
1870	**Metropolitan Water Act.**

1875	Public Health Act.
	Artisans' Dwellings Act.
1887	Lister discovered the use of blood serum to combat infection.
1890	Housing of the Working Classes Act.
1900–1914	'Garden City' developments.
1905	Metropolitan Water Board established.

QUESTIONS

(*1*) *What was the sanitary condition of London in the early nineteenth century and what measures were taken to improve conditions up to 1905?*

(*2*) *What important developments in medical science occurred between 1850 and 1900?*

(*3*) *What was the importance of the work of Florence Nightingale?*

CHAPTER FORTY-SEVEN

RELIGIOUS MOVEMENTS SINCE 1715

The Rise of Methodism

THE influence of the Church of England in the eighteenth century seriously declined, and it contributed little to solving the widespread moral problems caused by excessive drink (especially gin), cruelty and crime. *The Church was identified with the small ruling class and it became a field for 'careerism'.* The higher clergy were servants of the state and interested more in a good life (or bad one, according to one's viewpoint) and their incomes. The parish rectors and vicars held livings in several parishes at the same time— *'pluralities',*—and curates were employed to look after these parishes. In society in general, there was widespread loss of faith in Christianity itself, a trend which the Church apparently had no desire to combat. It was essentially as a counter to these social and religious conditions that **Methodism** arose.

At Oxford University **John and Charles Wesley** established a group dedicated to a pure life in contrast to prevailing standards both at the University and outside. The nickname **'Methodists'** was given them, and they accepted it. In 1739 John Wesley experienced a conversion through the influence of the **Moravian Church**, and from then on he spent his life in preaching throughout the British Isles. As a member of the Anglican Church he attempted to preach in churches, but when these were denied him he adopted *'field-preaching'*. In this work he was supported by his brother Charles Wesley and by another remarkable preacher, **George Whitefield**, who later left the Wesleys and established the Calvinistic Methodists.

John Wesley's organizing powers were immense. Although he always regarded himself as a member of the Church, the hostility of the clergy and the country squires, which led to frequent violence against him and his lay preachers, led him to organize numerous local groups throughout the country and to hold an annual Methodist Conference. Various groups of Methodists broke away from the parent body in the nineteenth century but they were mostly reunited in 1932.

Effects of Methodism

They helped to achieve a considerable decrease in drunkenness and crime through their direct appeal to the ordinary people and the example they set in their personal lives. Their belief in the possibility of immediate conversion through willing reception of the Holy Spirit had a direct appeal totally different from the class aloofness of the Anglican clergy. The Radicals tended to distrust the Methodists as 'taming' the more revolutionary spirit and channelling it into religion, but it is now clear that *a great deal of working-class and trade union activity had its origins in the Methodist communities of the industrial towns.* The Methodists made a great contribution to popular education and literacy and established a **Book Room** in London. During the nineteenth century their magazines not only published religious material but also the works of leading literary men—this, in fact, was one cause of the break-away of some groups who distrusted the moral influences of current literature, especially the romantic poets such as Shelley, Keats and Byron.

The Methodists strongly supported missionary societies, and their influence began to be felt in the Church itself through the activities of the **Evangelicals**. The new stirrings led on to the **Sunday School** movement of **Robert Raikes** and agitation for prison reform.

The Evangelicals

This movement within the Church is associated with the important work of such men as **William Wilberforce**, the **Earl of Shaftesbury, Bishop Ryle of Liverpool, Granville Sharp** and **Thomas Clarkson**.

Wilberforce (1759–1833) typified the evangelical approach to religious and social problems. He was converted to evangelism in 1784 when M.P. for Hull. In conjunction with Thomas Clarkson, he campaigned continuously against the slave trade and secured its abolition by Britain in 1807. These two men also became the leaders of the **Anti-slavery Society** established in **1823** and which led on to the **Emancipation Act** of **1833**. Their associates became known as the **'Clapham Sect'** from their practice of meeting in the houses of their supporters in that district, and they published the *Christian Observer* which carried on a constant campaign against public immorality, slavery, brutal sports (such as bull-baiting and cock-fighting), bad factory conditions, the harshness and brutality of the criminal code and the state of prisons. They advocated popular education, and Lord Shaftesbury became president of the **Ragged Schools Union**, a founder of the **Young Men's Christian Association** and the workingmen's institutes. He agitated for factory reform and succeeded in securing protection for badly exploited minorities, of which the most notable were the boy chimney-sweeps.

The effects of the Evangelical Movement were considerable. The Evangelicals stirred the conscience of the nineteenth century and much social reform is connected with them, though the Radicals (who distrusted them) and the Utilitarians could claim a greater influence. Their greatest influence was with the middle class rather than the labouring classes. This was partly due to their political attitudes rather than their religion—Shaftesbury distrusted democracy and opposed the Reform Bill of 1832, and his puritanical opposition to romantic literature of all kinds narrowed his appeal. Wilberforce was distrustful of the trade unions. On the other hand they had a healthy effect on the standards of the Church of England.

The Oxford Movement

In the early nineteenth century, the **High Church Movement** developed within the Anglican Church. It stressed the need to give new dignity to the Church by reviving ritual and stressing the importance of the bishops and of the priesthood. It was also concerned with Church doctrine. In 1833 some Oxford dons, of whom the most important were **John Henry Newman, John Keble, Hurrell Froude** and **Edward Pusey**, published the first of a long series of '*Tracts for the Times*' in which they stressed the connection of the Church of England with the Roman Catholic Church of the Middle Ages before the Protestant Reformation of the sixteenth century. In Tract Ninety, Newman argued that the Thirty-nine Articles of the Church of England did not conflict with the decisions reached by the Catholic Church in the sixteenth century. The Church of England had, therefore, remained a part of the Catholic Church. Newman was deprived of his fellowship and his position as Vicar of St. Mary's, and in 1845 he joined the Church of Rome. His influence on religious life in England became considerable, and his explanation of his motives for joining the Catholic Church in his *Apolgia pro vita sua* had a very wide sale. His writings on education and religion were also influential. In 1879 he was made a Cardinal. A number of his tractarian supporters of the Oxford Movement joined him, but Edward Pusey and others established the **Anglo-Catholic movement**.

The Christian Socialists

This movement was essentially an attempt to apply the doctrines of Christianity directly to industrial and political problems and to identify socialism with Christianity. Its leaders were **Thomas Hughes**, author of *Tom Brown's Schooldays*, **Charles Kingsley**, the novelist, **Frederick Denison Maurice, E. V. Neale** and others. Besides demanding the application of Christianity to social problems, they were *pioneers of the ideas of co-operation replacing capitalist competition*. They were pioneers of the **Co-operative movement** and established a '*wholesale agency*' which was the forerunner of the **Co-operative Wholesale Society**. They also succeeded in securing the full privileges of Friendly Societies for co-operative trading societies in 1852. Their early influence was small, but it revived in 1877 when the socialist **Guild of St. Matthew** was formed with the purpose of bringing the churches over to socialism. Before 1914, there were some hopes of this being achieved and a number of leading Anglican Bishops praised the aims of the early Christian Socialists. A new organization, the **Church Socialist League**, was formed to bring this about, but it failed to attain its object and was disbanded in 1923.

The early Christian Socialists were important pioneers of workers' education, and a number of them who were teachers at Oxford and Cambridge were the first to lecture to working men, without payment. In general, the Christian Socialist Movement, like other movements that preceded it, had a very healthy effect on the conscience of the Established Church.

The Salvation Army

Another important movement applying itself directly to the social evils of the times was the Salvation Army, founded by **William Booth** (1829-1912), who broke away from Methodism in 1861 and founded the *Christian Mission in Whitechapel*. In 1878 this became the Salvation Army and William Booth its first General. Its meetings were subject to mob attacks urged on by its opponents, and Booth himself at one time was imprisoned as a breaker of the peace. But by 1900 it was established in numerous countries, and the women's ministry had been organized by **Mrs. Booth**. In 1890 William Booth published his important work *In Darkest England and the Way Out*. He advocated religious conversion allied to direct social work and reform, through such agencies as farm colonies, poor men's savings banks and poor men's lawyers—all of which, together with direct work in homes through the '*household salvage brigades*' would lessen drunkenness, poverty and crime. Booth's social studies, if not all his methods, were of great importance in stimulating further social reform through Parliament before 1914.

Contemporary Problems

One of the great problems facing all religious movements in the twentieth century has been the spread of doctrines, especially Communism, which deny the validity of religion and postulate varieties of materialism. The conflict between religion and science which Darwinism produced was the first stage of this process, and the conflict continues in a variety of forms. Efforts to strengthen religion have tended towards a union of the churches; and in **1965**, the first steps towards a closer union of the Anglican Church and Rome were taken.

Summary

The decline of the Church of England in the eighteenth century contributed to the rise of the more challenging force of Methodism, whose effect on social and moral improvement was considerable. The Methodist contribution to literacy was also important. The Evangelicals also contributed much to social and religious reform and were prominent in securing the abolition of both the slave trade and slavery itself, as well as other serious social evils. Their most outstanding member was the Earl of Shaftesbury who, despite certain narrow eccentricities, was one of the most powerful forces for social reform in the nineteenth century. In the more purely religious and doctrinal sense, the Oxford Movement and Newman's acceptance into the Church of Rome were causes of great controversy. The Christian Socialists attempted to equate socialism and Christianity and at one time their influence within the Church of England was strong. Their influence was felt strongly within the workers' educational movement and the co-operative movement. The Salvation Army provided a new dynamic of moral and social reform which has had a wide appeal and achieved valuable social work. In the face of the materialist and secular challenge, the twentieth century has seen movement towards the closer union of the Christian churches.

Important Dates

1729 **Formation of the Methodists, at Oxford.**
1739 **Conversion of John Wesley.**
1780 **Robert Raikes established first Sunday School.**
1784 **First Wesleyan Conference.**
1787 **Clarkson and Wilberforce form Society for the Suppression of the Slave Trade.**
1807 **Abolition of Slave Trade by Britain.**
1823 **Anti-slavery Society formed.**
1833 **First of the Oxford Movement's 'Tracts for the Times'.**
      Abolition of slavery in the British Empire.
1844 **Y.M.C.A. formed.**
1845 **Newman joins Roman Catholic Church.**
1861 **William Booth forms Christian Mission, Whitechapel.**
1877 **Guild of St. Matthew formed.**
1878 **Salvation Army formed.**

1890 Publication of William Booth's 'In Darkest England and the Way Out'.

1923 Disbandment of the Church Socialist League.

QUESTIONS

(1) *What were the main reasons for the rise of Methodism?*

(2) *What were the religious and social results of Methodism?*

(3) *What was the importance of the Evangelical Movement?*

(4) *Give some account of the Oxford Movement.*

(5) *What was the importance of the Christian Socialists?*

(6) *Explain the origins and organization of the Salvation Army.*

(7) *Why do you think there were so many attempts to revive religious activity in the nineteenth century?*

CHAPTER FORTY-EIGHT

LABOUR AND CONSERVATIVE GOVERNMENTS, 1964–1981

Labour Government, 1964–1970

THE new government set up a number of important new organizations. **The National Board for Prices and Incomes** was to advise the government on the justice or otherwise of trade union demands for increased wages or demands by industry for higher prices. A **Regional Economic Planning Committee** was set up to supervise the work of development in the depressed areas of the country. In an effort to make Britain more up-to-date technologically the **Science Research Council** was formed, as also was the **Economic Research Council**. Even more important was the new **Industrial Reorganization Corporation** whose function was to help industries, with the aid of government funds, to bring themselves more up-to-date. To help workers who were made redundant by industrial reorganization, a system of redundancy payments was introduced.

In the election of March, 1966, the government's majority was increased to 97. It was soon forced to introduce a compulsory wages and prices 'freeze' to last for six months in order to reduce the rate of inflation, which was now becoming a serious problem. The pound was devalued in order to help exports by lower export prices. Efforts made to enter the **Common Market** failed, as also did those made to secure a settlement in Rhodesia based on the principle of majority rule.

The economic situation continued to get worse in 1967, with 500,000 unemployed and the balance of trade continuing against us. The Arab-Israeli six-day war resulted in the closure of the Suez Canal (not to be opened again until 1975), and the Arab oil producers imposed a temporary ban on the shipment of oil to Britain and the United States. The civil war in Nigeria also reduced Britain's oil supplies from that country. All this led to rising costs in industry and rising prices, with consequent labour unrest. Unofficial strikes in the Liverpool and London docks also hampered Britain's international trade.

To reduce the amount of purchasing-power in circulation and thus slow down inflation, the government increased taxation by £900 million in 1968. New charges were also placed on National Health prescriptions. Further economies were anticipated by the government's announcement of the withdrawal of all our forces from east of Suez by 1971, except Hong Kong.

A most important law of 1968 was the **Race Relations Act.** This arose from the problems caused by the influx of Asians expelled from Kenya who had not taken out Kenyan citizenship but held British passports. (Later, more were to enter from Uganda due to General Amin's policies, and also from Malawi in 1976.) In the first three months of 1968 more than 7,000 Asians, mainly Indian and Pakistani, entered Britain. This influx aroused much controversy in Britain. Even the Labour government was compelled to control the rate at which immigrants entered Britain. By the **Commonwealth Immigration Act** of 1968 a British colonial citizen holding a British passport could only enter if he had family ties here. The Race Relations Act made it an offence in law to discriminate against anyone on grounds of race in such matters as employment, housing, membership of trade unions, etc. The **Race Relations Board** was set up to supervise the operation of the act.

During the years 1964 to 1968 there was a great increase in unofficial strikes, with considerable loss of industrial output. The government appointed a Royal Commission on Industrial Relations, which reported in June, 1968. The government then issued a White Paper entitled **"In Place of Strife".** Its principal advocate was the Secretary of State for Employment and Productivity, **Barbara Castle**. Its main proposals were to give the Minister powers to delay an unofficial strike for four weeks, power to order a union ballot of its members before taking strike action, and penalties on workers and employers who failed to carry out the minister's orders. Fierce opposition to these proposals arose from the trade unions and from many members of the Labour Party itself, and eventually the government withdrew its proposals on an undertaking by the Trades Union Congress to use its influence more widely to bring about settlements of industrial disputes. The trade union movement had here shown the growing power which it was exerting in these years.

In 1969 industrial output was still low and unemployment high. International speculation against the pound sterling was reducing its value still further. More taxation was imposed, except that a million low-paid workers were now exempted from income tax altogether. However, a trading surplus of £360 million was achieved in December, 1969. It was partly the beginning of this improvement which decided Harold Wilson to call a **General Election in June, 1970**. He appeared confident that the Labour Party would be returned to power once again, and the various Opinion Polls seemed to bear this out. But, against all these expectations, Edward Heath and the Conservative Party won the election with a comfortable majority. The general conditions in the country told against Labour—increasing food prices, unemployment, industrial disputes, etc. Many disillusioned Labour supporters, and those complacently expecting Labour to win, also failed to vote.

Conservative Government, 1970–1974

Great problems faced Heath's government in this period. Conservatives wished to reduce the amount of nationalization, reduce government controls over industry wherever possible and appeal to the trade unions for voluntary restraint in wage claims. Pursuing the voluntary principal, the government abolished the Prices and Incomes Board. Despite the government's appeal for voluntary restraint in wage claims, the year 1970 saw large wage demands and more industrial disputes (strikes both unofficial and official) than in any year since the General Strike of 1926.

The government attempted to face up to the problems which the growing power of the trade unions involved, by altering the law relating to trade unions. The **Industrial Relations Act, August, 1971,** contained the following main clauses: (1) Agreements between employers and unions were to be enforceable at law; (2) Unfair practices, such as dismissal of workers without adequate notice, were to be illegal; (3) An **Industrial Relations Court** was set up with which unions could register and thus place themselves under the jurisdiction of the court in cases arising from the act; (4) The Secretary of State was given powers to order a 60-day cooling-off period where the government considered a strike would severely damage the national interest; (5) The minister also had powers to order a secret ballot of union members before a strike was called; (6) A guarantee was to be given to all workers of the personal right to choose whether or not to belong to a trade union; (7) A ban was placed on the 'closed-shop' principle—that is, the practice by which a firm would employ only members of a trade union.

Tremendous opposition to the Act arose from both the trade unions and the Labour Party. Many unions declined to register with the Industrial Relations Court and others refused to send representatives to the court in cases arising from the Industrial Relations Act. Several unions were heavily fined in consequence. A campaign of demonstrations and short strikes was organized. In 1975 a Labour Government repealed the Act. The whole episode showed the enormous growth in the power of the trade unions to defend their traditional position and to bring pressure upon the parliamentary system. They had, in fact, successfully maintained their old stance of free collective bargaining between unions and employers with a minimum of government interference. They had, in the course of seven years defeated both the Labour and Conservative governments' efforts to modify the traditional situation.

On January 1, 1973, Britain at last became a member of the **Common**

Market. After long and tedious negotiations with the Market, agreements were reached which attempted to safeguard the interests of Commonwealth sugar and dairy industries which had long held a favoured position in the English market. (The West Indies and New Zealand were particularly affected). The Labour Party and the trade unions and a number of Conservatives (of whom Enoch Powell was a leading member) came out against our entry on the terms agreed—especially against the amount of the annual financial contribution to the Market. There was also considerable fear that Britain would lose much of her sovereignty and independence as a member of the Market. However, Britain's entry was a triumph for Mr. Heath, who for long had been its most outstanding advocate.

Another menacing problem in these years was that of rising prices—**inflation.** After the failure of Mr Heath and the Trades Union Congress to reach agreement on a voluntary restraint in wage claims, and after the miners received a £90 million addition to their wages in 1972, the government introduced a ninety-day 'freeze' on wages, prices and dividends as Phase 1 of a new government policy, which really meant that they were abandoning the voluntary principle of which they had made much during the General Election of 1970. In April, 1973, Phase II limited wage increases to £1 a week or four per cent, and in November Phase III put the limits at £2.25 or seven per cent.

But the purchasing power of the pound sterling had fallen by 30 per cent since 1970 and the trade unions were restless. There were serious strikes by the gasworkers, civil servants and others. The government then set up the Prices Commission and the Pay Board to give some control. However, further sharp rises of prices occurred after the Arab-Israeli war of the autumn of 1973, when the oil supplies from the Arab states were drastically reduced. The miners' wage claims having been rejected by the Coal Board, their union imposed a ban on all overtime working. The power-station engineers followed suit. The nation suffered widespread electricity cuts in both industries and homes. Heath undertook further discussions with both the miners and the T.U.C., but no solution was found. The railway drivers' union (ASLEF) decided to operate a ban on all overtime from December 3, 1974. In these worsening national circumstances, in order to conserve fuel supplies and prevent a total breakdown in industry, the government introduced the **three-day working week** from January 3, 1974. At the beginning of 1974, with 2,000,000 unemployed, a three-day working week and a December trade deficit of £350 million the country was in its worst economic plight since the end of the Second World War. The Arab states had in the meantime quadrupled their oil prices. To make things even worse, the miners decided on an all-out strike to begin on February 9th.

In these circumstances Heath decided to call a General Election for

February 23, 1974, and based his campaign on the question 'Who governs Britain?'

Heath failed to gain the increased majority he had hoped and a minority Labour Government took office under Wilson. In October of the same year, 1974, another General Election slightly improved Labour's position with an over-all majority of 5. A new development in the election of February, 1974, was the return of 14 Liberal members with almost a quarter of the total national vote, **7 Scottish Nationalists** and **2 Welsh nationalists.**

The loss of two general elections in 1974 by the Conservatives led to criticism of the leadership of Mr. Heath and resulted in the election in February 1975 to the Conservative leadership of **Margaret Thatcher—** the first woman in British History to lead a major political party.

Labour Government, 1974–1979

The Labour government now set up an **Industrial Tribunal** to study the miners' claims, and it gave them all they asked for. They then returned to work. Soon afterwards the government returned the country to the five-day working week.

Wilson's government was still faced with all the problems which had afflicted Britain for many years. In the main, these problems were: (1) The low level of investment of money in industry, thus holding back production and profits. (2) A very small increase in the annual rate of industrial production—the smallest increase in Europe. (3) Very serious inflation. (4) The failure of several nationalised industries to pay their way. (5) The failure of a number of very important firms, especially in the motor industry. Even the previous government had nationalized **Rolls Royce** when it collapsed. The Labour government now felt compelled to assist **Leyland Motors** (British Leyland) to avoid imminent collapse, and government funds were made available on condition of government representation on the board of directors. Similarly, in 1974, **Burmah Oil** also had to appeal for assistance, which the government granted on condition of receiving a 51 per cent stake in the Ninian and Thistle oil fields in the North Sea. In 1975 the firm of **Chrysler (U.K.)** received a large government subsidy.

The government now entered into an agreement with the T.U.C. which became known as the **'Social Contract'**. By this the T.U.C. agreed to attempt to keep wage increases within reasonable bounds, but large wage demands and inflation continued to be a problem, and in 1975 the government succeeded, through the T.U.C. in gaining the agreement of all the major unions to the limitation of wage increases to £6 a week for one year, and this was followed in the summer of 1976 by a similar agreement to limit wage increases to $4\frac{1}{2}$ per cent for a further year. It was noteworthy that during the latter part of 1975 and the first half of 1976 the rate of inflation was declining and had reached a rate just below 20 per cent by June, 1976, as against 26 per cent a year previously.

In March, 1976, Wilson retired from the premiership and leadership of the Labour Party and was succeeded by **James Callaghan.** During 1976–1979 the efforts of the Labour government were especially directed to reducing the rate of inflation of the currency—a rate which at one point in 1976 had risen to 27 per cent. By the beginning of 1979 the inflation rate had been reduced to between 8 and 9 per cent—a reduction partly attributable to the success of the policy of wage-restraint demanded by the government. However, unemployment had increased to just under a million and a half at the beginning of 1979. Mr. Callaghan now attempted to get acceptance by the trade unions of a 5 per cent wage increase for the year 1978–1979. This was opposed by the Trades Union Congress, which demanded the return to free collective bargaining without government intervention. When the Ford Motor Company agreed to a settlement with its employees well above this limit, the government decided to impose sanctions of various kinds on the Company. When this was debated in the House of Commons, the government was defeated and was forced to withdraw the use of sanctions against employers. It also meant that the 5 per cent guideline was under attack.

The Conservatives now accused the government of weakness in the face of extreme trade union demands and of worsening inflation. Faced with increasing difficulties, James Callaghan was forced to call a general election. The Conservatives swept to victory with an overall majority of about forty M.P.s.

Conservative Government under Margaret Thatcher, 1979

The new government based its economic policy on the need for the nation to live within its means, and Margaret Thatcher's programme included drastic cuts in public expenditure and high interest rates. It was hoped that this '**monetarist**' policy would also lower the rate of inflation by reducing the amount of money in circulation.

The policy of reducing the money supply met with some opposition within the Conservative Party – there was special criticism of the high interest rates which hit not only small businesses but also homeowners with mortgages. However, Mrs Thatcher was determined to continue with a 'monetarist' policy and replaced some dissatisfied members of her cabinet. As a result, inflation had been reduced to 12 per cent by the beginning of 1982, but alarmingly the number of unemployed had risen to over three million.

The closure of many firms as a result of monetary stringency was attacked by the government's Labour opponents under their new leader, **Michael Foot**; but the position of the Labour Party was weakened by divisions between Left and Right and by the secession of some members, including most notably Shirley Williams, Roy Jenkins, David Owen and William Rodgers, to form the **Social Democratic Party** (SDP). In turn, the new party allied itself with the Liberals under **David Steel**. The SDP began to have important electoral victories which threatened the traditional two-party system: Shirley Williams was elected as Crosby's M.P. and soon after Roy Jenkins won the Glasgow Hillhead by-election.

The government again met strong criticism from the Labour Opposition when it introduced the Employment Bill, which encouraged the use of the secret ballot before strike action was taken and which protected workers refusing to accept the 'closed shop' on grounds of conscience. 'Secondary picketing', that is picketing of workers in firms not directly concerned in the strike, was made illegal. The trade unions saw this as an attack on them, while many Conservatives felt that the Bill should have curbed trade union power even further.

Changes in the immigration law introduced by the Home Secretary William Whitelaw were also criticized. These where designed to prevent the immigration of anyone who married a British national solely for the purpose of gaining entry to Britain.

In the summer of 1981, the government was faced with the problem of riots in London, Liverpool and Manchester. In some cases these were the result of racial tension, but in others both black and white youths joined forces against the police. The government appointed a commission of inquiry under Lord Scarman. The riots highlighted the problem of decayed inner city areas and high youth unemployment. The organization and personnel of the police were also brought into question.

In Northern Ireland, in 1981 several IRA members being held in the Maze prison went on hunger strike to demand political status. This was resolutely opposed by Mrs Thatcher, and after the deaths of a number of the hunger strikers the campaign ceased. There seemed to be no prospect of a solution to the Northern Ireland problem.

Mrs Thatcher's Common Market policy led to her fight to reduce Britain's financial contribution to the Community on the grounds that Britain paid more than other members in proportion to the size of her population and received less. After a long period of negotiation, her efforts were successful, and Britain's contribution was reduced for 1980 from £1000 million to £337 million and for 1981 to £445 million.

In these years Britain was developing a new source of strength for the future—North Sea oil, and in the autumn of 1975 the first supplies were piped ashore from the important **Forties Field.**

Another enormously expensive project, supported by both Conservative and Labour governments, was the Anglo French supersonic plane, **'Concorde'**. After many difficulties due to escalating costs in a world afflicted by inflation, in January, 1976, the first flights of the French 'Concorde' to Rio de Janeiro were inaugurated, and of the British 'Concorde' to Bahrein. This was followed in May, 1976, by the first flights to the United States. Another important project, the **Channel Tunnel,** the drilling for which had already begun on both sides of the Channel, was abandoned (or possibly suspended) on grounds of cost.

Summary

Both Labour and Conservative governments were faced in these years by enormous problems affecting the welfare of the people and Britain's position in the world. The basic problems were those relating to national production, to investment in industry, to the failure of important private firms leading to government assistance and increasing government control. Governments were forced to borrow huge sums from the **International Monetary Fund** in order to support the pound sterling and to continue a high level of social benefits for the people. Our adverse **balance of trade** was a continuing problem. Industrial disputes were numerous and damaging, and the attempts of both Labour and Conservative governments to bring more order into industrial relations by new legislation, proved a failure in face of determined trade union opposition. These years saw a great increase in the power of the trade unions, especially the transport workers, the engineers and the miners. Internationally, there were the problems arising from the growing military power of Russia, but at the same time a movement towards 'detente' between East and West. In Northern Ireland serious violence was continuous, and in London, Birmingham and elsewhere serious casualties were the results of IRA activities.

Important dates

March, 1966	**Compulsory Wages and Prices 'freeze'.**
October, 1967	**Closure of the Suez Canal**
	Ban on oil shipments to Britain.
1968	**The Race Relations Act**
	Government White Paper, 'In Place of Strife'.
June, 1970	**Conservatives win election under Mr. Heath.**
August, 1971	**Industrial Relations Act.**
January 1, 1973	**Britain enters the Common Market**
	Phases I, II and III in operation
	Oil supplies from Arab states drastically reduced
	Great industrial unrest.
January 3, 1974	**Britain on the three-day working week.**
February 24, 1974	**General Election results in a minority Labour Government.**

October, 1974	General Election gives Labour an over-all majority of 5 The 'Social Contract'.
1975	Agreement between government and unions to limit wage increases to £6 a week.
1975	Election of Margaret Thatcher as Conservative leader.
1976	The $4\frac{1}{2}$ per cent agreement 'Concorde' aircraft open up flights to Rio de Janeiro, Bahrein and Washington.
1979	Conservatives win General Election and Margaret Thatcher becomes Britain's first woman Prime Minister.

QUESTIONS

(1) *How would you account for the Labour victory of 1964?*

(2) *Why was the Race Relations Act of 1968 introduced?*

(3) *Why were attempts made by both Labour and Conservative governments to impose more regulations on the trade unions?*

(4) *Why did Mr. Heath's Industrial Relations Act arouse opposition from the trade unions and the Labour Party?*

(5) *State some of the Arguments for and against Britain's entry into the Common Market.*

(6) *What efforts were made in these years by both Labour and Conservative governments to meet the problem of inflation?*

(7) *Why did Britain go onto the three-day week in January, 1974?*

(8) *Why was government money spent to rescue such concerns as Rolls Royce, British Leyland, Chrysler and Burmah Oil?*

INDEX

Battles, sieges etc. are arranged alphabetically under 'Battles'; Treaties, 'pacts' and other international agreements under 'Treaties'.

426